Once upon an Oldman

Jack Glenn

Once upon an Oldman:
Special Interest Politics
and the Oldman River Dam

UBCPress / Vancouver

© UBC Press 1999

All rights reserved. No part of this publication may be reproduced, stored in a retrieval system, or transmitted, in any form or by any means, without prior written permission of the publisher, or, in Canada, in the case of photocopying or other reprographic copying, a licence from CANCOPY (Canadian Copyright Licensing Agency), 900 – 6 Adelaide Street East, Toronto, ON M5C 1H6.

Printed in Canada on acid-free paper ∞

ISBN 0-7748-0712-1

Canadian Cataloguing in Publication Data

Glenn, Jack, 1936-
  Once upon an Oldman

  Includes bibliographical references and index.
  ISBN 0-7748-0712-1

  1. Oldman River Dam Project (Alta.) 2. Oldman River Valley (Alta.) – History.
  I. Title.

TC558.C320435   1999   333.7'097123'4   C99-910374-1

This book has been published with a grant from the Social Sciences Federation of Canada, using funds provided by the Social Sciences and Humanities Research Council of Canada.

UBC Press gratefully acknowledges the ongoing support to its publishing program from the Canada Council for the Arts, the British Columbia Arts Council, and the Department of Canadian Heritage of the Government of Canada. We also wish to acknowledge the financial support of the Government of Canada through the Book Publishing Industry Development Program (BPIDP) for our publishing activities.

UBC Press
University of British Columbia
6344 Memorial Road
Vancouver, BC V6T 1Z2
(604) 822-5959
Fax: 1-800-668-0821
E-mail: info@ubcpress.ubc.ca
www.ubcpress.ubc.ca

We do not need a repeat of the vain political skulduggery
and general acrimony that accompanied the approval process
and ultimate construction of the dam on the Oldman River. The
fallout from that ugly confrontation still poisons the waters,
fields, grasslands and homes in the southern portion of the
province.

  – Editorial, 'Dam site better,' *Calgary Herald,* 4 October 1994

AUGUSTANA UNIVERSITY COLLEGE
LIBRARY

Contents

Illustrations and Maps

Illustrations

Maps

Preface

In 1986, the Alberta government began the construction of a dam on the Oldman River in southern Alberta. This sparked a controversy pitting the Alberta and federal governments and a well-organized and highly effective irrigation lobby against local landowners, environmental interest groups, and the Peigan Indian Band. At its peak in the early 1990s, the dispute featured a minor uprising on the Peigan Reserve, an environmental review by the federal government, and rulings by the Supreme Court, and it attracted the attention of the national media. *Once upon an Oldman* tells the story of that controversy from its beginnings in 1976 to the present day, and offers a critical analysis of how the participants dealt with some of the major issues at stake.

Most of the major incidents that marked the dispute were reported by the media as they occurred over the two decades from 1976 to the present. What was missing from these reports was a sense of continuity between events and an indication of what the outcomes might mean for the broader issues of environmental integrity and fairness to Indian people. My purposes in researching and writing this book were to provide a clear and coherent account of the Oldman controversy, to show how it revealed the disparities between what our governments say about the environment and Indian people and how they act towards them, and to illustrate the impotence of special interest groups in effecting changes that are contrary to the received wisdom.

In the writing of this account I have honestly tried to not favour one side or the other. It has been a struggle. If, in the judgment of the reader, I have failed in my attempt – and I expect many to so judge, I offer two reasons, neither of which can stand as excuses. The first is my inherent propensity to take the side of the underdogs – in this case the Peigan and the Friends of the Oldman River (FOR). Any person or group that takes on a government at any level automatically qualifies as the underdog, which takes care of FOR. As for the Peigan, despite their recent gains and more assertive (or aggressive) behaviour, Canada's Native people continue to reign as the nation's undisputed underdogs. The second is that after some thirty years of public service, I am more familiar with the Machiavellian ways of government than with what may well be the equally Machiavellian ways of public interest groups. This, together with the fact that the members of public interest groups are, for the most part, unpaid and otherwise unrewarded, at least in a material way, leads me to be less sceptical about their motives and declarations than those of politicians and government bureaucrats.

I make no claim to a particular knowledge of or experience with the cultural and spiritual beliefs of the Peigan people. As will be noted, the information presented and the interpretation of some of that information as it pertains to the Oldman River Dam controversy draws heavily on the work of others. If I've got it wrong, I apologize, but it is such an important part of the Oldman story that it couldn't be left out. I had some difficulty in obtaining information for the record from the Peigan. There were a number of reasons for this: I did not work with them long enough to win their trust; they could not be certain about what stand my manuscript would take on the issues pertinent to the Peigan; and, perhaps most important, Peigan politicians and officials had been cautioned by their lawyers to be extremely circumspect in what they said because of their pending legal suit against Alberta over rights to the water of the Oldman River.

In December 1992, the Alberta Department of Environment (Alberta Environment) became the Department of Environmental Protection. However, since the department was known as Alberta Environment during the time when most of the events recounted in this book occurred, I have used that term when referring to the department, its minister, and its various functionaries. For the same reason, the arm of the Alberta government responsible for administration of the Water Resources Act and all aspects of water management in the province, with the exception of water quality, is referred to as the Water Management Service. Its name, also, has changed several times over the years. Originally the Water Resources Division when it was in the Department of Agriculture, its functions were divided between the Environmental Engineering Support Services and the Policy, Planning and Research Services when it became a part of the newly formed Department of Environment in 1971. From the late 1970s until December 1992, it was known as the Water Resources Management Services. Following a reorganization in 1993, the name changed to Water Resources Services. In a 1995 reorganization, which reduced the number of assistant deputy ministers in the department from seven to four, it was combined with a number of other services under the name of Natural Resources. Although it has expanded and contracted over time, as bureaucracies are wont to do, its basic functions with respect to water management have not changed.

Similarly, the agency that exercises the federal government's responsibilities for Indians and Indian lands and which has, over the years, been included as an element in various departmental organizations – most recently the Department of Indian Affairs and Northern Development – is referred to simply as Indian Affairs. As a wise person once observed, changing the costume of the clowns does not essentially alter the nature of the circus in which they perform. Having served as one of the clowns, I can endorse that observation.

I am indebted to a great number of people for their assistance in compiling this account. I am particularly grateful to the following people who consented to my request for a recorded interview: Dave Anderson, Cheryl Bradley, Rod Chapman, the Reverend Peter Hamel, Joanne Helmer, Roy Jensen, Dr. Martha Kostuch, Dr. George Kupfer, Don Lebaron, Professor Chris Levy, Peter Melnychuk, Hilton Pharis, Dr. Brian Reeves, Dr. Stewart Rood, Dr. William Ross, Rick Ross, Dr. Dixon Thompson, and Cliff Wallis. Dr. Martha Kostuch gave me generous access to files on the Oldman Project and patiently answered my many follow-up queries; Commissioner John F. Thomas of the Canadian Coast Guard provided detailed answers to my questions about the federal response to the Oldman River Dam Environmental Assessment Panel's recommendations; and David J. Robinson and Jeff Stein of the Department of Fisheries and Oceans provided information about authorizations issued under the Fisheries Act. Others who answered questions or provided documentation or assistance included Paul Scott, Nadya Zavergenietz, and Patricia Woodward of FEARO's (now CEAA) Vancouver office; Joyce Ingram and Pat Cleary of NRCB; Olga Potter of the Alberta Energy and Utilities Board; Calgary Independent Reporters; Michel Blondin and Steve Varette, Indian Affairs; Ian Dyson, Alberta Environmental Protection; Roger Edwards, Canadian Wildlife Service; Tom Head; Doreen Kot; Louise Mandell; Pat Marshall, Archives, Sir Alexander Galt Museum; Al McPhail; James Penton; Kathy Pomeroy; Dale Russell, Western Heritage Resources, Saskatoon; Lorand Szjoka; Henry Theissen; Wendy Unfried; John Werring, Sierra Legal Defence Fund; Milt Wright, BC Ministry of Small Business, Tourism and Culture; the knowledgable and helpful staffs of the Calgary Public Library, the Lethbridge Public Library, and the University of Calgary's McKimmie Library and Law Library; and the host of federal and provincial public servants and members of the Peigan Band with whom I had off-the-record conversations. Thanks also to Jean Wilson, Holly Keller-Brohman, Randy Schmidt, Judy Phillips, and others at UBC Press whose patient guidance and careful editing helped to bring this work to fruition.

My special thanks to Dr. Jim Tagg, who read the manuscript and suggested many helpful revisions; to Gordon Glenn, who prepared the maps that appear in the book and who frequently bailed me out of difficulties with my word processor; to Peter Glenn, who patiently read early drafts of the manuscript and provided many helpful comments (and who was right about the length); and to Pat, who provided unflagging support and encouragement throughout.

Despite all of the assistance so generously offered and gratefully received, the opinions expressed in this book and the responsibility for any errors or omissions in the information presented are entirely mine.

Abbreviations

ADM	assistant deputy minister
AEN	Alberta Environmental Network
AF&GA	Alberta Fish and Game Association
AIPA	Alberta Irrigation Projects Association
ASA	Archaeological Survey of Alberta
AWA	Alberta Wilderness Association
AWRC	Alberta Water Resources Commission
BCR	band council resolution
CASNP	Canadian Alliance in Solidarity with Native Peoples
CEAA	Canadian Environmental Assessment Act/Agency
CEDF	Canadian Environmental Defence Fund
CEPA	Canadian Environmental Protection Act
CPAWS	Canadian Parks and Wilderness Society
CPTR	Committee for the Preservation of Three Rivers
CWF	Canadian Wildlife Federation
DF&O	Department of Fisheries and Oceans
DIAND	Department of Indian Affairs and Northern Development
EAC	Environmental Advisory Committee
EARP	Environmental Assessment Review Process
EARPGO	Environmental Assessment Review Process Guidelines Order
ECA	Environmental Conservation Authority/Environment Council of Alberta
ERCB	Energy Resources Conservation Board
ERT	emergency response team
EMC	Environmental Management Committee
FAN	Federation of Alberta Naturalists
FEARO	Federal Environmental Assessment Review Office
FOR	Friends of the Oldman River
IA	Indian Affairs
ID	irrigation district

INAC   Indian and Northern Affairs Canada
LAC   Local Advisory Committee
LNID   Lethbridge Northern Irrigation District
MD   municipal district
MID   Magrath Irrigation District
MLA   Member of the Legislative Assembly
MP   Member of Parliament
NRCB   Natural Resources Conservation Board
NWMP   North-West Mounted Police
NWPA   Navigable Waters Protection Act
O.C.   Order in Council
ORDEAP   Oldman River Dam Environmental Assessment Panel
ORSMC   Oldman River Study Management Committee
PFRA   Prairie Farm Rehabilitation Administration
PWSS   Department of Public Works, Supply and Services
PRIME   Prairie Rivers Improvement and Management Evaluation
RCMP   Royal Canadian Mounted Police
RID   Raymond Irrigation District
RSCC   Regional Screening and Coordinating Committee
SLDF   Sierra Legal Defence Fund
SAEG   Southern Alberta Environmental Group
SAWMC   Southern Alberta Water Management Committee
SMRID   St. Mary River Irrigation District
SSRB   South Saskatchewan River Basin
TID   Taber Irrigation District
TU   Trout Unlimited
WMS   Water Management Service

Introduction

Once upon a time, some farmers lived near a river in a dry and dusty land. Every spring, great quantities of water flowed down the river and on to the sea, and every summer, the farmers watched helplessly as their crops withered in the parched fields. If only we could spread water from the river on our land, they thought, our crops would not wilt and die. So, the farmers asked the prince who ruled over their land to build a dam on the river to hold back some of the spring flow so the farmers could irrigate their crops during the hot, dry summer. It so happened that the prince had made a lot of money selling oil and was looking for ways to spend it before the greedy king, who lived in the east and ruled over the whole country, took it from him. The farmers' idea sounded good to the prince, and his court agreed, so he sent his engineers and economists to find the best place to build the dam.

The engineers and economists looked very hard, and at last they chose a place where three rivers came together. Not everyone in the land agreed that this was the best place for the dam. The people who lived in the valley where the dam would flood their land didn't think so, and neither did some of the Indian people who lived downstream. People who fished in the river thought it was a bad place for a dam, and others worried about the birds and animals and trees in the valley and the ancient artifacts that would be covered with water. There were even some who thought there shouldn't be a dam on the river at all.

But most of the people that the engineers and economists talked to thought it was a fine place for a dam. So, the prince sent his lawyers, with bags of money, to talk to the people in the valley and the Indians downstream. The lawyers gave some of the money to the people who lived in the valley and helped them to find new places to live. They gave the rest of the money to the Indians and promised that they could use some of the water to irrigate their crops. Then the prince hired companies to build the dam, and to put rocks in the river to make it an even better place for fish, and to plant trees on the land around the dam where the birds and animals could live, and to gather up all of the artifacts. For many years, the companies dug and hauled and scraped and planted and gathered, and the prince's lawyers and engineers and economists and biologists and archaeologists watched to see that everything was done properly.

Finally, the dam was finished. It stretched across the valley, and the reservoir behind it filled with water to irrigate the farmers' lands. The river teemed with fish, and vast herds of deer and other animals roamed the forests on the uplands around the reservoir. The water that flowed from the dam ran deep and clear in the river, to the joy of people in the villages downstream and those who canoed and kayaked along the way. Everyone could see that they would prosper from the dam for years to come.

And the people lived happily ever after.

That was how it was meant to be; but as so often happens in life, the reality was different from the vision. Since the last ice age, 10,000 years ago, the Oldman River has flowed from the eastern slopes of the Rocky Mountains through the foothills and across the semidesert landscape of southern Alberta. In its natural state, fed by meltwater from glaciers and the mountain snowpack, the river flowed high in the spring and early summer, diminishing to a trickle for the rest of the year. In the spring of 1991, that natural condition was altered forever with the closure of a dam constructed at Three Rivers, just downstream from where the Oldman is joined by two of its main tributaries, the Castle and the Crowsnest Rivers (see Map 1). The Oldman River Dam now captures a portion of the river's flow in a reservoir that floods forty-three kilometres of the river valley and the lower reaches of the two tributaries. This is the story of how this dam came to be, and of the controversy that raged throughout the decades from its conception to its birth. Over the years, the Oldman River and the valley through which it flows have meant different things to different people.

For the Peigan tribe of the Blackfoot Indian Nation, they are a birthright and a homeland, an ancestral burial ground, a source of spiritual strength, and the thread that binds the Native people with the natural environment. They also offer the potential for economic development on the Peigan Reserve that could contribute to the well-being of its impoverished residents.

For southern Alberta's farming community, the Oldman is the prime source of water for the irrigation that is the basis for its existence in this perennially water-short area. And in the minds of many in this community, harnessing the waters of the Oldman offers the best hope for a prosperous future. For those whose farms were flooded by the dam, whose ancestors homesteaded there or who had chosen it as a retreat from the pressures and stresses of urban life, it was a haven, a refuge, a place where they had put down roots.

For environmentalists and anglers, the Oldman, the Castle, and the

Map 1 The Oldman River Basin in Alberta

Crowsnest provided some of the best trout habitat in North America, and the riparian cottonwood forests downstream from the dam site provided biologically diverse habitat in an otherwise treeless landscape. More than that, they were amongst the last untamed rivers in the southern prairies, remnants of a rapidly disappearing natural world.

For politicians on the government side in the provincial legislature, harnessing the Oldman meant strengthening their hold on the predominantly rural ridings in the southern part of the province. For engineers in government and in the consulting community, the unregulated river provided an opportunity to apply their ingenuity, their knowledge, and their technology to modify the harsh prairie environment, to enhance their professional reputations and further their careers.

For the vast majority of the people in Canada or even in Alberta, the Oldman River had no meaning whatever. Until the controversy surrounding construction of the dam began to heat up in the late 1980s, most were not even aware of its existence.

Over the course of the present century, dams have been built on most of the major rivers in western Canada. While few of these projects were completed without controversy, none experienced battles of the same intensity, or generated the degree of bitterness, that accompanied the construction of the Oldman Dam. Its timing and the coalescence of several volatile issues set the Oldman apart and aroused substantially more passionate levels of support and opposition than had its predecessors. Southern Indian Lake in Manitoba, the Gardiner Dam in Saskatchewan, the St. Mary, Bighorn, and Dickson Dams in Alberta, and the Columbia River and Bennett Dams in British Columbia were all built in the years between 1950 and 1980. Each shared one or more of the characteristics that were the focus of acrimony over the Oldman Project: resource development, environmental protection, Native rights. But by the late 1980s, sustainable resource development, thanks to the Bruntland Commission, was the focus of international attention, environmental interests were riding the peak of a wave of public support, and sympathy for Native Indians was at an unprecedented high. The three came together in the Oldman River Dam Project. As the controversy heightened, the project became the focal point of a province-wide power struggle between a development-oriented, primarily rural-based government and a conservation-minded, mostly urban-based environmental movement. It also became a pawn in federal-provincial wrangling over natural resources that is a significant element in Canada's ongoing constitutional battle.

In August 1980, nearly sixty years after it was first recommended by federal engineers as a means to provide a reliable water supply for irrigation in the Lethbridge Northern Irrigation District, Alberta's environment minister announced that his government was committed to the construction of a dam on the Oldman, preferably at Three Rivers. The first opposition to the dam came from landowners who would be flooded by the reservoir formed behind the dam, and from anglers, who felt that, if storage was necessary at all, it should be located offstream, rather than on the main stem of the Oldman River. In 1984, when the government finally decided that the dam would be at Three Rivers, the Peigan Indian Band, which had favoured a dam on its reserve, joined the opposition. When construction began in 1986, the landowners, the anglers, and the Indians were joined by an expanding coalition of environmental interests, the Friends of the Oldman River (FOR), in what was to become a determined, all-out fight to stop the dam.

At first, the project was given little notice beyond the region. But by late 1986, after both the Peigan and FOR had launched court actions challenging the provincial and federal governments on the legality of the project, the dispute began to attract national and international attention. Over the next few years, demonstrations, court actions, public debates, and reports, editorials, articles, and letters to the editor in both provincial and national news media proliferated. Meanwhile, construction of the dam proceeded without interruption. The level of protest peaked in 1990, when the Federal Court of Appeal ordered the federal government to undertake an environmental assessment of the dam and a group of Peigan Indians, inspired by their Mohawk counterparts in Quebec, tried to divert the river in an attempt to halt dam construction. By the end of 1991, the dam was completed, the reservoir had filled to its full supply level, and the Federal Environmental Assessment Panel had completed its public hearings and withdrawn to write its report. Media and public interest in the debacle grew sporadic, while supporters and opponents of the dam maintained an uneasy quiet, waiting for the panel's report and the next round in what promised to be a continuing drama.

In May of 1992, the federal panel submitted its report. It judged the project to be unacceptable and recommended that the dam be decommissioned. The federal government immediately rejected the idea that the dam be decommissioned, and Alberta moved ahead with plans for a grand opening celebration – a Festival of Life that was not to be. These events kept the controversial project in the news through the early summer of 1992. Thereafter, it faded almost entirely from the public eye, surfacing intermittently, and then only briefly, on events following from those of 1987-91, such as the federal government's 1993 response to the panel's recommendations. Yet, in 1997, more than a decade after the first sod was turned at Three Rivers, mention of the project still draws bitter comment from its opponents – not all of the people have lived happily ever after – and scepticism from more neutral observers. And a dam-related legal action mounted by the Peigan Indian Band against the Alberta government is still pending. Ironically, this law suit could have far greater repercussions for Alberta and for Canada than the event that sparked it.

This book is not for or against the Oldman Dam. Rather, it takes a critical look at the process by which, over the space of two decades, the dam evolved from a concept to a reality. It chronicles a conflict involving many actors: landowners, farmers, Indians, environmentalists, politicians, bureaucrats, businesspeople, journalists, academics, and jurists; and many issues: environmental protection, resource conservation, irrigation expansion, Native rights, and the unspoken issues of power, privilege, and profit that are at stake in most contemporary resource-use decisions. It reviews the confrontations, posturing, manoeuvring, and propagandizing that characterized the conflict. And, by examining some of the issues in the context of the events that transpired, it illuminates the roles played by the various parties and shows how their actions, reactions, or inactions contributed to the advent, the prolongation, and the outcomes of the conflict.

The governments of Alberta and of Canada, as represented by their politicians and bureaucrats, play a central part in this story. Alberta, the declared owner and manager of the Oldman River, and the proponent – now owner and operator – of the dam, initiated and controlled most of the elements in the process. Canada, by acting or, more frequently, not acting in areas where the dam infringed on its constitutional responsibilities, contributed substantially to the controversy. Both governments had the unqualified support of the southern Alberta irrigation community (represented by the Southern Alberta Water Management Committee) for which the dam and reservoir were created and which will be its greatest beneficiary. Arrayed in opposition were the Peigan Indians, across whose ancestral lands the river flows and whose sacred grounds were inundated by the water held behind the dam, and the environmental interest groups (represented by FOR), who took it upon themselves to defend the Oldman from what they perceived to be the wanton destructiveness of the provincial government and the studied neglect of the national government. Other featured players include the courts and quasi-judicial review bodies that found themselves in the unique position of assessing whether the provincial and national governments were complying with their own laws and policies and, when the governments were found wanting, rendering judgments or offering recommendations intended to correct their course, and the media, whose assumed responsibility it is to report upon and to provide knowledgable and unbiased interpretations of events that bear on the individual or collective well-being of its readers, listeners, or viewers.

In the decade preceding the construction of the Oldman Dam, agriculture and agriculturally based regional economies in western Canada experienced a steady decline. A submission to the Oldman River Dam Environmental Assessment Panel in 1991 observed that 'agriculture in Canada, and in the prairies in particular, has reached a point of crisis which is heart breaking for individual farmers and confusing for the public at large.'[1] The farm community was faced with steadily escalating costs, disastrously low agricultural commodity prices, due in no small part to the subsidies paid by the United States and the European Economic Community to their farmers, and declining world markets. Governments in Canada, both national and provincial, responded with a variety of subsidy programs intended to keep farmers on the land and producing. The Oldman Dam, though not always perceived as such, was a generous addition to the Alberta government's subsidy package for agriculture in southern Alberta.

The final phases of construction and closure of the Oldman Dam coincided with an active period in the Canadian Aboriginal peoples' struggle for recognition of their perceived rights to lands and to self-determination. This period was marked by demonstrations, violent or otherwise, by Indian people and their supporters in opposition to the exploitation by governments and other developers of lands and resources regarded by Native peoples as belonging to them. Lost to some extent in the furor and publicity surrounding the Mohawk Warrior's armed resistance at Oka in Quebec and the James Bay Cree's opposition to Quebec's Great Whale Project was the determined struggle by the Peigan Indian Band to prevent the trammelling of their interests in an out-of-the-way corner of southwestern Alberta.

Relegated to the back burner by the recession in the early 1980s, environmental conservation reemerged as a major issue in the latter part of the decade. Opinion polls at the time indicated that Canadians overall rated their concern about the environment at a level comparable with their concerns about the economy and nuclear war. In Alberta, this rejuvenation revitalized the environmental community and sparked a renewed interest in the Oldman Dam, by then in the early stages of construction. Convinced that the project would have dire consequences for the environment, FOR demanded that Alberta assess the environmental impact of the construction and operation of a dam at the Three Rivers site and that the federal government assess the dam's impacts on areas of federal jurisdiction. In the absence of what it considered reasonable responses to its pleas, FOR initiated legal actions against both governments.

The first half of the book begins with a very brief summary of the geography, history, and institutional arrangements critical to an understanding of how the Oldman Dam Project came into being, and of the controversies that continue to plague it. None of the voluminous documentation produced by the dam's proponent or by its supporters, opponents, reviewers, or critics frames the dam and the issues it raised in the context of the water-use and management policies and practices that have developed over time in this particular setting. Chapter 1, though it is no more than a brief sketch of one hundred years of human occupation and water management in the Oldman River Basin, provides some of this context. Subsequent chapters tell the story of the Oldman controversy as it unfolded from 1976 to the present day. Many of the events that make up this account were reported by the media as they occurred, usually in greater detail than has been possible here. I have relied heavily on newspaper reports of the day to supplement my recollection of the sequence of events and of who said what to whom. What I hope to have done in this brief narrative is weave these events into a story that provides the continuity understandably absent in isolated accounts of events, written by a succession of reporters, with a variety of backgrounds, as they occurred over a period of almost twenty years.

The second half of the book takes a closer look at the make-up, the motives, and the actions of the disparate groups engaged in the Oldman controversy: the governments of Alberta and Canada and their agencies; the Southern Alberta Water Management Committee; the Friends of the Oldman River Society; and the Peigan Indian Band. These are considered in the context of the major issues raised by the project: water management and irrigation development, the environmental impacts of the project, and its implications for the Peigan's culture and spiritual beliefs and practices and their claim to a share of the flow of the Oldman River. The contributions of the courts and review bodies called upon to resolve these issues are also examined. What emerges is a tale of confrontation pitting developers against environmentalists and Native people, along lines that have become so familiar to Canadians over the last quarter of the twentieth century.

Most citizens of liberal democracies expect their elected representatives to act as arbitrators in disputes over competing uses of publicly owned resources, working to find a balance or strike a compromise that is in the best interests of the country and its people as a whole, over the long term – the common good. Whatever our beliefs about the reality of the model that casts governments in this role, it is clear that this model was not in play when the fate of the Oldman River was being decided. Rather, what we see is southern Alberta's irrigation community, led by the Alberta government, lined up against a group of environmentalists and the Peigan Indian community, itself divided over whether to oppose or support the dam. The two sides became locked in a struggle over whether the common good was best served by damming the river, flooding a portion of its valley, and regulating its flow in the interest of economic development, or by abandoning the project in the interest of maintaining (not further degrading) the environmental status quo. Exactly where the Peigan fit into this equation became increasingly less clear with the passage of time. With the provincial government cast in the role of proponent, the federal government concluded, rightly, that the confrontation had become a political dispute. Not wishing to be caught up in a struggle between the government of Alberta and some of its people, the federal government also abandoned its role as arbitrator (and its fiduciary duty to the Peigan), leaving the field to the courts, whose powers are limited to ensuring adherence to the laws of the day.

All parties to the dispute, but particularly the governments, engaged in manoeuvres questionable from an ethical if not from a legal perspective to frustrate the moves of their opponents and selectively present, withhold, or manage the flow of information to favour their position, effectively denying neutral participants the opportunity to form objective opinions on the merits or otherwise of the project.

Although this struggle played itself out in a corner of southern Alberta somewhat remote, culturally and geographically from the rest of the nation, the events that took place were typical of those that characterize similar struggles – past or ongoing – in all parts of Canada. They happened on the Nemchaco River in British Columbia, in the James Bay region of northern Quebec, and they are about to repeat themselves at Voisey's Bay in Newfoundland and Labrador.

In many respects then, the Oldman River Dam stands as a metaphor for Canada in this final quarter of the twentieth century. Amongst the more prominent characteristics of the public affairs of the nation during this period are the ongoing constitutional struggles between the federal and provincial governments; concern for the environment and scepticism about government management of publicly owned resources and environmental issues; the increased assertiveness of Native people and the greater awareness and understanding of and sympathy with Native claims on the part of many Canadians; the continuing inability of governments and Native communities to reach accommodation on resource-use issues and the militant reaction to the resulting impasse by small bands of Native dissidents; a widespread loss of faith in the ability or willingness of governments and politicians to deal fairly with public issues; the consequent rise of single-issue interest groups, the growing tendency of those groups to turn to the courts to resolve those issues, and the inability of the courts to do so; governments, business, and special interest groups increasingly manipulating and controlling the flow of information to the public; and the unfortunate tendency of the media to focus on the more sensational events arising from disputes over issues, rather than on the issues themselves.

All of these were reflected in the Oldman controversy.

1
The Oldman River Basin

Everyone has a river in their life.

– Kevin Van Tighem, *Coming West: A Natural History of Home*[1]

The Oldman, the Crowsnest, and the Castle Rivers rise in the front ranges of the Rocky Mountains in southern Alberta. The three rivers flow east from the mountains and through the foothills, converging about ten kilometres northwest of the town of Pincher Creek. From there, the Oldman continues its eastward journey through the Peigan Indian Reserve, past the city of Lethbridge, and across the prairie to a point south of the town of Brooks that the early European settlers called the Grand Forks. There, its flow combines with that of the Bow River to become the South Saskatchewan River, which meanders past Medicine Hat and into Saskatchewan, where it joins with the North Saskatchewan River to flow into Lake Winnipeg, the Nelson River, and finally into Hudson Bay (see Map 2). The fact that the Oldman is a part of the Saskatchewan-Nelson River system adds another dimension to consideration of the Oldman Dam.

The mean annual volume of flow in the Oldman River is about three and one-half million cubic decametres.[2] By comparison with rivers in other parts of the country, that is not a lot of water. It is 10 percent of the mean annual flow of the Ottawa River in Ontario, and 5 percent of the mean annual flow of the Fraser in British Columbia. Variable is the word that Alberta water managers choose to characterize the flow of rivers like the Oldman that rise in the mountains and flow eastward across the dry southern plains. The annual cycle of flow in these rivers begins in early spring, when the snow begins to melt on the plains and foothills. By mid-June, when the weather warms enough to melt the snowfall that accumulated in the mountains over the preceding winter, the river flows begin to rise. Streamflows peak in early July, then recede steadily into late summer as the mountain snowpack disappears, and are sustained through the fall by run-off from glacier melt and whatever rain happens to fall. Winter sets in around mid-November, the ground freezes, the rains turn to snow, and river flows drop to their yearly minimums, where they remain until spring

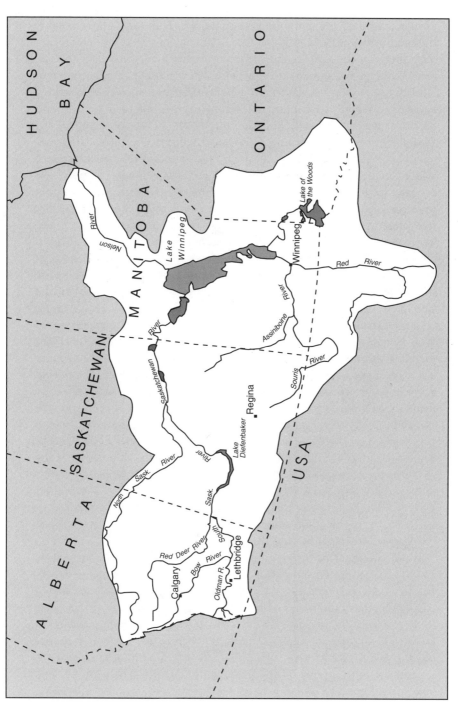

Map 2   The Saskatchewan-Nelson River system

returns. About 60 percent of their annual flow passes down these rivers in the months of June and July.

The flow in these rivers can also vary dramatically from year to year. Depending on the amount of snowfall in the mountains, streamflow can fall from near-record highs in one year to near-record lows the next. On occasion, streamflows remain well below average for periods of several years. When this happens, for example in the 1930s and again in the 1980s, summer rainfall is also well below the norm. Because of this variability, dams have been the favourite tool of the region's water managers. Water stored during the high flow period in early summer is available for use later in the year when the rivers begin to dry up or, in theory, during the next year should it be dry. In practice, so much of the water in most river systems is allocated for irrigation that there is rarely enough remaining in storage to meet demands in the second year of a dry cycle. That is why irrigation farmers are hit hard by water shortages during periods of drought and invariably raise the cry for more dams to capture and store the streamflow that is 'wasted' by being allowed to flow on through the system to Hudson Bay.

In the expanding economic conditions that followed the Second World War, irrigation and hydroelectric development proposals in the three prairie provinces posed the potential for conflict over the use and management of the river system. In 1948, the three provinces and the federal government established a Prairie Provinces Water Board (PPWB) to recommend the best use of the waters of the Saskatchewan River system, and how it should be allocated amongst the provinces. This arrangement, which began in a spirit of cooperation, broke down when provincial interests overcame the concept of an integrated plan for the development and use of the rivers. Because the PPWB was unable to agree on the relative merits of proposals put forward by the provinces, it was decided to adopt a formula for sharing the flow. The sharing arrangement was formalized in 1969, when the four governments reconstituted the PPWB, and ratified the Master Agreement on Apportionment.[3]

Although somewhat more complex in its details, the basic proviso of the apportionment agreement is that Alberta and Saskatchewan are each entitled to consume 50 percent of the flow of the Saskatchewan River system that flows into or originates in that province. The residual flow must pass to the downstream province. The agreement does not constrain the use of water in Manitoba. The agreement affords Alberta the option of considering the Red Deer River to be tributary to the South Saskatchewan in Alberta for the purpose of apportionment.[4] Alberta has exercised this option continuously since the agreement came into effect and, in 1976, the province adopted the policy of managing the three tributaries that contribute to the flow of the South Saskatchewan – the Red Deer, Bow, and

Oldman – 'in concert' to meet its flow commitments to Saskatchewan.[5] Because of these arrangements, the Oldman River Dam Project will have implications not only in the Oldman River system but also in the Bow and Red Deer systems. In particular, taking more water from the Oldman system to support the irrigation expansion that was the rationale for the project will limit future withdrawals from the Bow and Red Deer systems and threaten instream uses of water in those rivers.

The South Saskatchewan system in Alberta is intensively used and highly regulated. Each of the headwater tributary systems features one or more large onstream dams or diversion works, the operation of which affects the pattern of downstream flow in a major way. As of 1999, there are twenty of these with more in the offing. These dams and diversions are, as a general rule, operated to satisfy the water requirements of their owners or of the predominant water use that the dam or diversion was built to serve. For example, TransAlta Utilities' dams on the Bow River system are operated almost exclusively for the generation of hydroelectricity. Virtually all of the remaining structures, most of which are owned and operated by the provincial government, are operated primarily to support irrigation. Though the government claims that the provincially owned structures are operated for 'multi-purpose use,' when the weather is hot and dry and natural streamflow is low, they are only rarely operated for purposes other than to supply water for irrigation. Under Alberta's water law, instream uses are of the lowest priority, and structures are operated to provide flow in excess of what these uses require for bare survival only at times when natural streamflow is abundant. During low flow periods, extreme public pressure sometimes forces managers to operate structures on some rivers to maintain flow at some minimum level at which the destruction of fish and other aquatic organisms is 'minimized.'

The Oldman River Basin, the land area drained by the Oldman River and its tributaries, encompasses an area of about 26,000 square kilometres (see Map 3). The upper one-third of the basin lies in the mountains and foothills, where the river valley is deeply incised. The well-vegetated banks and bottomlands provide habitat for large and diverse populations of wildlife. Black bear, mule deer, and white-tail deer, moose, elk, fox, coyote, and various smaller mammals range the valley and the surrounding uplands, while beaver and muskrat make their homes in the river and its banks. The cold water in the streams in the upper reaches of the watershed are home to mountain whitefish and various species of trout, of which the rainbow, an introduced species, provides the greatest attraction for anglers, who consider these rivers among the best trout streams on the continent. The bull trout, a species increasingly rare in southern Alberta streams, is found in limited numbers in the Oldman. The river also has one threatened fish species, the shorthead sculpin.

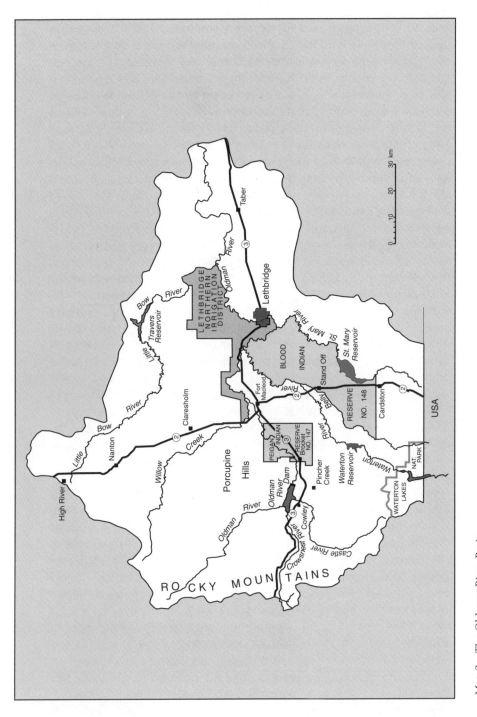

Map 3 The Oldman River Basin

Downstream from the dam, towards Lethbridge, the river enters the plains region, which comprises the lower two-thirds of the basin. The river water is warmer in the downstream reaches, and the coldwater fish species give way to pike and walleye, which are less appealing to dedicated sports fishers. The river in this region continues to flow in a deep valley, but the vegetation becomes sparse. The most common trees in the valley bottom are varieties of poplar, including the narrow-leaf and plains cottonwoods, the balsam poplar, and hybrids of these three species. These are the dominant species in the riparian forest ecosystems of the river valleys. Much has been made by environmentalists of the uniqueness and value of the cottonwoods and of the impact that regulation of the flow of the Oldman would have on their reproductive capability. The uplands in the lower watershed, before their occupance by farmers and ranchers, were predominantly grasslands, the range of vast herds of plains bison. Most of this land is now cultivated, and that which is not is used to graze the herds of beef cattle that are the staple of southern Alberta's ranching industry.

Precipitation in the mountains and foothills varies between 500 and 600 millimetres per year, much of it coming in the form of snowfall during the winter months. The Oldman River Dam is located towards the eastern end of this region. Precipitation in the downstream region decreases from about 450 millimetres around Lethbridge to less than 300 millimetres where the Oldman meets the Bow. This region receives an abundance of heat producing sunshine, which translates into a three- to four-month growing season. However, the combination of meagre summer rainfall, daytime temperatures in the 30-degree Celsius range, and almost constant dry westerly winds means that there is rarely enough moisture in the soil to allow farmers to take advantage of the otherwise excellent growing conditions. This, of course, is why irrigation was first introduced into the region, and why it remains so popular.

The first human occupants of what is now southern Alberta were the ancestors of the various tribes of the Blackfoot Indian Nation. According to archaeologists, these people emigrated from the Asian continent towards the end of the last ice age, about 12,000 years ago, by way of a land bridge over the Bering Sea and an ice-free corridor along the eastern slopes of the Rocky Mountains.[6] According to Blackfoot origin myths, the first people to make their homes in southern Alberta were put there by Napi, the Old Man, who made the world and everything in it. When Napi had finished his work of creation and taught the people how to hunt and live, he withdrew to the high mountains in the headwaters of the river that now bears his name – the Oldman. Whatever their origin, the Indian people occupied southern Alberta for centuries prior to the arrival of white settlers. The Oldman and its tributaries were the hunting grounds of the Peigan, the largest of the ancient Blackfoot tribes, who 'followed the buffalo and lived by the hunt.'[7] The first Europeans wandered into Blackfoot territory in the mid-1700s. Historian Hugh Dempsey reports that Anthony Hendy first met with tribes of the Blackfoot Nation in 1754.[8] Since the Peigan did not do much trapping, there was little early contact with the fur traders; the nearest fur trading posts were at Rocky Mountain House, on the North Saskatchewan, and on the Missouri River system in Montana.

Until the white settlers arrived in force in the late nineteenth century, the Peigan led a nomadic existence, dictated by their reliance on the buffalo for most of the necessities of life. A fur trader in the early 1800s reported that the Peigan controlled all of the hunting grounds within 160 kilometres of the mountains.[9] The seasonal pattern of their life saw them following the migration of the buffalo onto the plains in the spring, breaking up into small bands to follow and raid the herds on foot throughout the summer. In the fall, the small bands gathered in the area of the Porcupine Hills where they undertook to kill larger numbers of buffalo to sustain them through the winter. Before they acquired horses, buffalo jumps were favoured for the larger kills. With the arrival of snow and colder weather, the Peigan retreated to the valley of the Oldman, where they remained in sheltered campsites until spring and the beginning of a new seasonal round. The valley in the vicinity where Crow Lodge Creek flows into the Oldman River was one of the Peigan's most favoured overwintering areas. And it was there that they were destined to live on a permanent basis after the arrival of the white man and the disappearance of the buffalo.

The first non-Indians to take up residence in the Oldman basin were American whiskey traders from the Montana territory. These early-day entrepreneurs built a number of 'whiskey forts' in the area around present-day Lethbridge in the early 1870s, and entered into trade with the Peigan and Blood tribes. In 1874, the Dominion government raised the North-West Mounted Police (NWMP) and sent a force west to put an end to the whiskey trade and bring order to the Territories. The Mounties established a divisional headquarters at Fort Macleod, outposts along major rivers, and patrols throughout the region. The whiskey forts were soon transformed into legitimate trading posts. The first white settlers arrived in the Mounties wake, and by 1876 there were a number of farms and ranches in the area around Fort Macleod.

In 1877, the chiefs of the Blackfoot tribes in Canada, including the Peigan, and representatives of the government of Canada signed Treaty 7. Under the terms of this treaty, the Blackfoot surrendered all of their land, including the entire Oldman River watershed, to the Crown. In return, the government agreed to allow the Blackfoot to hunt throughout the area and to reserve a block of land for occupation by each tribe. The Peigan were assigned Reserve No. 147, a 181.4-square-mile (470-square-kilometre) tract of land straddling the Oldman River west of Fort Macleod.[10] For several years after 1877, the Peigan continued to follow the buffalo herds, hunting for food and for hides to trade with the white man. But by the early 1880s the buffalo had disappeared from the Canadian plains, and the Peigan, their numbers reduced by starvation and disease, were forced to abandon their traditional way of life. They withdrew to their reserve, where they were encouraged by Indian Affairs and the NWMP to take up farming. For the next twenty years, the Peigan struggled to grow potatoes and grains in a climate that was not suitable for either. They also tried raising cattle, at which they were marginally more successful, but the Peigan never became farmers on any scale. Once settled on the reserve, and in constant contact with white society, the Peigan population, which numbered about 1,000 in 1880, was steadily reduced by tuberculosis and other diseases. By the time the 1918 influenza epidemic was over, the population had dwindled to only 250 persons.[11] The reserve population recovered in subsequent years, and now numbers about 2,000.

Neither the Palliser nor the Dawson expeditions, efforts by the British and Canadian governments in the 1850s to obtain more useful information about the vast interior of western Canada, held out much prospect for agricultural settlement in the southern plains. Palliser's scientific expert, Dr. James Hector, described this arid country as 'deficient in wood, water and grass'; Palliser himself dismissed it as a 'desert.' Henry Yule Hind, a geologist in Dawson's camp, called it 'permanently sterile and unfit for the abode of civilized man.' Despite these assessments, agriculture – farming, ranching, and the processing and service industries that go along with them – is now the basis of the economy of this sparsely settled region. Fewer than 150,000 people, most of them on farms and in small towns, lived in the entire basin in the mid-1980s. Lethbridge, with fewer than 60,000 residents, was the largest urban centre. At the heart of this agricultural economy are the nine irrigation districts that draw water from the Oldman River system. Between them, they irrigate almost 285,000 hectares of land. The five largest districts – the Lethbridge Northern (LNID), St. Mary River (SMRID), Magrath (MID), Taber (TID), and Raymond (RID) – together account for over 90 percent of this total. The LNID draws its water supply from the Oldman River, through headworks located on the Peigan Indian Reserve. The other four large districts are supplied from the St. Mary headworks system, which draws water from rivers that are tributary to the Oldman – the St. Mary, Belly, and Waterton Rivers.

In 1893, a British-based coal mining company joined forces with a group of Mormon settlers to form the first of a series of companies that financed and constructed works to divert water from the St. Mary River for irrigation with a view to attracting more settlers to the region. The seeds of this development were sown in the 1880s when the Northwestern Coal and Navigation Company obtained substantial land grants from the Dominion government to construct railway lines from Lethbridge to Medicine Hat and south into Montana. The Mormon settlers, recent immigrants from Utah where irrigation was well established, purchased portions of this land and brought in more settlers. In 1912, the Canadian Pacific Railway (CPR), owner and developer of two large tracts of irrigated land on its main line between Medicine Hat and Calgary, purchased control of the company (by then The Alberta Railway and Irrigation Company).

In the early years of this century, the federal government worked very closely with the CPR to colonize western Canada.[12] This cooperation was an integral part of the national policy introduced by Sir John A. Macdonald's Conservatives in the 1870s and maintained in different forms by successive federal governments. The objective of the national policy was to solidify the Canadian nation by developing a national economy, in part to counter US ambitions to exercise its 'manifest destiny' to control the entire North American continent. The establishment of a system of protective tariffs, the construction of a transcontinental railway, and the agricultural settlement of the western plains served both the national economy and the CPR. Agricultural development of the west provided produce for shipment to the processing and manufacturing centres in eastern Canada and a market for goods of eastern manufacture. The CPR owned large tracts of land in the west and shipped goods in both directions.

The Department of the Interior was the major federal government agency involved in irrigation development. By the late 1800s, officials of the department were doing whatever was in their power to ease the way for irrigation. They were led by William Pearce, the superintendent of mines for the North-West Territories, located in Calgary, and Colonel J.S. Dennis, the chief inspector of surveys in Ottawa. The department drafted the North-West Irrigation Act, which became law in July 1894.[13] The act, which was the model for Alberta's water management legislation, gave ownership and all rights to surface water in the Territories, and the authority to allocate the use of that water to the federal Crown. The act also authorized federal engineers to design irrigation works and survey potential dam sites to store water for irrigation. Departmental field staff actively promoted irrigation in what is now southern Alberta and Saskatchewan. The Dominion Land Act was amended in 1898 to make land that was to be developed for irrigation available for one-fifth the going market price. Patterned after similar legislation in the United States, this measure, which became known as the 'irrigation system,' sparked much apparent interest in irrigation, but was abused by speculators more interested in acquiring the land than in growing anything on it.

The various interests promoting irrigation development in the west joined voices in the Western Canada Irrigation Congress – the earliest manifestation of the Iron Triangle discussed in Chapter 15. This happy band of politicians, railway officials, land developers, and government engineers reached its prime in the years immediately before and after the First World War. Its executive was composed of cabinet-rank politicians and senior officials of the governments of Canada and the four western provinces and representatives of the railway and land development companies. The interlocking nature of this relationship was reinforced when Pearce and Dennis moved from their government posts to senior positions with the CPR.

Despite some agitation for more government involvement in funding irrigation development, it was widely accepted that irrigation would pay its own way. In the early years, both the federal and provincial governments stood firm in their determination to avoid any direct financial involvement. Though they stopped short of direct funding, their generous assistance in kind laid the foundation for the public subsidization of irrigation that has continued to the present day. The depression of the 1930s all but bankrupted the provincial governments, leaving their fledgling water management agencies with no money and no staff to put to work at water development. The CPR, with the bulk of its lands taken up by settlers and its revenues reduced by the depression, lost interest in its irrigation projects. Unable or unwilling to spend the money needed to maintain its water distribution works, the CPR scrambled to get out of the irrigation business, selling its aging and disintegrating works to the farmers on its projects, or to the Alberta government, at bargain-basement prices.

In the wake of the Second World War, a new force arrived on the irrigation scene. In 1935, the federal government passed the Prairie Farm Rehabilitation Act, establishing an advisory committee to advise 'as to the best methods to be adopted to secure the rehabilitation of the drought and soil drifting areas in the Provinces of Manitoba, Saskatchewan and Alberta.'[14] By the 1950s, the advisory committee had blossomed into a full-blown bureaucracy, the Prairie Farm Rehabilitation Administration (PFRA), with the authority to 'develop and promote' water supply and land utilization systems – a Canadian version of the US Bureau of Reclamation.[15] For the first ten years of its existence, PFRA's scientists and engineers were fully absorbed in the task of preventing western Canada's topsoil from migrating to Ontario. Its water development activities were limited to the construction of farm ponds and dugouts to catch and store water for stock watering and the domestic needs of farm families. During the Second World War, PFRA's activities, like those of most government agencies not providing services or material for the war, were curtailed because of shortages of money and staff. But PFRA was not without its visionaries, and those left behind spent their war years designing 'shelf projects' that would come to life as public works projects in the post-war period.

Canada emerged from six years of war with an army of returning veterans and a backlog of displaced farmers driven from marginal prairie lands by the drought of the 1930s. The federal government selected irrigation development as one way to get these men back to work. PFRA was ready and willing to lead the way. The St. Mary Project, begun in the late 1940s, the Bow River Project, an irrigation resettlement scheme launched in the 1950s, and the Gardiner Dam, started in 1958 and completed in the early 1960s, were the major water development schemes built by PFRA. As work on the Gardiner Dam began to wind down in the mid-1960s, Canadians and their governments experienced the awakening of the environmental movement. Coincident with this phenomenon, the federal government began to realize, as had the CPR thirty years earlier, that irrigation in western Canada was a money-losing proposition. The federal emphasis in regional development switched from agriculture, particularly from irrigation and big water development to the industrial and service sectors, and PFRA faded from the water scene. Its place as the lead federal water agency was taken by the Water Sector of the Department of Energy, Mines and Resources, the agency that was later to be the nucleus of Environment Canada. Meanwhile, the Alberta economy, sparked by the discovery and development of several major oilfields, began to grow and the Department of Agriculture continued to prop up a number of irrigation districts that had fallen on bad times during the depression.

As the federal government manoeuvred to get out of the irrigation business in the 1970s, the Alberta government, determined to exercise greater control over Alberta's destiny, set out to diversify the provincial economy. Fortified by rising oil revenues, the government was in an expansionary mood, ready and willing to invest in infrastructure that would foster diversification. Fortunately for irrigation interests in southern Alberta, the government chose to focus on established sectors, where it believed Alberta had an economic advantage. One such sector was agriculture, in particular irrigation, which produced feed for livestock and so-called specialty crops, like corn, potatoes, and carrots, both of which could support an expanded food-processing industry. The vacuum left by the reduced federal presence in water development was gradually filled by the provincial agency, the Agriculture Department's Water Resources Division. As was to be the case with the federal Water Sector, the Water Resources Division became the nucleus of Alberta's new environment department. Throughout the 1970s, the agency expanded rapidly to deliver the water management programs required to support the irrigation expansion to which the government was committed.

In 1973, Canada agreed to transfer ownership and control of the extensive

network of federal irrigation works in Alberta to the provincial government.[16] In 1975, Alberta announced its Water Management for Irrigation
Use policy, which expanded its commitment to irrigation development
and consolidated its control over the system of dams, diversions, and
canals that supply water to the irrigation districts.[17] The policy included
commitments to reserve more water for irrigation; take over, rebuild, and
expand all district-owned headworks; and increase its investment in the
rehabilitation of district-owned water distribution systems. A key element
of the policy was a commitment to provide additional regulation of the
Oldman River – a commitment that evolved into the Oldman River Dam.

A scheme to divert water from the Oldman River to irrigate land north of
Fort Macleod was a 'live issue' as early as 1910.[18] In 1913, the federal
Department of the Interior completed surveys and a feasibility study for
the Lethbridge Northern Irrigation Project. The point selected for diversion from the Oldman was on the Peigan Indian Reserve. In 1916, with the
Lethbridge Northern Project still no more than a concept, engineers in the
department's irrigation branch were considering the possibility of a dam
on the Castle River to support 'further extension' of the project.[19] In 1919,
farmers in the area north of Lethbridge established the Lethbridge Northern Irrigation District (LNID) under the terms of Alberta's new Irrigation
Districts Act, and the Department of the Interior approved an allocation of
water for the project from the Oldman River. In 1922, the district purchased a 205-acre (83-hectare) right-of-way on the Peigan Indian Reserve
from the federal government and began construction of works to divert
water from the Oldman to the LNID. The Peigan have since maintained
that this purchase transpired without their consent and in contravention
of the provisions of the Indian Act. Construction of the works – a diversion weir, a canal, and a flume across the Oldman River – was completed
in May 1923. This canal, which was routed through a Peigan burial
ground, was destroyed by flood waters later in the same year. The LNID
borrowed from the Alberta government to rebuild the works, and the district finally began operations in 1924.

This diversion project marked the beginnings of both the ongoing dispute between the Peigan and the LNID and the never-ending flow of cash
out of Edmonton to subsidize irrigation in the Oldman River Basin. Farmers in the district were unable or unwilling to pay the high rate levied by
the district to repay its government loan, and the district was soon in serious financial difficulty. In 1926, the Alberta government absorbed the
debt, and placed the district under the control of a provincially appointed
trustee. This arrangement continued until 1968, when the district reverted
to the control of a board of directors elected by the ratepayers.

Irrigation of district lands, which peaked at 32,000 hectares in 1950, had fallen to less than 20,000 hectares by the late 1960s. Encouraged by a provincial program, introduced in 1970, to share the costs of rehabilitating capital works in the districts, the LNID embarked on a period of expansion, and, by 1975, it was committed to supply water to 44,000 hectares. At this level of development, however, the district was unable to supply the water demands of its irrigators in dry years and was forced to introduce rationing. Recurring shortages led the district board and the water users to put pressure on the provincial government to make more water available to the district.

2
In the Beginning

> Alberta Environment's strategy is to identify most of the excess
> water throughout the Southern part of the Province for
> agricultural use on a priority basis.
>
> – Alberta Agriculture and Alberta Environment,
>   *Water Management for Irrigation Use*[1]

In 1971, Peter Lougheed's Progressive Conservatives took control of the
provincial legislature, forcing the Social Credit Party into opposition after
thirty-five years in power. Campaigning on a ticket that included shelving
government plans for diverting water from north to south – a concept dear
to the hearts of the irrigation community – the Tories had taken forty-nine
of the seventy-five seats in the August election but were completely shut
out of the twelve constituencies in the irrigation belt, south and east of
Calgary. Determined to make inroads in the south before the next election, the new government threw off its concerns about inequity in government subsidization of irrigation and water development and set out
both to diversify the agricultural sector and to win favour with the irrigation community.[2]

Irrigation interests in southern Alberta began to lobby the new government to do something to increase the amount of water available to farmers in the Oldman River Basin. The LNID had been forced to ration water
among its users and many drylanders within reach of the district's canals
had added their names to the ever growing list of farmers hoping to
obtain irrigation water. Because of the substantial irrigation withdrawals
upstream, flows in the river at Lethbridge were chronically low during the
summer months, with the result that water quality was deteriorating.
Environmental interests and sports-fishing enthusiasts were suggesting
that the irrigators should take less water and use it more efficiently. The
solution favoured by the farmers and the government's water managers
was a dam on the Oldman River, and in June 1974, Alberta's Water Management Service (WMS) launched a study to investigate potential dam sites.

In the 1975 election campaign, Conservatives promised public money
for rehabilitating irrigation district infrastructure and increasing water
supplies for irrigation, including regulation of the Oldman River. The
strategy worked. In the March 1975 election, the Tories captured nine of
the twelve seats in the irrigation belt. In the wake of the election, the

government confirmed its promises by adopting a water management policy developed by Alberta Environment and Alberta Agriculture. The policy, published under the title *Water Management for Irrigation,* gave irrigators first crack at the water in the South Saskatchewan River system and cleared the way for the Oldman River Dam.[3]

The new water management policy established the responsibilities of each department in the area of irrigation water management – a move necessitated by the earlier transfer of the Water Resources Division, and the administration of the Water Resources Act, from Agriculture to the new environment department. Environment would be responsible for the 'operation and maintenance of all headworks to deliver water to Irrigation Districts and other [unspecified] users'; Agriculture would be 'concerned with all aspects of irrigation farming and water distribution systems within District boundaries.' The policy committed Environment to 'maintain a secure and continuous supply of water to Irrigation Districts and all other users.' To achieve this, the department would undertake 'additional regulation of the South Saskatchewan River System,' with regulation of the Oldman River as 'the first priority.' Environment was committed to spend $44 million to rehabilitate and enlarge its irrigation headworks and $65 million for storage on the Oldman. Agriculture would spend $90 million to rehabilitate and enlarge the irrigation districts' distribution systems.

In June of 1976, Alberta Environment produced a five-volume report on its Oldman investigations, recommending a detailed analysis leading to construction of a dam at the Three Rivers site.[4] The construction of a dam somewhere on the Oldman system was the only water supply alternative that had been considered. The department's planners, most of them engineers who had served their apprenticeship with Alberta's Water Resources Division or with PFRA, had investigated nine potential dam sites. Though Three Rivers had ranked as only the sixth most suitable in terms of potential environmental impact, it was rated the most suitable site overall 'mainly because of its ability to meet the needs of the LNID through gravity diversion at the lowest cost.'[5] The department made no attempt to disguise the fact that the study was primarily concerned with providing water for irrigation, solemnly noting that it had been done in accordance with the government's 1975 Water Management for Irrigation Use policy. In fact, the study, initiated in 1974, anticipated the policy, introduced in 1975.

It is interesting to note at this point that there is no suggestion in the Phase I study reports that a dam on the Oldman would have any impact on the Peigan Indian Band. Though the terms of reference for the studies called for 'a sociological and socio-economic evaluation, including benefits and disbenefits to people in the area,' there was no specific requirement to consider the Peigan.[6] The archaeological studies noted frequent occurrences of artifacts and other evidence of former Indian occupation in buried campsites and buffalo jumps at the various sites, but there was no suggestion that these might have any connection to contemporary Indian residents in the area or be of any significance to their culture or spiritual beliefs and practices.[7]

The previous year, the department had released a report recommending that the government construct a dam on the Red Deer River, upstream from the city of Red Deer.[8] That recommendation had been rejected by the province's Environmental Conservation Authority (ECA) after public hearings in the fall of 1975. But after a second round of studies by the department, followed by a second round of public hearings and a second rejection by the ECA, the provincial government announced it would build the dam anyway. The recommendation to dam the Oldman, coming while the province was still struggling to overcome the adverse public reaction to its decision to dam the Red Deer, created a predicament for the government. It could have handled the situation by simply not releasing the Oldman report, but its recommendations were common knowledge in the Lethbridge area and the irrigation community was pressing the politicians to make the report public. Reluctantly, Environment Minister Dave Russell released the report on 14 July 1976, emphasizing that the government was anxious to determine the public's reaction to the recommendations. During the next few months, there were over seventy responses to the minister's request for feedback.

The irrigation community was supportive. The chairman of the LNID board of directors observed that 'this is the reason we have been pressing for upstream storage for the past 10 years.'[9] The manager of the SMRID, Jake Theissen, who in a later incarnation as a government employee was to serve as construction manager for the Oldman Dam, welcomed a dam at Three Rivers but noted that offstream storage that would support another 40,000 hectares in the SMRID could be built for one-eighth of the cost.[10] The *Lethbridge Herald,* long a proponent of large-scale water development, urged the government to 'build the dam.'[11]

Farmers whose homes or land would be flooded by a reservoir at Three Rivers opposed the idea. They joined forces to establish the Committee for the Preservation of Three Rivers (CPTR) to lobby against the dam. The Peigan Indian Band reminded the government that, in their interpretation, Treaty 7 gave the rivers to the Indians and served notice that any development on the Oldman must be done in consultation with them.[12]

Given the decidedly mixed reaction, the government decided that more study was needed to provide the information it would need to defend a decision to build a dam. It would also delay that decision, which meant the government wouldn't have to do battle with the anti-dam faction on two fronts simultaneously. In November, the government announced that there would be Phase II studies to investigate the other potential dam sites, including the Brocket site, in more detail. Peter Melnychuk, the assistant deputy minister who headed up the Water Management Service (WMS), told the *Lethbridge Herald,* 'We certainly feel our procedure for testing the public with the Phase I report was a good one. Now we will begin the Phase II studies so we have every last bit of information with absolutely no missing parts when the public hearings begin.'[13] The extent to which this goal was realized was to be the focus of debate in open forums, in public hearings, in the media, and in the highest courts of the land for years to come.

The Phase II program 'to consider additional water *supply* alternatives [emphasis added]' was under the direction of the Oldman River Study Management Committee (ORSMC).[14] Irrigation interests were well represented on the ten-person committee by three irrigators and the three senior civil servants, each of whom had spent all or most of their career in the agriculture department.[15] Notably underrepresented were environmental interests, people who used the river for recreational purposes, and the Peigan Indians. The committee hired a member of the Peigan Band to provide liaison with the Peigan Reserve.

The committee was chaired by Peter Melnychuk, an engineer who had spent his entire career with the provincial government's water agency. A proponent of supply-side water management, Melnychuk's philosophy was summed up in a 1980 interview that appeared in a departmental publication: 'We have many water management problems, but we always start with our basic one – that is the problem of seasonal variation in flows in our rivers ... Of course we can't use the water, nor do we really need it for the six weeks in early spring when we have peak flows. When we do need it, in summer and fall, we don't have it ... So we need to implement some kind of man-made regulation on our streams ... to capture our share of the water ... With respect to reduction of consumption, we do not have anything specific in that regard, in terms of an operational program.'[16]

The Phase II studies began in February 1977, and on 26 August 1978, the Management Committee released a report recommending a 'strategy for water and land management' in the basin, the key element of which was a dam on the Oldman River. The strategy was presented largely in the form of a program of 'integrated irrigation and water development,' essentially a blueprint for implementing the 1975 Water Management for Irrigation Use policy in the Oldman basin.[17] It prescribed a step-wise approach to the construction of the dams, diversions, and canals required to support irrigation expansion in the Oldman basin. The water storage capacity in the system was to be increased by some 600,000 acre-feet (740,000 cubic decametres), and the irrigated acreage was to increase by nearly 300,000 acres (121,000 hectares) to 850,000 acres (344,000 hectares) by the year

Figure 1   Peter Melnychuk, head of Alberta's Water Management Service

2005. It required a start on construction of a dam on the Oldman River sometime between 1985 and 1990, so the dam could be 'fully operational' between 1990 and 1995.

The committee recommended that the dam should be constructed at either Brocket or Three Rivers. A third site – Fort Macleod – had been rejected for a number of reasons, but the deciding factor was that water could not be conveyed from a reservoir at this location to the LNID via a gravity diversion, and, in an era of escalating energy charges, the cost of pumping water uphill to the LNID would be prohibitive. Noting that Brocket and Three Rivers were roughly comparable from technical, economic, and environmental perspectives, the committee left the final choice of a site to the politicians.

The Management Committee made no mention of the possibility that a dam on the Oldman could have any adverse impact on the culture or the spiritual beliefs and practices of the Peigan.

Although they were not saying so publicly, provincial government officials were not anxious to see the dam built on the reserve. In 1976, WMS had advised the Peigan that it wished to obtain additional reserve land in order to increase the capacity of the LNID headworks and requested access to the reserve to conduct engineering investigations (see Map 4). Research undertaken by the Peigan had convinced them that the 1922 transfer of reserve land to the LNID for its original headworks was invalid because the federal government had not adhered to the requirements of the Indian Act. The Peigan replied that they were willing to negotiate access to the reserve and a land transfer, but only if they were adequately compensated for past use of the land on which the existing headworks were situated. Alberta took the position that the matter of ownership and compensation for past use of the land was a separate issue that should not be tied to its request for access to the reserve and the transfer of land for the proposed headworks expansion.

WMS continued discussions with the Peigan and, in March 1978, the band issued a permit granting the Service access to the reserve for three months to carry out surveys and engineering investigations. In May, dissatisfied with the inaction on the compensation issue, the Peigan revoked the permit. Led by then chief Nelson Small Legs Sr., they established a blockade that denied Alberta Environment and LNID officials access to the diversion weir. The LNID, desperate for water, obtained an injunction from the Alberta Supreme Court preventing the Peigan from obstructing access to the weir. The immediate problem of water for the LNID was resolved, but the more pressing problem for WMS of obtaining the access and the land required for the headworks expansion remained. Since a dam on the Oldman River would be of little value to the LNID if the capacity of the headworks was not increased, the province reluctantly agreed to negotiate compensation with the Peigan.

Not all of the Peigan people were happy with these developments. Some warned that if negotiations did not go their way, they would construct works to divert the Oldman River around the LNID weir – a warning not taken seriously at the time, but one that returned to plague Alberta and the LNID twelve years later.[18]

This uneasy peace was still in effect when the ORSMC completed its studies and submitted its recommendations. Although it recommended that Brocket should be considered as a location for the dam, the committee signalled its reservations, observing that 'the extent and complexity of the jurisdictional and political problems associated with the development by the province of a major reservoir on Indian lands cannot be fully assessed by the committee, and is a matter for resolution by the Peigan Indian Band and the provincial and federal governments.'[19]

3
The ECA Review

The Environment Council is convinced that an onstream dam is not required at this time, nor in the foreseeable future.

– Environment Council of Alberta, August 1979

Simultaneous with his release of the ORSMC's report, Environment Minister Russell announced that he'd asked the Environment Council of Alberta (ECA) to convene public hearings on the report and submit their findings as soon as possible.[1]

The Environmental Conservation Authority, later known as the Environment Council of Alberta, was established by Alberta's Social Credit government in 1970. Its title notwithstanding, the ECA had no authority. Its mandate was simply to conduct public hearings on matters related to the environment and to act in an advisory capacity to the cabinet. The ECA described itself as 'a non-partisan body without vested interests, at one length removed from the government itself.'[2] The perception that it was at one length removed from government eventually brought the Authority into disfavour with its political masters and led to its demise.

The ECA's difficulties began in 1974 when it took a stand against a proposal by Alberta Environment to build a dam on the Paddle River in the Barrhead constituency of Tory legend Dr. Hugh Horner, then deputy premier and minister of Transportation.

The Paddle River had a history of overflowing its banks during spring run-off, with the result that landowners adjacent to the river were frequently unable to get onto the land in time to seed a crop that would reach maturity in the limited growing season of north-central Alberta. To solve this problem, Alberta Environment proposed the construction of four dams on the Paddle and its tributaries upstream from the town of Barrhead. After holding public hearings on the proposal, the ECA recommended that the three tributary dams not be built and that the dam on the Paddle itself be scaled down.[3] Although its recommendations did not deter the government from building the Paddle River Dam, they did turn the political spotlight on the project, thus earning the ECA the enmity of Horner, which opposition politicians hinted was a factor in its eventual downfall.[4]

Undaunted, the ECA, in 1976 and again in 1977, dug in its heels in opposition to a WMS proposal to dam the Red Deer River, attracting national
attention in the process and placing the government in the difficult position of publicly opposing the views of its own environmental watchdog.

Its final report on the Red Deer proved to be the final utterance of the
Environmental Conservation Authority. By the end of the year, the province had legislated the death of the Environmental Conservation Authority and the birth of the Environment Council of Alberta. The creative
choice of a name for the new body allowed the continued use of the
departed Authority's acronym, and allowed all who cared to do so to pretend that nothing had changed. In fact, a great deal had changed. The permanent four-member executive of the former Authority had been replaced
by the Council's single chief executive officer and the government would
appoint temporary panel members for each public hearing that the Council might be asked to convene. NDP Opposition Leader Grant Notley predicted the government would appoint panel members 'most likely to reach
the conclusion the government would want.'[5] It was this new ECA that the
government mobilized for public hearings on the Oldman.

To counter rumours that panel members would be selected on the basis
of their pro-dam sentiments, the government invited eighteen different
groups to nominate candidates for the three panel positions, but tipped its
hand by indicating it was looking for panelists with some knowledge of
farming, water storage, and community interest in irrigation.[6] Knowledge
of the environment or Indians were not prerequisites. After weeding out
the nominations, the government appointed Dr. Arnold Platt, a professional agrologist and farmer from the Cardston area, to chair the panel.
The other members were Alistair Crerar, chief executive officer of the new
ECA, Thomas Sissons, a Medicine Hat businessman, and Dr. Dixon Thompson, an associate professor of environmental design at the University of
Calgary. Between 6 November and 29 November 1978, this panel sat for a
total of ten days in eight different communities, listening to 205 briefs presented by landowners, environmentalists, Indians, anglers, irrigators, local
governments, chambers of commerce, academics, consultants, students,
religious groups, and just plain citizens. Another 33 briefs were filed with
the ECA after hearings, bringing the total number to 238.

In the end, opinion divided along predictable lines between those
favouring and those opposing the dam. Numerical differences merely indicated which interests had the time and resources to present their briefs at
hearings in the greatest number of centres. The Alberta Irrigation Projects
Association (AIPA) and the Committee for the Preservation of Three
Rivers, for example, each presented essentially the same brief at several different hearings, as much to engender a broad base of public sympathizers
as to inform the panel. A controversial brief taking a strong position for or

against the dam was usually guaranteed a post-hearing interview by reporters and, in the larger centres, an appearance on the television news.

After deliberating over the winter and through the following spring, the panel delivered its report and recommendations to the environment minister in August 1979.[7] It offered seventy-four recommendations in all, on matters as diverse as the quality of storm water run-off and the purchase of land for crop research, but it was its recommendations on a dam on the Oldman River that were the most controversial. To the dismay of the government, the irrigation community, and the critics of the new ECA, the panel concluded that 'an onstream dam is not required at this time, nor in the foreseeable future.'[8] It is important to understand that although the panel recommended against a dam on the Oldman River, it did so not because of the impact that a dam would have on the environment or on the Peigan Indians, but because it concluded that an onstream dam was not needed *to support irrigation expansion to the level that the panel recommended.* The panel accepted without question that the irrigated acreage in the Oldman basin should be increased, but it scaled the ORSMC's recommended expansion limit of 850,000 acres (344,000 hectares) down to 786,000 acres (318,000 hectares) on the grounds of economic feasibility.[9] To provide the water to support expansion to that level, the panel recommended the construction of a series of offstream reservoirs that, in the aggregate, would store 210,000 acre-feet (259,000 cubic decametres) of water.

Over the years that followed, opponents of the dam frequently misrepresented the panel's preference for offstream storage as support for their claim that as much water could be provided by offstream storage as by a dam on the Oldman River.[10] Whether they did not understand or chose to ignore the fact that the panel's conclusion assumed the irrigation of less land (therefore requiring less water) than had been recommended by the ORSMC was never clear. In fact, the ECA panel never did make an outright rejection of a dam on the Oldman River. Though it said a dam would not be needed for the foreseeable future, it left the door open by adding that 'should a dam [on the Oldman] become feasible, only the Brocket and Fort Macleod sites [should] be considered.'[11] The panel rated Three Rivers as the least preferable site because it would have the greatest environmental and social impact and had no appreciable engineering or cost advantage over the other sites.

The panel had little to say about the potential environmental impacts of a dam on the Oldman, and even less to say about potential impacts on the cultural or spiritual values of the Peigan. To a large extent, this is a reflection of the type and quality of information that was presented to the panel for review, though it also suggests that most of the issues that were later raised in opposition to the dam – the maintenance of biodiversity, the cultural and spiritual rights of the Peigan – were not major issues in 1979. The

panel adopted a largely homocentric view of 'environmental considerations within the basin,' noting that they ranged from 'a concern for the
uniqueness of the ecosystems of the western end, through concern for
preservation of a largely man-created environment in the central portion
of the basin, to primarily an interest in what can be done to enhance the
environment for human habitation towards the eastern end of the system.'[12] Its sole recommendation under the heading 'Environment' was
that 'landowners should be encouraged to maintain areas *unsuitable for
cultivated crops* in ways which would add diversity and provide shelter for
wildlife [emphasis added].'[13] As far as impact of a dam on the river and the
river valley was concerned, the panel limited its observations to generali-
ties. It noted that the Three Rivers site was 'a sheltered corridor ... [that] ...
provides a wide range of habitats and is an important transition zone for
the animals of the mountains and the plains, the grasslands and the
forests,' and that the environmental losses from a dam at that site would
be 'substantial.'[14] The Brocket site had 'major environmental values' and
was also in a transition zone, but 'a less important one' than Three Rivers,
while a dam at the Fort Macleod site, since 'it [was] not in a terrestrial transition zone [and lacked] important corridor features ... would cause less
environmental disturbance' than a dam at Brocket.[15]

The panel measured the social impact of a dam entirely in terms of effects
on landowners who would lose their homes, land, or property, whose farming operations would be affected, or who would otherwise be inconve-
nienced or lose their sense of community. It did not comment on how a
dam might affect the cultural or spiritual values of the Peigan, beyond noting that 'one brief from the Peigan people pointed out the importance of
the river to the Band's way of life.'[16] Even in that brief the only reference
to matters cultural or spiritual was contained in a single rhetorical question: 'What price can be set on our spiritual and cultural values and on an
ecological ethic for our natural environment?'[17] Eloquent, but empty.
What was to become a critical issue once construction of the dam was
underway was either not understood or not perceived to be important by
the public, the media, the government agencies, the ECA, or even by
Indian spokespersons during the period when information was being presented that would be the basis for a decision about a dam on the Oldman.

The panel members were not insensitive to social and economic conditions on the Peigan Reserve. While the panel believed it was beyond its
terms of reference, it noted that 'nowhere in the basin did the Council
find a more urgent need for opportunities that would give hope to the
young people [than on the Peigan Reserve],' and recommended that 'a
partnership be established between a sensitive Alberta government and
the Peigan peoples' to search out such opportunities.[18] Ironically, since
1979, the Peigan leaders and the provincial government have more often

been adversaries over dam-related issues than partners in seeking opportunities to better the lot of the Peigan.

Dam opponents, like the Committee for the Preservation of Three Rivers, were 'cautiously optimistic' about the ECA's conclusion that onstream storage was not needed. People in the irrigation community admitted to some disappointment with the ECA's position but indicated that they were not about to give up on the idea of damming the river. They took some consolation from the public reaction of Environment Minister Jack Cookson, who told the *Lethbridge Herald* he was yet to be convinced that a dam on the Oldman would not be required sometime in the future – a response that the *Herald*'s editorial writers found to be 'less than satisfactory.'[19] In the same interview, Cookson promised a decision on the ECA's recommendations within a year. He maintained that a decision to dam the Oldman would not put the government in a situation comparable to that in which it had found itself two years earlier when it opted to dam the Red Deer, contrary to the advice of the ECA, an indication of how badly Cookson and his department underestimated the strength and determination of the interests opposed to a dam on the Oldman.

Cookson spent the winter of 1979-80 parrying demands by the irrigation community for an early announcement favouring a dam. He repeatedly assured opposition MLAs that he would make an announcement in the spring of 1980, while the legislature was in session, but kept finding excuses for not doing so. Foremost among these was the government's on-again, off-again negotiations with the Peigan over access to the LNID weir. The irrigation community continued to take heart from signals put out by the government that the decision, when it finally came, would be good news for them. In March, the speech from the throne heralded that the government would be making a major decision on water resource development in the Oldman River Basin and that this decision would be 'the first stage of a renewed emphasis on the development of Alberta's water resources and [would] be an important element in the government's recognition of the importance of food production and the specialized nature of irrigation.'[20]

In April, Cookson said he would soon propose 'a new 20-year plan for water use in southern Alberta' to the provincial legislature, focusing on Alberta's thirteen irrigation districts and costing more than $200 million.[21] In the debate on his department's estimates that same month, Cookson assured the legislature that a 'public statement of policy [would be forthcoming] that would deal pretty well with the whole irrigation situation in southern Alberta.'[22] In a newspaper interview published in June, Cookson blamed the stalled negotiations with the Peigan for the delay in announcing a decision on the dam.[23] In another interview for the same article, Peter Melnychuk took issue with the ECA's conclusion that there was no need for a dam on the Oldman, saying that the ECA had looked only at the short term, while his ORSMC had considered the long term and concluded that a dam on the Oldman was a necessity.

As spring turned to summer, it became apparent that the government would adhere to custom and delay the announcement of what was bound to be a controversial decision until the legislature was in recess. The weather throughout the prairie region continued hot and dry through July and into August. Farmers bemoaned the lack of moisture, and irrigation districts threatened to ration the water in their canals. Newspapers and television screens showed pictures of farmers kneeling in their parched fields under the blazing sun, sifting the powder-like soil through their fingers. Still the government dithered, and at a mid-August ceremonial signing of an understanding with the Peigan that would ensure government access to the LNID weir, Cookson maintained that his department had still not resolved whether a dam on the river was necessary.[24]

4
A Dam on the Oldman

The persistence of water management agencies in seeing their
dreams to fruition is remarkable.

– Richard C. Bocking, *Canada's Water: For Sale?*[1]

On the last Friday in August 1980, Jack Cookson and his colleague Agriculture Minister Dallas Schmidt flew to Lethbridge to announce that the government would indeed build a dam on the Oldman River. Although the government preferred the Three Rivers site, Cookson said the allocation of funds for dam construction would be deferred to give the Peigan time to submit a proposal for a dam at the Brocket site. They also committed the government to an ambitious construction program designed to make it possible to divert substantially greater amounts of water from the South Saskatchewan River system for irrigation. These decisions, said the ministers, were simply 'a continuation *and an expansion* of the major policy decisions made in 1975 concerning the management of water resources, the need to rehabilitate existing irrigation systems and the *requirement* of future expansion [emphases added].'[2]

The decision to build a dam on the Oldman meant that the government had opted to allocate enough water from the Oldman River to expand irrigation in the basin to 850,000 acres (344,000 hectares) as recommended by the ORSMC – 285,000 acres (115,000 hectares) more than were irrigated in 1980, an increase of 50 percent.[3]

Mike Cooper, speaking for the landowners at Three Rivers, criticized Pincher Creek-Crowsnest MLA, soon to be environment minister, Fred Bradley for not representing the interests of people in his constituency opposed to the dam. Bradley expressed sympathy for the landowners, calling the decision 'the most difficult that I've had to participate in.'[4] However, like other southern rural MLAs on both the government and opposition benches, he defended the dam as necessary for irrigation over the long term. NDP Opposition Leader Grant Notley, whose party held no ridings south of Edmonton, condemned the decision because the ECA had proclaimed a dam unnecessary and because 'it puts another nail in the coffin of the ECA and ... of public participation in environmental matters.'[5]

The ECA's chief executive officer, Alistair Crerar, said the government's decision was 'indefensible' and that he would seek some clarification of the decision and its ramifications for future ECA endeavours.[6] Former panel chairman Dr. Arnold Platt observed that 'our terms of reference didn't include political considerations, and obviously a government has to take that into account.'[7]

Crerar and the members of the by then dissolved panel met with Cookson in October, and, although they left the meeting still questioning the government's economics, they informed a press conference that while they hoped the government would reconsider before starting construction, they did not intend to prolong the debate. Neither the ECA nor the panel members voiced any concern about the environmental implications of the decision.

Concluding from newspaper reports that the government was about to announce in favour of the dam, former panel member Dixon Thompson had written to Cookson in July, raising a number of questions that he believed would have to be answered before a rational decision could be made in favour of a dam. Cookson's response, tendered after the government's decision had been made public, included a statement that indicated how little the opinions of the ECA panel, or anyone else outside the irrigation community, weighed in the government's considerations: 'The decision to proceed with an onstream dam was based on the need for an assured water supply for the residents of the Oldman River basin, many of which are dependent upon the irrigation industry. Other benefits from flow regulation, such as improved water quality ... assured water supply for municipalities, and ... the Apportionment Agreement were recognized, *but were peripheral to the decision to proceed* [emphasis added].'[8]

To the surprise of many observers, the *Lethbridge Herald,* which at the culmination of the Phase I studies in 1976 had shouted 'build the dam,' was apparently having second thoughts.[9] The *Herald*'s impression was that the Oldman Dam decision was political and 'owed its existence to the province's surplus of money rather than to hard-headed analysis of the water situation.'[10] The *Calgary Herald,* venturing the opinion that a dam might 'make sense eventually,' reminded its readers that 'agriculture is one of Alberta's major industries ... to which we must look for continued prosperity when our petroleum production goes into decline.'[11]

The Peigan, having earlier informed the government of their interest, responded positively to Cookson's announcement that the government was prepared to consider building at the Brocket site rather than at Three Rivers. The government said it would allow fifteen months for the Peigan to submit a proposal for a dam on the reserve; the Peigan said they were 'prepared to see what they [the province] have to offer.'[12] Having kept the province on the hook for over two years on the question of access to the LNID weir, the Peigan were not about to be stampeded into a hasty deal over a dam on their reserve. In light of the difficulties that the province had experienced in operating the LNID diversion works on the Peigan Reserve, Cookson's observation that 'the biggest problems with the proposed Brocket site are constitutional, regarding the surrender of Indian land' was not surprising.[13] It was a clear indication that unless the province could obtain clear title to the land on which the dam and reservoir were to be located and unobstructed access to that land, there would be no dam on the reserve.

Until the LNID headworks on the reserve were enlarged to allow the LNID to increase its rate of diversion from the river, a dam on the Oldman would be of no benefit. Consequently, the government had delayed its decision to build a dam until it could be confident that the Peigan would allow work on the headworks to proceed. The negotiations that the Peigan and Alberta had agreed to enter into following the 1978 blockade did not formally begin until the fall of 1979.[14] In the meantime, the Peigan had filed a statement of claim in the Alberta Court of Queen's Bench against the LNID and Alberta Environment, asking the Court to declare the 1922 transfer of reserve land for the headworks right-of-way invalid. In October 1979, Peigan Chief Nelson Small Legs and Alberta Environment Assistant Deputy Minister Henry Theissen sat down to begin the negotiations, a process that would require some forty meetings over the next two years. On 5 August, Chief Small Legs and Environment Minister Cookson signed a memorandum of understanding that set out the terms for a proposed agreement. In exchange for a cash settlement of $2.5 million, and a further $1 million to be held in trust at prime plus 1.5 percent interest, the Peigan would grant Alberta 'irrevocable proprietary interest' in the 4.1 acres (1.7 hectares) of riverbed and 50.8 acres (20.5 hectares) of reserve land taken up by the rehabilitated headworks.

Since many Peigan people opposed the 'surrender' of reserve land, the proposed agreement was hotly debated during the campaign leading up to the band elections in January 1981. Following the elections, the new band council made it clear that any suggestion of surrender of reserve land for the headworks was not acceptable. The negotiations were resumed, Alberta upped the ante, and at a meeting on 30 April 1981, mediated by Chief Justice Mulvain of the Alberta Supreme Court, the negotiators reached a final agreement. Ratification of the agreement by the Peigan, Alberta, and the federal government was announced in June.

Under the terms of the April 1981 agreement, Alberta agreed to make an initial payment of $4 million to the Peigan, and annual payments of $300,000 (in 1981 dollars) thereafter for the life of the agreement. Alberta also agreed to provide technical advice and support for irrigation development on the reserve as well as advice on the construction of a dam at the Brocket site, to develop training programs for Peigan workers, and to erect fences to prevent Peigan livestock from straying onto the right-of-way and into the canal. The Peigan agreed to provide Alberta 'unquestioned and continued control of and access to' the headworks and right-of-way, the use of 32.1 acres (13.0 hectares) of reserve land for four years for headworks construction, unhindered access to the headworks for all government employees, and to withdraw its August 1979 statement of claim against Alberta and the LNID and any previous claims.

One consequence of the April 1981 agreement was a commitment by the province and the federal Department of Indian Affairs to jointly fund a study, to be managed by the Peigan, to assess the potential impact on and the benefits and costs to the Peigan of a dam and reservoir on the Oldman at the Brocket site. The Weasel Valley Water Use Study, initiated in 1981 and completed in 1983, provided information on the implications and opportunities posed by a dam for the resources, economic activity, and social conditions on the reserve.[15] The Peigan used the findings and recommendations of the study as the basis for a proposal for the joint development of a dam at Brocket. In November 1983, Chief Yellowhorn forwarded the proposal to Environment Minister Bradley with the advice that the band was prepared to begin negotiations.[16] The Peigan proposal made it clear that the province would not have sole ownership and control of the dam.

As the spring of 1984 turned to summer, and the Peigan waited for the government's response to their offer to discuss joint development of a dam at Brocket, dryland farmers in southern Alberta watched their crops shrivel and their fields turn to dust under the rainless sky. Soil moisture and precipitation conditions that summer, the eighth year of a drought that began in 1977, were the worst experienced in the area since 1916. By mid-July, there had been no measurable precipitation at Lethbridge in over three weeks. Even irrigators, whose crops had to that point been spared, began to worry as the LNID prepared for the fifth time since 1977 to shut off the flow in its canals while it restored the level in its main reservoir.

On Sunday, 15 July, prayers for rain dominated the liturgy in Lethbridge and district churches, although some, like United Church clergyman Reverend Bill Mayberry in Fort Macleod, didn't believe that 'our faith in God is such that if we shout loud enough, we'll get rain.'[17] For those of like mind or who doubted the efficacy of prayer, there was always the government to shout at, and the Picture Butte and District Chamber of Commerce invited southern MLAs to a meeting on 16 July with just that in mind. For several hours on a stiflingly hot July evening, a half-dozen government MLAs, led by Agriculture Minister Leroy Fjordbotten, were jammed into a school auditorium with 500 angry farmers, where they were harangued for their inaction on construction of the long-promised Oldman River Dam.

Whatever message the beleaguered MLAs took back to Edmonton, whether concern for the plight of the farmers or concern for the future of the Conservative Party, it had an obvious impression on Premier Peter Lougheed. In the second week of August, accompanied by Environment Minister Fred Bradley and several other southern Alberta MLAs, Lougheed descended on the south for a helicopter tour of the drought-stricken cropland, and to unveil a hastily assembled $30-million drought-relief package. For *Lethbridge Herald* columnist Joanne Helmer, the premier's mercy mission conjured up 'the ridiculous vision of Lougheed dropping sacks of money from the helicopter as he was flying over the farms.'[18]

Lougheed capped off his visit at a press conference in Lethbridge on 9 August, where he announced that the construction of a dam on the Oldman River, at Three Rivers, would begin in 1986. To avoid sharing the limelight with a forewarned and forearmed opposition, the government had not given the landowners at Three Rivers or the Peigan advance notice of its decision.

The Peigan, still awaiting some word from the government on whether it was prepared to negotiate joint development of a dam at Brocket, learned of the decision to build at Three Rivers through the media. Environment Minister Bradley told the press conference that the Brocket site had been rejected because a dam there would have 'higher construction costs' and because the Peigan wanted 'significant economic compensation.' In a 1994 interview, Peter Melnychuk said, 'To be honest, another factor was the long-term security of the site.'[19] Official notification for the Peigan came later in a letter from Bradley to Chief Yellowhorn, dated

Figure 2 Premier Peter Lougheed. His government made the decision to build the Oldman River Dam.

9 August, the day of Lougheed's press conference.[20] Two days later, Yellow-horn announced that, if they could get financial backing from the federal government and the private sector, the Peigan were prepared to build their own dam at Brocket.[21] Claiming ownership of the water in the Oldman and reminding the government that the river flowed across reserve land, Yellowhorn observed that the Peigan also had the option of applying for a court injunction against development on the river or of diverting the flow of the river around the LNID headworks.

Environmental interests charged that the government had ignored concerns that the dam would destroy the sports fishery in the upper Oldman and the lower Castle and Crowsnest Rivers.[22] The government stood by its decision on the grounds that the dam would bring greater stability to southern Alberta agriculture. Bradley promised that the landowners would be 'treated fairly and equitably' and forecast that the social and economic benefits that would flow from the dam would outweigh any environmental impacts.[23] Government press releases claimed the fishery upstream from the reservoir would be 'unaffected,' the fishery downstream would be 'enhanced,' and 'recreational facilities *compatible with the operation of the reservoir for irrigation* will be developed to accommodate boating, sailing and fishing [emphasis added].'[24]

The *Lethbridge Herald* took the government to task for choosing to build a dam to increase the water supply for irrigation, while slowing the pace of canal rehabilitation that would permit more efficient use of water, noting that the water rates charged to irrigation farmers had not increased and that 'there has not been a noticeable interest in conservation among local municipalities.'[25] The *Herald* also intoned what was to be a prophetic warning: 'The dark clouds hovering overhead cannot be ignored. The initial questions about the need for a dam and its location will not disappear simply because the government has made a decision. Neither will opposition forces simply pack their tents and go away without a fight ... Its decision could also have high costs in terms of relations between the Native and non-Native community [sic].'[26]

5
Interlude

The Oldman River Dam has the potential to be an economic
and environmental disaster. The dam's only benefit may be
political, ensuring by its largeness that southern Alberta remains
solidly Tory.

– Edmonton Journal[1]

Eight days after the Lougheed announcement, Environment Minister
Bradley released the report of his department's South Saskatchewan River
Basin Planning Program.[2] Bradley announced that the information provided in this new report would be the basis for public hearings in the fall
of 1984.

Determined not to run the risk of again locking horns with its old nemesis the ECA, the government decreed that these hearings would be
presided over by the Alberta Water Resources Commission (AWRC). This
newly anointed body included two MLAs, four assistant deputy ministers
from line departments, four citizens appointed by the government, and an
executive director. The presence of the two MLAs and five senior public
servants virtually assured that the AWRC would be more in sympathy with
government policies than was the ECA, and that its recommendations
were less likely to be at odds with those policies.[3]

In 1984, the AWRC was chaired by the Honourable Henry Kroeger, MLA
for Chinook, a constituency in drought-prone, east-central Alberta.[4] In
1979, Kroeger had served as co-chairperson of an informal, government-
sanctioned committee, later formalized as the Water Advisory Committee,
that championed large-scale diversions of water from rivers in the northern part of the province to the southern Alberta drylands.

The commission's hearings on the South Saskatchewan program ran
through November and December of 1984. As was inevitable, they became
a forum for debate on the Oldman Dam issue and many of the interest
groups and individuals that were to play prominent roles in the battle over
the dam fired their first shots during the South Saskatchewan hearings.

Roy Jensen, an irrigation farmer from Shaughnessy who was to become
the main spokesperson for the irrigation community in the late 1980s and
early 1990s, presented several briefs on behalf of the LNID. Jensen was
elected to the board of directors of the LNID in 1968, and in 1978, became
its chairman, an office he held for the next fifteen years. For about five

years, at the height of the Oldman controversy, he was also chairman and director of operations of the AIPA.[5]

In his first appearance before the AWRC panel, Jensen applauded the government for its support of irrigation and for standing up to 'verbal outbursts from erratic environmental thinking and/or anti-growth people.'[6] Singling out Agriculture Minister Fjordbotten, Environment Minister Bradley and Chairman Kroeger for particular thanks, he expressed the 'hope that your type of thinking will be prevalent in future decisions.' Jensen staked out the high ground for the irrigation community by suggesting that one of Alberta's objectives should be 'to utilize our God-given resources of water and agricultural land to the best of our ability that we may help feed the nations of the world.' This claim had earlier been dismissed as 'good fertilizer' by the *Tabor Times,* which said, 'Sugar beets do not feed a hungry world. They don't even result in good nutrition. They provide empty calories for people who already eat too much sugar. And feed grains don't feed a hungry world. They fatten cattle for consumption by people who already eat more meat than is good for them. The same goes for alfalfa. And what about crops that are grown for the making of alcoholic beverages? Food for a hungry world?'[7]

The Alberta Wilderness Association (AWA), Federation of Alberta Naturalists (FAN), Trout Unlimited (TU), and Alberta Fish and Game Association (AF&GA) all presented briefs that questioned the utility of irrigation expansion and the damming of rivers. The AF&GA advised the panel that it was 'opposed in principle to the building of dams in Alberta rivers,' a position that raised the hackles of AF&GA members involved with irrigation.[8] Several people who were to be founding members of FOR – Martha Kostuch, Cliff Wallis, Andy Russell, and Gordon Merrick – submitted briefs that opposed the Oldman Dam and took the government to task for its poor water management.

When the AWRC reported in October of 1986, over a year and a half after the hearings, its only comment on the Oldman River Dam was that it supported the government's efforts to include mitigative measures in the design and management of the dam.[9]

Facing an election in 1986, the government took steps to consolidate local support for the dam. Alberta Environment established an information centre in the town of Pincher Creek, a few kilometres from the Three Rivers site, appointed a local advisory committee (LAC), with representation from the rural and urban communities in the immediate vicinity, and sponsored open houses in a number of local communities to present information about the project. WMS began work on the final design of the dam and, forced to take some action to counterclaims that the dam would wreak havoc on the environment, it initiated a highly publicized mitigation planning program. WMS promised that the product of this program, an 'Environmental Mitigation and Opportunities Plan,' would 'focus on the ways and means of avoiding or at least reducing any negative impacts' of the project.[10] It would include plans for 'salvaging' archaeologic artifacts and historic buildings, providing alternative habitat for the birds and mammals driven from the land flooded by the reservoir, and creating artificial fish habitats above and below the reservoir.

The Peigan Indian Band, having lost its bid to have the dam built on its reserve, set out to cut its losses and secure whatever benefits it might derive from a dam at Three Rivers. By 1986, the Peigan had a new chief, Peter Yellowhorn, a university-educated, former oil-company executive. Yellowhorn kicked the new year off with a press conference at which he declared that 'the Peigan Nation is engaged in a battle for its survival.'[11] He called the provincial government's plans for a dam at Three Rivers the latest threat in a history of 'trespass, confiscation and suppression,' that would destroy the Peigan people 'economically, culturally and spiritually.' He claimed that the province's plan for use of the water stored by the dam 'ignores our prior and superior rights to the use of water' and accused the federal government of neglecting its responsibility to protect the land and water rights awarded to the Peigan in Treaty 7. He served notice that 'the Peigan people will take any necessary action to safeguard and maintain jurisdiction over our lands and resources so that future generations of Peigan people can continue to enjoy them as we have.' Yellowhorn warned that, though Chief and Council – the official decision-making body and administrative authority on the Peigan Reserve (see Chapter 21 for further discussion) – would prefer to resolve these issues through the courts, some more militant Peigans might not have the patience to wait out lengthy court battles.

On 20 January, the Peigan Band Council issued a 'proclamation' stating that the Peigan had a reserved right to all of the natural flow of the Old-man River and had a right to compensation for any damages resulting from changes in natural rates of flow or water quality in the river and for use of the river channel to transport water through the reserve.[12] Indicating that the Peigan might yet accept the dam if they were adequately compensated, Yellowhorn invited Alberta's new Premier Don Getty to sit down with the Peigan and negotiate 'a deal.'[13] Meeting with Yellowhorn on 18 March, Getty and his cabinet agreed in principle to fund a Peigan study to determine the impacts of a dam at Three Rivers on reserve residents. On 28 March, the Peigan submitted a proposal for a $750,000 study, but before the proposal got onto the cabinet's agenda, the band initiated the first of the many court actions launched by opponents of the Oldman Dam.[14]

The Peigan had engaged Vancouver lawyer Louise Mandell and former BC Supreme Court Justice Thomas Berger, commissioner of the federal government's 1977 Mackenzie Valley Pipeline Inquiry, to prepare a court challenge against the dam. On 11 April, the Peigan filed a statement of claim against Alberta in Court of Queen's Bench, claiming rights to water in the Oldman River, ownership of the bed of the river as it flows through the Peigan Reserve, potential damage to the reserve from construction and operation of the Oldman River Dam, including the destruction of spiritual values, and asking for an injunction that would restrain the province from building the dam.[15]

In June, the Peigan filed a claim in Federal Court against Canada and the minister of Indian Affairs. In this action, the Peigan claimed ownership of and exclusive right to the use of the waters of the Oldman in their present quality and quantities as they flowed through the reserve, that the construction of the Oldman Dam would cause damage to the band and the reserve, and that Canada and the minister were obligated to protect the band's 'rights and interests' in the Oldman River by preventing the construction and operation of the dam.[16]

In early May, the people of Alberta had gone to the polls and elected the Conservatives for a fifth straight term. With Don Getty, fighting his first election as party leader, the Conservatives took 51 percent of the popular vote and sixty-one seats in the legislature. Though it was a substantial drop from the 62 percent of the popular vote and seventy-five seats it had captured in 1982, the government still commanded an overwhelming majority. The opposition parties won only twenty-two seats. On 26 May, the premier introduced his new cabinet. Ken Kowalski was named to replace Fred Bradley as environment minister.

Figure 3   Premier Don Getty. His government built the Oldman River Dam.

In 1974, Ken Kowalski left his job as a high school social studies teacher in Barrhead, Alberta, to become executive assistant to Dr. Hugh Horner, Conservative MLA for the Barrhead constituency, at the time deputy premier and minister of Agriculture. In 1978, Horner moved to the Transportation portfolio. Kowalski went with him and was appointed deputy minister of regional transportation services. When Horner opted not to run in the 1979 election, Kowalski inherited his candidacy in the Barrhead riding and retained it for the Conservatives by a narrow margin.

Kowalski assumed political responsibility for the dam just as the preliminaries to its actual construction began in earnest. Alberta had applied to Transport Canada on 10 March for approval to construct the dam under the Navigable Waters Protection Act, the final design of the dam was nearing completion, and government contractors had started work at the Three Rivers site. Access roads and a camp to house and feed the work crews were being built in preparation for a start on the first major construction contract: digging two 900-metre-long tunnels through which the river would be diverted while the dam was under construction.

The detailed design for the dam submitted in July, by UMA Engineering Ltd., carried a price tag that brought the total cost of the project to $349.6 million (in 1986 dollars). Inflation and design modifications over the years had increased the estimated cost of the project from $114.5 million in 1978 to $200 million by the time the Three Rivers site was selected in 1984. Continuing inflation plus safety considerations that dictated the dam must have a larger spillway and a broader base to provide flatter slopes brought the 1986 cost to three times the original estimate. Despite the cost escalation, the province was able to report that the project remained economically feasible.[17] An updated economic analysis revealed that although the cost had tripled, the benefit had doubled. A benefit-cost analysis using the 1986 information yielded a benefit-to-cost ratio of 2.17:1, compared to 3.2:1 in the 1978 analysis. Such is the magic of economics.

The farmers and ranchers whose lands and homes were located in the area that would be inundated by the water captured behind the dam had posed a formidable obstacle to construction at Three Rivers. United under the banner of the Committee for the Preservation of Three Rivers (CPTR), most had actively campaigned against the dam, hoping that the politicians could be persuaded to choose another site. The committee presented briefs in 1976 and 1977, demanding that the government rethink the irrigation expansion-water management issue and hold 'public hearings examining all aspects of water management in southern Alberta' before building any dams.[18] In 1978, CPTR member Audrey Westrop produced a recording, which she sent to fifty-four MLAs, seventy-one radio stations, and fifteen newspapers, in the forlorn hope that by publicizing the government's intentions she could provoke enough sympathy and public indignation to shame the government into backing away from its decision to dam the river and inundate the homes of the valley landowners. The two songs on the disk lament the government's destruction of the land and the heritage bequeathed by the original Native inhabitants and the pioneers for purely political purposes.[19]

Over the next six years, committee members appeared at public hearings, gave interviews, wrote letters to the media, and lobbied their MLAs. Ron Buchanan, one of the landowners, served for a few months as a member of the ORSMC. He resigned when it became apparent that the government was interested only in building a dam, not in alternative ways of managing water.[20]

The government was no more sensitive towards the landowners than it had been towards the Peigan. The sixteen families faced with being forced from their homes learned that the government had finally decided their fate only after Lougheed addressed his 9 August press conference.[21] Though few had believed that their pleas would be heard, they were not prepared for the sudden shock of Lougheed's public announcement. The government later maintained it had 'dispatched letters' to the landowners 'immediately prior' to Lougheed's announcement. Even had the letters reached them before the press conference, the decision to advise them by mail rather than by personal contact was indicative of the government's callous and uncaring attitude. Peter Melnychuk says there was no need to give those who would lose their homes personal notice of the site decision. 'It was common knowledge,' he said, 'so they weren't contacted individually.'[22]

Even after Lougheed's announcement, there were those, like Audrey Westrop, who clung to the belief that the government might not go ahead with construction. For Westrop and others like her, this period of denial and self-deception ended abruptly when the land acquisition program kicked into gear. Some of the landowners attempted to have the government deal with them openly and as a group. However, the government opted to divide and conquer, approaching each landowner individually, controlling the flow of information, and establishing the process and timelines for land acquisition. Besieged by lawyers and government land agents, confused by the process, and harried by the pressure to conform to the schedule imposed by itinerant bureaucrats from Edmonton, the landowners struggled to attend to the day-to-day operations of their farms and the routines of family life.[23] In the prevailing climate of uncertainty and with the threat of expropriation constantly looming over them, they soon abandoned any attempts to maintain a common front in their dealings with the government.

As the CPTR disintegrated, the landowners and their problems faded from the news. By the time construction was ready to begin in earnest, in 1987, the government had acquired all of the land needed for the project.

The politicians and bureaucrats were adamant in maintaining that all of the landowners received a generous price for their lands and few of the displaced landowners disputed that claim. Most, however, felt that they were not in any way adequately compensated for the massive dislocation imposed upon them and their families. Few in government seemed capable of understanding this distinction. A government study in 1994 revealed that many of the displaced landowners continued to be bitter about the project and the way the government went about acquiring their lands.[24]

In 1991, Dr. Marie Louise Million completed a study of the phenomenon of involuntary displacement as it affected families forced to move from the Three Rivers site to make way for the dam.[25] Anyone interested in obtaining a deeper insight into the problems and emotional upheavals faced by five of those families should read the in-depth interviews recorded in Million's study. Dr. George Kupfer, a sociologist who served as a technical specialist to the Oldman River Dam Environmental Assessment Panel (ORDEAP), says a reading of Million's work 'could assure that we never again assume that the forcible displacement of people has no significant consequences.'[26]

Excavation of the twin diversion tunnels got under way in the fall of 1986 and continued on schedule through the winter of 1986 and into 1987. With excavation and lining of the tunnels scheduled for completion by the spring of 1988, construction of the dam itself could start in the summer of that year. In the meantime, contracts were let to build a reservoir perimeter dike on the left bank of the river and two drainage tunnels, one on each bank of the river downstream from the toe of the dam. These tunnels, each three metres in diameter, would eventually carry seepage from under the dam back into the river about 700 metres downstream. Since construction of these tunnels required work in the river, in August of 1987, Alberta Environment quietly issued itself a licence, under the Water Resources Act, to construct the Oldman River Dam.

6
The Battle Joined

Mitigation is a euphemistic way to assuage the conscience.

– Luna B. Leopold[1]

In the summer of 1987, environmentalists in the Lethbridge area decided it was time they did something to stop the Oldman Dam. They agreed to meet in Lethbridge on 29 August and invited Dr. Martha Kostuch, an environmental activist from Rocky Mountain House, to help them get organized. Kostuch was raised on a farm near Moose Lake, Minnesota. Farm life and early experiences hunting big game in the company of her father and brothers sparked her interest in the outdoors and steered her towards a career in veterinary medicine. She graduated from the University of Minnesota in 1975, emigrated to Canada, and established a veterinary practice in the central Alberta town of Rocky Mountain House. In 1978, Kostuch spearheaded the successful opposition to the development of a convention-centre resort on Crown land in the Kootenay Flats west of Rocky Mountain House. She quickly developed a knack for planning campaigns to oppose projects and organizing people to put those plans into effect and got her first experience in dealing with the legal establishment and the court system.

Seventeen people attended the Lethbridge meeting. Among them were members of the Alberta Fish and Game Association (AF&GA), Alberta Wilderness Association (AWA), Canadian Nature Federation (CNF), Canadian Parks and Wilderness Society (CPAWS), Federation of Alberta Naturalists (FAN), and Trout Unlimited (TU). The upshot of the meeting was the formation of an independent group, Friends of the Oldman River (FOR), dedicated exclusively to opposing the Oldman River Dam. Cliff Wallis, a consulting biologist and president of the AWA, was elected president and Kostuch, vice-president.

In preparation for the Lethbridge meeting, Kostuch visited the Edmonton offices of Alberta Environment's Controller of Water Resources in mid-August. She found that WMS had applied for a licence to build the dam in 1985, but that it had yet to be issued. On a second visit, in September, she discovered that the controller had issued a licence on 18 August, and that he had done so without requiring WMS to give public notice of its application.[2] Shortly after Kostuch's discovery, FOR announced that 'based on the government's decision not to advertise the application for a permit to construct the dam, FOR is challenging, in court, the issuance of the permit to construct the Oldman River Dam at the Three Rivers site.'[3] The *Lethbridge Herald* welcomed FOR's challenge, noting that 'the Alberta government has never offered a satisfactory explanation of its decision to build the dam.'[4]

The Alberta government's experience with environmental groups had taught it that they were normally polite, if not downright timid; lacked a broad base of support; and, when presented with the slightest gesture of accommodation, were reasonable to a fault. Taken by surprise and shocked that an environmental group would have the audacity to challenge the government in court, Environment Minister Kowalski's reaction was typically bombastic. He dismissed the threatened court action as 'absurd, nonsensical and to the point of being ridiculous.'[5]

Some media reports claimed that Kowalski had called those behind the court challenge pot-smoking social anarchists – a statement he claimed was taken out of context and not directed at FOR members.[6] Whatever was said, the report set the tone for future relations between FOR and the minister. FOR needed a bad guy on whom it could focus its protests; Kowalski was tailor-made for the role.

FOR's statement of claim filed in Alberta Court of Queen's Bench in Calgary on 24 September 1987 claimed it had not been 'expedient, fit and proper' for the minister to waive the requirement to give public notice of

Figure 4   Alberta Environment Minister Ken Kowalski (left) and PC Caucus Irrigation Committee Chairman Alan Hyland (centre foreground)

the application to build the dam, that the province had failed to obtain the permission of the municipal district (MD) of Pincher Creek, the authority responsible for roads that would be inundated, and had failed to refer the application to the Energy Resources Conservation Board (ERCB), all of which are required by the Water Resources Act. The action sought an injunction against construction of the dam.

Mindful that taking the government to court would be a costly venture, FOR approached environmental groups beyond Alberta in the hope of gaining national and international support for their cause and obtaining the financial support they would need to pay their legal bills. FOR made a significant breakthrough at the national level, announcing in early November that it was to get help in fund-raising from the Canadian Environmental Defence Fund, a national body boasting a number of prominent Canadians as members of its honorary board of directors.[7] Included were Dr. David Suzuki, UBC biology professor, host of the weekly CBC-TV series *The Nature of Things*, and author of an environmental column syndicated in a number of large daily newspapers; Farley Mowatt, a prolific, Governor-General's Award-winning author and professed conservationist; and June Callwood, a journalist best known for reporting on social issues and championing the rights of underdogs.

With FOR's legal challenge of the construction licence looming, the first cracks began to appear in the government's highly touted mitigation program for the dam. In mid-October, the *Edmonton Journal* reported that a yet-to-be released archaeological study, done by a private consultant as the first step in the development of a plan for salvaging the historic and prehistoric artifacts in the dam and reservoir area, had recommended against construction of the dam. Alberta Environment's initial response to the leak of this study, which the department had kept under wraps since the previous February, was contradictory. Taken by surprise and with Minister Kowalski on a political junket out of the capital, a spokesperson for the dam project advised the press that the reports would be released when they were 'finalized.' The minister's executive assistant, on the other hand, claimed that 'we don't know what report is being referred to.'[8] By the end of the next week, with all damage control systems in place, Kowalski announced that the reports would be released by the end of the month. In the meantime, he said, Alberta Culture 'must determine and make a recommendation about the archaeological impact. They will tell us what sites are vital, and,' he added, with the characteristic Kowalski hyperbole to which dam watchers would soon become accustomed, 'we will undertake the largest mitigation archaeological program in the history of Western Canada.'[9]

On 18 November, Kowalski released the reports on the archaeological and historical resources of the Three Rivers area prepared by Lifeways of

Canada Ltd. The reports on the archaeological studies were authored by University of Calgary archaeologist Dr. Brian Reeves, who had indeed rec-ommended that 'the Three Rivers should be designated a Provincial His-torical Resource, and the Oldman River Dam should not be constructed.'[10] Kowalski announced that 'after an evaluation of the consultant's reports and further assessment of the sites themselves by experts in the field of history and pre-history,' Alberta Culture had recommended 'a strategy for the investigation and preservation of these resources.'[11] Culture Minister Greg Stevens said, 'In our view, the project area does not contain any single historic resource or sum total of historical resources which would necessitate designation of the area as a historic area.'[12] Just where this put Reeves, an internationally recognized expert on plains archaeology, was not spelled out in the government's statement, but it was evident that the 'experts' employed by Alberta Culture did not share his view of the impor-tance of maintaining the archaeological find in place.

Jack Ives, director of the Archaeological Survey of Alberta, explained that while many archaeological finds would be destroyed by construction of the dam or inundated by the reservoir and that though some people felt these finds to be of sufficient importance that the dam ought not to be built, 'we [Alberta Culture] do not consider that it is our role to determine whether the dam is built or not. Instead, we consider our role to be that of making responsible recommendations about what ought to happen to the historical resources which will be affected by the Oldman project, given that it does, in fact, go ahead. If we were to say that developments ought to be stopped when archaeological sites are present, much development as we know it would have to cease.'[13] While many who shared Reeves' view of the importance of maintaining archaeological finds 'in situ' would have considered it responsible to recommend that the dam not be constructed, and beneficial if 'much development, as we know it' were to cease, Ives' interpretation of Alberta Culture's role was an accurate reflection of the government's priorities.

The mitigation plan was to be 'refined in consultation with the Munici-pal District's Oldman River Historical and Archaeological Resources Com-mittee so that implementation of the plan can begin in 1988.'[14] Although the preponderance of the archaeological finds inventoried at the site – teepee rings, buffalo drive sites, campsites – were of Indian origin, there was no suggestion that the various Blackfoot bands, whose ancestors' life-styles and very existence were recorded by the finds, would be consulted on the mitigation plan.

As the public learned more about other aspects of the government's mit-igation plans, these too came under attack. Effort to reduce the project's impact on fish was to be directed at ensuring that there would be 'no net loss of recreational fishing opportunities' by managing fish habitat to increase fish populations elsewhere in the river system.[15] Critics were not optimistic that the government could successfully compensate for the stretch of natural river that would be inundated by the Oldman reservoir. The chairman of environmental science at a local community college predicted that the dam would change the river ecosystem such that what had been a 'rich, productive, cool water flowing system' would become a 'cold, barren, unproductive standing water system.'[16] A former director of the province's Fish and Wildlife Division, Martin Paetz, expressed doubt that the plan to improve fish habitat by adding boulders to the river bed would improve the quantity or size of fish. 'I can't understand how they can say there will be no net loss in those rivers,' said Paetz.[17] The government was also criticized for its plans to create new habitat for mule deer by planting trees on uplands adjacent to the flooded valley habitat and for assuming that the many species of animals and birds that would be displaced from the 2,800 hectares (10 square miles) of flooded habitat would simply move into adjacent habitats that were already occupied. Studies by Dr. Stewart Rood, a plant physiologist at the University of Lethbridge, had revealed dramatic declines in the stands of poplars in river valleys downstream from other dams in the region.[18] He predicted that the same thing was likely to occur downstream from the Oldman Dam and that the loss of the trees would severely damage the riverine ecosystem. Other researchers were quick to support Rood's theories.[19]

That opposition to the dam was attracting attention in the media was not lost on the irrigation community. Sensing the need to counter the anti-dam message and to shore up the government's resolve to push ahead with the project, the AIPA renewed its efforts to mobilize support for the dam. AIPA spokespersons accused 'well-motivated [but] mis-guided, mis-directed and mis-informed' environmentalists and the 'northern press' of turning the public and northern MLAs against the dam.[20] Lamenting that the AIPA had been 'too complacent' and had failed to offset the 'concentrated barrage of distorted, close-minded hysteria' generated by Calgary and Edmonton newspapers, the AIPA's public relations chairman pleaded for a 'massive display of support' from 'every city town and rural municipality south of the Red Deer River.'[21] According to one spokesperson, the AIPA needed the public to support the dam because 'we're always perceived as a self-interest group.'[22]

Chief Justice Kenneth Moore presided over FOR's first legal challenge to the dam and in a judgment issued on 8 December, he quashed the licence because the government had failed to obtain the required clearances from the ERCB and the MD. As to whether it had been 'expedient, fit and proper' for the minister to waive the requirement to publish notice of the licence application, he observed that the effect of that action had been 'to deny affected parties the opportunity to voice their concerns.' He concluded that it had not been 'fit and proper,' and could only have been meant to 'expedite the matter.'[23]

While dam opponents rejoiced and the opposition parties and the media called for Kowalski's resignation, the government attempted to play down the issue and adopt a business-as-usual attitude. Premier Getty said Chief Justice Moore had ruled the licence invalid on the basis of a legal technicality, and expressed 'tremendous confidence' in Kowalski. The attorney general announced that the government would appeal the judgment and that, since no stop order had been issued, construction of the dam would continue. Kowalski, while acknowledging ministerial responsibility for the actions of his department, claimed that he 'wasn't even involved,' implying that the decision to deny dam opponents the opportunity to file objections to this very controversial and politically sensitive project had been taken entirely by departmental staff.[24] Kowalski had, quite properly, delegated his authority for licensing water development projects to the Controller of Water Resources. Whether or not the controller's decision to waive public notice of the licence application was made without his concurrence, it reflected poorly on Kowalski. Applying the principle of ministerial responsibility quite literally, the *Calgary Herald* observed that 'between the lines of terse legalese in [Moore's] ruling the portrait of Kowalski as a sloppy bumbler is unmistakable.'[25] Kowalski concluded that he and his department had been 'made to look like blubbering idiots' and that the publicity 'makes us all look very stupid.'[26]

On 10 December, the Alberta Legislature set aside its regular business to engage in an emergency debate on whether, in the light of Chief Justice Moore's judgment, the government should continue with construction of the Oldman River Dam. The debate amounted to little more than an acrimonious exchange between government and opposition members.[27]

Moore stayed the execution of his order quashing the licence until the end of February 1988, or until the province's appeal had been heard, which meant construction would continue, pending some final disposition of the case. The hearing on the province's appeal was set for 9 February 1988. In mid-December, Kowalski announced that his department had applied for a new licence and that it was likely the controller would be able to process a new licence before the stay on the court order quashing the existing licence expired.[28] These disclosures suggested that the province would not likely proceed with its appeal of Chief Justice Moore's decision and that Kowalski was expecting, if not directing, the controller to again waive the requirement to post notice of the department's application. On 8 February, the province announced that it would not proceed with the appeal. It was revealed that on 5 February, the controller had issued the department a new licence to construct the dam, again waiving the requirement to publish notice of its application.[29] FOR announced that it would challenge the new licence in court. Kowalski was not surprised and, though he predicted that 'once again there will be a large amount of tax-payer's money wasted,' his duty was clear. 'They [FOR] are in the business to obstruct,' he said. 'I'm in the business to build.'[30]

FOR challenged the new licence on the grounds that the department had failed to provide the information required to support an application for a licence to build a dam for irrigation purposes and that the controller had improperly waived the requirement to give public notice of the appli-cation. The case was argued before Madam Justice Ellen Picard in April. The Crown countered FOR's claim that Alberta Environment had failed to support its bid for a licence for an irrigation project by pointing out that, in fact, the department had applied for and had been issued a licence to impound water for the general purpose of water management, not for the specific purpose of irrigation.[31] In response to FOR's charge that the con-troller should not have waived the requirement to give public notice of the application, the Crown argued that the controller's decision had been based on his consideration of information indicating that the public had, by other means, been afforded ample opportunity to become informed about and to register complaints about the project. FOR's application was denied.[32]

Chief Justice Moore's decision had ignited the pro-dam lobby. The AIPA chairman and the mayors of several southern communities were very critical of the decision and feared that FOR might succeed in blocking the project. One small-town mayor was reported to have said, 'I think the judge is nuts; he should be sued.'[33] Although encouraged that work on the dam was continuing, the irrigation community felt sufficiently threatened that it moved to form a coalition of dam supporters to counter the favour-able publicity that the court action had given to FOR's cause. In December 1987, a fledgling group calling itself the Southern Alberta Water Manage-ment Committee (SAWMC), chaired by Don Lebaron, a Lethbridge busi-nessman and city alderman who had co-chaired the southern Alberta sugar beet lobby group in the early 1980s, was formed to 'correct the false-hoods' that had been spread by opponents of the dam. This new commit-tee included representation from irrigation districts, towns, and municipal councils, chambers of commerce, engineering consulting firms, and the local academic community.

Three days before Christmas 1987, the SAWMC sent a sixteen-man del-egation, led by Lebaron and Roy Jensen, to Edmonton to urge Kowalski and Premier Getty to continue with the dam. The delegation also met with the leaders of the two opposition parties in the legislature, and the Edmonton media, some of whom, according to delegation spokespersons, 'had a lot of misconceptions and misinformation' about the dam.[34] SAWMC's concerns about the media's position on the dam were shared by

Figure 5 Southern Alberta Water Management Committee lobby group returning from Edmonton. Lethbridge Alderman Don Lebaron is third from left and AIPA President Roy Jensen is fourth from left.

the government. Kowalski's executive assistant, Jay Litke, told the press that the SAWMC delegation's visit was useful to the government, because its efforts helped to explain to people in northern and central parts of the province the importance of water management in the south. 'We [the government] understand water management,' said Litke, 'but we are not getting the co-operation expected through the media.'[35]

Despite the legal wrangling, work at the dam site continued unabated and on schedule. By late spring, the two diversion tunnels were finished and work on the drainage tunnels was well under way. In late February, Kowalski spoke at a breakfast meeting in Lethbridge sponsored by the SAWMC. In friendly territory and surrounded by admiring supporters, he announced the award of a $97-million contract for construction of the main dam.[36] Work under this contract began in May, and on 19 July, the river was diverted from its bed to flow through the diversion tunnels so that construction of the main dam could begin. For a brief while it looked like smooth sailing ahead for the government. But no sooner had the river been diverted through the diversion tunnels than FOR was back in court to initiate the longest running of its many legal actions against the province. On 2 August, Martha Kostuch appeared before a justice of the peace in Pincher Creek to lay charges under the federal Fisheries Act against Alberta Environment Minister Kowalski, the project manager, and

Figure 6   Construction begins, summer of 1987

the two construction companies for destroying fish habitat in the Oldman River.[37]

Kostuch thought she had obtained a commitment from the federal Department of Justice to prosecute the case, but when its jurisdiction was challenged by the province, the Department of Justice withdrew, opening the way for the Alberta attorney general to intervene and assume responsibility for the prosecution. He did so and promptly stayed the charges on the grounds that there was insufficient evidence to obtain a prosecution. FOR offered to provide the attorney general with the names of witnesses and other evidence to support the charge that an offence had been committed. The offer was declined. Instead, the attorney general asked the RCMP to investigate the charges and report its findings to the federal Department of Justice; a move that the head of the RCMP's commercial crime division described as 'unique.'

The RCMP completed its initial investigations in December and submitted a report to the Department of Justice, where officials proceeded to review the findings and ponder the legal questions. Thus began six years of legal manoeuvring, with FOR persisting in its determination to charge Alberta for violating the Fisheries Act and federal and provincial officials using every means provided by the justice system to prevent the case from coming to trial. At stake was not simply whether Alberta and its construction companies had destroyed fish habitat, which was evident to the most casual observer, but also larger questions pertaining to federal and provincial jurisdiction and the constitutional powers of the federal government.

Meanwhile, the government's mitigation program moved from the planning to the implementation stage. The historical resources mitigation plan, released in the fall of 1987, was approved by the Local Advisory Committee, and contracts were let for the first phase of the excavation and salvage of artifacts. Work began in June 1988. In May 1988, the plan for fisheries mitigation was made public. It was roundly criticized by anglers as a feeble and unpromising attempt to compensate for the fishery that would be lost on account of the dam. Undeterred, the government continued with the construction of artificial 'habitat enhancement structures' upstream from the reservoir area, in hopes that they would produce larger populations of fish in those reaches.[38]

In September, morale in the environmentalists' camp soared with the announcement that Premier Getty had shuffled his cabinet, moving their archrival Kowalski from minister of environment to minister responsible for career development and employment, and lotteries. With an election forthcoming, the premier obviously felt it expedient to move the outspoken minister to a less prominent post, where he would have fewer opportunities to embarrass the government. Although the environment had never loomed large as an election issue in Alberta, there was no political dividend due the government for maintaining a constant state of war with environmental interest groups.

The *Calgary Herald* cheered Kowalski's banishment from the sensitive environment post, observing that he and another demoted colleague 'did their jobs with all the subtlety of twice-removed cousins who show up in Hawaiian shorts at a formal wedding.'[39] Noting 'Kowalski's tendency to disconnect his tongue from his brain,' the *Herald* concluded that 'his new post in Career Development and Lotteries should put a cork on Kowalski.' And so it did, however briefly.

The premier used the occasion to announce another move calculated to deflect some of the criticism being directed at his government for allowing its Environment department to be both the proponent and the regulator of water development projects. To environmentalists, these conflicting mandates meant that irrigation and hydro development would always win out over ecological balance and habitat for fish and wildlife. The government had previously ignored these criticisms, but the highly publicized controversy over construction of the Oldman Dam was creating an embarrassing situation and what little credibility the department might have had as protector of the environment was rapidly eroding. Changes were required to improve the department's image. The trick would be to appear to resolve the conflicting mandate problem and move the environment department out of the line of fire without substantially altering the government's water management programs and priorities.

Acknowledging the existence of 'a conflict of interest in having an environmental minister who is also responsible for building dams,' the premier

AUGUSTANA UNIVERSITY COLLEGE LIBRARY

announced the transfer of responsibility for dam construction, including the Oldman River Dam, from the Department of Environment to the Department of Public Works, Supply and Services.[40] The move was disarmingly simple and, apparently, highly effective in creating the illusion that Alberta Environment was no longer responsible for the Oldman River Dam. Together with Kowalski's ouster from the environment portfolio, it made a favourable impression on some of the government's critics. Martha Kostuch's reaction to the news was fairly typical: 'They have taken dam building out of the environment portfolio and put it into public works where it belongs. Now the department will no longer be a proponent and evaluator of a project. It removes any reason for conflict within the department.'[41]

Not everyone was taken in, however. Lawyer, angler, and columnist Bob Kambeitz understood that transferring responsibility for construction of water projects to another department was nothing more than a public relations move: 'All that we would have is one arm of government making application to another arm of government for a permit, and anyone who thinks that would represent arms-length submission by a proponent to an unbiased and impartial adjudicator must be dead or in Edmonton.'[42]

7
The EARPGO Challenge

I conclude that the Guidelines Order was intended to bind the
Minister in the performance of his duties and functions.

– Mr. Justice Stone, Federal Court of Appeal[1]

In January 1989, the Canadian Wildlife Federation (CWF) filed a notice of
motion in Federal Court challenging a licence issued to the Saskatchewan
Water Corporation by the federal minister of environment, under the
International Rivers Improvement Act, for the Rafferty-Alameda Project in
southeastern Saskatchewan. The licence authorized the construction of
the Rafferty Dam on the Souris River and the Alameda Dam on Moose
Mountain Creek. The grounds for the challenge were that the minister had
issued the licence without having first subjected the project to review
under the federal Environmental Assessment and Review Process Guidelines Order (EARPGO).[2] Federal lawyers argued that since Saskatchewan
had done an environmental review that met the EARPGO requirements,
the minister had enough environmental information to support issuance
of the licence. The Federal Court, however, decided the provincial review
had not adequately addressed some areas of federal responsibility. On 10
April, the Court quashed the licence and ordered the minister to review
the project under the EARPGO before issuing a new licence.[3]

The decision got mixed reviews in Saskatchewan: Premier Grant Devine
was angry, local boosters and the companies building the dams were out-
raged, CWF officials were ecstatic.[4] The Saskatchewan Water Corporation
immediately launched an appeal. In Alberta, FOR interpreted the decision
in terms of what it might portend for the Oldman River Dam, concluding
that it could mark 'the beginning of the end' for that project. On 18 September 1987, the federal minister of transport had issued Alberta an
Approval to build the dam under the Navigable Waters Protection Act.[5]
Noting that the Oldman Dam had implications for the Peigan Indians and
for fish habitat in the Oldman River, both of which fell under federal jurisdiction, and that the federal minister had not applied the EARPGO before
issuing the approval, FOR announced it would take court action against
the federal government.

In April 1989, FOR filed an application in Federal Court for orders to quash the federal approval for the Oldman Dam and require a federal environmental impact assessment of the project. Environmental interest groups in Alberta had been laying the groundwork for this action since mid-1987. In August of that year, the Southern Alberta Environmental Group (SAEG) had written to the federal minister of fisheries and oceans, pointing out that the Oldman River Dam would have an impact on fisheries and fish habitat, areas of federal responsibility for which his ministry was responsible, and asking if the minister would, therefore, call for an environmental impact assessment of the dam.[6] The minister replied in August, advising that 'in view of ... the fact that the potential problems associated with the dam are being addressed, I do not propose to intervene in this matter.'[7] In December 1987, FOR wrote to the federal minister of environment, requesting that the Oldman Dam be subjected to the EARPGO. The minister's assistant replied that, because of 'administrative arrangements' with Alberta on fisheries management and environmental impact assessments, it 'would not be appropriate' for the federal government to intervene in the Oldman.[8]

The Peigan had also asked the federal government to bring the EARPGO into play. In March 1989, after several months of dithering, Indian Affairs Minister Pierre Cadieux responded to the Peigan's latest request that the minister order an environmental review of the project. Cadieux's response was not encouraging. Beyond promising that he would forward the request to Environment Minister Bouchard and that department officials would 'consult with' provincial officials, Cadieux could do no more than offer 'hope that a mutually acceptable solution to this issue can be found in the near future.'[9]

In February, representatives of FOR had met with the Peigan Band Council to discuss the possibility of coordinating their opposition to the dam. While they shared a common objective, they were unable to agree on a common approach to achieving that objective. The Peigan's lawyers preferred to address the issue in the context of Aboriginal and treaty rights, which left little room for collaboration with FOR. In the end they agreed to go their separate ways.

On 20 March, Alberta had gone to the polls and returned its sixth successive Progressive Conservative government – its majority reduced from thirty-nine seats to a still-comfortable thirty-five. On 13 April, Premier Getty announced his new cabinet. The Environment portfolio went to rookie MLA Ralph Klein, a former television reporter and mayor of Calgary. For the many who for years had been given to believe that Klein, if not a socialist, was at least a Liberal, his sudden shift to the right of the political spectrum was seen as opportunistic. This view of Klein's emergence as a born-again Conservative was shared by many of the PC old guard. Renowned both for his late-night stands at the St. Louis Tavern, a watering hole near Calgary's city hall and for his early morning fishing expeditions along the banks of the Bow River, Klein was seen as a man of the people and a friend of the environment. Environmentalists considered Klein's appointment to be good news; the bad news was the resurrection of Ken Kowalski. Having served his penance as minister in a forgettable portfolio, the bombastic MLA from Barrhead was back on the front bench as minister of public works, supply and services. Foremost among the responsibilities of his new portfolio was construction of the Oldman River Dam. The man who had claimed, while minister of environment, that 'my job is to build,' had found a home at last.

Red Deer lawyer and outdoors writer Bob Scammell offered a judgment of the two ministers that was shared by most environmentalists at the time. Borrowing a federal MP's description of the Saskatchewan government as an 'ignorant crew' on environmental matters, Scammell described Kowalski as 'that world-class coxswain on any ignorant crew.'[10] On the other hand, Scammell believed that Klein showed some promise and 'might even be able to protect us all, including even the federal government, from Kowalski.'

The day before filing its application with the Federal Court, FOR representatives met with Klein to discuss its plans for further legal action. Klein's comments after the meeting suggested that he was not yet in tune with his newly adopted party's position on the dam, environmental protection, or areas of provincial jurisdiction. Noting that the decision to go to court was up to FOR, Klein said, 'If there were deficiencies in the way the environmental concerns were addressed, I have faith in the courts.'[11] Klein's faith in the courts was short-lived. By mid-May, apprised of the views of his cabinet and caucus colleagues, he was declaring that, even if the Federal Court ruled in favour of FOR's application, the government would not stop work on the dam. Whatever the courts might decide, Klein was now convinced that damming the Oldman was the 'politically right thing to do.'[12] Faith in the party had transcended faith in the courts. Calling the Navigable Waters Protection Act 'offensive,' and accusing the federal government of encroaching 'in such a way as to give them authority to control provincial waterways,' Klein gave notice that the province would appeal any court decision it found to be unfavourable in what it considered to be a 'constitutional issue.' Perhaps reminded that, since responsibility for dam building had been transferred to the Department of Public Works, Supply and Services (PWSS), the Oldman Dam was no longer the concern of the minister of environment, Klein pointed out that, whatever the case, the dam was 'not in any way, shape or form in my portfolio. I can't do anything. It's strictly under Public Works.'[13] At this point, Bob Scammell must have begun casting about for a new protector.

Klein's posturing on the court issue hinted at what was soon to become apparent: the Alberta government feared that the Federal Court's ruling in the Rafferty-Alameda case had opened the door to federal intervention in other resource management decisions; decisions that Alberta maintained were entirely within the constitutional domain of the province. And while the federal government, conscious of its need for provincial support for other issues on the constitutional agenda, seemed reluctant to pass through that door, the decisions had given heart to environmental groups in their fight to force the federal government to defend the 'national interest.' With its megaprojects at risk, Alberta, as it had done previously over oil issues, prepared to go to the wall over what it perceived as its constitutional right to develop provincial resources without federal interference.

Alberta perceived a greater threat to its plans for logging and pulp mill and oil sands megaprojects in the northern part of the province, many of which would have an impact on federal lands and Indian communities, than to the Oldman Dam, which at that point was half-way to completion. However, the Oldman case provided a playing field on which the province hoped to win enough ground to provide a reluctant federal government with sound reasons for not intervening in provincial resource development projects. Of the most immediate concern to the province was a proposal by Alberta-Pacific Forest Industries Inc. (Al-Pac) to harvest trees from 73,000 square kilometres of Alberta's boreal forest and build the world's largest bleached kraft pulp mill, discharging its wastes into the Athabasca River.[14] The project would have impacts on fish habitat in the river downstream from the mill, through Wood Buffalo National Park, and into the Northwest Territories, and on Indian bands that used the river and the surrounding forests for hunting and fishing. The possibilities for impact in areas of federal jurisdiction were countless, and the federal government was under pressure from Indian bands and environmental interest groups to require that the project be subjected to a review under the EARPGO.

On 15 June, the Federal Court ruled that Alberta could intervene on the side of the federal defendants in FOR's challenge of the Navigable Waters Protection Act Approval for the Oldman Dam. The trial judge adjourned the hearing for six weeks to give Alberta time to prepare its case, to allow the Court to consider the outcome of the Saskatchewan Water Corporation's appeal of the Federal Court's decision on Rafferty-Alameda, and to give the federal minister of transport time to respond to Alberta's request to withdraw the approval under dispute.

In a desperate attempt to undermine the basis of FOR's challenge, Alberta PWSS officials had written to Transport Canada on 9 June, asking that the approval issued in 1986 be withdrawn, on the grounds that Alberta was not subject to the Navigable Waters Protection Act. Transport Canada referred Alberta's request to the Department of Justice for a legal opinion. The opinion, if any, was never made public, but the approval was still in force when the case came to court on 21 July, and it remained in force until quashed by the Federal Court of Appeal the following year.

On 22 June, the Federal Court of Appeal dismissed the Saskatchewan Water Corporation's appeal of Rafferty-Alemeda, ruling that the federal minister of environment was obliged to follow the EARPGO 'just as he is obliged to follow other laws of general application.'[15] For environmentalists, the ruling appeared to seal the fate of the Oldman Dam. Martha Kostuch called the decision 'terrific, absolutely tremendous.' Her euphoria was to be short-lived.

FOR presented its arguments before Associate Chief Justice James Jerome of the Federal Court's Trial Division, in Calgary, on 21 July. FOR maintained that, since the Oldman Project would have impacts on areas of federal responsibility, the minister of transport should have applied the EARPGO before issuing the approval. FOR also maintained that any work in the river that would result in harmful alteration of fish habitat must be approved by the minister of fisheries and oceans, and that the province had neither applied for nor received such approval. FOR asked the Court to quash the approval and order the federal ministers to comply with the EARPGO. FOR claimed that the facts in its case were similar to those in the Rafferty-Alemeda case, where such orders were issued. The federal government's lawyers argued that the EARPGO did not apply to the Navigable Waters Protection Act, and that the Department of Fisheries and Oceans was not bound by the EARPGO. For its part, Alberta claimed that a province does not have to obtain approvals under the Navigable Waters Protection Act, that it would welcome an order quashing the existing licence, and that if the Court did quash the licence, Alberta had no intention of reapplying.

Mr. Justice Jerome delivered his judgment on 11 August. He ruled that, since there is no requirement for an environmental assessment under either the Navigable Waters Protection Act or the Fisheries Act, neither the minister of transport nor the minister of fisheries and oceans had a statutory obligation to deal with environmental considerations and had either required that the EARPGO be complied with, he would have exceeded the authority granted to him.[16] He concluded that the Oldman case was 'significantly different' from the Rafferty case because the International Rivers Improvement Act, the legislation at issue in the Rafferty case, required approval prior to construction, whereas the Navigable Waters Protection Act did not, and because the duties of the minister of environment, the defendant in Rafferty, extended to protection of the environment, while the duties of the ministers of transport and of fisheries and oceans did not. He turned down FOR's application.

Acknowledging that the judgment was a major blow, Kostuch vowed that FOR would continue its fight against the dam. The immediate problem was money. Kostuch estimated that FOR had spent $70,000 on court actions to date, and would need another $50,000 to appeal Jerome's decision. FOR's biggest fund-raising event had been a benefit concert, billed as a 'celebration' of the Oldman, held at Maycroft Crossing on the banks of the upper Oldman River in June of 1989. Organized by country and western singer Ian Tyson, a self-styled, southern Alberta rancher, the benefit attracted a crowd of from 8,000 to 15,000 people, depending upon whose estimate was to be believed. They came from all over Alberta, and from British Columbia, Saskatchewan, Manitoba, and Montana, many combining the concert with a camping holiday at one of the local campgrounds. Though it rained in the early morning, Sunday, 12 June, turned out to be a warm, sunny day, perfect for lounging on the grass and listening to some of the country's favourite entertainers perform, free of charge.

The concert opened with blessings offered by Peigan spiritual leader Joe Crowshoe and Anglican priest Peter Hamel, an environmental activist from the church's national office in Toronto. Then came the music and the speeches. Tyson and his ex-wife and former singing partner, Sylvia Flicker, were reunited for the day to provide the harmony that made Ian and Sylvia a big draw in the late 1960s. Murray McLauchlan sang the 'Farmer's Song' and Gordon Lightfoot sang his 'Railroad Trilogy.' In between the musical offerings, speakers urged the crowd to take a stand in defence of the environment, and against the Oldman Dam. David Suzuki delivered an emotional speech, exhorting the crowd to 'keep up this fight' to save the environment from 'the bottom line.' Other speakers included FOR's Andy Russell and Lorne Scott, president of the Saskatchewan Wildlife Federation, the provincial arm of the group that took the federal government to court over the Rafferty-Alameda Project.[17]

In an interview after the concert, Martha Kostuch said, 'In our wildest dreams we never imagined a turn-out like that.' People had not only supported the protest by attending the concert, they had contributed generously when the hat was passed. Kostuch estimated that the event brought in over $20,000 in much-needed cash, and many had added their names to a petition calling for the government to change directions on the dam. By the end of the day, the petition boasted 10,000 signatures.

In September 1989, FOR launched its appeal, and on 13 March 1990, the Federal Court of Appeal overturned most of Associate Chief Justice Jerome's rulings.[18] The Appeal Court quashed the Navigable Waters Protection Act Approval and ordered the minister of transport and the minister of fisheries and oceans to comply with the EARPGO. The Court also ruled that Alberta was not immune from the approval requirements of the Navigable Waters Protection Act, which meant that further construction, without a new approval, would be a breach of federal law.

Figure 7   Crowd gathered for Friends of the Oldman River benefit concert,
Maycroft Crossing, June 1989

Figure 8
Ian and Sylvia at
Maycroft Crossing
concert

Figure 9
Gordon Lightfoot
at Maycroft
Crossing

Figure 10
David Suzuki at
Maycroft Crossing

8
Carry On Regardless

Will [the Minister of Public Works] do the right thing and order
that construction be stopped until this matter is settled?

– Alberta Opposition Leader Ray Martin[1]

The Appeal Court's decision sent panic through the ranks of dam supporters. Government politicians and bureaucrats scrambled to come up with
reasons to rationalize continued construction of the dam and to delay
making decisions about the future of the project. Federal Environment
Minister Lucien Bouchard voiced the dismay of the federal government,
claiming that 'for years people had thought that this was just a guideline
so that governments were not legally bound to comply with them.'[2]

Opposition parties in both the federal and provincial legislatures, none
of which had representation or even any good prospects for representation
in southern Alberta, called on both governments to put a stop to construction. They were joined by Alberta's major daily newspapers. The *Lethbridge
Herald*, citing fiscal and moral grounds and noting that 'environmental
responsibility requires more than soothing words in a throne speech,'
called on the province to respect the law and stop construction.[3] The *Calgary Herald* maintained that for Alberta to continue work on the dam under
the circumstances was 'unconscionable.'[4]

Alberta continued to claim it didn't need federal approval to build the
dam. Environment Minister Klein observed, fatuously, that the Court's
decision was 'against the federal government and not the province of
Alberta'; Public Works Minister Kowalski, pointing out that the Court had
not issued a stop-work order, told the legislature that he had 'been advised
by numerous legal counsel that the province of Alberta is not in breach of
the Navigable Waters Protection Act.'[5] Premier Getty vowed to continue
construction on the dam, and the attorney general advised the legislature
that Alberta would seek leave to appeal the Federal Court of Appeal's order
to the Supreme Court of Canada.[6]

The government's response to the Appeal Court's decision prompted yet
another emergency debate in the Alberta Legislature.[7] Opposition members tried in vain to get the government to admit that its decision to proceed with dam construction in the face of the Appeal Court's order was, as

Liberal Grant Mitchell put it, 'blatantly breaking the laws of this country.'[8] But the government stuck to its line that, since the Court had not issued a stop-work order, Alberta was not obliged to cease construction, putting the onus on the federal government to enforce its law, if it wished to do so. Deputy Premier Jim Horseman claimed that the very 'survival' of southern Alberta hinged on the completion of the dam.[9] The *Lethbridge Herald* called Horseman's rhetoric 'a blatant political attempt to create hysteria among southern Albertans.'[10]

Alberta Public Works, Supply and Services (PWSS) officials voiced fears that with the main dam still at only one-third its final height and with an above-average run-off forecast, flood flows could overtop the dam, posing a serious threat to the structure, to residents of the Peigan Reserve, bridges, and other property downstream. Dan Bader, the senior PWSS official in charge of building the dam, said there was a legitimate and significant concern for the safety of the project if construction was halted.[11] He claimed that the potential threat to public safety could be avoided only if construction continued until the dam reached its designed maximum height. In fact, the flood risk, estimated at 2 percent, was the same as it had been the previous spring, when, as the *Lethbridge Herald* pointed out, no one in an official capacity had voiced any concerns about safety and no warnings were issued to people living downstream.[12]

The cry for continued construction was taken up by the hordes of provincial and federal politicians who descended on the area. Concern for public safety became the accepted rationale for continuing in the face of what appeared to be a moral obligation on the part of the two governments to call a temporary halt to the project. Most politicians agreed that the onus was on the federal government to prevent disaster by not interfering with construction. It seemed not to occur to them that the province, as builder and owner of the dam, might have a responsibility to take steps to protect the people and property put at risk by the presence of what was, in essence, an illegal structure. If the fuss was good for anyone, it was the airline industry. The cadres of MLAs, MPs, parliamentary secretaries, and cabinet ministers flying south and west to Lethbridge were passed in mid-air by lobbyists flying north and east to Edmonton and Ottawa, all adding handsomely to their frequent-flyer points.

The SAWMC led the parade. Its first response to the Appeal Court's decision was to call an 'emergency' meeting of dam supporters to plot a strategy for promoting continued construction of the dam. Attended by over 100 mayors, reeves, and other elected officials, and a bevy of provincial civil servants, the meeting provided a platform for anyone with an argument that supported continuing construction. Among them was Jake Theissen, PWSS's project manager for the dam. *Lethbridge Herald* columnist Joanne Helmer reported that Theissen's predictions of the flood damage

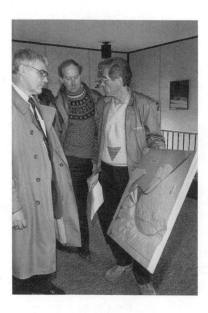

Figure 11 Environment Parliamentary Secretary Lee Clark (left), Macleod MP Ken Hughes (centre), and PWSS Oldman River Dam project manager Jake Theissen (right)

that could occur if construction was stopped 'just about built a case for hysteria.'[13] Having convinced themselves that dam construction must continue, the assemblage agreed to petition federal Environment Minister Bouchard to tour the project before making any decisions about the dam's future. With a supporting cast of irrigation farmers, businesspeople, engineering consultants, and politicians in tow, SAWMC chairman Don Lebaron trekked off to Ottawa to bend the ears of any MPs or senators who would listen.

Lucien Bouchard was the first prominent federal politician to enter the fray, and the elected official whose decision would determine the fate of the dam, at least in the short term. Encouraged by southern Alberta MPs and the entreaties of SAWMC, Bouchard decided to visit Alberta to talk with the interest groups and to gauge the likely political implications of whichever decision he would soon be forced to make. After testing the waters, Bouchard retreated to Ottawa, promising a decision within days. His parting message to southern Alberta was that a decision to shut down work on the dam was 'a matter of balancing the environment, the economy and the needs of the local people.'[14] He might have added that it was also a matter of judging whether the provincial government would accede to or defy a federal stop-work order. A soon-to-be-former Mulroney crony, with a greater interest in the independence of Quebec than the environmental integrity of Canada, Bouchard made no bones about the fact that he found himself in the kind of situation that politicians strive to avoid. It was one thing, he said, to know you have to apply strong environmental

Figure 12   Environment Canada Minister Lucien Bouchard (right) reviews a
report on the dam

rules for future projects, but quite another thing when it comes to addressing ongoing projects.[15]

On 23 April, Bouchard announced that he had ordered the federal government to complete an environmental impact assessment on the Oldman
Project, and was looking for people to appoint to a panel to review the
assessment. Bouchard said he would not call a halt to construction until
federal officials advised him that it would be safe to do so. On 21 May,
Bouchard resigned as minister of environment and as a member of the
Tory party to devote himself to the cause of Quebec separatism. The following day, Transport Minister Doug Lewis announced that he would not
order a halt to construction of the Oldman Dam. Said Lewis, 'We have
maintained all along that we wanted them to continue work on the dam
until it's safe to stop. I haven't been advised that we're at that position, or
that I should issue a stop work order.'[16]

The federal government's struggle to maintain some credibility for its
environmental stance, while at the same time avoiding a head-on clash
with Alberta, was complicated by developments in other parts of the country. In January 1990, Bouchard had called a halt to construction on
Saskatchewan's Rafferty-Alemeda Project after the Federal Court ruled that
he must appoint a panel to conduct a public review of the project.
Although Saskatchewan agreed to stop work on the dam until the review
was completed, work was resumed on some elements of the project in late

April, breaking the spirit if not the word of its agreement with the federal government. Following Alberta's example, Saskatchewan claimed it had resumed construction for 'safety reasons.'[17]

Meanwhile, in Quebec, the James Bay Crees had launched legal action to prevent Hydro Quebec from proceeding with the second phase of its James Bay hydro development project. Environmental interests had joined the Cree in objecting to some aspects of the environmental impact assessment arrangements agreed to by Canada and Quebec. Looming over all was the impending 'crisis' over the Meech Lake Accord, a proposal for amendments to Canada's constitution that required ratification by the legislatures of each province and the federal Parliament prior to 23 June 1990. With the credibility of the prime minister and his party hinging on the successful closure of the Meech Lake deal, there was a reluctance in Ottawa to take any action that might alienate a provincial government.

In May, Alberta released its long overdue Water Management Policy for the South Saskatchewan River Basin.[18] This policy had been gestating in the offices of senior Alberta Environment officials since the AWRC had submitted its report and recommendations four years earlier. Though not immediately apparent, some elements of the policy had significant implications for the allocation of water in the Oldman River system and, by extension, for the future operation of the Oldman River Dam. One such element required that the government 'establish' the flows required for instream uses of a river – for example, for fish habitat – and manage regulated rivers, such as the Oldman, to maintain these 'instream flows.' Another required that the government 'establish' the maximum water allocation for irrigation purposes in the Red Deer, Bow, and Oldman basins. Included with the policy were Irrigation Expansion Guidelines for the South Saskatchewan River Basin, which limited the area that could be irrigated with water from the Oldman River system to 884,000 acres (358,000 hectares). This was 34,000 acres (14,000 hectares) more than the ORSMC had recommended as the ultimate irrigated acreage to be supplied from the Oldman system, *with the Oldman River Dam in place.*

Meanwhile, FOR's efforts to prosecute Alberta Environment for destroying fish habitat in the Oldman River were going nowhere. Exasperated by the province's foot-dragging on the action she had initiated in 1988, Martha Kostuch decided to start over again. On 11 January 1990, she laid new charges, and in February, Ken Kowalski and the construction companies were summoned to appear in provincial court on 26 April. On the appointed day, counsel for the provincial attorney general applied to intervene and assume responsibility for prosecution of the case. FOR promptly filed a motion requesting that the court refuse the Crown's application. Judge W.J. Harvie dismissed FOR's application but ordered that the parties appear for trial on 13 July, with the prosecution in the hands of the attorney general.[19] On 10 July, the federal minister of justice, Kim Campbell, announced that she had decided not to prosecute the Alberta government on charges of destroying fish habitat in the Oldman. 'I do not believe that any proceedings by way of prosecution would serve the interests of the proper administration of justice,' Campbell said.[20] The next day, the Alberta attorney general, finding himself in full agreement, again stayed the charges.

While the politicians dithered, construction of the Oldman Dam continued apace. By July, the dam had risen to a height of forty metres, over halfway to its final height of seventy-six metres. PWSS claimed that the project was 80 percent completed.

In early March of 1990, some 3,000 kilometres to the east, a small group of Mohawk Indians began the occupation of a wooded area between the Mohawk community of Kanesatake and the town of Oka, a few kilometres north and west of Montreal. This little-noticed event marked the beginning of what was to become known as the 'summer of discontent' for Canada's Indians. The occupied area, known as the 'Pines,' long claimed by the Mohawks as tribal land, had been approved for development as a golf course by officials of the town of Oka. While the rest of the country was transfixed by the political manoeuvring under way to win final approval of the Meech Lake Accord, the Warriors barricaded both ends of a dirt road bisecting the Pines, and denied access to all but Native people. In June, the town of Oka obtained a court injunction ordering the removal of the barricades, which was ignored by the Mohawks, prompting the town to appeal to the province and the Sûreté du Québec for help.

On 21 June, Manitoba MLA Elijah Harper, a Cree Indian, sat in the Manitoba Legislature, eagle feather in hand, and refused to give the unanimous consent required to permit the Assembly to debate and vote on the Meech Lake Accord. Harper's defiant stand, motivated by his belief that the accord did not adequately recognize Indian rights, effectively killed any chance that the accord would be approved before its 23 June deadline.

By early July, the occupation at Oka had developed into an armed confrontation between the Mohawk Warrior Society and the Sûreté du Québec. In the early morning hours of 11 July, the Sûreté attempted to remove one of the roadblocks, turning the confrontation into a shoot-out, which resulted in the death of a member of the Sûreté. Indian leaders throughout the country expressed sympathy with the Mohawks. Though not happy with the Warrior's methods, they understood their frustration, and refused to condemn their actions. The Mohawk protest, together with the stand taken by Native leaders in opposition to the Meech Lake Accord, inspired Native groups across the country to 'take to the streets,' both in support of the Mohawks and in protest over the many long-standing injustices to which they believed they had been subjected. From one end of the country to the other, Indian demonstrators threw barricades across highways, logging roads, and rail lines that crossed reserve lands; confronted loggers; and staged sit-ins at airports and legislatures.

On 5 August, Quebec Premier Bourassa issued an ultimatum giving the Warriors forty-eight hours to lift the barricades. On 8 August, with the Warriors still defiant, he called in the army. When the 5th Mechanized Brigade replaced the Sûreté at the barricades on 20 August, supported by armoured personnel carriers, helicopters, and overflights by CF-15 fighter aircraft, media coverage of events at Oka intensified. The 'Oka Crisis,' as it was dubbed by the CBC, dominated the national news until 26 September, when the confrontation ended.

Meanwhile, back in Alberta, far from the glare of the national media, a group of Peigan Indians, inspired by the Mohawk Warriors, acted to defend their traditional homelands from destruction at the hands of the Alberta government. Styling themselves the Lonefighters Society, this ragtag group, unarmed and, by Warrior standards, unorganized, was determined to stop construction of the Oldman Dam.

9
The Lonefighters

When no other option appeared available, the Lonefighters acted
as a last ditch effort to protect the rights of the Peigan people and
to bring attention to the unfair actions of Alberta.

– Peigan submission to the Environmental Review Panel[1]

When the Federal Court of Appeal quashed the Navigable Waters Protection Act Approval for the dam in the spring of 1990, the Peigan assumed that the province would be compelled to stop work, at least until it either successfully appealed the Federal Court's ruling or until the dam had passed a federal environmental review. By late March of 1990, it became apparent that Alberta intended to continue construction without the federal approval and that the federal government was prepared to stand by and watch. Chief Leonard Bastien demanded that Ottawa shut down the dam and band councillor Albert Yellowhorn threatened action on a local level, hinting at a dam blockade if construction continued.[2] The province, having seen similar Peigan threats amount to nothing in the past, ignored the warning.

Meanwhile, Milton Born With A Tooth, frustrated by the continued failure of attempts to obtain consideration of Peigan concerns by going the established route, decided to try something different. Born With A Tooth was born in the Oldman River valley, on the Peigan Indian Reserve, in 1957, the third youngest in a family of fifteen children. He left school in his early teens and thereafter lived an itinerant existence on and off the reserve. His first involvement in the politics of protest came in the late 1970s in the United States, when he joined in the Longest Walk, a cross-country march by American Indians to protest the US government's plan to dissolve its Indian treaties. His opponents and the right-wing media, drawing on shadowy accounts of Born With A Tooth's scrapes with the law in the United States, characterized him as a thug and a criminal.[3]

Whatever his past, Born With A Tooth had many supporters, both on and off the reserve, perhaps because, as one Indian activist put it, 'With native people, we are what we are today. We don't accept people or reject people because of past sins.'[4] Encouraging southern Albertans to look beyond personalities and focus on the issues, Joanne Helmer reminded her readers that 'southern Albertans don't have to accept the particular messenger to recognize the validity of the message.'[5]

After consulting with friends and some tribal elders, Born With A Tooth decided to put the Peigan's long-standing threat to divert the river to the test. He rounded up a group of followers, enlisted the support of a spiritual leader (a 'pipe carrier'), and approached the band Chief and Council in the hope of getting their backing. The majority of council members were cool to Born With A Tooth's proposal, but he and his confederates, who had taken to calling themselves the Lonefighters – a traditional Peigan clan to which Born With A Tooth and some of his associates claimed an ancestral tie – decided to press on.[6] The most prominent of Born With A Tooth's fellow Lonefighters were spiritual advisor Develon Small Legs, the son of former Chief Nelson Small Legs, and Glen North Peigan. This triumvirate made the major decisions and acted as spokespersons for the Lonefighters.

On Friday, 3 August, the Lonefighters moved to play what the Peigan called their 'ace in the hole.'[7] Media representatives invited onto the reserve that day for a 'ground breaking ceremony' were escorted to the west bank of the Oldman River, a short distance upstream from the LNID weir (see Map 4). There they watched as a bulldozer, rented by the Lonefighters 'for irrigation work' from a construction company working on the dam, cleared bush from an abandoned oxbow channel. The Lonefighters explained that they hoped to divert flow from the Oldman into the abandoned channel then back into the river at a point below the LNID weir. If they could channel sufficient flow around the weir, they reasoned, they could prevent water being diverted into the headworks canal for delivery to the LNID. At a press conference held at nearby Head-Smashed-In Buffalo Jump following the bulldozer demonstration, Born With A Tooth explained that the Lonefighters' diversion efforts were directed at forcing the provincial government to stop construction of the Oldman Dam. The Lonefighters, he said, were acting to protect the traditions and way of life of the Peigan Nation.

Cliff Wallis told the press conference that FOR endorsed the Lonefighters' 'lawful and non-violent' action and had backed their endorsement with a donation of $5,000. Peigan Band Chief Leonard Bastien said that, though he supported their objectives, the Lonefighters did not have the backing of the band council, the majority of whom still believed that Peigan concerns could be resolved through negotiation with the province. He said he would call a meeting of all reserve residents to determine how they felt about the Lonefighters and their activities.

Following the press conference, the Lonefighters returned to their diversion site, where they promptly mired their bulldozer to the top of its treads. After sixteen hours of digging with spades, the determined band freed the bulldozer from its trap and got it back to work. The high water table in the oxbow channel created marsh-like conditions which seriously delayed the Lonefighters' excavation. Some observers later reported that

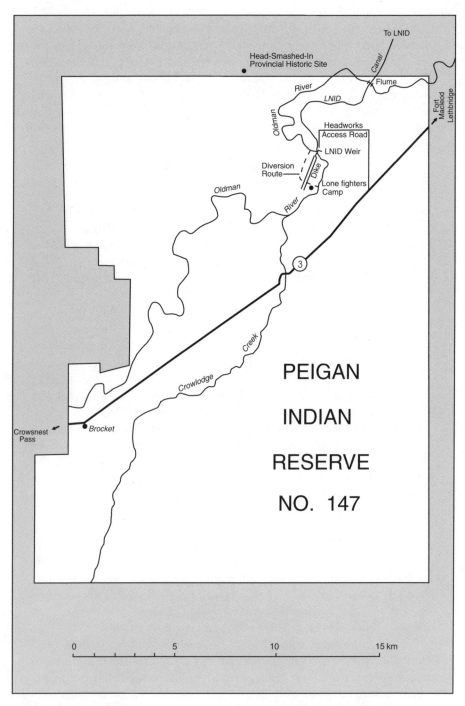

Map 4   Lethbridge Northern Irrigation District headworks and Lonefighters'
diversion

Figure 13   Lethbridge Northern Irrigation District weir on Oldman River; the
canal to the LNID is at left and the dike breached by Lonefighters is at right.
The Lonefighters' camp is located upstream in the top right-hand corner of the
photograph.

the bulldozer spent more time stuck in the mud than it did clearing the
diversion route.

The RCMP, moving quickly to get a handle on developments, contacted
local WMS officials and accompanied them on reconnaissance flights over
the Lonefighters' encampment. To get the opposing parties talking, the
RCMP arranged for Alberta Environment officials to meet with the Chief
and Council and Indian Affairs officials on 7 August. Bastien sought assurances from Superintendent Owen Maguire, the officer in command of the
RCMP's Lethbridge Sub-Division, that the RCMP would not enter the
reserve with a large force as they had done at the time of the LNID weir
blockade in 1978. He obtained a commitment that the RCMP would only
go to the Lonefighters' camp or to the diversion site in the company of the
chief or a band councillor.[8]

On 7 August, a party of Alberta Environment officials, including Deputy
Minister Vance MacNichol, WMS head Peter Melnychuk, and Minister
Klein's executive assistant, Rod Love, journeyed south to meet with the
Peigan. During the morning, MacNichol and Melnychuk joined local WMS
officials on their daily reconnaissance flight. They flew over the LNID
headworks, just as the Lonefighters' bulldozer rammed its way through a
dyke that extended from the west end of the diversion weir and across the
dry channel down which the Lonefighters hoped to divert the river. Any

doubts that the government might have had about the Lonefighters' determination were put to rest. That afternoon, the Alberta Environment contingent and two senior Indian Affairs officials from Edmonton sat down with Chief Bastien and his council in the Peigan Administration's offices in Brocket. Bastien requested written assurance that a tripartite committee, representing the band and the two levels of government, would be established to deal with environmental concerns and economic development.[9]

Following the meeting, Melnychuk and Indian Affairs Regional Director General Garry Wouters accompanied Bastien and some band councillors to the Lonefighters' camp. There, perched on lawn chairs in an 'arbour' (a large meeting-house constructed of cottonwood boughs), they met for several hours with Born With A Tooth and other Lonefighter leaders. Melnychuk later described the meeting as a 'threatening experience.'[10] Although they were unable to squeeze any concessions from the provincial representatives, the fact that there had been a meeting at all was sufficient to convince the Lonefighters that they had the government's attention and that their actions would force the province to the bargaining table.

On Monday, 13 August, the Chief and Council discussed matters with reserve residents at an open meeting attended by about one-half of the more than 600 voting members of the band. Opinion on the reserve was divided between what one observer called the materialists, who favoured economic development and growth for the reserve, and the traditionalists, who preferred the maintenance of a more traditional lifestyle and the cultural and spiritual practices associated with that lifestyle.[11] The former, who believed that the reserve could yet benefit from the Oldman Project and favoured the maintenance of good relations and continued negotiations with Alberta, were reluctant to cast their lot with the Lonefighters. The traditionalists, many of whom supported the Lonefighters, had little hope that the Peigan would ever benefit from the dam and feared that the social and cultural impacts of the dam would be harmful to the Peigan in the long run.

There were also some immediate financial concerns. Many who opposed the Lonefighters feared losing the annual $300,000 (indexed) payment that the band received from Alberta under the 1981 agreement. It was also rumoured that Alberta had threatened to withhold a grant promised to fund a Peigan Cultural Centre, which the band hoped would attract tourists to the reserve. The materialists feared that supporting the Lonefighters meant forfeiting the grant. The traditionalists believed that the Peigan 'should forget about building a cultural centre to educate tourists about Peigan life; they should protect Peigan life, and live it.'[12]

After consulting the various interests, the Chief and Council were no closer to taking an unequivocal stand. Chief Bastien, though personally sympathetic to the Lonefighters' cause, preferred that the protest come to a halt. He still believed that there was more to be gained by negotiation than by confrontation. He had been advised that a cabinet-level committee, comprised of Klein, Kowalski, Lands and Forests Minister Leroy Fjordbotten, Attorney General Ken Rostad (who was also minister responsible for Indian matters), and MLA Fred Bradley, had been appointed to enter into the negotiations that Bastien had requested on 7 August. He had also been advised that there could be no negotiations as long as the Lonefighters continued work on the diversion. In his first official statement on the issue, delivered on 14 August, Bastien said that the Chief and Council, 'from a legal perspective,' did not endorse the Lonefighters' actions, but stopped short of condemning them. Support for the Lonefighters from band members appeared to be increasing with time. Bastien advised Indian Affairs on 17 August, that, if a vote were taken on the reserve that day, it was likely that a majority would have backed the Lonefighters.[13]

Plagued by equipment breakdowns and frustrated by the slow progress of their diversion efforts, the Lonefighters mounted a verbal offensive to bolster their own morale and to garner public sympathy for their cause. Provincial ministers were regularly subjected to verbal abuse and accused of persecuting the Peigan Nation. In an interview with the *Kainai News,* Born With A Tooth attacked Environment Minister Ralph Klein in particularly vitriolic terms. Klein, who prided himself on his close association with Native communities, was accused of committing 'a genocidal act.' In a burst of rhetorical excess, Born With A Tooth said he considered Klein 'to be in the same category as Hitler himself ... who just went ahead and destroyed a culture.'[14]

A number of environmental groups – FOR, Greenpeace, Alberta Wilderness Association, International Rivers Network, Friends of the North – and several Native organizations – International Treaty Council, the Blackfoot Band in Montana, Cold Lake First Nations – had spoken out in support of the Lonefighters. There was, however, little support or understanding for their cause in the local community beyond the reserve. In an attempt to correct this imbalance, the Lonefighters opened their camp to anyone who wished to visit. In particular, local farmers, irrigators, and businesspeople were encouraged to drop by for a chat and a guided tour.

If those who accepted the invitation – mostly reporters and people sympathetic with the Peigan position – expected scenes comparable to those being flashed into their living rooms each evening from Oka, they were disappointed. What they saw – several teepees and an arbour, truck-mounted holiday campers, women preparing food over open fires or relaxing in the shade, children swimming in the river and playing on its banks – was more reminiscent of a family holiday resort than a battlefield. Traditional and religious ceremonies were important elements in the daily routine of camp life. The Lonefighter leaders took their visitors on guided tours of the camp and explained the part played by the river and its valley in the history of the Peigan people and the religious ceremonies and traditional practices essential to the maintenance of the Peigan culture. Their basic message was that in building the dam, the government was taking from the Peigan people something that they already possessed – their traditional cultural and spiritual attachment to the Oldman River – in exchange for the hope that economic benefits might flow to the band once the dam was a reality. Born With A Tooth called this 'a ploy to entice the poor people.'[15]

Dam supporters called press conferences to demand that the province not allow itself to be held to ransom by a small group of 'renegade Indians.' Not convinced that the renegades were capable of devising and implementing a plan to divert the river, Roy Jensen claimed that FOR was behind the Lonefighters' actions. 'If something happens, we hold the Friends of the Oldman River responsible ... It's just like they went and bought and paid somebody to do this.'[16]

Jensen and Don Lebaron, both of whom had lobbied strenuously to convince the Alberta government that it should continue construction of the dam in defiance of federal law, were reincarnated as disciples of law and order. Jensen voiced the fundamental contradiction in the dam supporter's position when he advised the provincial government that 'whatever you do, you don't stop work on the dam ... You apply the law.'[17]

The Lonefighters believed their actions were entirely legal. Since Alberta was not being denied access to or use of the LNID weir, there was no breach

Figure 14   Preparing a meal at the Lonefighters' camp

of the 1981 agreement. The diversion channel they hoped to create would be located entirely on Peigan land and, according to their lawyer, the dike they breached was not included in the 1981 agreement. Superintendent Maguire said on 16 August that he was not aware that the Lonefighters had broken any laws. The RCMP would not be involved 'unless there is a criminal offence,' he said. 'The last thing we want is a confrontation.'[18]

Neither WMS nor the RCMP were convinced that the Lonefighters were making any substantial progress in their attempt to divert the river. As if to reinforce the Alberta government's growing reputation for nondiplomacy, cabinet ministers waded into the fray. Attorney General Ken Rostad, the minister responsible for Native affairs, announced that the Peigan Band was not serious and that the diversion attempt was 'going nowhere.'[19] Minister of Advanced Education John Gogo told a public meeting, 'If they touch that river basin, things are going to happen.'[20] One minister ridiculed the Lonefighters, likening them to 'children playing with Tonka toys.'[21]

Privately, the government was taking a firm but less offensive approach, which gave Bastien reason for optimism. A 21 August letter from Deputy Premier Jim Horseman appeared to provide assurance that the province was committed to enter into negotiations with the Peigan, on the condition that the Lonefighters put down their shovels. In setting out the province's position on negotiations, Horseman wrote, 'It is not appropriate for the Alberta government to agree to participate in any negotiations with the Peigan Band while there are continuing threats to divert the waters of the Oldman River. *Once efforts to divert the river have ceased*, the Alberta government will be pleased to commence discussions with you and your Council on the issues you raised in the meeting on August 7 [emphasis added].'[22]

Not convinced that the Lonefighters could be persuaded to accept Horseman's condition, Bastien wrote to Horseman on 22 August to 'counter propose' a meeting, 'to discuss various issues of mutual concern ... as soon as possible regardless if the proposed diversion of the Oldman River is halted or continues ... Perhaps, during these deliberations the whole matter of controversy may be resolved.'[23] But that same day, Environment Minister Klein announced that a previously scheduled 31 August meeting with Peigan Chief and Council had been called off. It would be rescheduled only if the Lonefighters ceased work.

In late August, the Lonefighters got a shot in the arm, when an anonymous donor lent them a backhoe. Thanks to Indian Affairs' heavy equipment operators training programs, there were several qualified backhoe operators in the Lonefighters' ranks. On 27 August, with the media reporting that only a few more hours of work were required before the diversion channel broke through the bank and into the river, the backhoe broke down. Lonefighter spokespersons claimed this mechanical failure could delay their final breakthrough to the river by as much as three days. With the actual worksite closed to inquiring eyes, it was not possible for visitors or the media to verify the Lonefighters' claim that they had all but achieved their goal. WMS's Doug Clark, an experienced engineer who observed the diversion work from the air on an almost daily basis, was in the best position to assess the progress of the Lonefighters' work and its threat to the river. His opinion on 27 August was that the Lonefighters were a long way from being able to divert the river.[24]

While they waited for the final breakthrough, the Lonefighters were treated to news of a highway blockade on the neighbouring Blood Reserve and of demonstrations in Calgary. The Blood blockade, involving about twenty-five reserve residents, cut off access to the intersection of two provincial highways, one leading to Lethbridge, the other to the US border. The demonstrations in Calgary, in which at least 200 people took part, included a brief sit-in on a bridge crossing the Bow River into the downtown core, which tied up morning rush hour traffic, followed by a seventy-two-hour vigil at a downtown site. Ironically, both of these demonstrations had been in support of the Mohawks in Quebec.

Late on Tuesday, 28 August, the Lonefighters broke through the bank of the Oldman, and by Wednesday, a meagre but steady flow of water was reported to have pushed its way almost a kilometre down the diversion canal. The *Calgary Herald* and the *Globe and Mail* both reported, incorrectly, that the Lonefighters were diverting about 'a third of the flow' from

Figure 15   Glen North Peigan with Lonefighters' bulldozer and backhoe

the river into their diversion channel.[25] Reconnaissance flights over the area revealed that, although the river bank had indeed been breached, the minuscule quantities of water being diverted posed no threat to water users served through the government's headworks. When Environment's Clark monitored the flow above the reserve and at the LNID headworks, he concluded that there was 'no noticeable diversion.'[26] It is likely that most of what reporters took to be flow diverted from the river was ground water seeping into the channel. The media never had a complete understanding of how the Lonefighters' diversion would be accomplished, nor did they ever have unfettered access to the worksite.

Aerial reconnaissance on 29 August revealed that the Lonefighters were bulldozing sand and gravel into the river in an attempt to raise the water level and force more flow into their diversion channel. However, this material was being washed away almost as fast as it was being placed in the channel and it was evident to Clark that, unless they used solid materials, the Lonefighters would not be able to create an effective diversion.[27] Nevertheless, senior government officials were convinced that the longer the situation was allowed to persist, the greater the risk that the diversion would become effective and the greater would be the cost of restoring the river to its former condition. Any increase in river flows, whether because of heavy autumn rains or spring snowmelt, could erode the breach and scour the channel to the point that substantial flows might be lost to the diversion. Late on Wednesday, 29 August, the province applied to the Alberta Court of Queen's Bench in Edmonton for an injunction prohibiting the Lonefighters from further work on the diversion. The Crown was able to convince Mr. Justice J.B. Feehan that an emergency was imminent. That evening he issued an ex parte injunction forbidding anyone from preventing Oldman water from entering the LNID weir intake or obstructing the maintenance and operation of the headworks system.[28]

The following morning, RCMP officers arrived at the diversion site to serve the injunction. This force was reported by the media to number fifty men, an estimate later contradicted by RCMP spokespersons, who said only twenty-two officers had participated in the exercise. Whether twenty-two or fifty, the number of police officers on the scene was bewildering to the Lonefighters, who accepted the injunction without incident and pulled their equipment off the job. Although the Lonefighters had, to that point, not threatened violence, the RCMP, perhaps anticipating a confrontation like those beamed onto their television screens nightly from Oka, were taking no chances.

Born With A Tooth, in Edmonton with Chief Bastien to attend an emergency meeting of Alberta Indian chiefs when the injunction was served, was under the mistaken impression that, since Indians are a federal responsibility, Indians are obliged to honour rulings of the Federal Court only.

Subsequent consultation with their lawyers convinced the Lonefighters that they were indeed bound by the injunction. With the exception of a brief flurry of bulldozer activity the following morning, which the RCMP dismissed as a 'media event,' the Lonefighters kept their machinery away from the river. Meanwhile, Born With A Tooth set off for Montreal to solicit the support of the Mohawk Warriors.

Word was received that Indian Affairs Minister Siddon would meet with Treaty 7 chiefs in Alberta on 6 September, kindling hope that he would intervene to work out a settlement. However, an Indian Affairs spokesperson announced that the Lonefighter diversion issue was not on the agenda for the meeting. He did not rule out the possibility that Siddon might discuss the matter privately with Chief Bastien. On 5 September, Siddon's visit was postponed 'due to the urgency of the situation in Quebec.'[29]

10
7 September 1990

The Alberta government sent in the Canadian cavalry to intimidate the Indians.

– Joanne Helmer, *Lethbridge Herald*[1]

It's a good day to die!

– Milton Born With A Tooth[2]

Visitors to the Lonefighters' encampment had swelled its numbers to around 200 on Labour Day, but with mothers and children heading home for the start of another school year, those numbers dwindled in the following days. RCMP Superintendent Maguire and his team maintained a close watch over the Lonefighters' diversion site during the days following the issuance of the injunction.[3] Maguire was ready to take action should the Lonefighters opt to continue their work, but he was determined to stay off the reserve unless there was clear evidence that the injunction had been breached. There was no sign of work on the diversion during daylight hours in the first week in September, though there were rumours that the Lonefighters had been working under the cover of darkness. RCMP officials later testified that they had been unable to verify that the Lonefighters were working nights.

In Edmonton that same week, senior Environment Department officials were making plans to enter the reserve to repair the damage done by the Lonefighters. Sometime between 2 September and 4 September, they decided to do the job on Friday, 7 September. Just who made the decision to do the repairs at that time, and why, is not clear. According to Peter Melnychuk, 'many people were involved.' Given the political implications, the final go-ahead must have been given by the provincial cabinet. In an affidavit sworn for the 29 August injunction hearing, Alberta Environment engineer Doug Clark said that if the damage done by the Lonefighters was not repaired before the 1991 run-off, the Oldman River might erode a new channel. Superintendent Maguire testified at Milton Born With A Tooth's trial that he recalled having been told by Peter Melnychuk that, if necessary, repair of the damage done by the Lonefighters could wait until the following spring. Melnychuk's recollection was that he felt it important that the damage be repaired before freeze-up in 1990.

Once the decision had been made to go in on 7 September, Melnychuk asked the RCMP to provide an escort to ensure the 'security and safety' of the Alberta Environment personnel. The government did nothing to advise the Peigan of its plans. On 5 September, Maguire received orders from K Division headquarters, in Edmonton, to draw up a plan for accompanying Alberta Environment onto the reserve on 7 September. The purpose of the RCMP escort was to prevent any breaches of the peace and to arrest anyone seen violating the terms of the injunction.

According to Maguire, his plan was to infiltrate the Lonefighters' camp on the night of 6 September to determine the Lonefighters' status and whether they were working on the diversion in violation of the injunction and, on the morning of 7 September, to escort the Alberta Environment personnel to the LNID weir, contact the Lonefighters to advise them what was going on and seek their cooperation, provide protection for Alberta Environment work crews repairing the damage, and arrest anyone who breached the 29 August injunction. Though he anticipated only 'passive resistance' from the Peigan, Maguire was to muster a force of almost ninety RCMP to put his plan into effect. That force comprised a sixteen-member emergency response team (ERT) to infiltrate the Lonefighters' camp and worksite, a thirty-six-member escort for Alberta Environment work crews, a thirty-member tactical troop (commonly referred to as riot police) to control demonstrators, several female RCMP members to look after any women or children who might be involved, and at least two photographers.[4]

Born With A Tooth's lawyers later referred to the assembling of this 'minor expeditionary force ... which entered the Reserve like an invading army,' as 'a huge overreaction.' Maguire disagreed. Though RCMP intelligence had advised him that Born With A Tooth was in Montreal, Maguire believed that in the climate created by events at Oka, Born With A Tooth's threats that the Lonefighters would use weapons to repel 'invaders' had to be taken seriously; to do otherwise, he believed, would have been irresponsible. He also felt that a large force would be necessary to control demonstrators and to identify and arrest anyone violating the injunction.

A critical element of Maguire's plan was a meeting with Peigan Chief Leonard Bastien to give him the greatest possible advance notice of what was about to occur. This was consistent with the RCMP's earlier commitment to give the Peigan Chief and Council two days' notice of any intended visits to the Lonefighters' camp. Attempts to meet with Bastien on 5 September were unsuccessful, but Maguire was able to arrange a luncheon meeting for the following day. When Bastien failed to show for lunch on 6 September, Maguire decided that he would go to the chief's office in Brocket on the morning of 7 September to advise him of the impending operation. The commitment to give the chief prior notice was abandoned.

Shortly after midnight on the morning of 7 September, the ERT, in camouflage and armed with automatic weapons, entered the reserve and took up positions on the east bank of the river, across from the Lonefighter encampment. From there, they observed the camp and the diversion site for about an hour and a half. They reported no movement in the camp and no work under way on the diversion.

Early on the morning of 7 September, the RCMP contingent and the Alberta Environment personnel and work crew assembled at the community arena in Fort Macleod. Shortly before 8:00 a.m., Superintendent Maguire, accompanied by Sergeant Mills, departed for the Peigan Administration's offices in Brocket to inform Chief Bastien of the operation, which had been under way since just after midnight when the ERT entered the reserve. At the same time, the Alberta Environment crew and its RCMP escort set off for the LNID headworks. The ERT, its task completed, was dispatched back to Calgary; the tactical troop remained in reserve at Fort Macleod.

When Maguire and Mills arrived at the Peigan Administration offices at about 8:30 a.m., Bastien was not there and his whereabouts were unknown to the office staff. Attempts to contact him by phone were in vain. Maguire's plan was beginning to go awry. Meanwhile, the Alberta Environment crew with its heavy equipment, under Water Management Service Assistant Deputy Minister Melnychuk, and the RCMP escort, under Staff Sergeant Campbell, supported by a fleet of vehicles, including ambulances, set out from Fort Macleod. Some observers took the presence of the ambulances to mean that the RCMP expected bloodshed. The RCMP

Figure 16   Camouflaged RCMP officer under cover near Lonefighters' diversion site, 7 September 1990

entered the reserve on the headworks access road from Highway No. 3, establishing roadblocks in their wake to control entry to the area, and arrived at the weir at about 8:20 a.m. As the RCMP officers approached, they saw two people run across the weir and west along the main dike in the general direction of the Lonefighters' camp.

And then the wheels fell off Maguire's plan. Shortly after arriving at the weir, the Alberta Environment contingent decided to continue across the structure and along the dike to observe the damage the Lonefighters had done to the dike. According to testimony later offered by Maguire, Staff Sergeant Campbell ordered the RCMP escort to accompany the government party to accommodate Alberta Environment's wish to recce the dike.[5] A vanguard of six Alberta Environment staff, including Melnychuk and Clark, and six RCMP officers led the advance. Four teams of six RCMP followed the lead party at intervals of from fifteen to twenty yards. The remaining team of six RCMP remained at the east end of the weir to guard the vehicles and equipment. Neither party made any attempt to contact the Lonefighters before making their move.[6] Maguire later testified that, had he been at the weir at the time, he would have made contact with the Lonefighters before advancing onto the dike. But Maguire was not at the weir; he was in Brocket trying to locate Chief Bastien.

When word that 'an army of RCMP' was approaching reached the Lonefighters' camp, it was received first with disbelief, then with a sense of urgency bordering on panic. Having previously been told that the government would not move to repair the damage caused by the Lonefighters without giving prior notice, the Lonefighters were caught completely off guard. There were still women and children in camp, and the Lonefighters had not formulated a plan for how they would react to a visit by government personnel, let alone an armed incursion led by the RCMP. The camp was roused, and the women and children were hastily moved to high ground.[7] The Lonefighter men, led by Born With A Tooth, who had returned from Montreal the previous evening, made for the main dike. One of the Peigan women, Evelyn Kelman, slipped down to the river to offer prayers for the safety of her people.

As the Alberta Environment party with its RCMP escort arrived at the breach in the dike around 9:00 a.m., a group of about ten Lonefighters appeared on the opposite side. The Lonefighters hollered at the intruders, calling them trespassers and ordering them off reserve land. Some of the government people shouted back. When their warnings went unheeded, the Lonefighters began to throw rocks at their tormentors. In the meantime, the Lonefighters' bulldozer clattered into position on the Lonefighter side of the breach, and its idling engine, together with the incessant beat of a Lonefighter drum and the drone of an RCMP helicopter hovering overhead, added to the general sense of confusion and unreality that pervaded the scene. In the midst of this, two shots rang out. By his own admission, Born With A Tooth had fired the shots, which he claimed were aimed into the air as a warning to the intruders. The RCMP later claimed the shots were directed at them. Heeding this warning, the Alberta Environment personnel, wisely, if belatedly, withdrew to the east side of the river. The RCMP escort scrambled down the sides of the dike to cover.

When Maguire was informed of the shooting, he departed for the scene, leaving Sergeant Mills in Brocket to await Bastien's appearance. The ERT, by then en route to Calgary, was recalled and deployed on a hillside over-looking the river. The RCMP brought several .308 calibre rifles and twelve-gauge shotguns forward for use, if necessary, by members remaining in forward positions on the dike. At 10:00 a.m., Melnychuk directed the Alberta Environment equipment and personnel to leave the reserve. On the Lone-fighters' side of the breach, the bulldozer excavated a bunker, into which the Lonefighters filed to take up their vigil. Thus began what the media were to call an 'armed stand-off.'

According to *Lethbridge Herald* columnist Joanne Helmer, who visited the Lonefighters' camp later in the day, 'The people in the camp were terri-fied, there's no question. One of the [Lonefighter] guys said they felt every minute like they had a target attached to them ... This was around the time of Oka and they didn't know what would happen.'[8] At about 10:30 a.m.,

Figure 17   Milton Born With A Tooth and his sister Lorna in Lone-fighters' bunker on dike, 7 September 1990

Peigan Councillors Leander Shot With A Gun and George Little Moustache, both Lonefighter sympathizers, arrived at the Lonefighter camp. After consulting with the Lonefighters, they crossed the breach and made their way to the weir, where they entered into negotiations with Superintendent Maguire aimed at bringing an end to the hostilities. Beginning at about 11:00 a.m. and continuing throughout the day, other Peigans, non-Native supporters, and news reporters made their way to the Lonefighters' position. The RCMP had set up a roadblock on the west road giving access to the Lonefighter camp, so the new arrivals simply came across country. The non-Native visitors were an eclectic assortment, including members of FOR and other established environmental interests and representatives of newly formed groups such as the Alberta Coalition of Concerned Citizens, whose concern was for the welfare of Native people. There was also a group of United Church ministers, intent on monitoring the situation and hoping to keep things from getting out-of-hand. A message of encouragement from the Mohawk Warriors read, in part, 'You know in your hearts and minds that you are right. Don't ever surrender.'

Among those arriving late on the scene was Peigan Chief Leonard Bastien, who joined in the negotiations with Maguire at the weir. It turned out that Bastien had been in Calgary. He first learned of the Alberta Environment/RCMP operation when he placed a telephone call to the Peigan Administration office at about 10:30 that morning and was connected to RCMP Sergeant Mills. That evening, the Peigan Chief and Council, greatly distressed over their 'betrayal' by the government and the RCMP, passed a band council resolution ordering both Alberta Environment and the RCMP off the reserve.

The next day, the Lonefighters' lawyer, Drew Galbraith, filed a notice of motion in Court of Queen's Bench seeking to quash the injunction issued against the Lonefighters. On 8 September, Mr. Justice William Egbert, after agreeing to hear arguments for and against the motion on the following Wednesday, warned both parties that they must, in the meantime, maintain the status quo and refrain from further confrontation at the diversion site. He promised that the Court would deal severely with 'any breaches by anyone on either side of this volatile and dangerous situation.'[9] At 5:00 p.m. that day, in response to the judge's order, Maguire ordered his men to withdraw from their positions, and by late evening, they had left the reserve. Thus ended the 'armed stand-off.'

Once back in Lethbridge, the RCMP obtained a warrant for the arrest of Milton Born With A Tooth on charges of unlawful use of a firearm. Sometime on the night of 8 September, Born With A Tooth slipped out of the Lonefighter camp and off the reserve.

That same weekend, thirty rifle-toting members of a white-supremacist group calling itself the Aryan Nations roughed up demonstrators and reporters at a public cross burning on a farm near the village of Provost, Alberta, some 700 kilometres northeast of Brocket. An RCMP cruiser made 'a couple of passes' by the cross burning; otherwise there were no police in evidence. No one was arrested. Civil rights lawyer and Liberal MLA Sheldon Chumir called it a 'total abdication of the policing responsibility.' Observing that the Alberta government had ignored the white-supremacist rally, Joanne Helmer asked, 'If society doesn't recognize its real enemies, how will it defeat them?'[10]

11
In the Aftermath

I'm going to continue what I'm doing, to slowly mentally and
physically dismantle this dam.

– Milton Born With A Tooth[1]

One outcome of the RCMP-supported Alberta Environment venture onto
the reserve was a substantial increase in support for the Lonefighters from
within the Peigan community. From the beginning, the Lonefighters had
been denied the support of the band Chief and Council that they sorely
needed to lend credibility to their protest. This situation changed somewhat in the wake of the 7 September confrontation and the surge in reserve
support for the Lonefighters. On Monday, 11 September, Chief Bastien
announced the band council's official support for the Lonefighters. Reading from a prepared statement, he said that Chief and Council backed the
Lonefighters' 'lawful efforts to stop construction of the Oldman Dam until
a further and proper study has been done upon the effects the dam will
have upon the Peigan Band, its people, culture, lands and religion ... [but]
not violence or other aggression, [or] ... the breaking of any laws of the
Peigan Band, the federal court or the provincial court.'[2]

On Wednesday, 12 September, most of the Lonefighters and many of
their supporters travelled to Calgary to be on hand when Mr. Justice Egbert
delivered his decision on their motion to quash the injunction. They
descended on the courthouse in downtown Calgary. The Lonefighters'
lawyer argued that the injunction should be lifted because it rested in part
on the question of who owned the water in the Oldman as it flowed
through the reserve, a question still to be decided by another court, and
because no evidence had been presented to prove that the presence of the
diversion would prevent other users from obtaining any water. Arguing
that the injunction should remain in effect, Crown lawyers said the diversion interfered with the province's ability to use the LNID weir, as guaranteed by the 1981 agreement, and claimed, with the mock seriousness
reserved for those in attendance at the bar, that construction of the diversion had caused environmental damage. The judge reserved his ruling for
the following day.

There was no sign of Milton Born With A Tooth, but later that evening he was apprehended at the home of friends in another part of the city and taken into custody by the RCMP. Around midnight that same night, the owner of the bulldozer used by the Lonefighters to do most of the work on their diversion canal entered the reserve at the invitation of an unidentified reserve resident to remove his machine. He was accompanied by an RCMP escort, armed with shotguns. The sole Peigan at the site chose, wisely, not to intervene. When news of the recovery operation reached Lonefighter leaders in Calgary, they reacted with bitterness and surprise, asking why the owner had not retrieved his machine when he had visited the camp to service it the previous day and claiming that the RCMP was in contempt of Mr. Justice Egbert's order to maintain the status quo. The RCMP issued a press release saying it had accompanied the bulldozer owner to the diversion site 'to prevent a breach of the peace.' The bulldozer's owner said he had acted because he was concerned he might never collect the $27,000 in rental charges the Lonefighters still owed him. The Lonefighters received another setback when Egbert, concluding that the people entitled to receive Oldman water would 'suffer irreparable damage and harm' if that water was withheld, denied the Lonefighters' application to quash the injunction.

On Tuesday, 18 September, Born With A Tooth was arraigned in provincial court in Lethbridge on charges of possession of a weapon for purposes dangerous to the public peace and pointing a firearm. He was to be held in custody until his preliminary hearing, at a date to be established. In denying bail, Judge Arthur Wood said that since Born With A Tooth had vowed to stop construction of the Oldman Dam, he posed a risk to society, and it was in the public interest that he be detained until brought to trial. At the preliminary hearing on 27 November, Born With A Tooth was ordered to stand trial on two weapons-related charges. In the meantime, he was to remain in custody. In the two and one-half months following his arrest, Born With A Tooth was refused bail on three occasions. His continued incarceration prompted his supporters to suggest that the province was making every effort to keep him in jail, not because he was a risk to society but because of concern that, under his leadership, the Lonefighters might launch some new form of protest that might hold up work on the dam. The New Democrat opposition party claimed that Born With A Tooth was a 'political prisoner,' a charge echoed by several groups concerned about how the justice system dealt with Indians.

On 12 October, two Alberta cabinet ministers, Leroy Fjordbotten and 'Boomer' Adair, met with the Peigan Chief and Council. The ministers announced that Alberta intended to repair the damage done by the Lonefighters and that, once the repairs were completed, the province would be prepared to begin negotiations on the issues the band had raised in

August.[3] The Chief and Council responded by passing a band council resolution (BCR) prohibiting any activity at the diversion site by either the
Lonefighters or the province for six months, and requesting an immediate
start to negotiations. Premier Getty acknowledged receipt of the BCR in a
letter to Chief Bastien on 2 November.[4] Getty assured Bastien that he was
'eager to enter into discussions' on the issues raised by the Peigan, but
Getty also advised him that Alberta would be 'moving quickly to the business of repairing the breach in the main dyke of the headworks.' He ended
in a positive mood, noting, 'We believe that immediate discussions will
provide the Peigan Band with the forum it is seeking, and at the same time
allow us to fulfill our responsibilities ... I look forward to getting on with
these solutions as quickly as possible.' While it was clear that Alberta
intended to proceed with repairs to the dike, despite the BCR, the reassur-
ing, nonthreatening tenor of Getty's closing words conveyed the impression that, at the least, the discussion of issues and the repair of the dike
would occur simultaneously.

A copy of Getty's letter went to federal Indian Affairs Minister Tom
Siddon. In early November, Siddon wrote to Alberta Attorney General Ken
Rostad to say he was pleased that Alberta was prepared to begin discussions with the Peigan. He advised Rostad that the Peigan were 'frustrated
that no direct negotiations have yet taken place even though the attempts
of a protest group to divert the Oldman River ceased several weeks ago.'[5]
This was a subtle reminder to Alberta that the condition earlier established
by Deputy Premier Horseman as the key to opening discussions had been
met.[6] In addition, he wrote that while he could appreciate Alberta's wish
to repair the dike before it was damaged further, he could also appreciate
Chief Bastien's wish 'to see evidence of good faith on the part of both
governments through immediate commencement of serious negotiations.'
Siddon said he 'would like to explore the possibility of establishing a mediation or bridge-building process' similar to that which had been used
effectively in a recent dispute between the Sarcee Band and Canadian
Forces Base Calgary.

Bastien and his council were invited to meet with Rostad and his committee of provincial ministers at Government House in Edmonton on 14
November. At Bastien's invitation, Develon Small Legs and other Lonefighter representatives made the trip to Edmonton, with the intention of
sitting in on the meeting. Unwilling to accord the Lonefighters any legiti-
macy, Rostad's committee refused to meet with them. The meeting proceeded without them, but the province's treatment of the Lonefighters did
nothing to improve relations with the Peigan. According to Bastien, the
province's decision to exclude the Lonefighters 'created further challenges
for the band council and the community.'[7] There were no signs of progress
towards a negotiated solution. Rather, each side emerged from the meeting

issuing blustery statements intended to convince anyone who might be listening that it had the upper hand in the struggle. Rostad spoke of immediate action to repair the dike and Fjordbotten suggested heavy equipment could be moved to the site the following week. Bastien responded by saying the Peigan's ban on access to the diversion site was still in effect and if the province hoped to repair the dike, it would be obliged to prove when and how it came into possession of the land on which the dike was located. The Lonefighters retreated to the diversion site, announcing that they would remain there over the winter and would prevent anyone from coming onto the reserve to repair the dike.

Rostad did not reply to Siddon's early November letter until 28 November, by which time plans for a joint Alberta Environment-RCMP incursion onto the reserve on 30 November had been finalized. Rostad's letter advised that the mediation process Siddon had suggested was not necessary, since Alberta and the Peigan had agreed 'to explore fully the possibilities of direct discussions' and to 'enter into these discussions without precondition.'[8] This assessment put a much more positive spin on the 14 November meeting than was supported by the public statements issued by the two sides following the meeting, and it gave no warning to the federal minister that the province was about to move onto the reserve. In fact, the province struck before Rostad's letter reached Ottawa. As many as seventy RCMP, armed, camouflaged, and accompanied by dogs, led an advance onto the Peigan Reserve at first light on Friday, 30 November. A quick sweep of the

Figure 18   RCMP at Lonefighters' diversion site, 30 November 1990

Lonefighter camp confirmed that there was no one on hand to oppose the dike repair. Once the RCMP had secured the site, Alberta Environment officials and their earth-moving contractor moved in. The repairs were completed and the crew withdrew from the reserve on 2 December.

Peter Melnychuk told reporters it had been essential to complete the repairs before the ground was too deeply frozen. And while there was some truth in that explanation, the fact that the federal government had appointed the Oldman River Dam Environmental Assessment Panel and the panel had scheduled information meetings to begin in December must have weighed heavily in the government's decision to move onto the reserve when it did.

Chief Bastien was first informed of the government's action by reporters from the *Calgary Herald,* and it was only after work was well under way that a government minister, Leroy Fjordbotten, contacted him to explain what was going on. Bastien described the government's move as 'another broken promise ... [showing] total disregard and lack of respect for the Peigan people.'[9]

On 17 December, Born With A Tooth was arraigned on six additional weapons-related offences stemming from the 7 September confrontation, a move his lawyer, Karen Gainer, called 'overkill.' Gainer, a Calgary criminal lawyer and sometimes federal Liberal candidate with an interest in Indian justice and a reputation for defending the underdog, had been brought into the picture in late November when it was obvious that Born With A Tooth's case would go to trial. He was to be tried on the two original weapons offences before a judge and jury in Court of Queen's Bench in Fort Macleod, beginning on 25 February 1991. A preliminary hearing on 7 February would determine if he would also be tried on the six new charges.

On 19 December, after spending three months in jail awaiting trial, Born With A Tooth was released on his own recognizance on condition that he could not own a firearm, could not come within 1.6 kilometres of the LNID headworks, and could not have any association with the Peigan Band Council, other than for day-to-day activities on the reserve. The release came despite the judge's observation that, during the course of the hearing, lawyer Gainer had not provided relevant evidence and had skirted the issues.[10] The judge who rendered the observation was Mr. Justice Laurie MacLean, who was to preside over Born With A Tooth's February trial. His critical comments on Gainer's conduct at the bail hearing were a portent of what was to come in Fort Macleod.

At the 7 February preliminary hearing, Born With A Tooth was ordered to stand trial on the six additional charges along with the two original charges at the trial scheduled for 25 February. Gainer moved to have the trial location changed from Fort Macleod – considered territory hostile to the Peigan – to Edmonton or Calgary, where, she argued, a fair trial would be more likely. Gainer claimed that in the larger centres, media coverage of the events leading to the charges being laid had been less intense and public emotions were less prejudicial to the interests of her client. Court of Queen's Bench Justice Frank Quigley denied the request on the grounds that publicity and editorial comment on the events, both favourable and unfavourable to Born With A Tooth, had been widespread and there was insufficient evidence to convince him that there was prejudice against Born With A Tooth in Fort Macleod.[11] The Crown had argued strenuously that the trial venue should not be changed.

The trial opened in Fort Macleod on 25 February, as scheduled, with Mr. Justice Maclean presiding. The first day, given over largely to jury selection, did not, in Born With A Tooth's view, bode well for his future. Of the twelve jurors selected, six were men and six were women; all were white. Two prospective Native jurors had been approved by Gainer but rejected by the Crown prosecutor.

Testimony by prosecution witnesses differed as to whether two or three shots had been fired, and whether the shots had been fired in the air or in the direction of RCMP and government officials. There was, however, agreement among the witnesses that the shots had been fired by Born With A Tooth. Nor was this testimony denied by Born With A Tooth's lawyer, who conceded that the Lonefighter leader had, indeed, fired rifle shots, but that he had done so in lawful defence of Peigan land against 'a small military invasion.' Gainer made little progress in her attempts to present evidence pertaining to the spiritual aspect of the Lonefighters' actions. This evidence was critical to her defence, which was based on the presumption that the Lonefighters were in peaceful occupation of what they believed to be Peigan land. According to press reports of the trial, Maclean admonished Gainer on several occasions for attempting to introduce 'irrelevant evidence,' denied her permission to enter evidence pertaining to Peigan spiritual beliefs and the Lonefighters' spiritual ceremonies, and twice cleared the jury from the courtroom while he questioned the case being put forward by the defence.[12]

After hearing evidence for six days, the jury deliberated for nearly four hours on 5 March before delivering guilty verdicts on six of the eight counts. Gainer announced that, in light of some of the directions imparted by Maclean in his charge to the jury, she would be filing an appeal. On 25 March, Born With A Tooth was sentenced to eighteen months in prison. The sentence included a mandatory one year in prison for using a firearm in the commission of an indictable offence. The following week, the Alberta Court of Appeal agreed to hear an appeal of the 5 March conviction and ordered Born With A Tooth released from custody, on condition that he not go within 1.6 kilometres of the diversion site. The Crown objected to both moves, but to no avail.

Gainer cited sixteen separate grounds as the basis for her appeal, which sought to have the Court order a new trial, in a location other than Fort Macleod.[13] They included errors on the part the judge in instructing the jury, in interpreting the law, and in ruling on the admissibility of evidence. Other grounds cited were that the judge had interfered 'unduly' in the process of the case, 'disparaged' defence evidence while giving 'undue credence' to Crown evidence, refused to allow evidence on the 'spiritual significance' of the Peigan land or Native spiritual ceremonies, and repeatedly called defence evidence 'irrelevant.' She also submitted that the judge's instructions had 'implicitly placed the onus on the accused to justify his actions, and did not place sufficient emphasis on the fact that the burden of proof in the case was always on the Crown.'

Many observers expressed shock and anger over the conduct of the trial in terms more graphic than the dry and formal terminology in the appeal documents. Born With A Tooth's futile attempts to obtain bail and his lengthy pretrial incarceration had attracted the attention of Native sympathizers from well beyond southern Alberta. Among the many people who crowded into the Fort Macleod courtroom were observers from a number of national church and Native rights groups. They were appalled by the proceedings. A spokesperson for the Canadian Alliance in Solidarity with the Native Peoples (CASNP) said that MacLean's behaviour, 'from the standpoint of natural justice or even of good manners, was particularly outrageous.'[14] The Alliance filed a lengthy complaint about Mr. Justice MacLean's conduct with the Canadian Judicial Council, charging that MacLean's comments were 'gratuitously insulting to native people' and that his treatment of Born With A Tooth's lawyer could be 'characterized as harassment.'[15] The Southern Inter-Church Committee on Aboriginal Rights, representing a number of United Church groups, charged that the trial was a violation of Born With A Tooth's human rights and called for a federal public inquiry.[16] Lorraine Land, the Alberta director of Citizens for Public Justice, an organization affiliated with the Christian Reformed Church, attended the trial as an observer for the Ottawa-based Aboriginal Rights Coalition. She reported, 'I was there because there were some fundamental concerns about the way the justice system had treated Born before his trial. I was, however, completely unprepared for the overt bias and racist remarks made by the judge trying the case. Born With A Tooth was by no means treated justly by the legal system. The overtly hostile judge and the all-white jury who tried the case were in the end simply accommodating players on the much larger scale of a justice system seemingly unable to deal justly with aboriginal people.'[17]

An observer for the Mennonite Central Committee was left with the impression that 'here in a nutshell was what the native peoples have faced in the past 120 years.'[18] He concluded his report with the observation that 'the case demonstrated to me how inadequate the legal system is to deal with the problems facing natives.'

Indian Affairs Minister Siddon was inundated with letters urging him to express concern about Born With A Tooth's treatment. Some of Born With A Tooth's sympathizers lionized him to the point of martyrdom. *Calgary Herald* and *Windspeaker* columnist Richard Wagamese wrote that 'Milton Born With A Tooth poised at the lip of the Peigan diversion, rifle in hand, has become the quintessential symbol for the continued trampling of Indian rights in Canada.'[19] Others stretched credulity to the limits. Elizabeth May, then executive director of a group called Cultural Survival (Canada), explained in a letter to Indian Affairs Minister Siddon that the shots fired by Born With A Tooth had 'diffused a very tense situation and performed, in a fashion, a peacekeeping role.'[20]

At a meeting in Lethbridge in May 1991, Ken Kowalski dismissed suggestions that the Lonefighters continued to pose a threat to the project, saying that there was no indication of further protests by the group. Within days of Kowalski's speech, Born With A Tooth announced that the Lonefighters were planning 'direct action' at the dam site.[21] The direct action turned out to be a Peigan pipe ceremony performed atop the dam the following Sunday, 26 May. Indians from other provinces and representatives of non-Indian environmental groups and religious organizations joined in the ceremony, which Born With A Tooth said was held to 'tear the dam down spiritually,' and to 'remind the river that we haven't given up on it.'[22]

One of the non-Natives at the demonstration was the Reverend Peter Hamel, the Anglican Church's Consultant on Native Affairs, working out of the national office in Toronto. On the Friday before the demonstration, Hamel met with Born With A Tooth and Alberta Wilderness Association officials in Calgary. Alarmed at the news that, despite the absence of the federal approval, water was being captured behind the Oldman Dam, Hamel undertook to raise the alarm with federal MPs meeting in the area that weekend. On Saturday, he drove to Kananaskis country, west of Calgary, where he buttonholed the NDP's Jim Fulton and Tory cabinet minister David McDonald and demanded that something be done to stop the reservoir from filling. McDonald agreed to refer the matter to Ottawa.

Hamel attended the demonstration at the dam on Sunday and the next morning drove to Calgary to catch a flight back to Toronto. He was met at the Calgary terminal by RCMP officers and asked to accompany them to their offices in the terminal building where, in Hamel's words, he was 'interrogated' about the weekend's activities.[23] He arrived home in Toronto later in the day to find his wife upset because the RCMP had telephoned her on Saturday, enquiring as to his whereabouts. They told her they wished to speak to Hamel on an urgent matter but refused to give any more information. Later in the week, a *Calgary Herald* reporter interviewed Hamel about the weekend's events. Hamel confirmed that he had been interrogated by the RCMP about his involvement in the demonstration at the dam. 'It wasn't a very pleasant experience,' he told the *Herald*, 'but I think that its [sic] reality. It gave me a deeper understanding of what the aboriginal people face on a daily basis.'[24] Hamel did not lay a complaint and Calgary RCMP denied any knowledge of the incident.

Born With A Tooth's appeal was heard on 18 June 1992. The appeal judges concluded that the trial judge had indeed failed to admit evidence relevant to Born With A Tooth's defence, and, consequently, ordered a new trial.[25] In deciding that Mr. Justice MacLean's failure to admit evidence was sufficient grounds on which to order a new trial, the appeal panel excused itself from commenting on MacLean's alleged abuse and intimidation of defence counsel and witnesses – the behaviour that had led to the public outcry against MacLean. The Appeal Court did register the view that Gainer's conduct, while not excusing MacLean's errors, provided a partial explanation of why MacLean responded as he did. Gainer, wrote the Court, had failed 'to articulate compelling answers to [MacLean's] questions ... was at once argumentative and vague ... asserted positions but said almost nothing to explain them [and] defied the rulings by repeatedly leading evidence like that already excluded.'[26]

The Canadian Judicial Council held its consideration of the complaints against MacLean in abeyance until the Alberta Court of Appeal had dealt with Born With A Tooth's appeal. In April 1993, the executive director of the council advised the CASNP of the results of the council's review. She reported that the review panel had concluded that, 'Mr. Justice MacLean had displayed an insensitivity to cultural and religious differences, displayed discourtesy to defence counsel, characterized evidence with unnecessarily colourful and meaningful epithets and, generally, did not conduct himself in an appropriate manner for a trial involving sensitive and cultural issues.'[27] She further advised that MacLean, 'had responded to this complaint by unequivocally acknowledging that his conduct was unacceptable ... accepted full responsibility for his conduct ... expressed his regret that it had occurred ... and informed the panel that he had taken concrete steps to avoid such conduct on his part in future. [28] In the end, the panel concluded that 'public confidence would not be sufficiently undermined by the conduct in question to render [MacLean] incapable of executing the judicial office' and that a formal investigation into whether MacLean should be removed from office was not warranted.[29]

12
The Federal Review

Completion of the dam, now 80 per cent finished, will not make
any material difference in the nature of the enquiry being
undertaken by the panel, nor to the recommendations expected
to flow from its work.

– Dr. W.A. Ross, panel chairman[1]

With their leader in custody, their bulldozer reclaimed, and a court order
prohibiting them from work on the diversion, the Lonefighters' plan to
disrupt work on the Oldman Dam was effectively derailed. Their attempt
to win seats on band council in the January 1991 election also fell short of
the mark. At least ten Lonefighters and supporters ran for council; only
one, an incumbent councillor, was elected. Develon Small Legs and Glen
North Peigan, who shared the Lonefighter leadership with Milton Born
With A Tooth, were among the vanquished. Small Legs came close, finish-
ing thirteenth in the race for twelve council seats. Leonard Bastien, despite
bad reviews for his equivocation during the Lonefighter diversion episode,
was elected for a second term as chief. Members of the new council talked
of overcoming the turmoil resulting from the Lonefighters' action and
moving to resolve outstanding issues with the provincial government.
Among the priorities for the new council identified by Chief Bastien was
reopening the 1981 agreement on the LNID weir. There were some unre-
solved questions about land ownership and, in Bastien's view, the province
had not come through on the economic development promised in the
agreement.

Robert de Cotret, Lucien Bouchard's successor as federal environment
minister, seemed in no hurry to appoint a panel to review the Oldman
Project. In July 1990, a spokesperson for the Federal Environmental Assessment Review Office (FEARO) said that six names had been recommended
for the panel, but no appointments were immediately forthcoming.[2]

On 13 September 1990, the Supreme Court granted Alberta leave to
appeal the Federal Court of Appeal's ruling requiring the application of the
EARPGO to the Oldman Project. In October, an assistant to Environment
Minister de Cotret said that the EARP hearings were 'on ice' until the
Supreme Court handed down a ruling on the appeal.[3] Aware that if construction continued at its current pace the dam could be completed and
fully operational before the Court even heard the appeal, FOR filed a notice

of motion asking the Federal Court to order the minister to appoint a review panel for the Oldman. The move had the desired effect. The Federal Court was scheduled to hear the motion on 20 November; on 16 November, de Cotret's office announced the appointment of a six-member review panel. Dr. W.A. (Bill) Ross, a physicist, professor in the University of Calgary's Faculty of Environmental Design, and veteran of several federal environmental reviews, including the twinning of the Trans-Canada Highway and the CPR line through Banff National Park, was appointed panel chairman. Of the other five members, three were from the area: Jim Gladstone, a Blood Indian, lawyer, and professional rodeo cowboy, from Cardston; Helen Tremaine, the executive director of a museum in Crowsnest Pass; and Tracy Anderson, a retired Agriculture Canada research scientist, resident in Lethbridge. The remaining members, both from British Columbia, were Dr. Rolph Kellerhalls, a consulting engineer, with experience in large-scale hydro projects in Alberta and British Columbia; and Dr. Michael Healey, director of the Westwater Research Centre at UBC, formerly a fish ecologist with the federal Department of Fisheries and Oceans.

The panel was to review all of the studies related to Alberta's environmental review of the project and 'information prepared in accordance with the Navigable Waters Protection Act and the Fisheries Act,' and to obtain whatever further information it might need to 'fully understand the project and its potential impacts.'[4] To do its job, the panel was authorized to contract for studies to obtain additional information, make its information available to the public, and hold public hearings on the project. Having done these things, the panel was to submit its findings, conclusions, and recommendations to the federal ministers of environment, transport and fisheries and oceans – all of which to be completed 'as expediently as possible.'

Within a few days of the panel's appointment, an assistant to Alberta Environment Minister Klein announced that the province would not participate in the federal review. Alberta followed up with a last-ditch attempt to derail the process by applying for a Federal Court order to suspend the review until the Supreme Court had ruled on Alberta's appeal of the March 1990 Federal Court decision, scheduled to be heard in February 1991. On 20 December, Mr. Justice Paul Rouleau denied the application. 'If I choose to interfere with this panel, I would just further delay any good that they can do,' said the judge, which was exactly what Alberta had intended.[5]

The panel first met on 30 November and agreed on a plan for two rounds of public meetings to get the review under way. The first meetings, scheduled for mid-December, were simply to introduce the panel members to the public and to disclose their plans for the review. A second round of public meetings, to receive information and advice from the public, was scheduled for early January. Attendance at the December meetings was modest, but audiences of forty to fifty people in the last few days before Christmas indicated that public interest in the dam issue had not waned. Chairman Ross ensured those in attendance that, despite the fact that the dam was 80 percent completed, the review would be conducted with vigour, and that, should the impacts warrant it, the panel would not hesitate to recommend that the dam be decommissioned.

The second round of public meetings was to 'identify issues, concerns and gaps in information that the public would like to see the Panel address.' To a very great extent, these meetings were a preview of the public hearings that were to be the centrepiece of the review process. Each of the major interest groups – the Peigan, FOR, SAWMC – appeared at one or more of the meetings, and each filed a written submission with the panel.[6] They were joined by a host of minor players – interest groups, representatives of local governments, businesses, and individuals. Meetings were held in centres in the immediate vicinity of the project – Lethbridge, Brocket, Pincher Creek, and Picture Butte – and in Calgary and Edmonton. Generally, submissions at meetings in the region, where participation by individuals was the greatest, tended to support the dam; submissions in the larger centres, where the most participants represented interest groups, tended to oppose the dam. There were, however, advocates of both positions at every meeting. The principal pro-dam lobbyists made it their business to appear in both Edmonton and Calgary to counter the views of the environmental groups and to educate the 'big-city' media, which they believed had been unduly influenced by the anti-dam lobby.

The larger interest groups opposed to the dam identified issues and information gaps relating to fisheries, plants, and wildlife, particularly threatened or endangered species, and downstream riparian habitats. They were harshly critical of the provincial government. The AWA warned the panel that Alberta had demonstrated its 'intent to use any available means to complete this dam in spite of environmental impacts, legal questions or the legitimate demands of citizens of Alberta and Canada for an objective, thorough public review of the project.'[7] In addition to a litany of complaints about their treatment at the hands of both the provincial and national governments, the Peigan raised a number of issues specific to the Oldman Dam. Amongst these were concerns about the safety of the dam, Peigan water rights, and the impact of the dam on Peigan cultural, economic, social, and religious activities.

For dam supporters, the only issue was whether the dam would be completed and allowed to function as intended. Their submissions were largely of the booster variety, and they made the most of any opportunity to discredit the views of those opposed to the project. They expressed unquestioned confidence in the wisdom of the provincial government – politicians and civil servants alike. At the meeting in Lethbridge, one supporter said that the people who built the dam were 'educated engineers' and shouldn't be questioned.[8] The focus of the SAWMC's submission was an emotional plea to the panel: 'PLEASE DO NOT STOP THE DAM!'[9] George Snow, from Milk River, Alberta, probably expressed the frustrations of most long-time rural occupants of the region, more immediately concerned with scratching out a living from an inhospitable land than with abstractions like biodiversity and sustainable development: 'Are we who are trying to survive in this Palliser Triangle expected to just sit on our hands and do nothing to preserve the precious water that is wasted year after year in the Hudson Bay and the Gulf of New Orleans [sic]?'[10]

The panel recognized that while it could depend on interest groups to identify the issues at stake, it would not be able to rely solely on the public to identify the 'gaps in information,' particularly in the technical and scientific information. Consequently, it engaged a number of consultants, as technical specialists, to review and advise on the quality and completeness of the information upon which assessments of the environmental and socioeconomic effects had been based. They identified informational requirements in a number of areas, including vegetation, fish and wildlife, and economic and social impacts. The most serious information gaps were identified in the determination of impacts on fish and wildlife. Dr. Brian Horesji, the technical specialist on wildlife, reported that his preliminary review indicated 'the wildlife studies ... are deficient in almost every' informational category examined, which led him to conclude that 'a wildlife impact assessment of the Oldman River Dam project has not yet been undertaken.'[11]

A number of federal government agencies also offered their views on the adequacy of the available information. The Department of Fisheries and Oceans, whose minister had earlier maintained that 'the potential problems are being addressed' by Alberta, submitted the most extensive list of information deficiencies.[12] The department's submission also included an unequivocal statement of its minister's responsibility for fish habitat: 'The provincial government has responsibility for day-to-day management of the fishery. However, the Minister of Fisheries and Oceans remains responsible to Parliament for the conservation and protection of fish and fish habitat.'[13] Environment Canada advised the panel that the only operating plan for the dam available from Alberta Environment 'does not provide sufficient information to predict downstream flow conditions and therefore allow assessment of the possible impacts due to the change in flow conditions ... In order to fully evaluate the performance of the dam, it would be necessary to have access to a detailed operating plan, and i) review all of the input data, ii) be fully apprised of the specific demands incorporated in the various scenarios, and iii) review the output results.'[14]

Armed with this advice, the panel prepared a statement of the additional information that would be required for the review.[15] This document, over twenty pages in length, is testimony to the inadequacy of the information upon which Alberta's assessments and decisions about the Oldman Dam were based. The greatest amount of additional information was required to answer questions about the impacts of the project on fish, wildlife, and vegetation. To assist in assessing these impacts, the panel requested a 'detailed operating plan for the Dam and reservoir.'[16] The panel asked for more information pertaining to the socioeconomic and the archaeological and historical resources components, noting that 'much of what would comprise a socioeconomic study were [sic] not included in the earlier studies ... [and] the lack of emphasis on [sic] the early studies related to the social and cultural effects of the Project on both the Peigan and the ranching community in the Pincher Creek area.'[17]

The panel concluded that, since the Oldman is 'the Blackfoot Nation's holy river ... [and] central to the development and maintenance of Blackfoot religion and culture ... a summary of the knowledge of the spiritual and cultural significance of the river is required.'[18] Noting differences of opinion as to the value of the archaeological resources that would be lost when the reservoir was filled, the panel asked for an independent review of work to date, and a 'determination of the value placed on identified archaeological and historic sites by the Peigan.'[19]

The panel next set its technical specialists and advisors to obtaining the information. Questions that could be answered only by the project proponent were directed to the Alberta government. The technical specialists undertook to provide the remaining information, with help and advice from federal agencies. The panel was at pains to explain that the federal agencies would not do any 'impact assessment work' and that new information would be 'generated' only by the proponent or the panel's technical specialists. Federal agencies would, however, be asked to review existing information and any new information generated and to provide recommendations and analysis on the project.[20] The panel decided to schedule its public hearings only when it was 'satisfied that there is a sufficient basis of information on the areas of concern to the public and the panel.'[21] At the end of June, apparently satisfied that this condition would be met, the panel announced that its public hearings would begin in November.

While the panel proceeded with its work, Alberta took its argument that the EARPGO did not apply to the Oldman Dam to the Supreme Court of Canada. The case marked the first occasion upon which the Supreme Court had been asked to rule on an environmental assessment issue. Martha Kostuch called it 'the most important environmental court case in Canada so far ... the Meech Lake of the environment.'[22] Alberta, supported by British Columbia, Saskatchewan, Manitoba, Quebec, New Brunswick, and

Newfoundland, argued that the EARPGO infringed on provincial jurisdiction. Joining FOR in supporting application of the EARPGO were the Northwest Territories, several Native organizations, and a number of heavyweight environmental interest groups.[23] They argued that, since the environment does not conform to provincial boundaries, and since the federal government is responsible for Native peoples, the federal government must be able to protect the environment throughout the country. The federal government found itself in the uncomfortable position of arguing on both sides of the question. On the broader constitutional issue, it argued that the federal government has a right and a responsibility to assess projects that have impacts in areas of federal responsibility, such as fisheries and Indian lands. In the specific case at issue, however, the federal government stuck to the position it had taken in Federal Court that the ministers of transport and fisheries and oceans were not bound to apply the EARPGO to the Oldman Dam. After sitting for two days in February 1991, the Court reserved its judgment.

That same February, the Alberta Fish and Game Association (AF&GA), at the urging of association members from southern Alberta, dropped its opposition to the Oldman Dam. A founding member of FOR, the AF&GA had written to Premier Getty in 1988, criticizing his government's handling of the dam issue and demanding a comprehensive environmental review of the project. Subsequent events, however, had convinced some members that the association should soften its stand against the dam. At its February 1991 convention, the membership debated a motion calling for the AF&GA to support the construction of the Oldman Dam at the Three Rivers site. Southern Alberta delegates urged support for the motion, suggesting that if it was not passed, AF&GA members might have difficulty obtaining permission to hunt and fish on private land in that part of the province and southern Alberta clubs might withdraw from the association – suggestions in-coming president Niels Damggard considered 'blackmail.' The motion passed by a three to one majority.

Determined to take the spotlight off the federal review, Environment Minister Klein announced to faithful Conservatives gathered for the annual McDonald-Cartier dinner in Calgary, on 11 March, that the government intended to revise the Water Resources Act and would encourage the public to participate in the revision process. Klein said revised legislation would be ready by the spring of the following year. A series of workshops to facilitate the public participation process was scheduled for the fall of 1991. People who had for years demanded public debates on the Oldman Dam and on other water management issues in Alberta were faced with trying to do justice to both during one hectic month in November of 1991.[24]

Over the spring and summer of 1991, the panel's technical specialists, aided by federal government 'resource people' and staff from FEARO's Vancouver office, laboured to provide the additional information required for the review. The fruits of their labours were published and presented to the panel and the public in September 1991.[25] The work of those who compiled the response was hampered by Alberta's reluctance to be forthcoming with information. In the introduction to the published information, the authors note that 'it was a challenge for the contributors ... to base their response ... on information provided by the proponent.'[26] Some of the information requested of Alberta could not be provided because it had never been collected. To further frustrate the process, some of the information that Alberta did provide 'changed over time, or was delivered to the reviewers too late to be incorporated' into the response, and the panel's technical specialists were denied access to provincial employees and contracted consultants who might have been able to answer questions about the information that was available.[27]

The panel held its public hearings during the first weeks of November 1991, at four centres in the vicinity of the Dam – Lethbridge, Pincher Creek, Picture Butte, and Brocket – and in Medicine Hat, Calgary, and Edmonton. Over the course of ten days of hearings, the panel listened to over 100 presentations by its technical specialists, interest groups, and interested individuals, and received 137 written submissions. The hearings did not draw large audiences, nor did they attract more than normal media attention. Every session was transcribed for reference by the panel and 'to provide a permanent record of the proceedings.'[28]

All of the written submissions were published by FEARO.[29] They ranged from highly technical analyses of information to statements of support or opposition based on emotion, logic, or common sense. The greatest number of written submissions, fifty-eight, were offered by interest groups: thirty by interests supporting the dam, focusing on its potential economic returns; twenty-eight by interests opposed, concentrating on its social, economic, and environmental impacts.[30] The Peigan tabled thirteen written submissions. Thirty, mostly critical of the project, were submitted by federal government agencies and the panel's technical specialists. The remaining thirty-six were submitted by individuals.[31] Taking advantage of public funding provided under the EARPGO, the interest groups engaged consultants to provide much of their review and analysis and, in some cases, to make presentations to the panel. UMA Engineering Ltd., the firm under contract to Alberta to manage construction of the dam, did most of the consulting work for interest groups supporting the dam. The groups opposed to the dam relied heavily on consulting firms from British Columbia or the United States.

Alberta did not participate formally in the hearings, but PWSS mounted a 'truth squad' to shadow the panel. At each hearing site, PWSS staff manned a display and information centre, whenever possible set up under the same roof as the panel, where they distributed information about the project and the mitigation program. Though Alberta refused to allow the panel's technical specialists contact with its staff and consultants, several consultants then or previously under contract to PWSS for work on the project appeared before the panel to speak in support the project.

The public hearings wrapped up on 20 November in Lethbridge, and by the end of December 1991, the last written submission had been received. The public portion of the federal review was at an end, and the panel withdrew from the public eye to consider the information received and draft its recommendations to the federal ministers.

In January 1992, while the panel debated its options, the Supreme Court of Canada legitimized all that the panel had done over the preceding year. In an eight-to-one decision, the Court denied Alberta's appeal of the March 1990 Federal Court of Appeal ruling that obliged the federal government to apply the EARPGO to the Oldman River Dam Project. The Court ruled that the constitution empowers the federal government to order environmental assessments of any project that has an impact on any aspect of federal jurisdiction. Martha Kostuch was again 'ecstatic'; Ken Kowalski was not. Putting the best possible interpretation on the ruling, Kostuch concluded that 'the Alberta government has to apply for federal approval or tear down the dam.'[32] Offering a more moderate view, and signalling that not too much should be expected of the federal government, Environment Canada Minister Jean Charest predicted that the dam would survive the Court challenge. Ken Kowalski, voicing the fears of the five provinces that had intervened in the case in support of Alberta, worried that the ruling would scare off foreign investment in resource megaprojects and threaten the development of Quebec's James Bay II hydro project. But as far as the Oldman Dam was concerned, Kowalski was prepared to put his money on Charest's prediction.

In April, with no fanfare, ownership of the dam was transferred from Alberta PWSS to Alberta Environment.

13
The Panel Reports

The Panel is convinced that it received enough information
to allow it to reach proper conclusions and that the
recommendations in this report are sound.

– Oldman River Dam Environmental Assessment Panel[1]

In early May 1992, the panel submitted its report and recommendations to
the federal ministers. The panel said the project was 'not acceptable' and
recommended that the dam be decommissioned. It concluded that the
environmental impacts of the project would be severe. The loss of fishery
resources would be significant, greatly outweighing any potential gains
from the project, and there was no certainty, in the panel's estimation, that
the loss of the riparian cottonwood ecosystems downstream from the dam
could be avoided. Because of the inadequacy of Alberta's work, the panel
had been unable to determine the full extent of the project's consequences
for wildlife and biological diversity. While noting that Alberta Culture had
implemented an 'ambitious' program to salvage archaeological and historical artifacts from the reservoir area, the panel observed that 'the scientific
and cultural value of these artifacts is diminished when the artifacts are
taken out of context.'[2] Coming down firmly on the side of the government's original consulting archaeologist, Dr. Brian Reeves, the panel concluded that 'the existence of a record of the unique cultural achievement of
the bison hunters, in situ, is important provincially, nationally and internationally. The irreversible loss of an area which contains so much historic
and prehistoric information is a significant cost of the project.'[3]

The panel believed that the project had, and would continue to have,
significant adverse social and cultural consequences for the Peigan. It
found that the Peigan were not sufficiently involved in decisions about
the project, one outstanding example of which was that no Native people
were interviewed during the course of the historic sites studies. The panel
called this oversight 'inexcusable,' because it 'overlooks a very important
source of local information.'[4] It found that cottonwoods, fish, game, and
willows – resources important to Peigan culture – would be affected by the
project, that mercury contamination of fish downstream from the dam
would be a threat to the health of the Peigan, and that sites within the
reservoir area with cultural and spiritual value to the Peigan would be

flooded. The panel said the failure of the Peigan and Alberta to come to terms over the project was one of its 'most significant and unacceptable features.'[5] Though it suggested that Alberta, Indian Affairs (IA), and the Peigan themselves each bore some responsibility for the 'inadequacy' of the consultations that led to this impasse, the panel concluded that 'the Peigan were not treated fairly in the decision making, planning or implementation phases of this project.'[6]

The information and arguments presented by dam supporters did little to convince the panel that the project had any substantial social or economic merit. It concluded that the dam would be 'very difficult to justify on economic grounds,' and that while 'existing irrigation in Southern Alberta is important and valued ... the need for increased irrigation acreage was not convincingly demonstrated.'[7] The project was found to have disrupted the lives of the landowners it displaced and created polarization in the community of Pincher Creek. The panel found that to reach 'balanced conclusions' about the project from a sustainable development perspective, 'environmental and social matters had to be viewed in concert with economic considerations.' Its overall conclusion was that 'the environmental, social and economic costs of the project are not balanced by corresponding benefits.'[8]

The first, and 'preferred,' recommendation offered by the panel was to decommission the dam, which meant leaving the structure intact, but 'opening the low level diversion tunnels and permitting unimpeded flow of the river.'[9] However, since it 'recognized' that acceptance of this recommendation might 'pose insurmountable inter-jurisdictional difficulties,' the panel presented 'a secondary set of recommendations directed toward minimizing the environmental and socio-economic impacts of the dam if it were to be operated.'[10] These recommendations, four in number, required that federal approval of the project be conditional on Alberta reaching agreement with the Peigan on the operation of the dam and establishing and funding an Environmental Management Committee with full authority to mitigate the environmental impacts of the project, and on the establishment of a process by which Alberta and the Peigan could negotiate agreement on mitigation and compensation for the environmental, social, and cultural impacts of the project.[11] Should Alberta fail to comply with these recommendations, the dam was to be decommissioned. The panel added a number of recommendations specifying actions to be taken to prevent or mitigate the impacts of the project on vegetation and fish and wildlife habit, to improve the lot of the Peigan, and to increase the effectiveness of environmental management generally.

The panel did not believe that the project would provide a solution to the region's water shortage problems in the long term. It concluded that, 'should all the proposed acres for irrigation be developed ... the situation would quickly become the same as it was in the early 1980s,' in which case instream uses of water could be expected to bear the brunt of the shortage.'[12] To avoid that, the panel recommended that a reserve of water in the reservoir should be set aside for 'conservation purposes (such as minimum fisheries flows and flows sufficient to ensure protection for riparian cottonwood forests).'[13]

On 21 May, Transport Minister Corbeil and Environment Minister Charest released the panel's report and recommendations. An accompanying news release made it clear that the ministers were having nothing to do with the panel's recommendation to decommission the dam.[14] Corbeil said, 'We are confident, based on the evidence presented to the panel, that environmental impacts can be and are being mitigated effectively. Therefore, we are rejecting the option of decommissioning the dam.' He did not say what evidence had so inspired his confidence in the effectiveness of Alberta's mitigation plans. People who had followed the review and were familiar with the information presented to the panel were unable to recall that anyone, other than Alberta's consultants and spokespersons for the irrigation lobby, had expressed any degree of confidence in or satisfaction with Alberta's mitigation program. The panel's technical specialists had been particularly cautious, and any of their comments favourable to the mitigation program were well qualified. Trout Unlimited (TU), FOR, and the AWA had declared that the mitigation plans would be ineffective. Most considered the minister's professed confidence in the success of mitigation was designed to allow him to avoid the admission that there was no way the federal government could compel Alberta to decommission the dam without inviting an insurrection – the 'insurmountable inter-jurisdictional difficulties' alluded to by the panel.

Alberta politicians made it clear that they had every intention of disregarding the panel's recommendations. Public Works Minister Ken Kowalski, who labelled the panel's report 'technically adolescent,' said 'There is no way the dam will ever be shut down.'[15] Panel chairman Bill Ross was reported to have said he didn't have a great deal of difficulty with the rejection of the panel's first recommendation, which prompted Kowalski to 'wonder what really the veracity was with the recommendation in the first place.'[16] Environment Minister Ralph Klein, sounding somewhat more diplomatic than his colleague, said, 'We honestly feel at this particular point that we have addressed most of the concerns.'[17] When asked a few weeks later if Alberta could operate the Oldman Dam without a federal licence, Klein replied, 'Of course we can ... we're doing it now.'[18]

Environmentalists were pleased with the panel's recommendations and, though not surprised at the provincial response, they were disappointed by the federal government's hasty rejection of the decommissioning option. Cliff Wallis, speaking for both the AWA and FOR, promised to use the panel's report to support another attempt to obtain a court order to shut down the dam. Elizabeth May, speaking for the Sierra Club, called the panel's report a 'strong and unequivocal' condemnation of the project.[19] Roy Jensen said the panel's recommendation to decommission the dam was 'unbelievable,' and Don Lebaron urged members of the SAWMC to take part in a letter-writing campaign in support of the federal decision to reject the recommendation.

Peigan Chief Leonard Bastien said that the federal government would have to do more than pay lip service to the recommendations to ensure that the Peigan's interests would not 'continue to be eroded by the provincial government.' Fed up with governments, including the Peigan Chief and Council, and with the courts, Milton Born With A Tooth's response was, 'I'm going to do it my way.' Although somewhat equivocal on timing, he warned that 'if the valves [in the dam] are not open in the next few days or weeks, they'd better kill me before I get home because I'm willing to die for this.'[20]

The *Calgary Herald* called on the Alberta government to make a public apology for its 'chicanery' and the 'affront to fair play, honesty and good judgement it showed in pig-headedly plowing ahead with the dam in spite of legitimate environmental and jurisdictional concerns.'[21]

Despite its criticism, the *Herald* supported the decisions by federal and provincial governments to not decommission the dam, concluding that 'letting the dam do what it was designed to do – once the appropriate concerns are met – is the only reasonable course of action.'[22] *Calgary Herald* columnist William Gold said the panel's report posed some moral questions for all Albertans: 'Do we believe in treating Indians fairly? Do we believe in having a federal government?'[23]

By the time the panel's report reached the streets, the Oldman River Dam was fully operational and plans were under way for a big blow-out to officially commemorate the birth of the project. The previous August, Public Works Minister Kowalski had announced that committees were at work, planning activities for a 'multi-day celebration' to accompany the official opening. Exercising his celebrated talent for over-elaboration, Kowalski had christened the event 'A Festival of Life – A Celebration of Water.'[24] The 'celebration' was to begin on 16 July, with Premier Getty presiding over the official opening ceremonies. In addition to the official opening, the four-day program was to include recreational boat tours, wild water rides, a children's carnival, a canoe and kayak whitewater competition, demonstrations of old-time threshing, a 500-seat dinner for dignitaries, a two-day beer garden for the common folk, a concert by Canada's top country band – Juno Award winner Prairie Oyster – and a church service.

As he might have expected, not everyone shared Kowalski's enthusiasm for the Festival of Life. The Peigan announced that they would not be participating and several environmental groups took exception to the government spending the taxpayer's money to celebrate its victory. Martha Kostuch said the event was misnamed. 'It should be called a festival of death – the death of three rivers,' she said.[25] This led Kowalski to link Kostuch's name with the possibility of violence at the festivities, which in turn prompted Kostuch to demand that the minister retract his remarks and apologize to her for suggesting that she was an advocate of violence. Kostuch eventually received a letter from Kowalski, that she said was 'as close to an apology as Kowalski will ever get.'[26]

As the big day drew near, organizers began voicing concerns about security. Ministers Kowalski and Klein replaced Premier Getty on the agenda, whether because of the security scare, because the intended feel-good event had turned into the kind of controversy that the premier preferred to avoid, or simply because of scheduling conflicts was never explained. On 30 June, Prairie Oyster delivered what many supporters feared would be a death blow to the festival. The Toronto-based band had been booked by a local Lions Club for what it understood was to be a charitable function. When it was revealed that the booking was for the Oldman festival, Prairie Oyster withdrew. Lead singer Russell de Carle said, 'We don't support the project and we don't want to get involved in anything like this.'[27]

In early July, Milton Born With A Tooth called a radio talk show to say that he was prepared to lay down his life in opposition to the dam. His declaration struck fear in the hearts of the organizers, many of whom were apparently hearing it for the first time. Arrangements for the show proceeded on schedule, but plans for even heavier security were announced. Kowalski said, 'I will not be intimidated,' but some of his colleagues were rumoured to be of fainter heart.

On 4 July, Kowalski threw in the towel. At a news conference in Lethbridge, local organizers announced that threats of violence had forced them to cancel the festival. The threats, attributed to Born With A Tooth and environmentalists, were said to have scared off government officials, who 'felt they were too highly exposed,' and without whom the festival would have 'been a flop.'[28] Roy Jensen was one of those who advised the minister to 'drop the celebration, because I really believed [Born With A Tooth] would do anything to make himself a hero.'[29]

Dam opponents regarded the cancellation as a rare, albeit minor, victory following a long string of defeats. To them, the festival was simply another blatant act of self-aggrandizement on the part of the Tory government, masterminded by Kowalski. That the government, which had for years run roughshod over all opposition to the dam, doing all in its power to intimidate and discredit every dissenting voice, should now be cast in the role of victim, particularly the victim of the forces that it had so recently overwhelmed, was the ultimate irony.

Kowalski, calling the cancellation 'an embarrassment for democracy,' and determined to find someone to blame, reported that he had unearthed a conspiracy to disrupt the festivities, involving both old and new enemies: Indians, environmentalists, labour, and the United Church. In response, the church said it had indeed expressed concern that the dam had gone ahead without an environmental assessment and had written to Kowalski questioning the appropriateness of the opening celebration, but it denied any association with violence and demanded an apology. After meeting with church officials, Kowalski called a news conference to 'make it very clear that the government of Alberta does not perceive the United Church of Canada as an enemy.'[30] Kowalski noted that one definition of a conspiracy was a scheme to act in harmony towards a lawful end, implying that it was this that he had in mind when he accused the church of conspiracy.

Cliff Wallis dismissed the charges as simply a case of Kowalski 'blowing smoke.' The *Calgary Herald* advised Kowalski to 'put up or shut up.'[31] Noting that no evidence had been offered to support the suggestion that 'a vast network of dam opponents are ... working to threaten the ceremonies,' the *Herald* concluded that 'Kowalski's conspiracy theory looks more like a public relations attempt at damage control.' There were no further reports on the conspiracy from the minister's office.

At dawn on 23 July, a contingent of sixteen flag-bearing horsemen staged their own dam-opening ceremony. Accompanied by a member of the Alberta Legislature, the gallant band spurred their mounts across the top of the dam, a gesture that *Alberta Report* described as 'a respectful affirmation of their support for water management in southern Alberta and their contempt for the threats of violence that have prevented a public celebration.'[32]

14
And Thereafter

> Rearranging Creation is easy when you see rivers as lines on
> maps, and consider them merely water resources.
>
> – Kevin Van Tighem, *Coming West: A Natural History of Home*[1]

With the dam in operation, the official opening debacle over, and another round in Canada's perpetual constitutional debate to be faced, the Oldman Dam controversy began its steady descent from the front pages of the daily news to the backwaters of history.[2] Although most issues surrounding the controversy were far from resolved, they resurfaced only infrequently and didn't attract the attention that they did when there was still a possibility that the dam might not be completed. Alberta continued its efforts to legitimize the dam and to discredit those who stood in opposition to progress. The federal government continued to dodge whatever bullets came its way.

In August 1992, Alberta's Water Management Service (WMS), having fulfilled to its own satisfaction the conditions of its interim licence, issued itself a final licence to operate the dam.[3] And on 7 December, it issued new licences to seven irrigation districts in the Oldman basin that allow them to divert an additional 387,000 cubic decametres of water from the Oldman River system.

Martha Kostuch and the Friends of the Oldman River continued their battle against the dam. Nearly a year after it released the Oldman panel's report, the federal government had taken no action on the panel's recommendations. In January 1993, concerned that federal authorities intended to back off from their responsibilities, FOR applied to the Federal Court for an order requiring the minister of transport to implement the panel's recommendations. The application was heard by Mr. Justice Marshall Rothstein at sittings in Calgary in May, and in Vancouver in June, and concluded by way of a conference call in September. The Court ruled that the minister was required to take action only on those panel recommendations that the federal government agreed should be implemented, but that he was obliged to 'move the matter forward.'[4] At 10:00 a.m., Pacific Daylight Time, on 2 September, the hearing was reconvened in the form of a conference call, at which time federal lawyers revealed that the federal response to the panel's recommendations had been released to the press one-half hour earlier. Satisfied that progress was being made, Rothstein adjourned the hearing.

The federal Response addressed each of the panel's twenty-three recommendations, indicating in each case the then current conditions or activity related to the recommendation and what further action was contemplated by the federal government.[5] It was, Corbeil claimed, 'a reasonable and appropriate answer to the recommendations of the Panel's report.'[6] The Response confirmed the federal government's earlier rejection of the panel's first recommendation – that the dam should be decommissioned. The responses to Recommendations 2 to 5, the package served up by the panel as the alternative to Recommendation 1, were more equivocal.

On Recommendation 2, that federal approvals be conditional on Alberta reaching an agreement with the Peigan and making a commitment to mitigate impacts, the Response promised that conditions pertaining to mitigation would be attached to any approvals issued. However, because it was anticipated that negotiation of an agreement between Alberta and the Peigan 'could take some time,' the Response indicated that Transport Canada 'may approve the permit before the negotiations are completed.' In fact, the Navigable Waters Protection Act Approval was issued the same day that the Response was released to the public.[7] The 'conditions considered necessary for the protection of fish and fish habitat' were to be 'addressed' at some unspecified time in the future.

The Response to Recommendation 3, the appointment of an Environmental Management Committee with *full authority to mitigate* the environmental impacts of the project, endorsed the Environmental Advisory Committee appointed by Alberta to *advise* the WMS on matters related to the operation of the dam and the mitigation program.

Recommendation 4 called for the establishment of a process through which Alberta and the Peigan could negotiate mitigation and compensation for the dam's impact on the Peigan. The Response indicated some considerable progress in this respect. In fact, it was not until February of the following year that the Peigan and Indian Affairs signed a memorandum of understanding defining a process by which they would negotiate with Alberta and an agenda of items to be negotiated. To date, Alberta has not agreed to either a process or an agenda for negotiations, though IA advised the Peigan in May 1997 that Alberta had indicated it was ready to begin negotiations.

Recommendation 5 said that, should Alberta fail to comply with Recommendations 2, 3, and 4, the dam should be decommissioned. It was meant to be the lever that would force Alberta to meet the panel's bottom line. The federal Response was that it would 'consider' decommissioning under s. 6(1) of the Navigable Waters Protection Act, which precludes the requirements of the panel's Recommendations 3 and 4 and possibly those of Recommendation 2 as conditions for leaving the dam in place. The federal government had, for all practical purposes, rejected Recommendation 5 and, in the process, signalled its lack of resolve on Recommendations 2, 3, and 4.

Transport Canada said it and 'colleague departments' had worked with Alberta Environment to 'address these issues.' In fact, the federal Response was simply a deal struck between the two governments.

In July 1993, having obtained assurances of federal support, WMS had announced the appointment of the Oldman River Dam Environmental Advisory Committee (EAC) to advise on matters related to the operation of the dam and the implementation of the mitigation program. This, claimed the government's news release, would 'fulfill recommendation number three of the Environmental Assessment Review Panel.'[8] Exactly how appointment of a committee to advise on mitigation would fulfil the panel's recommendation for a committee with 'full authority to mitigate' was not explained, but it was accepted by the federal government and by the media, which reported it without comment. The EAC members were appointed by Alberta to represent 'interest groups directly involved in the area.'[9] Local governments, the LNID, the University of Lethbridge, the AF&GA, and the Alberta Environmental Network (AEN) were represented on the committee. The Peigan Band and the federal government were each given one place. After some delay, the federal seat was occupied by a representative of the Canadian Coast Guard; the Peigan declined representation.[10]

To keep FOR president Cliff Wallis, a Calgary resident nominated as its representative by the AEN, off the EAC, it was decreed that only persons resident in the basin could be appointed to the committee. Despite appeals to the minister of environment, this situation persisted until April 1994, when WMS, acknowledging it could not maintain the pretense of an environmental advisory committee on which environmental interests were not represented, agreed to Wallis' appointment for a three-year term.

In June 1994, the EAC recommended that the Operational Strategy (June 1994) for the dam should be 'presented to the Controller for implementation,' although, as is evident from the letter of recommendation, the committee was uncertain about many aspects of the strategy, including instream flow needs and reservations of water in storage to meet the conditions of the Navigable Waters Protection Act Approval.[11] In October 1996, the committee recommended that the first priority for the use of water stored in the reservoir should be for protection of the aquatic ecosystem downstream from the dam.[12] The minister's response, finally delivered in 1998, was, at best, ambiguous. He accepted the committee's recommendation but indicated the reservoir would continue to operate in accordance with the Operational Strategy (June 1994). This strategy incorporates minimum flows for fish habitat that are substantially lower than those specified in the January 1989 operational plan and which were found wanting by the ORDEAP. As of the fall of 1998, the EAC is still meeting regularly under the watchful eye of WMS, but, since April of 1997 when Cliff Wallis' three-year term expired, without representation from the environmental community. Though the EAC had recommended that Wallis be reappointed, the minister chose not to do so.

In October 1993, in an open letter to the minister of Indian affairs, Peigan Chief Leonard Bastien expressed 'disgust with ... [and] tremendous concern' about the federal Response, which showed 'contempt for the Crown's obligation to our people.'[13] Bastien pointed out that in issuing an approval for the dam prior to any agreement between Alberta and the Peigan, the federal government had overridden seven of the panel's recommmendations. In February 1994, the Peigan and Indian Affairs signed a memorandum of understanding setting out a process and an agenda for negotiation with Alberta.[14] Among the items proposed for negotiation with Alberta were Peigan water rights. The legal action over water rights initiated by the Peigan against Alberta, which has been at the 'discovery stage' since 1986, is scheduled to go to trial in January 2000. Alberta has recently indicated that it is finally prepared to enter into negotiations with the Peigan as recommended by the federal panel in 1992. It remains to be seen whether these negotiations get under way before the water rights issue comes to trial and whether Alberta is prepared to negotiate water rights for the Peigan.

There were some notable changes in the government ranks at both the federal and provincial levels in the post-dam construction era. In December 1992, Don Getty stepped down as premier of Alberta, to be replaced on a second ballot of the Tory faithful by Environment Minister Ralph Klein. The following June, Klein led the Tories to a seventh successive victory. Ken Kowalski, whose own leadership aspirations had been squelched by a lack of enthusiasm in the party caucus, was appointed deputy premier and minister of economic development as his reward for rallying second ballot support for Klein's leadership bid in rural areas of the province. Less than two years after his appointment, Kowalski's star had fallen. A rumoured casualty of a power struggle within the Tory ranks, he was stripped of the deputy premiership and dropped from the cabinet. The once influential Kowalski, the political handmaiden of the Oldman River Dam, and the scourge of Alberta's environmentalists, faded into the anonymity of the back benches.[15]

Peter Melnychuk, for sixteen years the driving force behind the Oldman River Dam, moved up to become deputy minister of environment and Jake Theissen, project manager for construction of the Oldman Dam, inherited

Melnychuk's old job as assistant deputy minister in charge of WMS. In the general shake-up and government downsizing that became the hallmark of the Klein administration, Alberta Environment absorbed the Fish and Wildlife Division – the only provincial agency that had ever offered any opposition to the water development projects touted by WMS. Thus did the goat's watch over the cabbage patch become less onerous.

In the 1993 federal election, the Liberal Party routed the Conservatives from office. Amongst the things that the new government inherited from its predecessors were the federal Response to the panel's recommendations and the cadre of public servants that had supported Alberta throughout the years when the Oldman Dam was under construction. That these people might easily be moved to alter the federal position, on the uncertain assumption that the new government might be inclined in that direction, was a dubious proposition. These were the same senior bureaucrats who had resisted application of the EARPGO and made it possible for projects like Alcan's Kemano Completion, Hydro Quebec's Great Whale, the fixed link to Prince Edward Island, and low-level training flights over Labrador to avoid all but the most rudimentary and self-serving environmental assessments. Nor was there much hope that a change of government would alter the attitude of the Department of Indian Affairs towards the Indian people – an attitude entrenched during the long years of Liberal rule before the Tories came to power in 1983.

The leadership of the Peigan Band also changed. Leonard Bastien, burned out according to some of his supporters, according to others the victim of a loss of support because of his failure to negotiate any benefits from the dam, chose not to stand for a fourth term as chief. In the 1995 elections, the office went to Philip Big Swan, and in 1997 it passed to Peter Strikes With A Gun.

Martha Kostuch, on behalf of FOR, continued her legal action against Alberta for destroying fish habitat in the Oldman River. On 24 July 1990, two weeks after the attorney general had for the second time stayed the prosecution of charges against the Crown, Kostuch swore new information against Alberta and its construction companies. For the next two years, Alberta engaged in a series of legal manoeuvres, including appeals to the Court of Queen's Bench and the Court of Appeal, which succeeded in keeping the charges from coming to trial. Finally, on 22 March 1993, the hearing resumed before Provincial Court Judge Fradsham.

Appearing for the Alberta attorney general was a lawyer from the Manitoba Attorney General's Department. In an attempt to demonstrate impartiality, Alberta had asked the Manitoba attorney general to review the evidence and advise whether charges laid by Kostuch should be prosecuted. The Manitoba lawyer, having concluded from his review that it would 'not be in the public interest' to proceed with the prosecution, had been directed by the Alberta attorney general to intervene on his behalf and stay the charges.

Kostuch applied to the Alberta Court of Queen's Bench for an order preventing the Alberta attorney general from thwarting her attempts to prosecute the province on the grounds that his action violated her rights under the federal Charter of Rights and Freedoms. In August, Queen's Bench Justice Power denied the application, ruling that the attorney general had done nothing that could be found to have violated Kostuch's Charter rights. Kostuch appealed to the Alberta Court of Appeal, which upheld the Queen's Bench ruling. In November, Kostuch applied to the Supreme Court of Canada for leave to appeal the Alberta Court of Appeal's decision. With funding from the Canadian Environmental Defence Fund and renowned criminal lawyer Clayton Ruby arguing its case, FOR hoped to establish the right of a citizen to proceed with a prosecution over the objections of the attorney general. Environmental interest groups from across the country, recognizing the significance of the case, pledged their support and lined up to intervene on Kostuch's behalf. On 9 May 1996, the Supreme Court announced that it would not hear Kostuch's appeal. As is customary, the Court gave no reasons for its decision. Prevented by politicians and the justice system from bringing Alberta to account for violating the law, FOR is not planning any further legal action against Alberta for destroying fish habitat in the Oldman.

In another action, FOR applied to the Alberta Court of Queen's Bench for an order quashing the new water licences issued to the IDs in December 1992, claiming that Alberta's Controller of Water Resources had not complied with the requirements of the Water Resources Act. In November 1993, satisfied that the controller had been 'in substantial compliance' with the act, Mr. Justice V.W.M. Smith dismissed the application.[16] FOR appealed the ruling. The Alberta Court of Appeal allowed the licences to stand, noting that they were 'limited by their own terms' to authorizing delivery of the water allocated through District works existing at the time of the allocation.[17] In August 1996, claiming to have evidence that land was being irrigated with water supplied by works built on the strength of the new allocations, FOR laid criminal charges against the St. Mary River Irrigation District (SMRID) for violating the Water Resources Act. The Alberta attorney general intervened and ordered an RCMP investigation, which revealed that since WMS had given the SMRID the go-ahead to irrigate new lands from the new works, there was little chance of a successful prosecution against the SMRID. In the spring of 1997, the attorney general stayed the charges.

FOR then applied to Court of Queen's Bench for an order requiring WMS to enforce the law either by requiring the SMRID to apply for a licence for its new works in accordance with the Water Resources Regulations or by declaring those works illegal and ordering that they be closed down. After many delays, the case was scheduled to go to trial in January 1999.

On 22 February 1994, Milton Born With A Tooth's new trial opened in Court of Queen's Bench in Calgary and Born With A Tooth, eagle feather in hand, took his place in the dock. After listening to evidence and legal arguments for three weeks, the jury pronounced Born With A Tooth guilty of the five counts on which he was charged. The trial judge, Mr. Justice Willis O'Leary, bent over backwards to accommodate the presentation of defence evidence and allowed the use of a traditional Blackfoot pipe ceremony, administered by Born With A Tooth's Lonefighter co-conspirator Develon Small Legs, in place of the customary oath on the Bible or solemn affirmation to swear in witnesses. The hordes of supporters and observers in evidence at Born With A Tooth's first trial were conspicuous by their absence.

O'Leary listened to arguments for and against employing a traditional Indian 'sentencing circle' to decide on Born With A Tooth's punishment. Though indicating agreement with the process in principle, O'Leary rejected it in the particular instance because Born With A Tooth gave no indication of remorse and because O'Leary did not believe that the Peigan could adequately supervise whatever sentence might be agreed upon by the circle. The 9 September sentencing hearing was held in Fort Macleod, to make it easier for Peigan petitioners to appear on Born With A Tooth's behalf. Only four did so, including his sister Lorna, Develon Small Legs, and Evelyn Kelman, 'housemother' at the Lonefighter camp during the diversion attempt. O'Leary sentenced him to periods of up to four months in prison on each of the first four charges, to be served concurrently, plus the mandatory one year on the final count – sixteen months in all. He was released after serving the mandatory twelve months of his sentence.

Both the federal and provincial governments have continued to be active in reviewing and amending environmental policies and laws, much of which activity is related in one way or another to past or ongoing experiences with the Oldman River Dam.

In October of 1994, the federal government finally proclaimed its Canadian Environmental Assessment Act.[18] First proposed by the Tories in 1988 and given fresh momentum when the Federal Court declared the EARPGO to be 'a law of general application,' the new act, opposed by both environmentalists and environmentally unfriendly provincial governments, was slow to come to fruition. Most provinces opposed it for the same reason they had joined in Alberta's appeal of the Federal Court of Appeal's 1991 ruling on application of the EARPGO to the Oldman Dam – because they considered it to be a federal infringement on provincial jurisdiction. Environmentalists opposed it because they believed it was too narrow in scope, had no teeth, and gave the federal minister too much discretion in deciding what projects should be reviewed. Steve Hazell, chairman of the Canadian Arctic Resources Committee, called an early version of the act 'a law which has the force of guidelines.'[19]

After amendments that made it somewhat more acceptable to environmental interests, the new act was passed by Parliament in June 1992 and proclaimed in October 1994. This was good news for environmental interests that depended on strong federal laws to protect the environment, but there were other moves afoot that threatened to undermine whatever successes had been realized. The new Liberal government, caught up in the prevailing wisdom of deficit reduction, deregulation, and less government, and under pressure from the provinces and the corporate community, has entertained a number of 'initiatives' that would severely limit its effectiveness as an environmental watchdog.

Since November 1993, the Canadian Council of Ministers of Environment (CCME) has been working towards finalization of a National Accord on Environmental Harmonization, including a subagreement governing environmental assessments. Billed as a move to avoid overlap and conflict in the conduct of environmental assessments by different jurisdictions, the accord would severely limit the scope of federal assessments. Although governments rationalize joint reviews as a means of avoiding 'unnecessary duplication, delays, and confusion,' they make no bones about them denying environmental and other interest groups the opportunity to 'play off one level of government against another.' Peter Melnychuk says when environmental impact assessments are harmonized, 'environmentalists will no longer be able to whipsaw between the feds and the province.'[20] What politicians see as playing off one level of government against another, environmental groups see as a legitimate appeal to a higher level of authority or, at least, to an authority that views the impacts of projects in a broader context. Though it encountered strong opposition from environmentalists, the House of Commons Standing Committee on Environment and Sustainable Development, and over sixty public health, Aboriginal, environmental, and labour organizations, the Harmonization Accord was signed by Canada and all provinces but Quebec in January 1998.

In the summer of 1994, the federal Department of Fisheries and Oceans opened discussions on the possibility of transferring responsibility for all aspects of the Fisheries Act that pertain to the freshwater fishery in the 'inland' provinces, including s. 35, to the provincial governments. Whether such a transfer is possible without a constitutional amendment is not clear. In 1961, Bora Laskin, who was later appointed Chief Justice of the Supreme Court of Canada, said, 'Canadian constitutional law forbids the delegation by Canada to a province (or vice versa) of legislative power where this would enlarge the delegatee's competence beyond the authority specified for it in the BNA Act.'[21] DF&O continues to pursue this initiative, but has so far been unable to reach agreement with the provinces about what responsibilities would be transferred to their jurisdiction. In the meantime, DF&O adopted the practice of issuing Letters of Advice to proponents of projects that might harm fish habitat in lieu of an authorization under s. 36 of the Fisheries Act to avoid triggering an environmental assessment under the Canadian Environmental Assessment Act (CEAA). Despite being chastised by a Federal Court judge for a practice that he called 'a transparent bureaucratic attempt at sheer evasion of binding statutory [sic] imperatives,' DF&O is still issuing Letters of Advice rather than complying with the CEAA.[22]

In November 1996, with the help of the Sierra Legal Defence Fund, Friends of the West Country, an environmental interest group led by Martha Kostuch, initiated legal action against DF&O for issuing approvals for two bridges on a logging road built by a logging company west of Rocky Mountain House that has interfered with fish habitat.[23] In July 1998, the Federal Court quashed the approvals because the environmental assessment on which they were based looked only at the impact of the bridges, whereas it should have examined the impact of the entire road.[24] In September 1998, DF&O filed notice that it would appeal the ruling. On 23 November 1998, the Federal Court of Appeal dismissed the federal government's appeal.[25]

Alberta, too, has been active in the environmental area in the post-dam era. On the legislative front, Alberta has consolidated much of its environmental law, including environmental impact assessment, into the Environmental Protection and Enhancement Act, proclaimed in September 1993.[26]

Alberta has created a Natural Resources Conservation Board (NRCB) to review the social, economic, and environmental effects of resource development proposals and recommend to cabinet whether they would be in the public interest.[27] The board can refuse to grant its approval for a project, or, with cabinet approval, it can grant conditional approval. The only water development project reviewed to date is the Pine Coulee Project, discussed later in this chapter.

The review of Alberta's water management policies and laws, launched by WMS in 1991, proceeded in fits and starts over the ensuing years. A new water act to take the place of the Water Resources Act was finally passed by the legislature in 1996. Described as 'long and complex' by one reviewer, those who persevere in working their way through the new legislation eventually come to understand that it contains nothing new that is of any substance. It provides no meaningful resolution to Alberta's most pressing water management problems: the protection of instream flows, the compartmentalization of water quantity and quality management, the dual role of Alberta Environment as developer and regulator of the water resource, Aboriginal water rights, public input into allocation and management decisions, and environmental assessment of water development projects. Promulgation of the new act has been delayed, unaccountably, for over two years.[28] In the meantime, the Water Resources Act remains the authority for water management in Alberta.

An important limitation that appears in all three of these new Alberta initiatives is the requirement that only persons 'directly affected' by a project may submit formal objections or concerns about a project that must be considered by the authorities granting approvals and licences or hearing appeals. While it is argued that this limitation is necessary to prevent 'frivolous and vexatious' appeals or interventions, it is most effective in perpetuating – even strengthening – the current situation where influence in government decision making is largely concentrated in the hands of government agencies and local interests. The NRCB has discretion as to who may be allowed to intervene at a board hearing, but intervenor funding is available only to those who, in the board's opinion, are 'directly affected' by the project.[29] Since the collection and analysis of information, the preparation of submissions, and appearance in the role of intervenor at a hearing can be very costly, in terms of both time and resources, the denial of intervenor funding can effectively prevent the intervention of broadly based environmental interest groups, which for the most part consist of unpaid volunteers.[30]

At NRCB hearings, which are conducted in a formal, quasi-judicial environment, intervenors commonly find themselves opposed by government agencies or private developers, supported by consultants and phalanxes of lawyers. Intervenors who have not been granted funding to engage lawyers and consultants are put at a distinct disadvantage in compiling and analyzing information, in presenting it to the hearing, and in undergoing cross-examination by proponents. This is particularly the case where the proponent is a government agency that may have spent years in the design of a project, has virtually unlimited funds at its disposal, and is supported by lawyers provided by the Department of Justice.

Other measures undertaken or scheduled in Alberta, as part of the Klein government's ideologically driven program to reduce the role of government, will dramatically reduce opportunities for public involvement in government decisions about the management of the environment. Government agencies that have been phased out in recent years include the ECA, the AWRC, and the Round Table on Environment and Economy. Interference and repressive measures by successive governments prevented any of these agencies from realizing their full potential as vehicles for citizen input into public policy about management of resources and the environment. Nonetheless, they provided a forum for public debate which occasionally had an influence on government direction. Contrary to the professed intent of reducing the role of government in people's lives, the absence of these agencies increases the unfettered power of politicians and bureaucrats.

One of the more controversial government manoeuvres in the environmental area was a joint effort involving Canada and Alberta. Following the Federal and Supreme Court rulings on the EARPGO, Alberta still had a number of resource development proposals up its sleeve, among them the Pine Coulee and the Little Bow dam and river diversion projects, both announced during the run-up to the 1989 provincial election. In a move designed to avoid repetition of the friction that developed between them over the Oldman River Dam, the two governments entered into an agreement to cooperate in the conduct of environmental assessments. The Canada-Alberta Agreement for Environmental Assessment Cooperation, signed in August 1993, was one of a number of last-ditch measures implemented by the federal Tory government in the final days before the 1993 election.[31] Environmental groups were caught off guard when the agreement was announced. It had been negotiated entirely in secret by government bureaucrats, with no public consultation.

In June 1994, the NRCB and FEARO entered into an agreement to conduct a joint review of WMS's Pine Coulee Project. A joint review panel – styled an NRCB/EARP Joint Review Panel – with one federal and two provincial members was appointed and began work in June 1994.[32]

Four intervenors applied for funding: two groups of local farmers (one opposed to and one supportive of the project), the Peigan Band, and the Pine Coulee Coalition, a blanket organization representing a number of environmental interests. The two local groups were deemed by the board to be 'directly affected' by the project and received a portion of the funding applied for – 75 percent in one case and 50 percent in the other. The Peigan Band was found to be directly affected and received 10 percent of its requested funding. The Pine Coulee Coalition, in the board's view, was not directly affected but received about 4 percent of its requested funding because the board believed it would be more efficient if the coalition acted on behalf of its members than to have each group involved independently.[33]

The Joint Panel sat for nine days of public hearings in the fall of 1994. This was only two days fewer than the federal hearings on the Oldman, which said more about the nature of the two different hearing processes than about the relative impacts of the two projects. The Oldman hearings were informal, with direct participation of intervenors and other interested persons, and moved along with reasonable dispatch. The Pine Coulee hearings, quasi-judicial in form, with lawyers leading participants through their paces, were as drawn out and as tedious with irrelevant detail as the gaggle of lawyers on the proponents' side could make them. It became evident as the hearings progressed that relations between the Peigan and Alberta had not improved since the Oldman Dam controversy, nor was Indian Affairs any more willing to support the Peigan intervention than it had been to support the Peigan's opposition to the Oldman River Dam. The Joint Panel reported in February 1995.[34] Having concluded that it was 'in the public interest,' the panel recommended conditional approval of the project. Alberta has since authorized the project and construction is under way.[35]

In the summer of 1997, the same process was put in motion to review the Little Bow Project-Highwood River Diversion Plan. Public hearings were held in November, and the decisions of the Joint Panel were released in May 1998.[36] The panel approved construction of all major components (dams, diversions, canals) of the project but deferred 'consideration' of an operating plan for the diversion, pending the receipt of additional information. Both levels of government have accepted the Panel's recommendations.[37] There is no reason to believe that Alberta will not authorize construction of the works to proceed. Once the project is built and water is allocated to irrigate the lands the project was designed to support, whatever consideration NRCB/CEAA might give to an operating plan for the diversion will be inconsequential.

The Fisheries Act Authorization issued by DF&O for the dam in August 1994 requires Alberta to operate the dam 'in accordance with the operational parameters defined in the Operational Strategy [1994].'[38] The 'operational parameters' for fish habitat in the 1994 Operational Strategy are defined by a fish rule curve developed by Alberta Environment. It would, thus, appear that federal Fisheries have bought into the fish rule curve, which has more to do with politics than biology.[39] The authorization further requires that 'Alberta will, in making real time adjustments to the Operational Strategy, *take into account* the protection of fish habitat [emphasis added]' – whatever that means. Since there is no public reporting on the progress of the mitigation program or on the results of mitigation monitoring, it is difficult to know what impact the construction and operation of the dam have had on the environment.

The Oldman Dam itself is functioning much as the WMS had always intended. By 1997, the latest year for which figures are available, the acreage served by the five largest irrigation districts in the basin had increased by about 13,500 hectares since the dam came into operation in 1991.[40] This is about 13,000 hectares below the expansion ceiling specified in the South Saskatchewan Basin Water Allocation Regulation, but is probably pretty well on target.[41] Use of the recreational areas around the dam and reservoir is close to capacity during most of the summer months.

The summer of 1995 witnessed what was perhaps, but not necessarily, the final irony in the Oldman controversy. In 1991, fisheries experts had advised the ORDEAP that the Oldman River Dam posed an insurmountable obstacle to bull trout attempting their upstream migration. And in the fall of 1994, a magazine article reported that 'Alberta's last remaining population of prairie dwelling bull trout now teeters on the brink of extinction below the Oldman Dam.'[42] In May of 1995, the Alberta Legislature, with the almost unanimous support of its members, proclaimed the bull trout as one of Alberta's 'official emblems.'

15

The Iron Triangle and the Oldman River Dam

> Mercy on your soul! You have been assailed by the Southern
> Alberta water lobby (... the 'Iron Triangle' of dam building
> bureaucracies, politicians wooing votes via pork barrel projects,
> and beneficiaries – irrigators, contractors, merchants, local
> politicians and sundry opportunists).
>
> – Owen G. Holmes in a letter to the Honourable Lucien Bouchard,
>   federal minister of environment, April 1986[1]

From the earliest days of European settlement, water management in western North America has been characterized by an ongoing struggle between the development imperative and a conservation ethic. There is little about water management in Alberta that is not driven by the development imperative. In southern Alberta, and particularly in the Oldman River Basin, water development means irrigation.[2] The law that governs water allocation and development in Alberta is the Water Resources Act, a semi-modern variation on the North-West Irrigation Act, introduced by the federal government in 1894 to manage water for irrigation to support the agricultural settlement of western Canada. The policies that interpret that law have evolved at the hands of development-oriented governments, susceptible, particularly during dry periods, to lobbying by the irrigation community. The agencies that put the law and policies into practice are dominated in their executive ranks by civil engineers, whose training, work experience, and professional associations favour resource development over conservation or environmental protection.

In the quotation at the beginning of this chapter, former University of Lethbridge professor Owen Holmes refers to this triumvirate as an iron triangle. Robert Gottlieb defined the iron triangle in the United States as a 'three-way interlocking network of interests – Congress, the water agencies, and the local water industry groups,' each benefiting in its own way from the efforts of the other two.[3] The politicians back water projects to buy the votes and goodwill that help them to get elected and, thus, to exercise the powers of government and realize the perks and privileges of public office. The water agencies benefit through acquisition and control of funds to finance ever more ambitious programs, which in turn allow them to expand their bureaucratic empires and to consolidate their influence with and, to some extent, their control over their political masters. The elements that comprise the third side of the triangle – Holmes's irrigators, contractors, merchants, local politicians, and sundry opportunists – are the end users and the intermediaries who manage to latch onto some of the largesse at various stages in the development process. I refer to this group as the irrigation community or, when they are actively engaged in soliciting public support for irrigation, as the irrigation lobby.

By the 1970s, the federal government had moved out of irrigation development. A series of studies underwritten by Alberta Agriculture in the early 1960s led to the adoption of a new Irrigation Act in Alberta and the establishment of a cost-shared program for rehabilitating the decaying works of the irrigation districts, to which the Alberta government contributed 86 percent of the funding and the districts 14 percent. By the mid-1970s, Alberta had taken over all of the federal irrigation works in the province, bailed out and propped up the irrigation districts, and adopted its Water Management for Irrigation Use policy, with its promise of increased water for irrigation and continued funding of district rehabilitation programs.

A new 'Iron Triangle' began to take shape in the province, one that would eventually become the driving force behind the Oldman River Dam. On the political side were the MLAs from the irrigation belt, most of them on the government benches, the governing Conservatives' internal irrigation lobby group, officially designated as the Caucus Irrigation Committee, and, at the cabinet table, successive ministers of environment, agriculture, and public works, whose departmental budgets bankrolled the water development programs. On the water agency side, the lead players were Alberta Environment's Water Management Service (WMS), Agriculture's Planning and Development Sector, and, after 1987, Public Works' Reservoir Development Group.

The irrigation community included the irrigation districts and their lobby organization, the Alberta Irrigation Projects Association (AIPA); agricultural producer groups like the Alberta Sugar Beet Growers Association; the civic governments of virtually every city, town, village, county, and municipal district in the irrigation belt; farm organizations like Unifarm; chambers of commerce; and equipment suppliers, businesses, and engineering consultants reliant on irrigation for some portion of their trade. In 1986, when the battle for the Oldman Dam began in earnest, the various elements of the irrigation community consolidated under the umbrella of the Southern Alberta Water Management Committee (SAWMC).

The Iron Triangle's objective for the Oldman River Basin was to substantially increase the amount of land under irrigation. To achieve that objective it chose to build a dam on the Oldman River at Three Rivers and to ensure that the lion's share of the water captured behind the dam would be allocated to support irrigation expansion in the basin. The politicians and the water agencies took the lead, breaching federal laws and ignoring and manipulating provincial laws and policies with impunity. Three instances stand out.

The first was the decision to do an end run around Alberta's Environmental Impact Assessment Guidelines during the planning and approval phase of the project.[4] Though virtually unnoticed at the time, it set the stage for much of the controversy that followed. The Environmental Impact Assessment Guidelines were published in February 1977 and 'adopted as policy directives' the same year.[5] The guidelines required 'government departments and agencies with responsibilities for the construction and operation of capital works ... to prepare environmental impact assessment reports in accordance with these guidelines.'[6] The assessment process included public involvement to 'provide adequate exchange of information to allow identification of potential impacts and concerns, to provide for adequate assessment of their community significance, and to ensure evaluation from the public perspective of the alternatives and potential gains and losses involved in proceeding with a proposed development.'[7]

The public was to have 'adequate opportunity to review the overall implications of the proposed development and to indicate ... whether or not the proposal is within the limits of public acceptance ... [and] the specific views of the public should be incorporated as an integral part of the final environmental impact assessment report submitted to government.'[8] The entire process was to be completed *before* the department applied for a licence to build the dam.[9] However it was left to the discretion of the minister of environment to order an environmental impact assessment if he or she believed a project would 'result in surface disturbance' but only if he or she 'considers it in the public interest to do so.'[10]

In 1980, four years before the decision to build at Three Rivers, Alberta Environment published its Water Resource Management Principles for Alberta. While there was clearly some ambiguity as to the status of statements set down in the glossy sixteen-page document, variously called guidelines, policies, or principles, it was obviously meant to clarify and communicate how the department exercised its responsibility for managing the province's water. One of the 'principles' enunciated was that 'an Environmental Impact Assessment is prepared for water management projects that have a major impact on the environment.'[11] It would be difficult to argue that a dam on the Oldman River did not fit this description. When asked why Alberta Environment did not prepare an environmental impact assessment on the Three Rivers site, Peter Melnychuk, an assistant deputy minister in the department when the guidelines were issued in 1977, when the principles were published in 1980, and when the decision to build at Three Rivers was made in 1984, said that at the time 'there was no understanding of what the environmental requirements in Alberta were.'[12]

That the guidelines existed and were not adhered to is indicative of the dichotomous character of Alberta Environment during that period. The guidelines reflected the thinking of the conservation-oriented staff of the department's Environmental Co-Ordination Service and the environmental concerns prevalent in society in the mid-1970s. The decision not to adhere to the policy set out in the guidelines reflected the dominance within the departmental hierarchy of the development-oriented WMS and the political influence of the irrigation lobby. The outcome of the decision to dispense with the guidelines is a reflection of the closed nature of the decision making process in the Lougheed Conservative government. Had WMS been required to submit an environmental impact assessment on the Three Rivers site and had the government considered that assessment before approving the proposal to build at Three Rivers, one of two different outcomes might have resulted: The government might have decided not to build a dam at Three Rivers, or, in the more likely event that it chose to build at Three Rivers anyway, it might have avoided the costly legal challenges, the inter-governmental and inter-regional acrimony, and the ill-treatment of the Peigan and the environmental interest groups.

The second notable example of Alberta's willingness to play fast and loose with its laws in the interest of expediting the Oldman River Dam was the process it followed in issuing itself a licence to build the dam. The Water Resources Act, administered by WMS, set out the conditions under which a licence could be obtained to divert (withdraw), impound, or otherwise 'use' water for a range of 'purposes' and to construct any works (dams, weirs, canals, etc.) that might be required.[13] It also enabled the minister of environment, when 'in his absolute discretion [he or she] considers it advisable and in the best interest of Alberta,' to construct and operate works for any purpose he or she considered 'proper.'[14] WMS had made liberal use of these provisions in the past to allocate substantial amounts of water to irrigation districts, frequently at the expense of other users, and to build and operate dams and a network of irrigation headworks for the benefit of the irrigation districts. In 1986, it used them to launch the Oldman River Dam Project.

The act directed the minister (in this case, the Controller of Water Resources to whom the authority had been delegated) to require anyone applying for a licence to build a dam to give public notice of the application.[15] Persons opposed to the application could file their objections with the minister, who was to consider them before granting a licence.[16] However, if the minister considered it 'expedient, fit and proper,' public notice need not be given at all.[17] As was earlier noted, the Water Resources Act was somewhat of an anachronism. Modelled on the North-west Irrigation Act of 1894, its provisions predated the dawn of environmental awareness; it generally favoured the development imperative at the expense of the conservation ethic. If public notice of an application was required, it needed only to be posted at the site of the works, in the office of the municipal district in which the works were to be located, or in a newspaper published in the neighbourhood. It was intended only to inform residents and landowners in the immediate vicinity, the only people assumed to have a stake in the matter. This was not an unreasonable assumption in 1894; it was entirely unrealistic in 1986.

FOR had been counting on the opportunity provided by these sections of the act to press its case against the dam. If WMS could be required to post public notice of its application, FOR could file a formal objection. It would be FOR's first and perhaps last opportunity to formally object to a dam at Three Rivers. All previous invitations from the government to register dissent had been tendered before a site for the dam was selected. FOR believed that its best hope for stopping the dam was to somehow force a reconsideration of the decision to proceed and that the best way to do that was to bring public pressure to bear on the government.

The controller first issued WMS a licence to construct the dam in August 1987.[18] This licence was quashed by the Alberta Court of Queen's Bench in December 1987. In February 1988, the controller issued WMS a new licence which withstood the scrutiny of the Court.[19] In processing the applications for both of these licences, the controller waived the requirement to post public notice. In so doing, he denied those opposed to the dam their only opportunity to lodge a formal objection before construction began, and allowed WMS to avoid a public accounting on questions specific to the Three Rivers site.

Alberta Environment has always made much of the special status and independence of the controller implied by the Water Resources Act. The department's claims aside, the controller, as head of the Water Rights Branch of WMS, was a line employee accountable for his performance to the director of the Water Resources Administration Division and to the assistant deputy minister in charge of WMS. His independence was qualified by the reality of his situation. It is inconceivable that the controller would court the displeasure of senior managers to whom he was beholden for both his existing position and his future security by inviting the public review that WMS had used all of its artifices to avoid.

FOR took the controller to court, charging that he had exceeded his authority in issuing the licence before all the requirements of the Water Resources Act had been fulfilled and that in waiving the public notice requirement he had abused his discretion. In the controller's defence, the government's lawyers argued that, since there had been a lot of publicity surrounding the project and since *local* residents had provided their concerns during the *initial* stages of the project, posting public notice of the application would have served no real purpose. They also noted that the controller's staff had advised him to waive public notice because of the importance of the project. It was precisely because of the importance of the project and because the only opportunities for formal public input on the project had been at the initial stages, before a site for the dam had been selected, that many people, substantial numbers of whom were not local residents, wished to register their objections to a dam at Three Rivers. WMS had not released some studies that were critical of the project, for example Reeves' archaeology study, or an operating plan for the dam, without which it was not possible to assess the impact on fish habitat and the riparian ecosystem downstream.[20]

None of this was lost on Alberta Court of Queen's Bench Chief Justice Kenneth Moore, who adjudicated the challenge to the first licence. The reasons for the waiver offered by the Crown, wrote Moore, 'do not support the conclusion that it was 'fit and proper' for the controller to have waived the notice and publication requirements and in effect to deny affected parties the opportunity to voice concerns over a project of this magnitude. Hence, the only possible purpose behind the controller's decision must have been to expedite the matter.'[21] He concluded that, 'given the magnitude of this project and the potentially significant ongoing effect it will have *on the Province of Alberta and its citizens*, it is, in my view, unreasonable to say that notice of the application would serve no real purpose.'[22]

Despite his obvious disapproval, Chief Justice Moore did not overturn the controller's decision to waive public notice of the application.[23] He quashed the licence because certain other requirements of the act had not been complied with.[24] Nevertheless, some legal reviewers suggested that the controller's decision to deny those affected by the project the opportunity to formally object to the application was a major consideration in Moore's decision to quash the licence.[25] Jonathon Scarth, for example, observed that: 'While it is not perhaps surprising to see a court read down subjective language governing a statutory power, the scope of the judgement on this point is nonetheless impressive and encouraging from a policy standpoint ... the implication of the learned Chief Justice's comments on this issue is that public information cannot be substituted for public participation in the decision-making process.'[26]

Before applying for a new licence, WMS corrected the oversights that had prompted quashing of the first licence. FOR's application for an order to quash the second licence charged that the controller had again abused his discretion by waiving the public notice requirement. The Crown responded with arguments similar to those offered in the first case. It claimed that, since there had been so much documentation available to the public, so many public information sessions, and so much publicity about the project, there had been adequate opportunity for those opposed to the dam to voice their opinions. Stacks of documents were entered into evidence to support the Crown's contention. They were sufficient to convince the judge that the controller had done no wrong. FOR's application was denied.[27]

Madam Justice Ellen Picard, who passed judgment on FOR's application, took a more literal view of the notice requirements than had Chief Justice Moore, noting that the act intended that notice be given 'in the area affected.'[28] The scope of Justice Picard's judgment on the waiver issue was substantially narrower than that of Chief Justice Moore, which Scarth had found 'impressive and encouraging.' Picard's observation that the controller 'had more information before him in coming to his decision in this case than he had in the earlier one' and that 'there was dialogue between the Controller and the applicant,' lent undeserved credence to the fiction that the controller acted independently of WMS. The information to which she referred consisted of 29 volumes of documentation produced by WMS, all of which was available to the controller at the time he waived the notice requirement for the first licence. Since none of the documents offered specific instruction on the impacts of the construction and operation of a dam at the Three Rivers site, a review of them might have suggested the need for, rather than the waiver of, public notice of the application. That the 'dialogue' with the applicant, his employer, convinced the controller that it would be 'fit and proper' to waive notice is not surprising.

Had WMS been required to post notice of its application, it could have used the opportunity presented by its consideration of the objections to challenge and refute FOR's contentions about the impact of a dam at Three Rivers and avoided the costly and acrimonious confrontations that were the legacy of its decision. By waiving the public notice requirement and, when challenged, insisting upon a narrow interpretation of that requirement, it twice turned its back on the opportunity and left the strong impression that it was not confident that its decision to dam the Oldman at Three Rivers could withstand public scrutiny. As Martha Kostuch points out, with some justification, 'Even when we lost in the courts, we won.'

FOR also challenged the new licence on the grounds that it authorized construction of the dam for the purpose of impounding water for water management. Anyone familiar with the government's reports or press releases pertaining to the project knew that the dam was being built to provide water for irrigation expansion.[29] In fact, the favourable benefit/cost ratio widely touted as the economic rationale for the decision to build the dam was based almost entirely on direct and indirect benefits attributable to irrigation expansion. However, had the government applied for a licence to build a dam for irrigation purposes, it would have been obliged to submit, and the controller would have been obliged to consider, detailed technical information on the irrigation aspects of the project.[30] Since this information, if it existed, had not previously been available to the public, it would have complicated the controller's decision to waive public notice of the application.

During the course of the hearing, one of the government's lawyers, tongue firmly implanted in cheek, offered to be 'candid' on the matter. In this vein, he informed the Court that while its sole purpose in building the dam was to impound water (wink, wink, nudge, nudge), WMS would not be surprised if, at some time in the future, someone applied to use that water for irrigation. In applying for a licence, he advised the Court, 'interested parties' would have to comply with the specific sections of the Water Resources Act and the Regulations that deal with irrigation. What the Court could not know was that by 1991, when the interested parties – the irrigation districts – applied to use the water, a generous and thoughtful government would have taken steps to ensure that the water was theirs for the asking.

Which brings us to the third example of the shell game operated by the WMS to ensure the success of the Oldman Project. In May 1990, Environment Minister Klein announced a policy, which, had it been adhered to, would have substantially limited WMS's freedom to operate the Oldman River Dam to supply water for irrigation. The policy was one of a number approved by cabinet as the government's response to the AWRC's 1986 recommendations on water management in the South Saskatchewan River Basin.[31] The pertinent elements of the policy read as follows:

2. Priority of Uses, Minimum Flows and Preferred Instream Flows

'Minimum' flows will be established on an individual river basis and these flows will be maintained to protect basic water quality and instream needs.

Two levels of instream flow requirements will be defined: 'minimum' to protect basic water quality and instream flow needs; and 'preferred' to protect desirable instream flow needs. *Regulated streams will be managed to meet preferred instream flows most of the time.* During low runoff periods, it is recognized that water shortages will occur and instream flows will occasionally drop below the preferred level. *On regulated streams, projects will be managed such that instream flow drops to minimum levels only for short periods of time under drought conditions* [emphasis added].[32]

The italicized sentences came to be known as the operational definition of the instream flow policy. With the Oldman River Dam constructed and in operation, the Oldman River would become a regulated stream, and the dam would have to be operated in accordance with this policy.

The package included another policy that was to have implications for the Oldman Project, though not in the straightforward way that a simple reading of it would indicate. The significant elements are as follows:

3. Irrigation

Maximum water allocation for irrigation purposes in the Red Deer, Bow and Oldman basins will be established with consideration to requirements for all other uses ... There is a need to establish guidelines for limiting irrigation expansion in the SSRB [South Saskatchewan River Basin], based on the water supplies available ... Ongoing work on instream flow needs will assist in refining the guideline for limiting irrigation expansion within individual Irrigation districts and other areas.[33]

'Irrigation Expansion Guidelines,' proposing expansion to 884,000 acres (358,000 hectares) in the Oldman basin, were included as an addendum to the policy statement.

In anticipation of the new instream flow policy, WMS developed a strategy for establishing the instream uses of a river and the preferred and minimum flows required to sustain those uses.[34] This strategy and the instream flow policy were first applied, in 1990, in the development of a plan to divert flow from the Highwood River to support irrigation expansion in the Little Bow River Basin. Of the various instream uses established for the Highwood, the defining flow requirement was for the maintenance of fish habitat. When the operational definition of the instream flow policy was applied with the instream flow needs for fish habitat in the Highwood River, it was revealed, to the dismay and consternation of the Edmonton bureaucrats who had designed the strategy and crafted the policy, that it was not possible to divert enough water from the Highwood to meet the needs of the Little Bow Project.

The potential implications for the Oldman River Project were obvious. Applied to the Oldman, the instream flow policy would render it impossible to divert sufficient water to support irrigation expansion to the level set out in the Irrigation Expansion Guidelines. The acreage targeted for expansion by those guidelines had been finalized only after intensive negotiations involving the established irrigation districts, WMS, and Alberta Agriculture. In the minds of the parties that negotiated them and the government that approved them – the Iron Triangle – they were a commitment. To avoid being trapped by its own instream flow policy, WMS turned to a rarely used provision of the Water Resources Act that allowed the cabinet to 'reserve any unallocated water, ... determine how that water may be used to the best advantage, and ... authorize the allocation of ... the water so reserved ... as [it] thinks best in the public interest.'[35] In September 1991, on the recommendation of Environment Minister Klein, the Executive Council passed Order in Council 615/91, the South Saskatchewan Basin Water Allocation Regulation' (Alberta Regulation 307/91). In a nutshell, this regulation did three things: it reserved all of the water in the South Saskatchewan River system that was not already legally allocated, it specified the uses for which that reserved water could be allocated, and it established minimum instream flows for the three southern tributaries of the Oldman River.

The cabinet, in its wisdom, decided that it could best serve the public interest by allocating a sufficient quantity of the reserved water to irrigation districts and other irrigators in the Oldman River Basin to allow them to increase their irrigated acreage to the level set out in the Irrigation Expansion Guidelines.[36] Obvious by its absence from the list of uses for which the reserved water could be allocated was instream uses.[37] Thus, the regulation established two conditions essential to the success of the Oldman River Dam Project: the allocation of enough water to support irrigation expansion and the removal of any constraints on diversions and dam operations imposed by the instream flow policy.

In December of 1989, before analysis on the Highwood had fully revealed the impact of the new instream flow policy, WMS initiated a program to establish instream flow requirements for the lower reaches of the St. Mary, Belly, and Waterton Rivers, collectively referred to as the southern tributaries of the Oldman River. The program had made little headway before it was terminated in the wake of the South Saskatchewan Basin Water Allocation Regulation, which set the instream flows for the southern tributaries at what the ORSMC had identified as 'hardship' levels for fish.[38]

The sixteen-month-old Water Management Policy for the South Saskatchewan River Basin had also committed the government to 'full public consultation throughout the implementation of this water management policy ... [and] to ensuring that Albertans have every opportunity to understand and provide advice on water management decisions.'[39] In its haste to enshrine the new regulation, the government abandoned both of these commitments. The new regulation came to public notice, unofficially, during the course of the ORDEAP's public hearings. It came as a complete surprise to the interest groups that were contributing, in good faith, to Alberta Environment's public consultations on revision of the Water Resources Act. A spokesperson for Trout Unlimited said, 'It certainly makes us wonder about the effectiveness of public consultation, and whether we're going to really be listened to.'[40] In contrast, the Taber Irrigation District had reported to its ratepayers that 'all irrigation districts in Southern Alberta have met with Alberta Environment, Alberta Agriculture, the Water Resources Commission and the Irrigation Council to discuss irrigation expansion limits and instream flows.'[41] Consultation with the irrigation districts was consistent with the government's commitment to 'ensuring that Albertans will have every opportunity to understand and provide advice on decisions affecting our environment.'[42] Environmental groups and Indian bands were left to conclude that these opportunities were available only to 'some Albertans.'

Beginning on 19 August, a month *before* the regulation was approved by cabinet, the Controller of Water Resources wrote letters to each of the irrigation districts (IDs) in the basin, in which he 'advised the districts of the current status of their licences ... [which] provided the districts with the information needed to determine how much water to apply for if they intended to expand to the acreage limits that *had been* established by the regulation [emphasis added].'[43]

So that his letter could not be construed by the districts as direction from the government, the controller noted that 'whether or not your District intends to expand to the allowable maximum acreage is of course something decided [sic] by the District Board.'[44] The districts reacted quickly to this timely reminder and the controller's office responded with unprecedented efficiency. By 26 August, the five largest IDs in the Oldman had filed applications for an additional 310,000 acre-feet (382,000 cubic decametres) of water and by 6 September, two weeks before Order in Council 615/91 reserving the water was approved by cabinet, four of them had published notice of their applications in the *Lethbridge Herald*.[45]

Several objections to the applications were filed and, presumably, considered by the controller, though none of the objectors was ever advised of his reaction. On 7 December 1992, the controller issued licences to divert the additional quantities of water for which the IDs had applied in August 1991.[46] The water allocation was determined by the controller, with no assistance whatever from the work on instream flow needs.

In early 1993, Martha Kostuch became involved in a frustrating and generally unsuccessful struggle to obtain information from the controller concerning the procedures followed in issuing the new licences. Even the provincial ombudsperson, who intervened in response to a plea from FOR, was unable to compel the controller's office to provide all of the information that Kostuch wanted. She was, however, able to obtain enough information to deduce that the controller had issued the new licences without requiring the IDs to comply with the requirements of the Water Resources Act as the Crown's lawyers had told the Court of Queen's Bench in 1988 would be the case.[47] As recounted in Chapter 14, FOR lost a court challenge over the licences, but subsequently laid charges against one of the IDs for using the water allocated by the licences to irrigate land served through works built after the licences were issued, contrary to the Appeal Court ruling. When an RCMP investigation revealed that WMS had authorized the district's action, Alberta's attorney general intervened and stayed the charges.

16

The Environment and Its Friends

Once participation declines, once the lateral associations that
were its vehicles wither away, the individual citizen is left alone
in the face of the vast bureaucratic state and feels, correctly,
powerless.

– Charles Taylor, *The Malaise of Modernity*[1]

The term environmentalist is used pejoratively these days. It wasn't always
so. In the prosperous 1960s and 1970s, in the wake of Rachael Carson, the
environmentalists were on the side of the angels. In the uncertain 1990s,
with its economic recessions and jobless recoveries, neoconservative ide-
ology, and big business agenda, those who are unwilling, in Canadian
philosopher Charles Taylor's words, 'to savage a forest habitat at the drop
of a balance sheet' are considered unrealistic.[2] This has happened despite
the emergence of a multitude of serious environmental problems: destruc-
tive logging practices in British Columbia, Ontario, and Alberta; the loss of
the North Atlantic cod fishery and the threat of a similar fate for the West
Coast salmon fishery; and the spectre of global warming. In a poll taken in
Alberta in the spring of 1995, only 1 percent of respondents identified protection of the environment as an important issue. Economic matters – the
deficit, jobs, and spending cuts – were the issues of concern.[3] In 1995 and
again in 1996, *Maclean's* magazine's annual year-end poll found that fewer
than 1 percent of Canadians rated the environment as their number one
concern, compared to 18 percent who did in 1989.[4]

Environmental scholars have identified two waves of environmental
concern in North America, the first from the mid-1960s to the mid-1970s,
the second beginning in the mid-1980s and continuing into the 1990s.[5]
According to Robert Paehlke, a professor at Trent University and the
founding editor of the environmental journal *Alternatives,* the first of 'two
waves in the evolution of environmentalism' in Canada lasted from 1968
to 1976.[6] It was an outgrowth of the heightened awareness and concern
about resource management and water and air pollution that developed in
the stable and prosperous decade of the 1960s. The seeds of these concerns
were evident in two conferences sponsored by the Canadian Council of
Resource Ministers: Resources for Tomorrow, in 1961, and Pollution and
our Environment, in 1966. The wave crested in the early 1970s, with the
establishment of departments of environment in Ottawa and in many of

the provinces, and the cautious introduction of environmental impact assessments in some jurisdictions.

Alberta, which frequently reminds any who care to listen that it was the first province to have an environment department, appointed an Environment Conservation Authority in 1971 to act as a sort of public watchdog, and in 1976, as the first wave of environmentalism sunk into a trough, published its first environmental impact assessment guidelines.[7] Canada, not to be upstaged by the provinces, spawned its own environment department in 1971. By 1974, Environment Canada had introduced an environmental assessment and review process, which screened all federal government development and regulatory activity and recommended measures to reduce the environmental impact of projects in areas of federal jurisdiction. Although Environment Canada applied the process with vigour in the northern Territories, particularly to activities in the private sector, it had little affect in the provinces and, since adherence to the process by other federal departments was largely voluntary, they tended to ignore it whenever possible. In 1984, the federal cabinet passed an Order in Council that formally recognized Environment Canada's environmental assessment and review process.[8] The resulting Environmental Assessment Review Process Guidelines Order (EARPGO) came to play a prominent role in the Oldman controversy.

The few environmental interest groups that operated in Alberta during this period were either long-established and relatively compliant, like the AF&GA, or small, ad hoc groups operating at a local level and for the most part, ineffective. The public uproar over Alberta's decision to build the Dickson Dam on the Red Deer River erupted in the mid-1970s, just as public enthusiasm for the environment had begun to wane. Consequently, while opposition to a dam at the site preferred by the government was heated, it was motivated more by concern about social and economic impacts – the flooding of farm lands, the dislocation of farm families, the disruption of local communities – than about environmental impacts. In fact, neither the public nor the Environment Conservation Authority seriously questioned the need to dam the river; both recommended that the government consider alternative sites upstream, where the environmental impact was potentially greater.

The Oldman River Flow Regulation studies, the ORSMC's recommendations to dam the Oldman, the ECA's public hearings on the proposal, and the government's decision to build a dam at Three Rivers all occurred between 1976 and 1985, in the trough between Paehlke's first and second waves of environmentalism. The studies on which the decision to dam the river were based offered little information on the potential environmental impacts of the project. The ECA expressed no particular concern about the lack of information about environmental impact; its recommendations against a dam were based on economic rather than environmental considerations. There was no public opposition to the dam on environmental grounds. Alberta Environment's studies before the decision to build at Three Rivers were limited to 'overviews' of environmental conditions at the various potential sites. There were no assessments of the environmental impacts of a dam built at a specific site or of the downstream impacts of regulating river flow.

By the autumn of 1987, Canada's second wave of environmentalism, which, according to Paehlke, began in 1985, had overtaken the Oldman River Dam. The second wave focused less on pollution and end-of-the-pipe solutions and more on broader issues with more widespread impact, like global warming, depletion of the ozone layer, destruction of rain forests, and the impact of resource development projects on rapidly declining plant and animal species. The report of the UN's World Commission on Environment and Development (the Bruntland Commission) published in 1987 propelled the term 'sustainable development' into the popular vernacular.[9] And by the late 1980s, the maintenance of biological diversity, which in earlier years had been of concern only to academic biologists, had made its way to the top of the international agenda and into the media.[10] By the time dam construction was under way, biologists had begun to focus on ecosystems in their drive to protect species and maintain biodiversity. Prominent biologists like Harvard's Edward O. Wilson were saying that biodiversity 'is the key to the maintenance of the world as we know it' and that 'in thinking about biodiversity, the primary focus has moved from species to the ecosystems in which they live.'[11]

Another hallmark of the second wave was a new brand of environmentalism practised by a new breed of environmentalists, like the Alberta Wilderness Association (AWA), the Canadian Parks and Wilderness Society (CPAWS), and the Sierra Legal Defence Fund (SLDF). Unlike the public groups typical of the first wave, whose interests tended to be associated with a particular activity, such as hunting or fishing, or a particular area, such as national parks, the dominant second-wave groups focus more broadly on environmental protection on regional, national, and global scales, and on the protection of species and ecosystems that maintain biological diversity within those environments. Inspired by global activist groups like Greenpeace and Friends of the Earth, they are not reluctant to stand up to and speak out against governments, and, if necessary, to fight them in court.

The second wave also featured the emergence of environmental action groups formed to address a specific issue or to oppose a specific project. One such group, the Friends of the Oldman River (FOR), rode the crest of the second wave of environmentalism into the midst of the Oldman River Dam controversy. Well organized, with determined leadership, a broad base of public support, a clear plan of action, and an understanding of how to execute its plan, FOR provided the only effective opposition to the Alberta government's plans for the Oldman River. Fortunately for the government, unfortunately for those opposed to the dam, FOR was a late arrival on the scene. Had it joined the fray before Alberta announced its decision to build a dam at Three Rivers, it is entirely possible that there might be no Oldman River Dam today.

In the early 1980s, groups like the AF&GA and the AWA, concerned about a dam on the Oldman, approached the Committee for the Preservation of Three Rivers (CPTR) with offers of support. At that time, however, the landowners who dominated the CPTR were optimistic that they could convince the government to choose another site for the dam. Rather than confuse the issue by bringing environmental concerns into the debate, the CPTR opted to battle the government on its own. The environmental groups, reluctant to horn in on the landowners, withdrew to the sidelines. By 1987, the landowners had lost their struggle; the last holdouts had sold their land and construction crews were at work on the Three Rivers site. Environmental interests in the Lethbridge area, led by the Southern Alberta Environmental Group (SAEG), saw the landowners defeat an opening of a window of opportunity for another group to take up the fight against the dam. Discouraged by the negative response of federal ministers to their request that the federal EARPGO be applied to the project, they began to look for other ways to stop the dam. Enter Martha Kostuch. The SAEG invited Kostuch to Lethbridge to help organize environmental opposition to the dam. The result was the Friends of the Oldman River Society (FOR), incorporated under Alberta's Societies Act in September 1987.

There are a number of reasons for forming a new, issue-specific group to wage war against a project like the Oldman Dam rather than marching under the banner of an established major organization. Mainly, it is easier to get agreement on and support for a plan of action from a small group formed for the purpose than from a large, established organization. It also avoids burdening the established organizations with legal costs. The AF&GA's on-again, off-again opposition to the dam illustrates how difficult it is to achieve unanimity on an issue like the Oldman River Dam in an organization with a large and diverse – in terms of both geography and interests – membership.

Kostuch emphasizes the importance of selecting the right name for an action group. Of the several names suggested for the new group, Friends of the Oldman River (FOR) was chosen because both the name and the acronym projected a positive image: *for* the river, rather than *against* the dam. In the years that followed, partly as a result of FOR's early successes, several environmental protest groups in Alberta adopted the Friends moniker (e.g., Friends of the North); so many, in fact, that Ralph Klein,

Figure 19
Martha Kostuch

on ascending to the Environment portfolio, remarked on the number of 'friends' he had acquired.

At its initial meeting, FOR developed and endorsed a plan of action that included information-gathering, membership and fund-raising campaigns, political lobbying, use of the media, demonstrations, and legal action. A six-person executive was elected, with Cliff Wallis as president and Kostuch as vice-president. Well-known author and filmmaker Andy Russell and Lethbridge journalist John Scott-Black were appointed to be the Friend's spokespersons. As the protest developed, Russell and Scott-Black, both resident in the Lethbridge area, came under the pressure of increasing criticism for their role in FOR.

By the end of FOR's first year of operation, Scott-Black had stepped down because of poor health and because his children were being harassed at school. Following the 1987 release of his book *Life of a River,* Russell limited his appearances on behalf of FOR to demonstrations, fund-raising, and membership campaigns. Kostuch, from Rocky Mountain House, and Wallis, from Calgary, became FOR's front-line spokespersons, which took some of the pressure off local members. Though neither Scott-Black nor Russell had reserved their criticism of the dam or its proponents, the move also gave FOR more freedom in its exchanges with project supporters, most of whom were from rural areas in southern Alberta. At the same time, it lent credibility to the claims of dam supporters that most of the opposition to the dam was coming from 'outsiders.'

In Kostuch's view, the volunteer leadership of a volunteer organization can either devote itself to the task of informing and consulting with its membership, or it can concentrate on executing the plans of the organization. Rarely is there the time and energy available to do both to equal effect. Deciding which course to follow is largely a matter of defining objectives and assigning priorities – in the case of FOR, whether to service the membership or to stop the dam. FOR's members recognized this and,

Figure 20
Cliff Wallis

from the beginning, gave Kostuch carte blanche to act on FOR's behalf, with the understanding that she would seek approval from the executive for any deviation from the approved action plan. She was, de facto, chief operating officer for the society. While she frequently consulted Wallis, and he shared some of the work, Kostuch operated largely on her own, particularly in handling the numerous legal actions in which FOR became involved. No one who has been involved in a volunteer organization will doubt that this arrangement had a lot to do with whatever success FOR achieved.

There were two areas in particular where prompt and decisive action was critical: responding to the government's initiatives – whether announcements, legal actions, or construction-related activities – and giving day-to-day instruction to lawyers acting on FOR's behalf. Kostuch handled both areas with skill and dedication. She was always available for comment immediately after a government announcement or a court decision. In the case of the latter, FOR's reaction normally preceded that of the government (sometimes by days) and invariably put the government in the position of having to respond to Kostuch's statements as well as to the Court's decision. While not as colourful or outrageous as her nemesis Ken Kowalski, she was easily as controversial and an equally good source for quotations to add spice to a column or newscast.

In addition to dealing with the media, lobbying politicians, and organizing demonstrations and fund-raising activities, Kostuch spent uncounted hours planning court actions with FOR's lawyers, swearing affidavits, and filing informations, and seemingly endless days sitting in courtrooms following the progress of FOR's legal battles. Because FOR's budget for legal action was meagre, particularly in comparison with that of its principal adversaries, the governments of Alberta and Canada, she did most of the nonlegal research upon which FOR's legal positions were based, and prepared most briefs and depositions for presentation to the courts.

Both Kostuch and Wallis regret not having been able to do more to inform and consult with FOR's members. Despite what they describe as less than desirable communication with the membership, neither received any serious criticism. Their decision to back the Lonefighters cost FOR the support of some previously dedicated members, including John Scott-Black and Barney Reeves, both of whom believed that the Lonefighters' action was illegal. However, the hard core of the membership maintained its support throughout. Wallis is adamant that providing direct support to the Lonefighters was the right thing to do, and, under similar circumstances, wouldn't hesitate to do the same thing again.[12]

From the seventeen people who attended its first meeting in the summer of 1987, FOR's membership grew to a peak of about 500 individuals and organizations in 1991. Since many of the organizations that were FOR members, such as AWA, CPAWS, Sierra Club, FAN, and, off and on, AF&GA, claimed memberships ranging into the thousands, FOR could lay claim to a base of support far in excess of its recorded membership. With one exception, the names on FOR's membership list have been kept secret. Kostuch says one reason for this precaution is that many members, for example those who are public servants, fear that disclosure of their membership could result, if not in the loss of their jobs, at least in a serious setback to their career ambitions. Another is that Kostuch and some other known members of FOR have received death threats.[13] On one occasion, FOR submitted a partial list of its members to a judge to counter SAWMC's contention that FOR did not represent a substantial number of people. Kostuch obtained the permission of fifty members to submit their names to the Court. The list, which remained confidential, satisfied the judge that FOR was more than simply a front for Martha Kostuch.

FOR's funding came from many sources, but most consistently from individual members, whose donations ranged from $5 to $1,000. Some of the more generous members have donated $1,000 more than once. Member organizations have also been generous, whether in cash or in kind. AF&GA, a founding member, donated $5,000; AWA, CPAWS, and the Sierra Club helped with publications and mail-outs. The Canadian Environmental Defence Fund (CEDF), having judged FOR's legal actions to be both potentially precedent setting and likely to be successful, accepted FOR as a member organization eligible to receive tax-deductible donations using CEDF's charitable status. Availing itself of a loophole in Canada's income tax law, the Alberta Green Party, a registered political party, also accepted donations on FOR's behalf, for which it issued receipts that entitled supporters to claim their donation as a credit against their Alberta income tax. Those who took advantage of this arrangement did so with a clear conscience, since the Alberta government was paying its legal bills with taxpayers' money. The 1989 rally at Maycroft Crossing netted $21,000.[14] An indoor benefit concert the following year, billed as A Cowboy Song for the Oldman, featuring Ian Tyson and Michael Martin Murphy, attracted 700 people and cleared about $5,000.[15] The largest single contribution to FOR's bank account, $105,000, came from the Alberta government, which was ordered by the Supreme Court of Canada to pay the costs of FOR's defence against Alberta's appeal of the Federal Court of Appeal ruling on application of the EARPGO.

As of the summer of 1993, FOR had received about $200,000 in donations, and was 'just about in the black.' Its greatest expenses were the costs of its various legal actions. These were considerably less than might be expected, since many law firms worked for the Friends at cost, or less, to obtain experience in environmental actions. At least one veteran lawyer, a retired judge, provided services pro bono in the interests of 'establishing good environmental law.'

True to its action plan, FOR's opposition ranged from political lobbying and public demonstrations, to advertising campaigns, television appearances, and press releases, to its most concentrated and probably most effective activity, litigation. Litigation over environmental issues is old hat in the United States. It began in a big way in the 1960s on the heels of a successful legal action by the Sierra Club against the Walt Disney organization that went all the way to the Supreme Court and affirmed the right of private citizens to fight environmental issues in the US courts. This success gave rise to the Sierra Club Legal Defence Fund and a number of other litigating organizations, formed for the sole purpose of mounting legal actions in support of conservation and environmental protection in the United States. Similar organizations have become established in Canada, including the Canadian Environmental Defence Fund and the Sierra Legal Defence Fund, both of which were involved in legal actions against the Oldman River Dam initiated by FOR in the late 1980s.[16] Until then, Canada's courts had not been used to any great extent to address environmental matters. In Alberta, government water development projects had never been challenged in court.

FOR's legal strategy, once it succeeded in getting its adversaries in front of a judge, was to argue points of law, not scientific fact. This strategy was founded on the experience of environmental groups that had gone into court armed with what they believed were sound arguments, only to find that what appeared black or white in the laboratory or classroom blended into shades of grey in the courtroom. In Martha Kostuch's experience, it is very difficult to prove a scientific claim beyond a reasonable doubt. She quotes examples of cases lost where environmentalists were unable to prove that pesticides harmed health or that forestry practices in Alberta are not sustainable. In Kostuch's opinion, 'Courts are not designed to decide on scientific facts; courts are designed to decide on law. You have a judge who knows nothing about the issues ... it's a matter then of who can supply the most experts. Obviously, we're going to lose because we don't have enough money to out-expert the government. Far better to argue whether acts are binding and whether regulations and procedures were followed.'[17]

Partly because of this, FOR's first legal action was based not on environmental issues but on the Alberta government's failure to follow the requirements of its own legislation when issuing a licence to build the dam. Its arguments dealt with what provincial politicians called technicalities and were dismissed by the government and dam supporters as frivolous. This reliance on technicalities – if the propensity of both the federal and provincial governments to overlook their own laws can be considered a technicality – was to be the major feature of all of FOR's legal actions.

17
Archaeology

No medicine wheels, no rock art, no vision quest sites, no prehistoric or historic remains, no physical, scientific or archaeological traces of any kind were discovered or any sacred or religious
sites anywhere behind the Oldman dam.

– The Honourable Doug Main, Alberta minister of culture
and multiculturalism[1]

The dam will result in the greatest archaeological loss in the
province's history.

– Dr. Brian Reeves[2]

As the dam progressed from the conceptual to the construction phase, the
environmental impacts that became the focus of the most attention were
those on the fish habitat and the riverine cottonwood forest ecosystem
downstream from the dam, and on the complex of archaeological resources
that would be disturbed by the dam or inundated by the reservoir. The first
of these issues to come to public attention was the fate of the wealth of
archaeological materials in the area that would be inundated by the water
impounded in the reservoir behind the dam. The archaeology issue had
two facets: first, the importance of the area and the artifacts to the archaeological record, and thus to the interpretation of the history of the area
before the arrival of European settlers and the beginning of recorded history of the region, and, second, their importance to the cultural and spiritual beliefs and practices of the Peigan Indians. The principal protagonists
were, on one side, Dr. Brian Reeves and various spokespersons for the
Peigan Nation and, on the other, Environment Minister Ken Kowalski,
Culture Minister Greg Stevens, and the Archaeological Survey of Alberta
(ASA), headed at the time by Dr. Jack Ives.

During the course of his thirty years as a professor of archaeology at the
University of Calgary, Dr. Reeves, Barney to his friends, came to be recognized as the authority on Plains archaeology in Canada. He was instrumental in having Head-Smashed-In Buffalo Jump in southern Alberta dedicated as a UNESCO World Heritage Site.[3] Reeves was a founding member
of FOR and later participated in a number of FOR-sponsored events.
However, in his debates with Alberta Culture and in his submissions to
the Oldman River Dam Environmental Assessment Panel, Reeves acted on

Figure 21   Author Andy Russell and archaeologist Brian Reeves at aborted dam protest demonstration

his own behalf. FOR supported Reeves' position and incorporated his arguments into its overall objections to the dam.

In 1985, Alberta Environment contracted with Reeves' consulting firm, Lifeways of Canada Ltd., to assess the impact of the Oldman River Dam on prehistoric (archaeological) and historical resources, as required by Alberta's Historical Resources Act.[4] Although he had participated in earlier surveys of the area, Reeves says that until he did the impact assessment for Alberta Environment, he 'had no idea that the [archaeological] resource base was as important as it was.'[5] His assessment of evidence of Native occupation of the reservoir area, the earliest of which was at least 8,000 years ago, led him to conclude that the Three Rivers area was 'one of the two most important winter river valley settlement areas in the foothills of Alberta.'[6] In his 1987 report to Alberta Environment, Reeves concluded that 'the loss of the Prehistoric [archaeological] resource component [would be] an impact of Provincial, National and International magnitude ... [and] cannot be adequately mitigated or compensated for.'[7] He recommended that 'Three Rivers should be designated a Provincial Historical Resource and that the Oldman River Dam should not be constructed.'[8]

Reeves' stand on preservation of the Three Rivers area on archaeological grounds was supported by elements of the Peigan Indian Band, who claimed that sites and artifacts within the dam and reservoir area were an irreplaceable part of their cultural and religious heritage. Both Alberta Environment and Alberta Culture, the home of the Archaeological Survey of

Alberta, rejected Reeves' recommendation. Alberta Environment simply claimed that it was acting on the advice of Alberta Culture, the arbitrator on matters pertaining to archaeological finds. This put the onus on Culture to explain why Reeves' recommendation was rejected.

Alberta's Historical Resources Act provided the minister of culture with a number of options for dealing with archaeological sites. The minister could choose to do nothing, or he could invoke measures designed to protect the resources. These measures ranged from 'recovering scientific information from the site,' i.e., salvage, to requiring that a project avoid disturbance of the site, i.e., build elsewhere, to protecting the site by designating it a Provincial Historic Resource.[9] In the case of the Oldman River Dam, Culture opted for a mitigation plan calling for the salvage of selected material within a specified budget and time frame. Culture Minister Greg Stevens, attempting to rationalize the dam from a cultural perspective, observed that the dam 'has provided us with a unique opportunity to research, document and interpret the historic and prehistoric resources in this area.'[10]

It fell upon Jack Ives, the director of ASA, described by Reeves as the 'point man' for the government position, to explain why, from an archaeological perspective, the Three Rivers site did not merit preservation. According to Ives, the ASA's examination of the evidence led the agency to the 'professional opinion ... that [the sites] are not so important that they require preservation through designation of the project.'[11] Whereas Reeves had argued that the archaeology of the Three Rivers area was a unique representation of the Northern Plains bison-hunting culture, Ives and ASA maintained that, since there are a number of other locations in the province where information about the Plains bison-hunting culture can be recovered, Three Rivers was not 'of outstanding significance.'[12] Ives argued that ASA's mitigation plan for the Oldman 'provides sufficient benefits, in the form of increased knowledge and appreciation of the prehistory of this part of the province that it can adequately offset the effects of the project.'[13]

These arguments reflected two very fundamental differences in the philosophy and practice of archaeology: whether archaeological finds should be analyzed and assessed in a regional or site-specific context, and whether sites should be conserved in situ or excavated.

Reeves is of the school that believes that to obtain the most meaningful knowledge from archaeological evidence it must be considered 'in association' with other finds in a regional context. That is to say, that more and better information can be gleaned from archaeological finds if they are studied in relation to other finds with which they are in geographical, temporal, or cultural association. To do this requires that the archaeological evidence be considered in the broader context of the region in which it is found, rather than the more restricted confines of the 'project area.'

ASA, largely because it is a government agency and particularly when it is dealing with an initiative of another government agency, is compelled to operate within the geographic, budgetary, and time constraints imposed by the particular project. Consequently, ASA tends to take a site-specific, rather than regional approach to archaeological investigations. In Reeves' words, 'they want to look at specific sites; they don't want to look at cumulative things; they don't want to look at the big picture.'[14] Such was the case with the Oldman River Dam.

ASA's defence of its practice of limiting archaeological inquiries to the area bounded by a project – in the Oldman case the area to be occupied by the dam and reservoir – is essentially a denial of the concept of association. Reeves had suggested that the Three Rivers area and nearby Head-Smashed-In Buffalo Jump were both 'components' of the Peigan's seasonal migration pattern and that the 'relationship' between the two was an indication of the archaeological importance of Three Rivers. Ives rejected Reeves' argument on the grounds that there was 'no tangible evidence of [a] connection' between the two sites.[15] On the other hand, he appeared to use the notion of association between sites in the area when he suggested that there may be numerous other sites in the area with a connection to Head-Smashed-In that would render Three Rivers of lesser importance than assessed by Reeves. On this difference, a majority of the archaeological community are in Reeves' corner, though their presence is not always apparent. Most practising archaeologists, including many moonlighting academics, are in the employ of governments, consulting firms, or resource developers in the private sector. Consequently, while they may favour looking at 'the big picture,' their livelihood is tied to projects.

On the second issue, conservation versus excavation, the archaeological community is divided, though Reeves says that in the case of Three Rivers, he had 'quite a bit of covert support.' The ASA, because it is a government agency and because governments, universally, are pro-development, rarely recommends conservation over excavation if it means derailing a development project. Reeves has little sympathy for the ASA's position. He says ASA 'is the agency that is supposed to be responsible for conserving the resources ... [but] they have been more prone to mitigative excavation as an option.'[16] Neither does Reeves accept the argument of the many 'scientists' who favour excavation that 'we need the knowledge now; if we don't get it we won't learn.' In Reeves' view, 'that's not what it's all about; we're here to conserve it.' On the other hand, he sympathizes with the position of the consulting archaeologists, who cannot make a living doing surveys alone. To stay in business, they needed the excavation contracts, which, he says, 'provided a lot of work for a lot of people in bad years when there wasn't much.'[17]

There was no indication that Alberta Culture or Alberta Environment

paid the least attention to the Peigan's claim to an interest in the archaeological resources. A band council resolution passed by the Peigan in February 1989 required archaeologists to obtain a permit from the nearest tribe's
signatory to Treaty 7 before excavating sites and removing artifacts. This
resolution was ignored by both government agencies and their contractors.[18] Both the Alberta Historical Resources Act and the ASA exhibit
strange attitudes towards the interest of Native peoples in archaeological
resources located within the areas traditionally occupied by their ancestors.
The act claims all artifacts found in Alberta as the property of the Crown.[19]
It makes no allowance whatever for consultation with Indian people on
the interpretation of sites or artifacts; on their significance to Indian history, culture, or religion; or on the handling or management of any
archaeological materials found in areas of traditional Indian occupation.

Officials of Alberta Culture (now Community Development) and ASA
responsible for the administration of the act interpret its provisions as
they pertain to the interests of Native people in the narrowest possible
manner. This is apparent in evidence presented at the 1994 joint EARP/
NRCB hearings on Alberta's Pine Coulee Project. The director of the ASA
informed the hearing that the Peigan were neither advised of nor consulted on the possible impact of the project on Peigan interests because the
act does not require it and because ASA does not consider it the agency's
responsibility to do so. He also expressed ASA's view that it was not possible to associate the artifacts found in the Pine Coulee area with any particular Native group. He defended ASA's decision to limit the archaeological
study to the project area on the grounds that without evidence of integra-
tion between areas, the study boundaries could extend forever.[20]

The consulting firm that did the archaeological impact assessment for
the Pine Coulee Project recommended that Native groups should be interviewed 'to establish the spiritual/religious significance' of the project area.
In response, William J. Byrne, deputy minister of Alberta community
development, advised that 'it is not clear that the provisions of the Alberta
Historical Resources Act would allow us to require a program of interviews
... however, it would certainly be reasonable to carry out such interviews
during the mitigation stage.'[21] Of course the mitigation stage only occurs
after the decision has been made to proceed with the project and after a
mitigation plan has been approved.

At the Pine Coulee hearings, a panel member asked ASA Director Jack
Brink if ASA had ever consulted with Native groups during the design
phase of a mitigation project. Brink replied that he could not think of a
case where that had happened. In the vernacular, it might be said that
Alberta Community Development and the ASA have an attitude problem.
Alberta's management of historical resources as it concerns the interests of
Indian people contrasts dramatically with comparable laws and practices

in British Columbia, where Aboriginal people, in part because of their unsettled land claims and the absence of treaties, are able to exert more leverage on the government. In British Columbia, applications for permits to excavate in search of artifacts of Aboriginal origin are routinely referred to the Aboriginal community for comment, including advice on the disposition of any artifacts found during the course of the search. If a permit is issued, the permit holder may be required to 'consult with or obtain the consent of' the Aboriginal community whose 'heritage the property represents or may represent.'[22] The BC government may also enter into formal agreements with a 'first nation' to conserve and protect artifacts that are specified as being of 'particular spiritual ceremonial or other cultural value to the aboriginal people' represented by that first nation.[23]

In the case of the Oldman River Dam, the Peigan were not consulted on the interpretation or disposition of the materials discovered during the impact study or on the design and implementation of the mitigation program. Although consultation with residents was a requirement in the inventory and assessment of historical resources, consultation with Indian people was not included in the terms of reference for the archaeological resources.[24] The mitigation program for historical resources included taping interviews with 'community members who remember the area as it existed during the period under investigation.'[25] No attempt was made to record information from Native elders, whose oral histories might have added substantially to the evidence obtained from the archaeological salvage operation. A historical and archaeological resources subcommittee of the Local Advisory Committee (LAC) had some limited involvement in the implementation of the mitigation plan. The eight-person subcommittee included one Native person, a Peigan councillor who was not appointed until 1988, by which time the mitigation plan had been approved and was being implemented.[26] According to the LAC chairman, Hilton Pharis, the Peigan member of the subcommittee attended very few meetings.[27] Given the membership and interests of the subcommittee, and the state of relations between Alberta and the Peigan, a spotty attendance record should not have been surprising.

Federal authorities took a different view of the Peigan's interest in the archaeological resources in the reservoir area. Bill Yeo, chief of Historical and Archaeological Research for Parks Canada's Western Region, advised Environment Canada that, 'the simplest and *fairest* way to look at this question is to think of the Three Rivers Area as a cultural landscape. Even though the Peigan have lived on their nearby reserve for over a century, their recent history undoubtedly links them with several special areas outside the reserve boundaries, one of which is the reservoir site [emphasis added].'[28] However, since both the area and the resources were outside federal jurisdiction, there was nothing the federal authorities could do, and they do not appear to have been consulted by Alberta. Nor did Indian Affairs intervene with Alberta on the Peigan's behalf.

Reeves' earliest representation to the federal panel recommended that a third party – a 'Northern Plains Archaeologist knowledgable of the region and the subject matter,' who had never been and was not then a consultant to the Alberta government – should be appointed to review and advise the panel on the 'difference in opinion on the value of the Historical Resources.'[29] The panel, following Reeves' advice, hired Dr. David Meyer, then an associate professor of Archaeology at the University of Saskatchewan, to review Lifeways' (i.e., Reeves') work and recommendations. Meyer wrote a report on his review for the panel and spoke at the panel hearings. On the question of the relative importance of archaeological sites, Meyer explained that 'what is considered significant, important, of value, varies depending on the research orientation of the particular archaeologist.'[30] Nevertheless, in the case of Three Rivers, Meyer concluded that 'Reeves must be considered the expert and his views must be taken very seriously.'[31] Professional archaeologists, Meyer noted, 'are all too willing simply to recommend mitigation ... [which] often consists of excavation before the site is permanently lost. Whether [excavation] constitutes real mitigation is a moot point.'[32]

How heavily archaeological considerations weighed in the panel's recommendation to decommission the dam is not clear. By the time the panel began its deliberations, a lot of irreversible damage had been done: the removal of 175,000 artifacts from the site was complete and the reservoir area was partially under water. That it attached great significance to the archaeological resources of the area was, however, abundantly clear. In its final report, the panel said, 'The existence of a record of the unique cultural achievement of the bison hunters, *in situ*, is important provincially, nationally and internationally. The irreversible loss of an area which contains so much historic and prehistoric information is a significant cost of the project.'[33] The panel also recognized the Peigan's interest in the archaeological resources of the area. It characterized Alberta's failure to interview Native people concerning the archaeological sites and artifacts as 'an inexcusable omission,' and recommended that the Peigan be compensated for 'cultural and spiritual losses in the reservoir area.'[34]

The significant finds uncovered during the course of the salvage operation convinced Reeves that construction of the dam has indeed resulted in the greatest archaeological loss in the province's history.[35]

18
Biological Diversity

An ecosystem consists of the physical environment and all the organisms in a given area, together with the webwork of interactions of those organisms with that physical environment and with each other.

– Paul R. Ehrlich, *The Machinery of Nature*[1]

A thing is right when it tends to preserve the integrity, stability and beauty of the biotic community. It is wrong when it tends otherwise.

– Aldo Leopold, *A Sand County Almanac*[2]

The second environmental issue to emerge in the fall of 1987 was biological diversity. Attention was focused in this area when researchers in the scientific community raised questions about the likely impact of dam operations on the riparian cottonwood forests downstream from the project. Unlike the fate of the archaeological resources, which for all practical purposes was decided with the implementation of the salvage operation and the inundation of the reservoir area, the debate surrounding the fate of the riparian forest ecosystems continued throughout the period of dam construction, and remains at issue today.

The three species of poplars – balsam, prairie or plains cottonwood, and narrowleaf cottonwood – and the hybrid swarm produced by their interbreeding that grow in the Oldman River valley, are the only tree species native to river valleys in the grasslands of southern Alberta.[3] These trees are the dominant species and the anchors of the riparian cottonwood forest habitats or ecosystems that have been characterized as amongst 'the most threatened ecosystems in arid and semiarid regions of the world.'[4] Some of the highest densities of these forest ecosystems occur along the Oldman River. In the late 1980s and early 1990s, when the dam was under construction and the federal review was under way, there was a respectable body of available knowledge about the distribution, densities, and health of the cottonwoods and about many of the animal and plant species associated with the riparian forests. But there was surprisingly little information about the riparian forest ecosystem per se or about the interactions of the various components of that ecosystem.

Figure 22   Riparian forest downstream from Oldman River Dam

The idea that the riparian forests represented an ecosystem was apparently not foreign to Alberta Environment. In one of a series of brochures
pertaining to mitigation planning for the project, Alberta Environment
says that 'a natural ecosystem is a complex interrelationship between living
organisms and their environment ... [and] because of these interrelationships, vegetation [in this case cottonwoods] cannot be discussed in isola-
tion, but should be viewed as part of a larger system.'[5] However, with the
one exception discussed below, there is no indication in any of the department's reporting on either the project or the mitigation plan that it did
anything to enlighten itself about the complex interrelationships that
defined the riparian forest ecosystem. Nor were the project's opponents or
the various contributors to the federal review able to provide such information. As late as February 1991, a study reported that 'little is known about
the other [than poplars] floodplain species, their interrelationships and
requirements for successful establishment.'[6] And in May 1992, with the
dam complete, the reservoir area cleared of its riparian forest and filling
with water, a conservation and management strategy for the riparian
forests, produced by the Alberta government and the World Wildlife Fund,
reported that 'few data have been compiled on the [environmental] value
of riparian poplar forests in southern Alberta.'[7]

The information that could be pieced together suggested that, in addition to the various species of poplar, some of the plant and animal life most
likely to be associated with the riparian forest ecosystem of the Oldman

River valley included numerous species of clumped and thicket shrubs, which comprise the understorey vegetation, and herbaceous plants, which inhabit the forest floor; forty species of mammals, including deer, coyote, and fox; six amphibian and four reptile species; and numerous nesting and migrating bird species, including eagles, hawks, falcons, and various water-fowl.[8] Drawing from a body of research done in the 1970s and early 1980s, Bradley noted the interrelationships between riparian forest ecosystems and associated river ecosystems that provide improved fish habitat.[9]

The interrelationships between river flows and cottonwood regeneration became a contentious element in WMS's plans for operating the dam. The first public concern for the fate of the downstream riparian cottonwood forests was voiced by Dr. Stewart Rood, a plant physiologist and professor of biology at the University of Lethbridge, in October 1987.[10] Rood had just completed a five-year study that revealed the impact on riparian forests of dams built on the St. Mary and Waterton Rivers in the 1950s.[11] Rood's study documented a severe reduction in the 'abundance' of riparian cottonwoods downstream from both dams – 48 percent for the St. Mary and 23 percent for the Waterton. This correlated with similar research completed in Canada and the United States during the 1980s.[12] The various researchers, working independently, all arrived at the same conclusion: cottonwoods were dying out downstream from dams.

The research confirmed that cottonwoods are replenished mainly by the establishment of seedlings. As anyone who has experienced an early summer blizzard of airborne 'cotton' can testify, cottonwoods are prolific seed producers. The conditions required to ensure the germination of the seeds and the growth of the seedlings include beds of moist sand and silt, free of competing vegetation, and with abundant sunlight for several weeks in the first year. In the Oldman, which is fed from mountain snowmelt, the period of high flow that provides the moist seedbeds coincides with the dispersion of cottonwood seeds in early summer. Since cottonwoods are phreatophytes (deep-rooted plants that obtain moisture from the water table or the layer of silt just above it), a high water table is required to ensure adequate water supplies for their continued growth in subsequent years. Although they thrive in semiarid environments, cottonwoods are not well adapted to drought stress because in their natural habitat – river valley bottoms – they generally have an adequate supply of water from groundwater. Since the riparian groundwater table is closely related to the water level in the river, reduced flows mean a lower water table and less than optimum conditions for cottonwoods.

The regulation of streamflow through the construction and operation of dams reduces the likelihood of the flooding that produces the moist seedbeds and can reduce downstream flows and, consequently, lower water tables adjacent to the river. Channel meandering, which exposes new seedbeds, is also reduced. These conditions threaten the replenishment of the riparian cottonwoods; if they are allowed to prevail, the cottonwoods will die out, as has been the case downstream from the St. Mary and Waterton Dams. And, Rood concluded, 'if the riparian cottonwoods are permitted to die, so will the entire riparian forest ecosystem.'[13] There is no compensating tree to move in when the cottonwoods are gone.

Until Rood blew the whistle, Alberta's concerns for vegetation had been limited to the reclamation of areas disturbed by construction-related activities in and around the dam site, and a tree-planting program on the uplands adjacent to the dam, intended to replace the wildlife habitat that would be lost when the reservoir area was inundated. Whether Alberta Environment was aware of the potential impact of dam operations on cottonwoods is not clear. When dam construction began in 1986, the water needs of the riparian forest ecosystem had not yet been identified as a factor in operating the dam, nor were they a consideration in the first operational plan for the dam produced by WMS in January 1989.[14] In 1988, faced with the mounting research evidence and increasing public concern sparked by FOR's information campaign, PWSS engaged Rood to 'find the causes of cottonwood mortality and provide an understanding of the linkages between river flow regulation and cottonwood stress.'[15] Convinced that the dam could be operated so that the cottonwoods could be spared, Rood hoped to contribute to the development of an operational strategy for the dam that would 'enable irrigation expansion, but [would] also attempt to minimize environmental damage.'[16] In 1989, Alberta Environment hired Rood to assess how the riparian cottonwoods would fare if the dam were operated as indicated in WMS's January 1989 operational plan.

The research that Rood carried out under these contracts provided the basis for his submissions to the federal EARP Panel in November 1991. Rood reported that neither the reduced silt deposition nor the limited flood attenuation provided by the dam would be harmful but that reduced streamflow and consequent lowering of the groundwater table during the summer months would threaten the continued existence of the riparian cottonwood ecosystem.[17] He concluded that it was 'the pattern of flow regulation that is expected to determine the impact of the Oldman River dam.'[18]

The development of WMS's January 1989 operating plan was based on data produced by a computer simulation of the South Saskatchewan River system.[19] Rood's assessment of the operational plan, was that 'overall ... [it] will have relatively little net impact on Oldman River cottonwoods, *relative to the present situation* [emphasis added].'[20] The 'present situation' was not good, particularly in what is referred to as the Fort Macleod Reach – between the LNID weir and the confluence with the Belly River – where it was not uncommon for the flow to be reduced to zero at times during the summer months. In fact, if the minimum flows prescribed in the operating plan were adhered to, Rood anticipated a beneficial impact in the Fort Macleod Reach and a decline in the Lethbridge Reach [below the confluence with the Belly]. The bad news for the Lethbridge Reach would result from reduced flows in the Belly and Waterton and St. Mary Rivers, which led Rood to conclude that 'the greatest negative impacts ... on riparian cottonwoods are likely to occur along the Waterton and St. Mary Rivers.'[21] His final conclusion was that the operational plan 'is probably survivable, but not optimal for Oldman River cottonwoods.'[22]

This relatively rosy assessment was the basis for statements released to the public by the PWSS ghost squad shadowing the panel's public hearings. PWSS maintained that 'an opportunity exists to preserve and enhance the cottonwood populations in the area of the Oldman River Dam Project ... [and] the government of Alberta has taken steps to do so by developing an operation plan for the dam that provides the conditions needed by the cottonwood forests for survival.'[23] Just exactly how survival equates with enhancement was not explained. Nor was there any mention of the fact, of which Rood says he was unaware at the time, that WMS's March 1991 operational strategy for the dam recommended 'refinements' to the 1989 operational plan that included reducing the summer minimum flows in the Oldman below the LNID weir by one-half.[24] The panel's technical specialists reported that 'no objectives have been specifically made with respect to instream flow targets for vegetation' in the 1989 operational plan.[25] Nor were there any in the June 1994 operational strategy, the current modus operandi.

The impacts on the riparian forest ecosystem in the reservoir area and downstream were central to FOR's claim that the Oldman River Dam posed a substantial threat to the maintenance of biological diversity in the grasslands of the southern prairies. Just as the Peigan's aim was not to preserve specific isolated sites but to preserve their 'sacred geography' by preventing impacts on the entire region, FOR's aim was not to preserve specific species but to preserve biological diversity in the Oldman River and the valley in which it flows. Although it supported Rood's analysis as it pertained to the cottonwoods, FOR was concerned that Rood might lead the panel to believe that the downstream riparian ecosystems were not at risk. FOR argued that Rood's assessment, which concentrated exclusively on the habitat requirements of cottonwoods, offered no indications of how the operation of the dam would affect other elements of downstream riparian ecosystems.

FOR maintained that the impact of the construction and operation of the dam on 'vulnerable fish species' also posed a threat to biological diversity. The major impacts of the dam on fish are due to the obstacle that it poses to upstream/downstream migration and the potential for reduced downstream flows when the stored water is diverted for irrigation. One of the naturally occurring fish species in the Oldman River system, the short-head sculpin, is threatened in Canada.[26] A second species, the bull trout, while not at risk, has suffered severe declines in Alberta.

The bull trout begin their life cycle in headwater streams, migrate to richer feeding grounds downstream when they mature, and move back upstream to the headwaters to spawn. Before the dam was built, the Old-man was the last large river habitat in southern Alberta capable of catering to the migratory habits of the bull trout.[27] They have been eliminated in the reaches below dams on the North Saskatchewan, Red Deer, and Bow Rivers in Alberta. Alberta's Fish and Wildlife Division was aware of the tenuous state of bull trout in southern Alberta. In 1984, it set the goal of increasing all naturally reproducing populations of bull trout by maintaining and enhancing existing bull trout habitat and by maintaining critical spawning and rearing areas.[28] Construction of the dam effectively prevented the achievement of that goal in the Oldman. The federal panel's technical specialists observed that the Oldman program was 'launched on a totally inadequate platform of science,' one example of which was the lack of knowledge about 'the real significance of [fish] migration.'[29]

In his submission to the panel, research biologist David Mayhood wrote, 'Protecting bull trout adequately will require that it be restored to representative native habitat throughout its range. The Oldman River represents the last large river habitat in southern Alberta suitable for this purpose. The dam is destroying the last large river stocks of this fish in southern Alberta.'[30] Mayhood urged the panel to reject the immediate pre-dam condition as its basis for determining the impact of the dam on the Oldman River ecosystem. He told the panel it must recognize that there had been 'enormous damage' to the river ecosystem already, and that ignoring that fact in assessing the impact of the dam would be 'absolutely guaranteeing that the Oldman River ecosystem will be inexorably degraded by increments.'[31]

The second potential impact – reduced downstream flows – will be less evident in the short term. Until irrigation expands to the point where it requires substantial diversions of the water stored in the reservoir, the dam may be operated to provide better flows downstream than were experienced in the years before dam construction, when diversions to the LNID often reduced the flow in the river to almost nothing. In low flow years, however, streamflow will at times be reduced at least to the lower ranges of the fish rule curve adopted in the June 1994 operational strategy. Flows in this range are substantially less than the minimum 'targets' identified in the January 1989 operating plan, which WMS admitted would put 'fish populations at risk.'[32]

FOR responded to the panel's requests for more information about biodiversity by providing definitions and general discussions. Cliff Wallis says the response was general because FOR believed it was 'hard for the panel to get their heads around the concept of biodiversity.'[33] It seems more likely that the panel wanted information specific to the potential impact of the dam on biodiversity in the Oldman River Basin. Because of the dearth of information about the Oldman riparian ecosystems, FOR was unable to offer anything specific.

19
EARPGO and the Courts

The protection of the environment has become one of the major
challenges of our time.

– Mr. Justice Gérard La Forest, Supreme Court of Canada[1]

The only notable successes achieved by FOR's various legal actions were
those pertaining to application of the federal Environmental Assessment
Review Guidelines Order (EARPGO).[2] Reduced to its essentials, the EARPGO
required any federal department with 'decision making authority' for an
'undertaking' that 'may have an environmental effect on an area of federal
responsibility,' to consider the environmental and related social effects
and public concerns regarding those effects. Where these were significant,
the proposed undertaking was to be referred for public review by an Environmental Assessment Panel.[3]

In 1986 and 1987, the Southern Alberta Environmental Group (SAEG),
FOR, and the Peigan had each tried, in vain, to persuade the federal government to apply the EARPGO to the Oldman River Dam. FOR considered
taking legal action, but its legal advisors believed that the EARPGO was
unenforceable and that a court would not order compliance with its requirements. That changed in 1989 when Mr. Justice Cullen of the Federal
Court ruled that the minister of environment must apply the EARPGO to
the Rafferty-Alameda Project.[4] Cullen found that the EARPGO was an
'enactment or regulation' as defined in the federal Interpretation Act and
was, therefore, 'not a mere description of a policy or program,' as both
governments had argued, but a law of general application that the minister of environment was obliged to follow. In addition, his interpretation of
the definitions set out in the EARPGO led him to conclude that the minister's decision-making responsibility for issuing a licence for the dams
under the International Rivers Improvement Act meant that Environment
Canada was the 'initiating department' for a 'proposal,' and must, therefore, apply the EARPGO before issuing the licence. Cullen also found that
Rafferty-Alameda would have an impact on several areas of federal responsibility, including international relations, the Boundary Waters Treaty,
migratory birds, inter-provincial relations, fisheries, and federal lands, that
had not been covered in Saskatchewan's assessment of the project. He

concluded that application of the EARPGO would not be the 'unwarranted duplication' that the federal Crown had claimed it would be. In not applying the EARPGO, Cullen said, the environment minister had 'exceeded his jurisdiction.'

Overwhelmed by the potential implications of the judgment for a raft of resource development projects for which the federal government had similar responsibilities, the federal Crown filed an appeal. Many of the projects to which the EARPGO might have to be applied if the judgment stood were, like Quebec's Great Whale (James Bay II), provincial projects of great political import. While the federal government would be unable to avoid some involvement in such projects, it had hoped to avoid intervening on environmental grounds, an area of shared jurisdiction about which provincial governments were becoming increasingly more sensitive.

'There is a duty owed to the public – an essential part of the process – and it did not occur here,' Cullen had written of Rafferty-Alameda.[5] That statement expressed, precisely, FOR's view of the federal performance with the Oldman River Dam. Although there were some obvious differences between the two projects as they pertained to federal responsibilities, FOR was convinced that the situations were sufficiently similar that a ruling comparable to Cullen's could be obtained for the Oldman. The minister of transport had issued an Approval for the Oldman Dam under the Navigable Waters Protection Act (NWPA) and the destruction of fish habitat required the authorization of the minister of fisheries. In addition to its impacts on navigation and fish habitat, the construction and operation of the dam would affect migratory birds, the Peigan Indian Band, and the Peigan Reserve, all areas of federal responsibility.

FOR filed an application asking the Federal Court to quash the NWPA Approval for the dam and order the minister of transport and the minister of fisheries and oceans to comply with the EARPGO. FOR argued that the minister of transport, in neglecting to apply the EARPGO before issuing the NWPA Approval, had failed to perform his statutory obligations and that it was incumbent on the minister of fisheries and oceans, knowing that the dam posed a threat to fish habitat that he had a responsibility to protect, to apply the EARPGO.[6]

In its defence, the Crown argued that federal departments did not have to apply the EARPGO to a project 'just because' it might have environmental impact in an area of federal responsibility.[7] The Crown claimed that, though Alberta was subject to the NWPA, the act was concerned only with navigation and not with the environment, so the minister did not have to apply the EARPGO before issuing an Approval. It also argued that since the EARPGO required application 'before irrevocable decisions are taken,' it was inconsistent with the NWPA, which allowed an Approval to be issued after construction of a project. The Crown claimed that, since the minister of fisheries and oceans had not been asked to issue an authorization for destruction of fish habitat, he was not a decision-making authority on the project and, therefore, not compelled to invoke the EARPGO and, since the authorization concerned fish habitat and not the environment, the minister would not in any case have been obliged to comply with the EARPGO.

Alberta intervened in the case, arguing that, contrary to the federal view, the province was not subject to the NWPA and the fact that it had applied for and been granted an Approval under the act should not suggest otherwise. FOR responded that having obtained the Approval and used it 'as a signal to all concerned of Alberta's authority to construct the dam,' the province could hardly claim that it was not now subject to the act. Alberta agreed with the federal arguments concerning the minister of fisheries and oceans and offered that the fish habitat issue could be dealt with by the criminal courts. The latter was more than somewhat ironic in light of the Alberta attorney general's persistence in preventing FOR from prosecuting the province and its contractors for destroying fish habitat in the Oldman.

Alberta disputed FOR's legal right to challenge the government's actions on the grounds that neither FOR nor its members were directly affected by construction of the dam. This was the same argument that Alberta had earlier used in the Court of Queen's Bench to rationalize the controller's decision to waive public notice of its application for a licence under the Water Resources Act.[8] Alberta also argued that single-issue groups, like FOR, should not be allowed to challenge projects 'with impunity and without liability, thereby creating an uncertain climate for government and business.'[9]

Both governments told the Court that the environmental assessments and public reviews undertaken by Alberta were more than sufficient. The federal Crown maintained that application of the EARPGO would simply be a duplication of the province's efforts. Alberta, not to be outdone, claimed it would be a triplication.

While FOR saw a lot of similarity between the Oldman and the Rafferty situations, Associate Chief Justice James Jerome, who adjudicated the action, took a different view. He boiled the arguments requiring his judgment down to four issues: FOR's legal right to challenge the governments in court, whether the federal ministers were bound to invoke the EARPGO, whether Mr. Justice Cullen's judgment in the Rafferty-Alameda case applied in the Oldman Dam case, and whether he should exercise his discretion to grant the orders requested by FOR.[10] Since he was to rule against the other three issues, Jerome simply accepted FOR's legal right to press its case against the government.

On the second issue, Jerome ruled that neither minister was bound by the EARPGO. He found that the minister of transport, when issuing

Approvals under the NWPA, was limited to the consideration of 'factors affecting marine navigation' and that, since the Fisheries Act did not 'contemplate an approvals process' (i.e., provide for the issuance of a permit or licence), the Department of Fisheries and Oceans was not an initiating department. Since 'environmental factors are not raised under either of the statutes,' Jerome concluded that neither minister had the authority to 'trigger' the EARPGO.

Because he found the circumstances in the two cases to be 'significantly different,' Jerome held that the rulings in the Rafferty-Alameda case were not applicable in the Oldman case. In Rafferty-Alameda, the *prior* approval of the minister of environment under the International Rivers Improvements Act had been required; in the Oldman, approval of the minister of transport under the NWPA, was required, but could occur *after* the project was commenced. Furthermore, Jerome wrote, it was the minister of environment's statutory duty to consider 'environmental factors' that led directly to the application of the EARPGO to Rafferty-Alameda, whereas neither the minister of transport nor the minister of fisheries and oceans was obliged by statute to 'deal with environmental considerations.'

Although Jerome found that neither federal minister could be required to comply with the EARPGO, he, nevertheless, offered reasons for not exercising his discretion to order them to do so or to quash the NWPA Approval. First, he said, he could find no justification for the Friends not having launched their court action much sooner than it did. Second, noting 'the extent and the comprehensive nature of the environmental review carried out by the Province of Alberta,' he concluded, 'I am satisfied that the public review process carried out here has identified every possible area of environmental social concern and has given every citizen ... ample opportunity to voice their views and mobilize their opposition.'[11]

To order that the EARPGO be complied with, thus precipitating the possibility of further environmental assessments and public reviews, would, in Jerome's judgment, 'bring about needless repetition of *a process that has been exhaustively canvassed* over the past twenty years [emphasis added].'[12] Jerome was apparently convinced by the affidavits of Alberta Environment employees, the mounds of documentation entered in evidence, and the persuasiveness of the government's lawyers that all that could be known about the environmental and social implications of the Oldman Project had been determined and revealed by the province. This view was not supported by the federal panel after its 1991 review of the project. Jerome seems also to have been persuaded that public participation in the environmental assessment process was meaningful, despite that there was no independent public review process active at any time *after the decision to build the dam at Three Rivers.*

Had FOR been less determined, Jerome's judgment, devastating in its implications for environmental assessment, might have been allowed to stand. The Oldman River Dam would have come into existence without any meaningful environmental review, and governments would have been encouraged to continue only to pay lip service to the environmental values that they so religiously espouse but so diligently avoid practising. FOR, with the encouragement of other environmental groups alarmed by Jerome's judgment, filed an appeal.

The appeal was heard in December of 1989, and the following spring, the Federal Court of Appeal issued a unanimous judgment, written by Mr. Justice Stone, overturning each of Jerome's rulings.[13] The Court addressed itself to three issues raised by FOR: whether the EARPGO applied to an application to the minister of transport for an approval under the Navigable Waters Protection Act, whether the EARPGO applied to the decision making authority of the minister of fisheries and oceans concerning s. 35 and s. 37 of the Fisheries Act, and whether Mr. Justice Jerome had erred in deciding that it would not be appropriate to quash the Approval issued by the minister of transport or to order the federal ministers to comply with the EARPGO. To these was added a fourth issue, raised by Alberta: whether Alberta was subject to the rulings of the Federal Court and the approval requirements of federal legislation.

The Appeal Court disagreed with Jerome that the minister of transport, in deciding on an application for an approval under the Navigable Waters Protection Act, was restricted to considering factors of marine navigation only and had no authority to require an environmental review. The Court adopted the position, similar to that taken by Mr. Justice Cullen in the Rafferty-Alameda case, that, since it would have impacts on areas of federal responsibility and required approval under the NWPA, the Oldman Dam was a 'proposal' requiring environmental review under the terms of the EARPGO and the minister of transport, as the 'decision making authority' for the approval, was obliged to comply.

The Appeal Court also disagreed with the lower court's ruling that the EARPGO, which was to be applied 'before irrevocable decisions are taken,' was in conflict with the NWPA, which allowed an approval to be issued after construction of the project was under way. In the Appeal Court's view, the subsection of the NWPA that allowed the issuance of an approval after construction of a project had begun was meant to allow the minister to take remedial action when works had been built without approval and was 'clearly subservient to the fundamental requirement [of the act] that an approval be obtained prior to construction.'

On the question of whether the minister of fisheries and oceans was bound to apply the EARPGO, Mr. Justice Stone reasoned that the SAEG's August 1987 letter to the minister asking him to protect the fishery resources of the Oldman River required that the minister decide whether or not to intervene in the matter, 'and decide he did.' In deciding not to intervene, the minister became a 'decision making authority' on an activity that might have an environmental affect on an area of federal responsibility. According to the Appeal Court, the responsibilities of the minister of fisheries were also 'engaged' by the application submitted by Alberta for approval under the NWPA. In both of these instances he was obliged to apply the EARPGO.

The Appeal Court also rejected Jerome's view that application of the EARPGO would result in 'needless repetition.' In the Appeal Court's view, the Alberta review put 'much less emphasis on the role of the public in addressing the environmental implications' than did the EARPGO, and did not 'guarantee the independence of the review panel in any discernible measure.' Mr. Justice Stone observed that 'several of the non-governmental members of the last two committees [the ORSMC and the LAC, which Alberta had offered as evidence of public involvement] might have had a lesser degree of independence than that required by the *Guidelines Order* because, being ranchers and farmers, the creation of this new water resource might enure to their benefit.'[14] This observation might also have been applied to the governmental members of the ORSMC, who, as employees of the proponent and senior officials of agencies with a vested interest in managing water for irrigation, were arguably less independent than the farmer and rancher members.

On the jurisdiction issue, the Appeal Court ruled that Alberta was both subject to the jurisdiction of the Federal Court and bound by the federal NWPA.

Mr. Justice Stone, like Associate Chief Justice Jerome and Madam Justice Picard before him, appears to have been impressed by the 'voluminous record ... of detailed work and study [of] environmental impacts of the dam project' presented by Alberta.[15] Like the others, he was apparently not aware that, since these studies were not specific to Three Rivers, they were largely irrelevant, as was later confirmed by the federal review.

Concerned that the Appeal Court's verdict opened the door to federal interference in any provincial resource development project, Alberta sought leave to appeal the judgment to the Supreme Court of Canada. To bolster its appeal, Alberta solicited the support of the environment ministries of the other provinces and territories, seven of which shared Alberta's concern to the extent that they filed as intervenors.[16] Native and environmental groups, aware that a Supreme Court ruling in the provinces' favour would substantially reduce the arsenal of federal laws upon which they depend in their stand against provincial resource development projects, flocked to intervene on FOR's behalf.[17]

The Supreme Court agreed to hear Alberta's appeal, and in February 1991, while the federal environmental review of the project was under way, the opposing sides presented their arguments to the Court. Almost one year later, on 23 January 1992, the Supreme Court handed down its judgment.[18] The Court addressed four major issues:

(1) the statutory validity of the EARPGO and its consistency with the Navigable Waters Protection Act and the Fisheries Act,
(2) the obligation of the ministers of transport and fisheries and oceans to comply with the EARPGO, including the question of whether the Navigable Waters Protection Act was binding on Alberta,
(3) whether the EARPGO was constitutionally applicable to the Oldman River Dam, and
(4) whether the Appeal Court, in quashing the Navigable Waters Protection Act Approval and ordering the federal ministers to comply with the EARPGO, had wrongly 'interfered' with the discretion of the Trial Court judge, Associate Chief Justice Jerome, who had declined to do so.

On the first issue, the Court ruled that the EARPGO had been validly enacted by Parliament and was mandatory. The Court agreed with the Appeal Court that the subsection of the NWPA allowing the issuance of an approval after the construction of works was 'subservient to the fundamental requirement [of the act] ... that an approval be obtained prior to the commencement of construction.'

On the question of ministerial obligation to comply with the EARPGO, the Supreme Court followed the Appeal Court's reasoning in ruling that the minister of transport was so obligated, but differed with its reasoning as it concerned the minister of fisheries and oceans. In the Supreme Court's view, the minister of fisheries and oceans' discretionary power to request or not to request information about the project did 'not constitute a decision-making responsibility' as defined by the EARPGO.

Alberta had tried to avoid the federal EARPGO by claiming that it was not bound by the NWPA and, therefore, did not require approval under that act, reasoning that if it didn't need that approval there would be no basis for the feds to apply the EARPGO. The Supreme Court closed that door by ruling that since the federal Parliament has jurisdiction over navigation, Alberta requires statutory authorization from Parliament to erect a structure that interferes with navigation, and approval under the NWPA is 'the only practicable procedure available for getting approval.'

It was the constitutional question – whether the EARPGO encroached on areas of provincial jurisdiction – that had drawn so many lawyers representing provincial governments to Ottawa to intervene on behalf of Alberta. In their response to Alberta's plea for support, several provincial governments had expressed fears that the Appeal Court's decision raised the threat of federal interference in provincial development projects 'such as logging, pulp and paper milling, mining and municipal utilities.'[19] The collective position of the provinces appearing before the Supreme Court was summed up in a statement attributed to counsel for Saskatchewan's attorney general, who 'sought to characterize the *Guidelines Order* as a constitutional Trojan horse enabling the federal government, on the pretext of some narrow ground of federal jurisdiction, to conduct a far ranging inquiry into matters that are exclusively within provincial jurisdiction.'[20]

Alberta argued that the EARPGO gave the federal government such general authority over the environment that when applied to projects 'primarily subject to provincial jurisdiction,' like the Oldman River Dam, it infringed on the province's exclusive legislative domain.[21] The strength of this argument depended on Alberta's contention that the Oldman River Dam fell into the class of matters defined by the constitution as 'of a merely local or private nature in the province' and, therefore, despite that its construction and operation would have environmental impacts on several areas of federal jurisdiction, any attempt by the federal government to assess those impacts would infringe on Alberta's constitutional rights.[22]

The Court said Alberta's constitutional argument was wrong on at least two counts. The first was 'an erroneous principle' that assumes the existence of 'a general doctrine of interjurisdictional immunity to shield provincial works ... from otherwise valid federal legislation.' The constitution does not assign responsibility for legislating on the environment to either level of government, nor does the environment fit within those areas of responsibility that have been assigned 'without considerable overlap and uncertainty.' In the exercise of their existing powers, either level of government may affect the environment 'by acting or not acting.' Consequently, 'it defies reason' to claim that the constitution bars the federal government from considering 'environmental repercussions' when dealing with a matter within its jurisdiction – in this case, an approval under the NWPA. In considering the approval of works that interfere with navigation, such as the Oldman River Dam, the minister of transport would be expected to 'weigh the advantages and disadvantages resulting from the interference' and 'this could involve environmental concerns such as the destruction of fisheries.'

The second and 'even more fundamental fallacy' to which Alberta had fallen prey was that the implications considered in reaching a decision pertaining to a particular law may somehow detract from the fundamental nature or purpose of that law. Alberta had argued that the federal government cannot base decisions in matters under its jurisdiction on criteria 'that are not rationally connected to' those matters. Reduced to fundamentals, Alberta's argument was that a decision to prohibit construction of the Oldman River Dam under a law concerned only with navigation could not be based on considerations of environmental impact. Mr. Justice

Gérard La Forest of the Supreme Court of Canada called this 'the conceptual trap of thinking of the environment as an extraneous matter in making ... administrative decisions.' He drew an analogy with an Australian case to make the general point that while the environmental considerations may not, in themselves, pertain to navigation, they may 'induce' a decision about navigation, which would be constitutional because navigation is within the constitutional realm of the federal government. Thus, a decision to not approve a dam that interfered with navigation in the Oldman River under the terms of the NWPA, induced by consideration of the dam's impacts on fish habitat, would be constitutional because navigation falls within the federal constitutional domain. Moreover, the EARPGO directs the minister of transport in his capacity as decision maker under the NWPA, to 'consider the environmental impacts of the dam on such areas of federal responsibility as navigable waters, fisheries, Indians and Indian lands' – all areas of federal responsibility. 'Quite simply,' La Forest wrote, 'the environment ... [consists of] all that is around us, and as such must be part of what actuates many decisions of any moment.'[23]

'In essence,' the Court said, the EARPGO has two 'fundamental aspects': the first dealing with environmental impact assessment in making decisions pertaining to matters of federal jurisdiction under the constitution; the second, 'its procedural or organizational element' – regulating the manner in which federal agencies perform environmental impact assessments in cases that 'touch upon' areas of federal responsibility. As such, EARPGO was 'nothing more than an instrument that regulates the manner in which federal institutions must administer their multifarious duties and functions ... an adjunct to federal legislative powers ... [and] any intrusion into provincial matters ... [is] merely incidental.'[24] Alberta's appeal on constitutional grounds was dismissed.

The Supreme Court also upheld the Appeal Court's decision to override Jerome's discretionary refusal to quash the NWPA Approval and order the federal ministers to comply with the EARPGO. Jerome's refusal was grounded in FOR's alleged delay in taking legal action and in the 'futility' of a 'needlessly repetitive' environmental assessment. In citing FOR's delay, the Supreme Court said Jerome had failed to take into account FOR's 'concerted and sustained effort [to] challenge the legality of the process followed by Alberta to build this dam' and the 'acquiescence' on the part of the federal ministers that had allowed that process to succeed. As to 'futility,' the Court said it was a proper ground for refusal only 'where the order could not possibly be implemented,' which was not the case, adding that 'it is not at all obvious that the implementation of the *Guidelines Order* even at this late stage will not have some influence over the mitigative measures that may be taken to ameliorate any deleterious environmental impact from the dam on an area of federal jurisdiction.'[25] The

Court could not know, of course, that the federal ministers' 'acquiescence' would continue into the post-EARPGO period, disregarding any of the panel's recommendations that might have had an ameliorating effect on the environmental impacts of the project. In the end, the federal government was to prove that Jerome had been right to consider further assessment futile.

The Supreme Court dismissed Alberta's appeal, with the exception that it was unwilling to order the minister of fisheries and oceans to comply with the EARPGO.

In 1993, a year after the panel submitted its recommendations, FOR asked the Federal Court to order the minister of transport to make decisions on the implementation of those recommendations, which the panel had said 'must be fulfilled within a reasonable time.' The arguments in defence of the minister's tardiness that federal lawyers submitted to Mr. Justice Marshall Rothstein led him to conclude that there had been no delay by the minister that 'could be characterized as unreasonable' because there were no recommendations on which the minister 'could make decisions independent of the Peigan Band or the environmental management committee.'[26] Yet when the minister released the federal Response and issued the NWPA Approval for the dam on 2 September, he did exactly that.

20
FOR and the Attorney General

An Attorney General, confronted with a government, especially
one of which he was a member, which was alleged to have
violated the law, might also have exerted on him or her
inappropriate pressure in respect of the prosecution of the
alleged offence.

– Alberta Provincial Court Judge A.A. Fradsham[1]

What might have been the most significant of FOR's legal forays, had it
borne fruit, was its attempt to prosecute Alberta for the destruction of fish
habitat in the Oldman River. This action evolved into a titanic struggle
between Martha Kostuch and the Alberta government over the right of the
attorney general to take control of a prosecution initiated by a private citizen. Had it been resolved in Kostuch's favour, it would have added substantially to the power of environmental interests to force governments to
adhere to laws pertaining to the conservation and protection of the environment. Kostuch called it 'the most important environmental law case,
so far, in Canada.'[2] Whether Alberta and its construction companies had
destroyed fish habitat in the Oldman River contrary to s. 35(1) of the Fisheries Act as FOR charged was never really at issue. It is simply not possible
to build a dam in a river without destroying fish habitat. What would have
been at issue, had the charges ever gone to trial, was whether Alberta had
committed a crime by destroying that habitat without the authorization
of the federal minister of fisheries as required by s. 35(2) of the act.

Canada's constitution assigns legislative authority for inland fisheries to
the federal Parliament, which it exercises, in part, through the Fisheries
Act.[3] Alberta claimed, and Canada was evasive in its response to that claim,
that Canada had delegated responsibility for administration of the Fisheries
Act, including s. 35, to Alberta under the terms of an agreement signed in
1987.[4] On numerous occasions prior to that, Alberta officials had sought,
and believed that they had obtained, assurances from federal officials to
that effect. A 1978 letter from the federal fisheries minister to the Alberta
environment minister stated that 'those parts of [the Fisheries Act] that
relate to alteration, disruption or destruction of fish habitat [are] important
parts of the overall fisheries management responsibility of those agencies
in Canada that administer the fisheries. In Alberta, this is the responsibility of the Provincial Government.'[5]

However, in submissions to the federal panel in 1991, Department of

Fisheries and Oceans (DF&O) officials emphasized that while Alberta 'has responsibility for the day-to-day management of the fishery ... the Minister of Fisheries and Oceans, remains responsible to Parliament for the conservation and protection of fish habitat.'[6]

It has since been conceded, implicitly through the actions of the two governments if not by frank admission, that the federal government did not delegate responsibility for s. 35(2) to Alberta. Nor did any federal minister of fisheries and oceans ever issue to Alberta an authorization to build the Oldman Dam under s. 35(2) of the Fisheries Act.[7] After dam construction was completed, Alberta applied to DF&O for an authorization under s. 35(2) and, in 1994, DF&O issued an authorization to *operate* the dam.[8]

The other issue that evolved out of FOR's attempted prosecution had implications extending beyond the Oldman River Dam. That issue concerned the powers of an attorney general to assume control of a criminal prosecution initiated by a private citizen. Criminal offences are usually prosecuted by lawyers on behalf of the federal or a provincial attorney general. However, private citizens also have the right to initiate the prosecution of a criminal offence.[9] Because we generally rely on governments to enforce the law, the right of a citizen to launch a private prosecution is of value in instances where governments themselves stand accused of offences or have failed to enforce the law. They can be of particular value in the enforcement of laws that governments are reluctant to enforce with any great enthusiasm, such as those pertaining to the protection of the environment. In this respect, private prosecutions have been called 'safeguards against inertia or partiality on the part of authority.'[10]

A private citizen may initiate a prosecution by swearing an information (laying charges) against an alleged offender before a justice of the peace. However, the citizen's efforts to obtain a conviction may end at that point because the right of the private citizen to continue the prosecution is limited by the power granted to federal and provincial attorneys general to intervene and take the conduct of a prosecution out of the hands of the citizen.[11] Having intervened, the attorney general may elect either to proceed with the prosecution, bring it to a halt by directing the court to stay the proceedings, or withdraw the charges.[12] Under certain conditions, a court may also stay a prosecution. The rationale for so empowering attorneys general and the courts is to protect citizens from 'unfounded and wrong-headed prosecutions edging into or arriving at persecution'[13] or, in the words of Canada's Supreme Court, 'to control prosecutorial behaviour prejudicial to accused persons.'[14] In Alberta, intervention by the attorney general is dictated by the government's blanket policy of intervening in *all* prosecutions that are not within the jurisdiction of the federal attorney general, in the interest of ensuring consistency in the conduct of prosecutions.[15] It has, on the other hand, been suggested that the reluctance of attorneys general to allow private prosecutions is borne of the experience that they can 'reveal so dramatically government ineptitude.'[16]

To withdraw charges, the attorney general must apply to the court, but an attorney general's discretion to stay proceedings is generally not subject to review by the courts, except where there is evidence of 'flagrant impropriety' in the exercise of that discretion. In either event, the courts have generally been very reluctant to interfere with the discretion of attorneys general.[17] There is no standard or universally accepted definition of flagrant impropriety. The criteria for determining the occurrence of flagrant impropriety in this series of cases was established by the late Alberta Court of Queen's Bench Associate Chief Justice Miller, who wrote, 'The degree of impropriety to be met before the court will intervene to reverse an action by the Attorney General ... must border on corruption by the Crown, violation of the law, bias against the particular offence or prejudice against the accused or the victim.'[18]

As a result of the actions of successive Alberta attorneys general, who on three occasions intervened to stay proceedings in the prosecution initiated by Kostuch, the question of whether it is legitimate for an attorney general to intervene to prevent the prosecution of his or her own government for violation of the law became a central issue. Resolution of this dispute in Kostuch's favour would have had immeasurable implications for the conduct of environmental law throughout Canada.

In the spring of 1988, Alberta Environment Minister Kowalski announced that Alberta had entered into a contract with two construction companies – W.A. Stephenson Construction (Western) Ltd. and SCI Engineering and Constructors Inc. – to build the Oldman River Dam. Since it was not possible to build the dam across the river with water flowing in the channel, a coffer dam was constructed in the river upstream from the site of the main dam, and, in July 1988, the river was diverted from its channel and conveyed through two large tunnels excavated for the purpose to a point about one kilometre downstream from the construction site, where it was returned to the channel. This diversion dried up the flow in the intervening reach of the river, effectively destroying the fish habitat. Martha Kostuch discovered that Alberta had not obtained authorization for the diversion from the federal minister of fisheries and oceans. On 2 August 1988, she 'swore an information' before a justice of the peace in Pincher Creek, charging that the Alberta government and the two construction companies had destroyed fish habitat in the Oldman River, in violation of the Fisheries Act.[19] As a general rule, both the federal and provincial governments in Canada are immune from prosecution. Such is not the case, however, for the commission of offences under the Fisheries Act, which specifically states that 'this Act is binding on Her Majesty in the right of Canada or a province.'[20]

Figure 23   Oldman River *before* and *after* diversion through tunnels
(top and bottom)

Regional officials of the federal Department of Justice tentatively agreed to prosecute the charges, but after further reflection and consultation with their masters in Ottawa, declined to do so. On the heels of that decision, the Alberta attorney general intervened and directed that the proceedings be halted.

The reasons for staying proceedings were set out in a statement sent to Kostuch's lawyer by Mr. Bruce Fraser of the Attorney General's Department – a statement that Provincial Court Judge Fradsham later said was 'as erroneous as it is patronizing and paternalistic.'[21] Fraser maintained that before a criminal matter can be prosecuted it must be investigated by 'the appropriate enforcement agency,' in this case, the Alberta government's Fish and Wildlife Division, and the results of that investigation reviewed by the Attorney General's Department, which would then decide whether to prosecute. Kostuch offered to provide evidence to support her charges. However, Fraser decided that he would review only evidence that was investigated and submitted to him by the Fish and Wildlife Division and, since that agency had not compiled any evidence for his review, Fraser claimed he was obliged to stay the proceedings.

Since the Fish and Wildlife Division was aware that the river had been diverted and fish habitat destroyed but had taken no action, it was clear to Kostuch that appealing to that agency would be a waste of time, and that her only hope was to manoeuvre the federal attorney general into taking on the prosecution. In September, FOR filed a complaint with the regional office of DF&O. If DF&O were to lay charges, the matter would then be in the hands of the federal attorney general. The Alberta Attorney General's Department, meanwhile, asked the RCMP to investigate the charges – to the dismay of both Fish and Wildlife officials and the RCMP. The investigation was assigned to the RCMP's commercial crime division and, over the course of the next several months, the division submitted a number of reports to the federal Department of Justice, which repeatedly asked for more information. Meanwhile, construction of the dam continued apace.

In January of 1990, eighteen months after first laying charges, Kostuch, in the words of Provincial Court Judge John Harvie, 'inferentially fed-up with what she regarded as foot-dragging by both Alberta and Canada,' laid new charges against the same parties.[22] On the day the parties were to appear on these charges, Alberta's attorney general applied to the Court for permission to intervene, claiming he was unable to decide, in the light of the RCMP's ongoing investigation, whether the prosecution should go forward.[23] Kostuch countered with a motion asking the Court to refuse the attorney general's intervention and allow the trial to proceed with her lawyer in the prosecutor's role. In effect, presiding Judge Harvie was being asked to rule whether the attorney general had properly exercised his discretion to intervene. In considering the issue, Harvie questioned the merit

Figure 24   Dam spillway under construction in the bed of the Oldman River

of Alberta's blanket policy of intervention, particularly in this case, *'because of the risk of perception* that justice may not appear to be done when the Attorney General of a province undertakes to show that either another minister of the provincial Crown, or the provincial Crown itself, has committed an offence.'[24]

Harvie also questioned the utility of the provincial policy that investigation by a law enforcement agency must always precede prosecution. In this case, he wrote, where the provincial government was 'indisputably putting the dam in the river and diverting the water so the old riverbed was dry, [an RCMP investigation] was at least arguably ... unnecessary.'[25] Nonetheless, Harvie was unable to characterize the attorney general's actions as flagrant impropriety, though he suggested that 'continued and persistent assertion' of the intervention policy might be 'of *itself* sufficient to constitute 'flagrant impropriety,' a proposition which Kostuch was later to test before the courts.

Judge Harvie revealed his discomfort at having been asked to pass judgment on an exercise of discretion by the attorney general, writing that there were grounds for 'serious contention' that the provincial court of Alberta was not sufficiently independent from the provincial government and the office of the attorney general to be considered 'an independent tribunal' in issues relating to the exercise of power by the attorney general. In Harvie's view, it was 'an affront to whatever dignity the hen may have to ask it to clip the fox.'[26] Interestingly, a few years later, when Alberta Premier

Ralph Klein ordered a 5 percent roll-back in the salaries of all provincial civil servants, including provincial court judges, Judge Harvie and his colleagues were not in the least reluctant to clip the fox. Claiming that Klein's assault on their pocketbooks threatened the independence of the justice system, they took the issue to court, where they were successful in preserving their income, if not their dignity.

In the end, Judge Harvie allowed the intervention, putting the prosecution once again in the hands of Alberta's attorney general. Summonses were issued requiring the alleged offenders to appear for a hearing on 13 July.

Shortly before 13 July, the RCMP's investigation reached its long-awaited conclusion. This coincidence made it possible for federal Justice Minister Kim Campbell to announce, on 10 July, that she had decided not to prosecute anyone for the destruction of fish habitat in the Oldman.[27] The official communique quoted Campbell as saying 'I do not believe that ... prosecution would serve the proper administration of justice.'[28] The next day, Alberta's attorney general instructed the clerk of the provincial court to 'stay' the proceedings in the case.

Kostuch laid new charges. In the eyes of the Alberta government, what to Kostuch was a determined pursuit of justice was nothing more than harassment. If the new charges came to trial, the attorney general could, as he had done on the two previous occasions, take the prosecution out of Kostuch's hands and stay the proceedings. However, that strategy had not kept the government out of court or the issue out of the news, nor did it appear to be dampening Kostuch's persistence. Although there had been no public criticism of the attorney general's unwillingness to let the case come to trial, 'continuous and persistent' intervention posed the risk of bad publicity for the government and public sympathy for Kostuch. The government opted for a different tack.

In the autumn of 1990, the two construction companies filed an application in the Court of Queen's Bench for an order that would prevent provincial court judges from compelling them and the government to appear in court to answer the most recent charges laid by Kostuch. The grounds for the application were that Kostuch's continued attempts to prosecute the charges were an abuse of the justice system. Alberta appeared as an intervenor in support of the companies' application. In October, Mr. Justice Sulatycky, having concluded that the matter fell within the jurisdiction of the provincial court and that that court was competent to deal with it, dismissed the application.[29]

Still determined to get Kostuch out of its hair and hoping it could get the court to do its dirty work, the province joined a bid by the construction companies to have the provincial court stay Kostuch's prosecution – an action that the late Associate Chief Justice Tevie Miller characterized as 'highly unusual, since the Crown has at its disposal the right to stay proceedings on its own discretion.'[30] The grounds for Alberta's request were that 'based on the conduct of the Respondent Kostuch to date,' forcing the government to defend itself against the charges that it had destroyed fish habitat in the Oldman 'constitutes an abuse' of the court's process. Since the two applications were essentially one, they were heard together by Provincial Court Judge A.A. Fradsham on 20 November.[31] Ironically, Alberta and the construction companies offered the attorney general's decision to stay Kostuch's earlier prosecution attempts as one of two reasons why further prosecution would be an abuse of the process. The second reason offered was the federal justice minister's declaration that prosecution of charges against the accused would not serve the interests of the proper administration of justice. Judge Fradsham found neither reason compelling, nor was he reluctant to review and reject opinions and actions of the Crown that appeared to contradict his [Fradsham's] definition of justice.

Fradsham's review convinced him that the attorney general's earlier decisions to stay proceedings had been founded on 'imperfect bases' and were not useful as reasons for preventing Kostuch's third prosecution attempt from proceeding. He found that the Court has the authority to permit a private prosecution in cases where 'there is sufficient support for the suggestion that the Attorney General is attempting to thwart a proper prosecution.' The attorney general's elections to stay proceedings had, in Fradsham's view, thwarted the prosecution and, though there had been no suggestion of bad faith on the attorney general's part, Fradsham observed that 'an Attorney General, confronted with a government ... of which he was a member, which was alleged to have violated the law, might also have exerted on him or her inappropriate pressure in respect of the prosecution of the alleged offence' – all of which seem to suggest very solid reasons for allowing a private prosecution.

Fradsham also examined the reasons offered by the federal justice minister to support her conclusion that prosecution in this case was not in the interests of 'the proper administration of justice.' One of those reasons, because 'Alberta had implemented a mitigation program designed to address the environmental consequences of the project,' Fradsham dismissed as 'a theory of the administration of justice which encourages violations of the law so long as the adverse effects of the violation can be minimized.' The second reason offered by the justice minister was the federal government's intention 'to subject the construction project to public review under the Environmental Assessment Review Process.' Since the damage to fish habitat resulting from dam construction would have occurred before the federal hearings were even under way, that process, in Fradsham's view, was 'doomed to ineffectiveness from the start.' In any event, he wrote, those hearings would 'not address the alleged violations and their consequences.' He concluded that the justice minister's decision was 'not based in logic and sound reasoning,' and was not sufficient reason to support the claim that Kostuch's pursuit of a private prosecution was an abuse of the court. 'If there are other reasons for her conclusion,' Fradsham added, 'they are not before me.'

There were, of course, other, more compelling, reasons for the federal government's unwillingness to press charges: a reluctance both to alienate a potential ally in Canada's ongoing constitutional battles and to earn the disfavour of a large block of supporters in rural southern Alberta, all in the name of a cause to which it was not particularly devoted – environmental conservation. These reasons were not before Judge Fradsham because they had more to do with the expedient practice of politics than with the proper administration of justice. He concluded that

> Dr. Kostuch has not attempted to abuse the process of this court. On the evidence before me she has, through her counsel, attempted to utilize, in the most proper and professional manner, those rights given to her under our legacy of common law and the provisions of the Criminal Code. On two occasions she has convinced judicial officers that a prosecution is warranted – on two occasions that prosecution has been *thwarted by the Attorney General* [emphasis added]. In both cases, the reasons behind the actions of the Attorney General, though not on the evidence before me motivated by mala fides [bad faith], were faulty. She again seeks the assistance of this court – that is not an abuse of the process, but a very proper use of the process.[32]

Both applications for a stay of proceedings were denied. The construction companies, with the support of the province, immediately appealed to the Court of Queen's Bench to set aside Judge Fradsham's ruling. The application was denied.[33]

The companies and the province then turned to the Alberta Court of Appeal. Their appeal was dismissed.[34] In the course of their judgment, the Appeal Court justices risked an opinion on the attorney general's future intentions, noting that, 'We do not think the fact that the Attorney General has on two previous occasions entered stays can be taken as an indication that he will do so in this case. His failure to intervene or express any intention to intervene suggests the contrary.'[35] This may have been subtle advice to the government against continued use of the justice system to process its dirty laundry.

After more procedural delays, the preliminary hearing finally opened in provincial court in Calgary on 22 March 1993, again before Judge Fradsham. Mr. George Dangerfield, QC, of the Manitoba attorney general's office appeared as an agent of the Alberta attorney general. In instances where a government or its officials have been accused of violating the law, attorneys general, in the interest of circumventing accusations of bias, sometimes ask a 'neutral' outside legal authority to investigate the circumstances of an alleged offence and offer recommendations as to what action the attorney general should take. In this instance, Alberta's attorney general had asked the Manitoba attorney general's office to review the evidence pertaining to the charges laid by Kostuch and recommend a course of action. While it can be argued that the Manitoba attorney general's office is an outsider, it can also be argued that, on matters pertaining to the management of natural resources and control of the prosecutorial process, Canada's provincial governments share sufficient common cause to cast doubt on that office's neutrality.

Dangerfield advised Alberta's attorney general that, since the public interest did not require that the case be prosecuted, the proceedings should be stayed. Acting on that advice, the attorney general instructed Dangerfield to intervene and direct the court to enter a stay of proceedings. In response, Kostuch filed an application in the Alberta Court of Queen's Bench for an order disallowing the attorney general's intervention and direction to stay proceedings, on the grounds that they were a violation of her rights under the Canadian Charter of Rights and Freedoms, and prohibiting the attorney general from intervening in and staying future prosecutions on the grounds of 'reasonable apprehension of bias' on the part of the attorney general.

The application was heard by Mr. Justice Power, who submitted his written ruling on 26 August 1993.[36] Apparently convinced that Alberta had, or believed it had, federal authorization to destroy fish habitat, Power concluded that 'there can be no suggestion in this case that the Attorney General failed to uphold the law or that he was acting out of improper motives for an improper purpose.'[37] In this respect he cited, among other things, federal Fisheries Minister Siddon's 25 August 1987 letter to SAEG. This letter, written in response to SAEG's request that he invoke the EARPGO, talks about DF&O staff having 'consulted with' provincial biologists and 'awaiting the formulation of mitigation and compensation proposals,' notes that the 'potential problems associated with a dam are being addressed,' and concludes with the advice that Siddon 'does not propose to intervene.' Power writes of this that 'from the statement contained in the letter of the Minister, one could conclude that the Minister authorized the project under s. 35(2) of the Fisheries Act.'[38] One could as easily conclude that the minister had done no such thing but had merely attempted to distance himself from the issue.

On the question of ministerial impropriety, Power judged the evidence before him in relation to criteria established by Associate Chief Justice Miller. Power noted that 'no such impropriety has been established' and, moreover, that Kostuch had 'made no allegations of impropriety' by the attorney general. He concluded that, 'absent flagrant impropriety by the [attorney general,] the actions in intervening in this prosecution and entering a stay do not violate [Kostuch's] rights under ... the *Charter*.'[39] He dismissed the application.

In his judgment, Power expressed an opinion that put him on-side with the earlier attempts by the Crown to prevent Kostuch from pursuing the prosecution: 'In the opinion of the court, it would be an abuse of process to allow this litigation to proceed further ... If the issues were permitted to be relitigated, it would raise the spectre of improper motive of the applicant to harass the respondent unreasonably.'[40] This view differed from those expressed by judges of Alberta's provincial court, the Alberta Court of Queen's Bench, and the Alberta Court of Appeal, each of which had, at one time or another, ruled to allow the case to proceed.

Kostuch appealed. At a hearing before the Alberta Appeal Court on 8 May 1995, Kostuch's lawyer argued that in staying the prosecutions, the attorney general had made 'unreasonable decisions and failed to uphold the law, and violated the fundamental principles of justice and the community's sense of fair play.'[41] He also claimed that the Alberta attorney general's interference with her right under s. 7 of the Charter to have a wrong redressed had caused her stress. The Appeal Court applied a test for the application of s. 7 established by the Supreme Court, which required that Kostuch demonstrate that she had been deprived of her right to life, liberty, and security of the person, and that such deprivation occurred in a manner not consistent with principles of fundamental justice. In the view of the Appeal justices, Kostuch failed the test. The Court noted that a private prosecutor's right to undertake a prosecution 'is clearly restricted by the provisions of the *Criminal Code* to cases where the Attorney General opts not to intervene.'[42] As this limitation related to Kostuch's Charter rights, the Court was of the opinion that, 'however broadly the right to "liberty and security of person" in s. 7 of the *Charter* may come to be interpreted ... it will not and cannot include the unrestricted right ... to continue a criminal prosecution in the face of an intervention by the Attorney General.'[43]

The Appeal Court agreed with Power that 'flagrant impropriety' as defined by Miller was the relevant test of the attorney general's conduct, and rejected Kostuch's claim that an 'unreasonable decision' could constitute flagrant impropriety. The Court noted that, in deciding to stay the prosecution, the attorney general had relied on the advice of 'independent prosecutors' – lawyer Dangerfield and an associate from the Manitoba attorney general's office. The Court ruled that it was acceptable for the attorney general to act on Dangerfield's advice, since Dangerfield had indicated, 'as an officer of the Court,' that he had formed his own opinion and there was no suggestion that he had been 'influenced in any manner by the Attorney General of Alberta or his agents.' Kostuch did not challenge Dangerfield's objectivity on the obvious grounds that, as a Crown attorney, albeit in another province, it was very much in his interest to defend the power of attorneys general to assume control of prosecutions initiated by private citizens. She says that FOR had decided to save that argument for the Supreme Court. In retrospect, that was a bad decision.

Concluding that flagrant impropriety on the part of the attorney general had not been established, the Court dismissed the appeal. In so doing, it continued the established practice of excusing itself from dealing with impropriety on the part of politicians on the grounds that the impropriety in question was not sufficiently flagrant to merit correction. One is left to wonder just how improperly an attorney general must act to satisfy the court's definition of flagrant, and why citizens should have to countenance *any* impropriety on the part of their attorneys general.

Kostuch applied to the Supreme Court for leave to appeal the Appeal Court's decision. The case had attracted the support, financial and moral, of a host of environmental groups. Clayton Ruby, one of the country's more prominent criminal lawyers, who frequently supports environmental causes, agreed to represent Kostuch in the Supreme Court at what Kostuch said was 'a significantly reduced rate.' The executive director of the Canadian Environmental Defence Fund referred to Kostuch's bid to rein in the attorney general as 'one of the most important law cases of the decade.'[44] The Supreme Court was not persuaded. In the spring of 1996, it announced that it would not hear Kostuch's appeal. As is customary, the Court gave no reasons for its decision.

21
The Peigan Indians

The history of [Aboriginal peoples'] relations with the
Government has left a substantial residue of suspicion and
distrust, based on a century or more of unfair, unjust and
oppressive government actions.

– The Honourable A.C. Hamilton[1]

Canada has a long and sorry history of exploitation of its Aboriginal population. Nowhere is this more evident than in the way the federal and the
various provincial governments have managed the development of the
country's natural resources with little or no regard to impacts – social, economic, and cultural – on Native peoples. What began with the beaver and
the buffalo continues to the present day. The management of surface
waters, which without exception are claimed by the Crown, is one area
where the abuse of Native peoples in the name of the public good has been
most flagrant. Some of the more notorious examples from recent times
include the Gardiner Dam in Saskatchewan, Southern Indian Lake in Manitoba, the Bennett Dam and the Kemano Project in British Columbia, and
the Bighorn Dam on the North Saskatchewan River in Alberta.

The Royal Commission appointed in 1951 to investigate and report on
various aspects of the proposal to build what was to become the Gardiner
Dam on the South Saskatchewan River gave no indication that it was even
aware that the water stored behind the dam would inundate a sacred rock
of great spiritual significance to the entire Cree Nation or that the changes
in flow regime resulting from operation of the dam would have devastating impacts on the Cumberland House Indian Band located downstream.[2]
By substantially increasing the level of Southern Indian Lake to serve its
generation expansion plans, Manitoba Hydro wreaked havoc on long-
established Cree and Metis communities along the shore of the lake and
upset their hunting and fishing economy.[3] W.A.C. Bennett's mighty monument on the Peace altered flow patterns and water levels downstream in
the Lake Athabasca delta, disrupting the trapping and fishing economy of
the Native community in and around Fort Chipaweyan.[4] Alcan's Kemano
Project flooded out burial grounds and the homes and traplines of a settlement of Carrier-Sikani Indians of the Cheslatta Band in British Columbia's
Nechako River valley.[5] Calgary Power's (now TransAlta Utilities') Bighorn
Dam flooded the traditional hunting grounds and the homes of Stoney

Indians living on the Kootenay Flats along the North Saskatchewan River in Alberta, destroying traplines and burial sites and driving the resident Stoneys from self-sufficiency to the welfare rolls.[6]

If Quebec's James Bay hydro development project and Alcan's Kemano Completion Project can be considered indicators, as indeed they must, the situation hasn't changed in any substantial way over the years. James Bay II would further decimate the traditional lifestyle of the Cree Indians in northern Quebec; the Kemano Completion Project would wipe out the salmon fishery on the Nechaco and have unknown effects on the Fraser River, with the Carrier-Sikani again an affected party. As these projects have demonstrated, governments continue to show great determination in their attempts to disregard or circumvent their own laws, and the courts have proven to be most inconsistent in their rulings as to the application of those laws. Though both have been sidelined, given the persistence of governments and industry, it would be folly to assume that they will not reappear.

Commenting on how resource development projects in Canada have generally proceeded with little or no consultation with the Native peoples who stood to be severely affected by them, Olive Dickason observes that 'the priority of development over local community well-being had never been seriously questioned, no matter what the degree of social disruption.'[7] The following, from a 1977 report by Alberta's Environment Conservation Authority, indicates how the general disregard of Native peoples has sometimes been reflected in the perspective of bodies established by governments as watchdogs to advise on the use and development of publicly owned resources:

> Before the arrival of the white man in the nineteenth century, herds of bison roamed the rich grasslands of the lower and central portions of the Red Deer River Basin ... The arrival of the settlers changed the character of land use in the lower and central Basin. The grasslands, settled soon after the turn of the century, were broken to the plough and the prairie grass was replaced by grain. Shortly thereafter, climatic variations brought the drought of the 'Dirty Thirties' and a plague of poverty fell across the lands of the lower Basin. Farms, abandoned to the sun and wind, suffered the serious erosion whose scars remain to this day. But the spirit of man is indomitable and his will to reoccupy the plains of the lower Basin initiated studies to provide additional water for the area.[8]

Purple prose aside, what is most remarkable about this description is how, by completely ignoring the presence of Indian people, it presents a distorted account of the historical use of the natural resources of the basin and of the impacts of the management or mismanagement of those resources. From the perspective of the Blackfoot Indians who had occupied the area for centuries before the arrival of the white man and lived by hunting the buffalo that roamed the rich grasslands, the plague of poverty fell upon the lands when the settlers arrived and replaced the prairie grass and buffalo with grain.

The ECA intended no malice; it was simply following the conventional practice of ignoring that the country was home to the Indians well before the arrival of the Europeans. Perhaps it took its cue from the eminent Canadian scholar and humorist Stephen Leacock, who wrote in a serious dissertation on Canada's history in 1941, 'With the close of the Norse voyages ... the [North American] continent remained as it had been for countless centuries, empty. We think of pre-historic North America as inhabited by the Indians, and have based on this a sort of recognition of ownership on their part. But this attitude is hardly warranted. The Indians were too few to count. Their use of the resources of the continent was scarcely more than that by crows and wolves, their development of it nothing.'[9] Canada has come some distance since 1941 – though not yet far enough for her Aboriginal population.

The Peigan Indians' experience with the Oldman River Dam project was no exception to the general rule.

The roots of the Peigan's on-again, off-again opposition to the Oldman River Dam are to be found in their struggle to lift the reserve and its occupants from the economically depressed state in which they have existed since the late 1800s, in their traditional cultural and spiritual beliefs and practices, and in their attempts to reclaim a portion of the legacy taken from them by Treaty 7.

Indian Reserve No. 147, the 'homeland' of the Peigan, straddles the Oldman River at the foot of the Porcupine Hills in southwestern Alberta (see Map 3). With the exception of the river valley, with its abundant willow and cottonwood forests, the reserve is a treeless, rolling upland, characterized by poor soils and low precipitation, and constantly buffeted by westerly winds. The only urban community on the reserve is the town of Brocket, where the Peigan Nation Administration has its offices and where virtually all of the reserve's central services – administration, schools, health services, public works – are located.

About one-third of the reserve's 2,000-odd residents live in the town of Brocket and its immediate environs; the remainder are scattered throughout the reserve. There are a large number of Peigan who, though they are status Indians, live in Calgary or Lethbridge, where employment prospects are better. In recent times, 70 percent of the potential workforce on the reserve has been unemployed. Average incomes hover around the poverty level and many reserve residents survive on welfare. Some who are better educated, more skilled, or better connected are employed by the Band Administration, by Indian Affairs, or by one of the few businesses on the reserve. A few Peigans are engaged in farming or ranching on reserve lands, mainly some sort of cow-calf operation, and some have found off-reserve employment, though infrequently of a permanent nature.

Despite widespread poverty, social conditions on the reserve have improved over what they were in the past. Still, housing conditions over-all are poor, and family break-up and alcohol and substance abuse con-tinue to be problems, though not to the extent realized on some reserves. In 1992, band officials reported that 200 families or individuals on the reserve were in need of housing.[10] That same year, with natural population growth creating a demand for twenty-seven new housing units each year and instances of as many as four families sharing a two- to three-bedroom house, Indian Affairs planned to build only three houses on the reserve.

Unlike the reserves of some of their more fortunate brethren, the Peigan Reserve is poor in natural resources. It has no extensive deposits of oil or natural gas, it has no minerals, no forests, and no large water bodies. High-way No. 3, the fabled Crowsnest route, passes through the reserve, and Head-Smashed-In Buffalo Jump, a UNESCO world heritage site, which the Alberta government has developed as a provincial historical resource site, is located just outside the reserve's northern boundary. These, in combi-nation with, ironically, the Oldman River Dam, offer some potential for employment and development of recreation-related businesses by reserve residents. Otherwise, the most likely opportunities for economic develop-ment on the reserve appear to be in agriculture, and, indeed, it was to farming that the Treaty 7 commissioners assumed that the Peigan would turn when they were restricted to their reserve.

Getting established in farming today is not as simple as it might have seemed to the treaty commissioners in 1877. Farming requires capital investment, and the Peigan, like many other Native people, have difficulty in obtaining financial backing. Reserve lands cannot be offered as security for loans, and the Peigan have no history of successful commercial opera-tions that might make them attractive to lending agencies, whether private or public. Farming has become a high-tech industry, which means that potential farmers require training before they begin and access to ongoing advice and assistance until their enterprise is on its feet. Despite having obtained apparent commitments from the province to that end, the Peigan have not succeeded in getting the training and assistance programs that are essential to a successful foray into agriculture. And, as the Peigan's neighbours have learned, with southern Alberta's limited and unreliable rainfall, irrigation is a virtual necessity for a successful farming operation. For the Peigan that means development of irrigation projects supplied with water from the Oldman River.

Falling under the constitutional responsibility of the federal government, but living in a province which administers many federal-provincial, cost-shared programs, the Peigan frequently find that they are unable to access support programs available to others in Alberta. In a paper submitted to the federal panel in 1991, the Peigan wrote:

> Often we approach Canada for assistance for a project only to be told that it is a provincial responsibility. When we talk to Alberta, they tell us that because we are Indians living on a reserve, it is a federal responsibility. We fall into a "crack" between Alberta and Canada. All around us our neighbours have access to Alberta programs to support economic development, agriculture, public works, adult education, utilities, etc. You only have to look around to see the effect of over 60 years of unequal access to programs by comparing the wealth and prosperity of our neighbours and the poverty of our people here on the Reserve.'[11]

The official decision-making body and administrative authority on the Peigan Reserve is the band council, sometimes referred to as Chief and Council. Under the terms of the Indian Act, the Chief and Council has powers of governance on the reserve somewhat comparable with those of a municipal council, but without any powers of taxation. In representing the interests of the Peigan to other levels of government and to the outside world, Chief and Council is the nominal official voice for residents of the reserve. The unofficial advisors on matters of tradition and culture are the elders, of whom there were about twenty on the Peigan Reserve in 1986. The elder whose name is most familiar to non-Natives is Joe Crowshoe, the Peigan's spiritual leader since the 1930s.

Various authors have attempted to define the difference in the way Native and non-Native peoples think about the environment in terms of opposing 'world views.'[12] In most of these interpretations, the traditional Native world view is ecological. The environment is simply the natural world; it has an intrinsic value; all things in nature, including human beings, are considered equal, and live in unity and harmony; the role of human beings is to practise stewardship, relying on wisdom, sharing nature's bounty with other creatures, and living within the limits of the ecosystem; spirituality is integrated with day-to-day existence in nature. In contrast, the non-Native's world view is seen as expansionist. It regards the environment as a collection of resources, to be owned and exploited for whatever value the market places upon them; human beings are superior to and exercise control over all else in nature and their role is to manage nature, relying on science, excluding other creatures, and expanding 'wise' use to and beyond nature's limits; spirituality is separate from the other things in life and materialism is the dominant philosophy. The differences in these two world views are most obvious in the decisions that flow from them. In the ecological world view, unless wisdom indicates that a proposed action is conducive to survival, that action should not be taken; in the expansionist world view, unless science can prove that a proposed action is harmful to survival, that action should not be constrained.[13]

Clearly all Native people do not subscribe to the ecological world view, but it is the view most consistent with Indian culture and traditional life. Similarly, all non-Natives do not subscribe to the expansionist world view, but it is predominant in our market-driven Western economies.

Native people argue that, because of their spiritual beliefs, their traditional way of life was in harmony with the natural world and that they took from nature only what they needed for survival. They looked on the land and on plants and animals not as resources but as 'part of a web of living systems that includes relationships among themselves and between them and human beings.'[14] They offer as evidence of their stewardship the fact that when the white man arrived on the plains, the buffalo herds were still as large as they had been since 'time immemorial,' and that other types of wildlife were to be found in abundance. Stoney Chief John Snow writes, 'Our people respected the Creator's beings, and as a result, in our long history of dominance on this continent, none of the animals we hunted ever became extinct.'[15] Because they viewed human occupance of the land as revolving, with future generations following in the footsteps of their predecessors, using and reusing the landscape in the same way, they developed the practice of 'walking softly' across the land, which meant 'not leaving a monument, but instead an undefiled terrain' and having little or no impact on the environment.[16] These claims were taken up and embellished by environmentalists and New Agers in the 1970s and 1980s, giving birth to a mid-twentieth century version of Rousseau's noble savage.

Not everyone subscribes to the theory of the Indian as the ultimate conservationist. Critics suggest that, far from being the good stewards that legend would have them be, North American Indians were potentially as exploitive of their environment as the Europeans who displaced them. That they did less damage is attributed to the limitations of their technology and to their small populations, which limited demand. Buffalo jumps, where as many as 600 buffalo were slaughtered in one stampede and the practice, when the herds were abundant, of taking only the most desirable cuts of slaughtered buffalo are offered as evidence of wastefulness. The North American beaver population, estimated to number thirty million at the time of Columbus, was severely depleted by Indian trappers in response to the insatiable European demand for beaver pelts. Disputes about the historical record aside, there are reasons to speculate about the extent to which contemporary Indians are concerned about living in harmony with the environment. Images of Mohawk earth movers tearing up the cemetery at Oka, billboards lining the highways through reserves, and attempts by Natives to extend their treaty rights to hunt and fish to commercial exploitation suggest otherwise. Recent forest management deals struck with provincial governments, the bid by the Meadow Lake Tribal Council in Saskatchewan to locate a nuclear waste dump on reserve lands, and excessive logging on the Stoney Reserve in Alberta in 1995 leave some environmentalists struggling to rationalize the actions of their allies.

The Peigan's cultural and spiritual linkage to the Oldman cannot be adequately described in a few short paragraphs, nor is it best attempted by someone outside the Peigan community. It is, however, vital to convey something of the elements of that linkage that were fundamental to the position adopted by those of the Peigan who opposed the dam on cultural or spiritual grounds. It is never easy for one person to explain another's cultural or religious beliefs; it is the more difficult when those beliefs are not well documented and when those who hold them have been reluctant to publicize them, even though they consider them fundamental to their cause.[17]

The spiritual beliefs of North American Indians focus to a large extent on the relationships between the people and their environment.[18] There is unity in the universe, such that all things are related and connected in some way with everything else. The physical world and the spiritual world, each governed by its own laws, are different aspects of the same reality, the same unified universe, and violation of the laws governing either world will have effects in both worlds. In the words of Stoney Chief John Snow, 'Our religion professes faith in one Creator, and acknowledges the unity and harmony of the Creation, the harmony of the whole environment – land, animals, birds, plant life, men.'[19]

Native spiritual beliefs attribute 'life, souls and spirits' to all things in the universe – humans, plants, animals, rocks, rivers, air. Peigan elder Reg Crowshoe says, 'When creator created all his creations, he gave them all equal authority to exist, and that's rocks, animals, plants, people; and through that sense the Oldman River was created. The Oldman River has a spirit like anybody else would have.'[20] The belief is not that there are 'little spirits' living within these objects 'like cartoon characters' but rather that objects can have powers that flow to those who use them. Treated with respect, these spirits or powers could become 'helpers' to the individual or to the band; to offend them is to run the risk that they might turn against the offending party.

It is because of these beliefs that those who practise them place such emphasis on the maintenance of harmony between and among humans and the relationships between humans and their environment. They give rise to this ethic, adapted from *The Sacred Tree:* 'Treat the earth and all of her aspects as your mother. If others would destroy our mother, rise up with wisdom to defend her.'[21] Spiritual beliefs are transmitted as part of Native culture, in part through legends and myths that are passed from one generation to another. In some cases, they are embodied in ceremonies and rituals, which themselves employ objects, such as medicine bundles or the branches of trees that form structures used in ceremonies that have, or take on, sacred qualities.

The Blackfoot have an origin myth in which Napi, the Old Man – sometimes referred to as the Creator, sometimes as 'a lesser Deity' – travelled north, populating the land with plants, animals, and people. At the Porcupine Hills, he taught the people how to hunt buffalo, and when his task of creation was finished, he went up the river which bears his name, the Oldman, into the mountains and to the Up Above World. A Blackfoot legend tells how the Blackfoot Confederacy came to be divided into the three tribes. Led by the Old Man, they left their homeland because they were starving and travelled east across the mountains to the buffalo country, where they split into three tribes – the Blackfoot, the Blood, and the Peigan – each led by one of the Old Man's sons. According to Reeves, this legend is supported by the archaeological record, which reveals that, about 5,000 years ago, a group of people from west of the mountains took up residence in the foothills and plains east of the Rockies.[22]

A Peigan story tells how Napi created the Oldman River. Napi had engaged the creator of the Westside People – the Kutenais and Flatheads – in a game of wheels and arrows. The game was played on a mountain meadow on the Eastern Slopes of the Rockies; at stake were the lands extending eastwards onto the plains and the plants and animals that resided there. After a long struggle, Napi won the game, and in celebration he created a river – Napi's river, the Oldman – to flow east from the mountains across the plains.

Because the Oldman is Napi's river, the Peigan hold it to be sacred. And because the Peigan have lived along their Creator's river for centuries, using its valley and resources both for their livelihood and in their ceremonies and rituals, it is both a provider and a place of spiritual significance to them. Many of the ceremonies and rituals practised by the Peigan take place in the Oldman River valley, and often the resources of the river and valley were, and continue to be, used in their conduct. Many plants, animals, and other objects, natural or manmade, and many sites along the river are thus considered by the Peigan to be sacred. The sun dance, one of the more important Blackfoot ceremonies, was for years outlawed under the Indian Act but was practised in secret. The lodge erected for use in the sun dance is constructed of cottonwoods taken from the riparian forests. The sweat lodge, used in the performance of purification rites, is constructed of willows and uses rocks taken from the river valley bottom.

Water drawn from the river is poured over the heated rocks to produce the steam essential to the ritual cleansing.

The Oldman and its environs frequently play host to vision quests, a ritual in which a young male treks to an isolated site, where he passes time in seclusion, fasting and praying in hopes of experiencing contact with the spiritual world. If his quest is successful, he will experience a vision in which he identifies that thing or object to which he can turn for spiritual help and guidance. Both the thing or object and the site where the vision occurred become sacred to him.

There are other aspects of Native culture that influenced the way the Peigan dealt with the problems posed by the Oldman River Dam. In some instances, these may have compounded the problems. Among them are the Native peoples' consensual approach to decision making, which requires that all voices be afforded a respectful hearing, and which, consequently, does not lend itself to haste or deadlines. Another is the tendency to avoid confrontation, which can, in cases where confrontation is inevitable, amount to avoiding an issue until it is no longer possible to do so. In practice, this can create the mistaken impression that a problem has been resolved, when, in fact, it has merely been postponed. Another is what Rupert Ross, an Ontario Crown Attorney who has written extensively on Native justice issues, calls the 'conservation-withdrawal tactic,' which involves backing off from a situation to consider all of its aspects in order to avoid an ill-considered or hasty response that might have an unfavourable result. This is the antithesis of the uninformed, knee-jerk responses typical of many of the non-Native political figures involved in the Oldman affair. As is always the case when citing general traits, these characteristics do not have universal application among the Peigan. For example, a convincing case could be made that the Lonefighters, once aroused, were not prone to avoiding confrontation.

22
The Peigan and the Oldman River Dam: I

> We begin to realize that race relations are not the issue, but that the nature of power, its maintenance and its abuse, is the most fundamental problem in our society.
>
> – Joan Ryan, *The Betrayal of the Urban Indian*[1]

Of the numerous themes that might be selected to characterize the Peigan's involvement with the Oldman River Project, four, in particular, stand out. These are the inconsistency over time of the Peigan's position on support for the project; the significance of the Oldman River to Peigan culture and spirituality and the inability to understand or unwillingness to accept this on the part of some non-Natives and their institutions; the emergence of Indian water rights as the focal point of Peigan opposition to the project; and the utter disregard with which the federal and provincial governments treated the Peigan throughout the course of events concerning the project. All of these are related. The inconsistency in the Peigan's stance towards the project owed much to differences amongst the Peigan over the primacy of cultural/spiritual beliefs or material rewards. It also reflected a reaction to federal and provincial government actions. Similarly, the emergence of water rights as an issue was a reaction to government indifference to the Peigan as reflected in Alberta's rejection of the Peigan's joint development proposal for Brocket and the federal government's refusal to intervene on the Peigan's behalf.

The Peigan's involvement with the dam project can be broken down into three distinct periods, each characterized by the nature and extent of the Peigan's support or opposition to a dam on the river. From 1976, when Alberta Environment first proposed a dam on the Oldman, until August 1984, when Premier Lougheed announced the dam would be built at Three Rivers, the Peigan supported the idea of a dam on the river and participated in various studies leading up to the choice of a site. From August 1984 to the summer of 1992, when the FEARO Panel issued its report and both the federal and provincial governments rejected its recommendation to decommission the dam, the Peigan pursued a policy of calculated opposition to a dam at Three Rivers. They officially opposed the dam but, apart from the unsanctioned Lonefighter uprising, made no attempt to prevent construction of the dam from proceeding.[2] Throughout this period, the band continued its attempts to negotiate some benefits from the project. From the summer of 1992 to the present, with the dam completed and operating, with the compliance and collaboration of the federal government, the Peigan have adopted a strategy of reluctant coexistence with the dam. They appear resigned to the fact that they are unlikely to obtain any direct benefits from the project. Their strategy appears to be focused on obtaining some rights to water from the Oldman.

From the late 1970s to the present day, the Peigan have held four, possibly five, what might be termed official (i.e., supported by Chief and Council) positions on the Oldman River Dam Project. At the same time, there were minority positions espoused by those not in positions of power on the reserve. The official positions ranged from support to opposition to the dam. A variety of reasons can be offered to explain why one position was superseded by another. Foremost amongst these was conflict between various factions, each of whom championed different approaches to accomplishing a common end – the betterment of life on the reserve. Whatever their motivation, in 1991, there were reported to be four factions on the reserve with opposing views as to how to resolve the Oldman controversy.

Forces and events outside the reserve also had an influence on the Peigan's position. Between 1976 and 1991, there was a virtual revolution in the confidence and assertiveness of Native people and their leaders, accompanied by a comparable rise in public interest in Native issues and sympathy towards Native grievances. In 1976, the Peigan had suffered the shock of the death of its chief's eldest son, Nelson Small Legs, Jr., a leader of the American Indian Movement in Canada, who had taken his own life after seeing yet another Indian initiative thwarted by federal bureaucrats and politicians.[3] Although significant progress towards recognition of their rights was being made by Indian people in the United States, progress in Canada had been much slower and for the Peigan, nonexistent. By the late 1980s, a number of Indian bands had fought their land claims to successful conclusions; Aboriginal rights had been entrenched in the constitution; and Indian spirituality, encouraged by events in the United States, had emerged from the closet to be embraced by a growing number of Indian people and a wave of non-Indian, New Age adherents.

These events were both driven by and responsible for a dramatic increase in the presence and effectiveness of Indian people in the conduct of national affairs – something that could not have been imagined twenty-five years earlier. This did not mean that Indian people were being heard and accommodated on all fronts. In more local issues, like the golf course at Oka and the Oldman River Dam, they continued to experience the steamrolling by governments and power groups that had long characterized their dealings with non-Native society. Despite the advances, Indian protest groups were still frustrated by their inability to gain concessions without going through lengthy and often fruitless bureaucratic processes, and had begun to take more direct and potentially violent action. The Indian protest movement, led by the Mohawk Warriors in Quebec, came to a head in the 'Indian Summer' of 1990. On the Peigan Reserve, the Lonefighters Society mounted their own action in protest against Alberta's handling of the Oldman River Dam controversy.

Finally, among the most compelling reasons for the Peigan's changes of heart towards the dam was the heavy-handed way in which the provincial government went about the business of selecting a site and stonewalling Peigan attempts to get a cut of the action, combined with the federal government's irresolute gestures in support of the Peigan cause.

These factors – conflicting opinions among groups and individuals on the reserve about what was best for the Peigan, growth in the confidence and assertiveness of Indian people and in the sympathy and support of non-Natives for Native causes, and the need to respond to perceived changes in government policies and approaches – taken in combination, account for the shifts in the Peigan's official position towards the project.

From 1976, when the ORSMC study began, until 1980, the Peigan cooperated with the WMS as it studied the possibilities for a dam on the river. With the exception of the impasse over access to the LNID weir in 1978, relations were cordial and, while the interchange of information between the study committee and the band was limited, the arrangement gave the impression that all was well. The Peigan seemed prepared to consider whatever the government might propose and expressed no concerns about the impact of a dam on the river on their economic, cultural, or spiritual way of life. However, because of the band council's complete control over all information pertaining to the study, both incoming and outgoing, and over access to the reserve, there was no direct communication between the study committee or its agents and the people on the reserve.[4]

In a 1978 presentation to the ECA public hearings on water management in the Oldman, spokespersons for the Peigan Chief and Council, though sceptical about the scale of potential benefit claimed by both the federal and provincial governments, supported a dam on the Oldman River in principle and indicated that Chief and Council were open to consideration of the ORSMC suggestion that it might be located on the reserve.[5] But a second brief, submitted by a reserve resident, served warning that not all Peigans were comfortable with Chief and Council's position, and that some were concerned about the environmental and cultural-spiritual impacts of the project.[6]

The dilemma facing the Peigan was described in a 1978 report to the ORSMC by the study's social impact consultants:

In attempting to effect their development plans the Peigan require considerable financial resources and yet the potential to secure these from their
own physical resources is very limited. Consequently, when the Province of
Alberta raised the possibility of a dam being constructed on their lands, the
economic and social implications of such a possibility came quickly to the
forefront of the Band's consciousness. The Peigans saw the proposed undertaking in terms of the total development possibilities that it might provide
... At the same time they recognized that the flooding of the river bottom
land would constitute a tremendous loss to them in social terms ... Thus,
the proposed dam presented an issue of major proportions for the Peigans,
perhaps one of the largest they had ever come to grips with as a developing
community seeking to become autonomous and self-governing.[7]

In the wake of Alberta's 1980 decision to dam the river, the Peigan
'welcome[d] the opportunity' to develop a position in response to the government's invitation to consider building the dam on the reserve.[8] Pro-
development forces on the reserve and on band council still predominated
over those concerned about the impact of the project. Although the band
recognized that the 'social and cultural organization of the Peigan people
could be changed radically' by a dam at Brocket, they were 'desirous of
expanding Band involvement in ... the water resource development under
consideration.'[9] With funding from the provincial and federal governments, the band launched the Weasel Valley study to evaluate the prospect
of a dam at Brocket.

In 1981, Chief Nelson Small Legs had negotiated a successful settlement
of the LNID weir dispute. The Alberta government's willingness to negotiate with the Peigan over the weir access issue and the terms, quite generous
to the Peigan, that it agreed to perhaps gave the Peigan the false notion that
they could negotiate a similarly beneficial deal for a dam on the reserve. If
that was the case, the Peigan badly underestimated both the extent to
which they had Alberta over a barrel on the weir issue and the extent to
which the situation was reversed on the dam site issue. That the Peigan
had been able to use their control over the land that Alberta needed for
the LNID weir to their advantage is evident in the annual payment –
$300,000, indexed to inflation – that the Peigan were able to extract from
Alberta in the 1981 agreement. As Barry Barton pointed out, this payment
'goes far beyond any level of rent that might be payable for the acreage
concerned.'[10]

In 1983, the band elected a new chief, Peter Yellowhorn, a businessman
with off-reserve experience in the oil industry, which, if anything, resulted
in the adoption of an even more development-oriented stance by band
council. The band's November 1983 proposal for development of a dam at
the Brocket site would have provided substantial benefits to the reserve.[11]

The proposal was that Alberta and the Peigan would enter into a joint venture to build a dam, and 'in return for the use of 4,200 acres (1,700 hectares) of land for the lifetime of the facilities, the Peigan would be given compensation for the loss of the 4,200 acres (1,700 hectares) of land, cost-free hydro power, assistance in the development of agricultural opportunities, and the development of an infrastructure to enable the members of the Peigan Band to participate in the socio-economic development of the Peigan Indian Reserve.'[12]

When Alberta announced, in August 1984, that the dam would be built at Three Rivers, the Peigan began to distance themselves from support for the project. The circumstances of the government's rejection of the Peigan proposal for Brocket – not only did Alberta not make any attempt to negotiate the proposal, it did not even acknowledge its receipt until after its public announcement that the dam would be at Three Rivers – brought the Peigan face to face with the reality that they were unlikely to reap any benefits from a dam on the Oldman. Despite the apparent shock of rejection, and Yellowhorn's face-saving response that the Peigan would build their own dam at Brocket, the transition to opposition to the dam was not immediate. Clinging to the faint hope that they could negotiate some benefit from a dam at Three Rivers, Chief and Council did not actively oppose construction of the dam for almost two years. In a brief presented to the AWRC in December 1984, the Peigan voiced no opposition to the dam 'regardless of where the Alberta Government builds [it],' but reasserted their claim to 'own and control the waters of the Oldman River as they flow through the boundaries of our reserve.'[13] Whatever leverage the Peigan hoped to achieve by brandishing their claim to Aboriginal and treaty rights to the Oldman was weakened by the fact that Indian water rights had never been recognized by government or adjudicated by the courts.

In 1986, with dam construction imminent, Chief and Council, still driven to negotiate some benefit from the dam but thwarted by government indifference, abruptly changed its strategy. In January, it issued a proclamation rejecting the province's plan for the dam and demanding that 1,023,000 cubic decametres of water be reserved for use by the Peigan. Alberta's response was to buy more time, granting the Peigan $750,000 for still more study of the impact of a dam on the reserve. In April, the Peigan filed a statement of claim against Alberta in Court of Queen's Bench, claiming that construction of the Oldman River Dam was in conflict with the Peigan's water rights in the Oldman River and asking the Court to declare that the Peigan owned the bed of the river through the reserve, had a right to use the water flowing through the reserve, and that Alberta could not operate the dam to interfere with flow through the reserve. The Peigan also asked for an injunction restraining Alberta from 'constructing the Three Rivers Dam and Reservoir.'[14] Amongst the reasons offered to support the claim were that the dam would 'cause ... destruction of the spiritual values of the Oldman River to the Peigan Nation [and] interference with the natural environment and ecological processes' of the river.

In June, the Peigan filed a similar claim against Canada in Federal Court, claiming damages and asking the Court to order remedies similar to those in its suit against Alberta.[15] In the federal suit, the Peigan placed more emphasis on Aboriginal and treaty rights, and on the federal government's fiduciary duties and obligations to the Peigan. In place of an injunction against construction, the Peigan asked the Court to order Canada to 'take the measures necessary' to ensure that the dam would not be built and operated. As in its suit against Alberta, the Peigan supported its claims with accusations that the project would 'destroy the spiritual values' of the river and damage 'the natural environment and natural resources of the Peigan territory.'

In citing spiritual and environmental damage as grounds for their claim, the Peigan were, in essence, indicating opposition to a dam on the river regardless of where it might be located. This marked an abrupt change in their position, which up to that time, had been to support a dam on the river on the grounds that it would bring some economic benefits to the reserve.

This change in position reflected a number of things. First, frustration that its attempt to negotiate some benefit from the project had been ignored by Alberta and its realization that the major beneficiaries would be the irrigation community to whom the water stored in the reservoir would be allocated, at the expense of allocations to the Peigan. Second, the growing confidence in the Indian community, encouraged by their legal advisors, that they could take a stand against governments on the basis of their Aboriginal and treaty rights with some chance that they would win if the dispute went to court. Third, the development of public support for Native causes based on both a greater awareness of past and continuing injustices perpetrated against Indians and new-found respect for Indian culture, spiritual beliefs, and traditional ways of life.

The reaction of the provincial government, which thereafter refused to enter into negotiations with the Peigan on matters related to the dam unless they dropped the court action, simply increased the distance between the two sides. The federal response was to focus more attention, at the officials level, on what was going on in southern Alberta.

The studies funded with the $750,000 provided by Alberta in 1986 (RDI Studies) provided the basis for a new Peigan position.[16] The new position was released in April 1987, in the form of a proposal for resolving major issues related to the dam.[17] The major issues were identified as 'allocation of water, protection and preservation of water rights, development of irrigation, protection and preservation of the environment, maintenance of health and welfare, and protection of the cultural and spiritual values of the Peigan people.'[18]

The measures proposed to resolve the major issues included the development of 2,670 hectares for irrigation; monitoring and investigation of river flow, water quality, riparian vegetation, and fish habitat; surveys and criteria for a flow easement (in effect, an arrangement to lease the portion of the Oldman channel on the reserve) and review of the dam design; and analysis of cultural and spiritual impacts. The proposal called for funding of $5.7 million, $5 million of which was for irrigation construction.[19] The RDI Studies had identified 21,500 hectares of reserve land as 'irrigable' by Alberta government standards, which they estimated would require a water allocation of 180,000 cubic decametres per year to irrigate.[20] The 2,670 hectares of land identified for development in the 1987 proposal would require but a fraction of the water claimed by the Peigan and of the funding that might ultimately be required.

Neither government responded to the proposal, although Alberta Public Works Minister Kowalski had claimed that funding the study upon which it was based would 'facilitate a full and open exchange of information between the Band and the Alberta Government.'[21] The federal government reviewed the studies with a view to using them as the basis for negotiations with Alberta, which never materialized. In December 1987, after Kowalski refused an invitation to meet with the Peigan and the minor officials sent in his stead were unable to respond to Peigan proposals, the Chief and Council announced their endorsement of FOR's efforts to stop the dam. In 1988, the Peigan stepped up their opposition by petitioning the federal government to apply the EARPGO to the Oldman Project.

The changes in Chief and Council's position on the Lonefighters' attempt to divert the Oldman River in the summer of 1990 reflected the shifting nature of public opinion on the reserve. The Lonefighters originally believed that they had the support of Chief and Council. Once the project was launched, however, reserve residents revealed themselves to be divided as to whether the band should support or oppose the Lonefighters. The division ran through the reserve population in general, as well as through particular groups, including Chief and Council. Consequently, Chief and Council adopted an official position that supported the Lonefighters' aims but opposed its methods, though it did nothing to prevent or discourage the Lonefighters' activity. Chief Bastien had revealed his personal views on demonstrations more than a year before the Lonefighters' action. He told the *Lethbridge Herald*, 'I believe there's a stigma attached to Indian activists that creates more harm and damage when they demonstrate against society. I think there are other means of reaching solutions.'[22]

Following the RCMP-supported Alberta Environment raid onto the reserve on 7 September, the majority opinion on the reserve swung to support the Lonefighters, with the result that Chief Bastien called a press conference to announce the band council's support for the Lonefighters. This move incited *Alberta Report* to dub Bastien 'Chief Walks Both Sides.' In the band elections of January 1991, Bastien was reelected chief, and all but one of the candidates for band council who supported the Lonefighter position were defeated. By summer, with the Lonefighters out of the news, Bastien was telling an international water conference that the Oldman Dam could be 'a boon for the Peigan.'[23]

In the summer of 1991, Alberta Environment moved to allocate the bulk of the water that would become available from storage in the Oldman River Dam reservoir to the irrigation districts. In reaction to this move, Bastien appealed to the federal government to exercise its fiduciary duty by intervening in support of the Peigan in its suit against Alberta and, in a scaled-down version of the 1987 proposal, he asked for $1.2 million to 'protect these resources [irrigable land and riparian habitat] and our population from failure of the upstream dam.'[24]

By fall, the dam was essentially completed, and the Peigan had, for all practical purposes, dropped its opposition. In its submission to the federal panel in November, the band's position remained essentially as outlined in the 1987 proposal, with emphasis on the Peigan's right to water to irrigate land on the reserve. Neither its report nor its verbal submission to the panel called for dismantling or decommissioning of the dam or for specific controls on its operation.

At the panel hearings, the official Peigan spokesperson revealed that there was still no consensus on the reserve as to whether to support or oppose the dam, or whether the exploitation of economic opportunity or the protection of cultural and spiritual values was paramount. By that time, the Peigan's opposition to the dam was more symbolic than real, as indicated by the following exchange between panel member Dr. Michael Healey and Peigan spokesperson Develon Small Legs at the panel's hearing in Brocket on 16 November 1991:

Dr. Healey [referring to a statement in the Peigan report to the panel]: That statement ... suggests that one of your principle [sic] concerns is for the band to have the right to develop the river as an economic resource rather than maintain it as a spiritual and cultural resource.
Develon Small Legs: There is a delicate balance between the two, and I think in terms of who we are as a Peigan Nation, we are the ones that can determine what that balance is. Like, there are individuals on this reserve who are wishing to develop in terms of the irrigation development and other economic opportunities related to water development.
Dr. Healey: Is it feasible that this delicate balance you speak about might

include something like the Oldman Dam, provided it was properly negotiated and discussed within the Peigan Nation?

Develon Small Legs: That's a theoretical question at this point in time. We have those proponents on the reserve wishing to benefit from that particular facility in terms of irrigation, like I said, and then we have some proponents that are directly against the overall facility.

Dr. Healey: Let's suppose you were able to enter into genuine negotiations with the province ... and if it [the dam] could be operated in such a way that the river bottom within the Peigan Reserve was protected from an environmental point of view, and you were to receive reasonable economic benefits from the dam, would that be a way you would be willing to proceed?

Develon Small Legs: Its [sic] a difficult question to ask ... we have to go to the membership and say, okay, what does the membership want.

Dr. Healey: So what I'm hearing you say is that ...

Develon Small Legs: It's a real possibility.

Dr. Healey: It's not inconceivable?

Develon Small Legs: It's not inconceivable, no.

Dr. Healey: So we're really looking at trying to establish a more fruitful communication relationship between your band and perhaps the provincial government, and also establishing some recognition of what you consider to be your aboriginal rights?

Develon Small Legs: Yes ... and the fiduciary responsibility of the federal government to the Peigan Nation.

Dr. Healey: So is it fair to say that at the moment the dam is kind of a symbol of the provincial and federal governments running rough-shot [sic] over those rights rather than an irritant that you would reject out of hand?

Develon Small Legs: Yes.[25]

In 1992, the Peigan Chief and Council accepted the federal and provincial governments' rejections of the federal Environmental Assessment Panel's 'preferred' recommendation to decommission the dam, opting to hang their hopes on the panel's alternative recommendations, which suggested a negotiated settlement between the Peigan and Alberta on water rights and compensation for cultural and spiritual losses. Chief Bastien described the Peigan position as 'prudent' but stressed that it was essential that the federal government 'enforce the recommendations.' The Lonefighters were critical of the official band position, and vowed to keep up their fight against the dam. Bastien, like his people, was torn between his wish to assert independence and his hopes for winning some economic benefit for the reserve. Frequently, as University of Calgary sociologist Rick

Ponting has observed, 'Pragmatic Indian politicians who are prepared to reach accommodations with non-Indian politicians, in order to extract the best deal possible ... to meet the pressing needs of their Indian constituents are dismissed as "sell-outs," who are merely paying rhetorical lip-service to the idea of opposing the government's scheme while actually collaborating with it.'[26]

Such was the case with Bastien – though he was able to win reelection in 1993, while Milton Born With A Tooth awaited his inevitable ascension to martyrdom.

In its December 1992 amendment to its statement of claim against Alberta, the Peigan deleted its request for an injunction against construction of the dam. This made sense, since the dam was by then completed and in operation. The Peigan did not, as might have been expected, request an injunction to prevent Alberta from operating the dam to store water until it had complied with the panel's Recommendations 2 to 4. Having accepted the completed dam as a reality, turned its back on the Lonefighters, and indicated its reluctance to take its water rights suit against Alberta to trial, the Peigan could do little but claim betrayal when, in September 1993, the federal government issued approvals for the dam, despite the absence of a settlement or even meaningful negotiations between Alberta and the Peigan.[27]

23
The Peigan and the Oldman River Dam: II

Since the beginning of time the river represented a way of life. In a few short years this thread of life has been severed by one of the most outrageous criminal acts against nature and original people.

– from 'The Last Will and Testament of the Oldman River'[1]

The cultural and ecological genocide of both the past and present of Napi's River and his People will be complete. The world will be the poorer for it.

– Dr. Brian Reeves[2]

As the Oldman controversy intensified, elements of the Peigan community increasingly emphasized the impact that the project would have on Peigan cultural and spiritual beliefs and practices. The response of many non-Natives and their institutions to this development indicated that they were unable to understand or unwilling to accept the significance or the relevance of these claims. In most cases, this was a reflection of the paternal attitude of Canadians and their European ancestors towards Native people; in others it suggests outright discrimination and racism. From the late 1880s until at least the late 1950s, Indian religion and spiritual beliefs were suppressed by the federal government in its drive to force Indians to assimilate, and by the churches, which regarded them as pagan. During that period those beliefs and customs went underground and were kept alive by certain elders and 'spiritual people' living on reserves.

In the 1960s, Indian people began to assert themselves and stand up for their culture and their rights. Traditional religious and spiritual beliefs and practices emerged from the closet and once again became a part of Indian life. The belief that passage of the American Indian Freedom of Religion Act in 1978 had legitimized the religious and spiritual practices of Indians in the United States crept across the border and strengthened the Indian religious movement in Canada in the 1980s. Simultaneously, mainstream churches in Canada, partly in response to the guilt heaped on them for the part they played in the residential school system that was a major element in the assimilation movement, began to seek accommodation with Indian religion and support Indian causes. Indian leaders involved in the rehabilitation and healing of Indian people who had succumbed to drug and alcohol abuse, focused their rehabilitative efforts on reestablishing traditional Indian values and instilling an understanding of and pride in Indian culture. The teaching of Indian spiritual beliefs played a big part in this process. Environmentalists and New Agers, who have embraced and promoted the traditional Indian beliefs of unity and harmony with the environment and respect for all living things, contributed to the spread of traditional Indian cultural and spiritual beliefs among non-Natives.

In the early stages of the Oldman River Dam developments, the Peigan gave no indication of concern that the project would be detrimental to their cultural and spiritual beliefs and practices. There were doubtless people of a more traditional bent on the reserve at that time who, had they had a clear understanding of the proposals, might have worried about the dam's impact, but they were not to be found amongst the band leaders. It was not until things started to go wrong for them in their dealings with Alberta that the Peigan voiced concern that the project would disrupt their spiritual life.

The first direct associations between the dam and the cultural/spiritual life of the Peigan appear to have surfaced in the Weasel Valley studies in the early 1980s, and the Peigan made passing reference to them in a brief to the AWRC in late 1984. However, it was not until 1986 that the impacts of a dam on Peigan spiritual beliefs became a serious issue. Interestingly, they became an issue largely as the result of the attention drawn to them by non-Natives, initially by Barney Reeves. In a break from tradition, some respected elders and spiritual leaders also began to publicize their concerns, focusing attention on the impact of the dam on Peigan spiritual practices. Joe Crowshoe presided over a number of 'sweats' in which other prominent Indians, environmentalists, and the media were invited to participate. For a brief period in the late 1980s, Crowshoe became something of a fixture on the environmental conference circuit, opening proceedings with a prayer to the Creator rendered in Blackfoot. Other Peigans with knowledge of spiritual matters frequently appeared as speakers at conferences and public meetings. These appearances and events, commonly brokered by environmental groups, most often FOR, were evidence of the informal liaison forged between environmentalists and dissenting Peigans.[3]

What were the spiritual 'things' that the Peigan claimed would suffer impacts from the Oldman River Dam? They ranged from the very general to the minutely specific; from the grand to the seemingly trivial. At the most general level, the Peigan claimed the Oldman and its valley – a vital part of their 'sacred geography,' the location of sacred and vision-quest sites of importance to both individuals and the Peigan as a whole – would be irretrievably altered. At the reservoir site, burial grounds, ancient ceremonial rocks, traditional camping sites, and past and present ceremonial

Figure 25   Peigan Chief Leonard Bastien (left) and Elder Joe Crowshoe (with eagle feathers) at Oldman River Blessing Ceremony

locations would be inundated. In one of his first public statements follow-ing his 1989 election as chief, Leonard Bastien, a prominent member of the Peigan spiritual community, said that 'whatever was or will be regard-ing our spirituality, because of the Oldman River Dam it will be totally gone.'[4] In trying to impress upon the federal panel the broad impacts of the dam, Milton Born With A Tooth spoke of a 'religious ecosystem.'

Operation of the dam means that the river will no longer have its sea-sonal pattern of flow, and seasonal patterns are central to Indian spiritual beliefs. Indeed, the prime purpose of the dam is to regulate the seasonal flow pattern that is so unsuitable for supplying water for irrigation. At the ceremonial level, the sun dance and sweat lodge ceremonies, 'the central spiritual institutions through which the Peigan exercise their spiritual practices and beliefs,' were identified as being closely tied to the Oldman because of locations where the ceremonies were performed, and because many of the natural materials used in the ceremonies are found in the valley.[5] Willows from which sweat lodges are built, the rocks heated for use in the sweat lodge ceremony, and the sacred cottonwoods – the only tree that can be used to build the medicine lodge used in the sun dance or burned to heat the rocks for the sweat lodge ceremony and from which punk is used to light the fires for ceremonial smudges and pipes – all of these are found most abundantly along the Oldman River, and are, in part, products of its seasonal pattern of flow.[6]

The introduction of the impact of the dam on Peigan spiritual beliefs posed a serious dilemma for many non-Natives – particularly dam supporters and neutral parties like the panel and their technical experts. Some were sceptical about the beliefs as presented or doubted the extent to which the Peigan themselves took them seriously; almost everyone had difficulty evaluating how important the alleged impacts might be. At the same time, it was not easy to take a firm stand in opposition to them. It is acceptable to question or even attack an individual's or a group's economic or political beliefs, but any attempt to dismiss or discredit the Peigan's spiritual beliefs was an open invitation to charges of discrimination and racism. It brought a new perspective that the process was simply not organized to deal with. In a sense, many regarded it as an unfair tactic. In a highly secular society, where the majority appear to have some difficulty in relating to the beliefs of Christianity, the faith which, when pressed, they are most likely to identify as their own, few were prepared to accept that the Peigan's spiritual claims were anything other than a red herring – a desperate last-ditch effort to block the dam.

Alberta's attempts to discredit Reeves planted some doubt in the public mind about the significance of the archaeological resources in the dam area and, by association, about the Peigan spiritual claims. Yet no one on the government side, not even Ken Kowalski, who was later prepared to accuse the United Church of Canada of involvement in a conspiracy against the dam, was prepared to debate the Peigan on the question of the impact of the dam on their spiritual beliefs and practices. The approach selected by the government was simply to ignore the Peigan claims, which served it well over the course of the controversy. No matter how frequently Reeves compared the spiritual desecration that would be wrought by the dam in Peigan eyes to the destruction of Mount Sinai in the eyes of the Judeo-Christian community, or how often Nelbert Little Moustache compared flooding of the Oldman valley to theft of the cup and chalice from the Christian Eucharist, the government maintained a condescending silence.

The federal environmental review panel, because it was obliged to consider all of the issues brought before it, could not so easily avoid the spiritual impact issue – nor did it try to do so. The panel's approach, which simply reflected the nature of the process and to some extent the background of the panel members – scientific, academic, and bureaucratic – was to urge, even to pay, the Peigan to document the issue and to provide the panel with hard evidence and specific examples of the dam's potential impact on their spiritual beliefs. An exchange between the panel chairperson and Milton Born With A Tooth at one of the public hearing sessions in Calgary is illustrative of the vast differences in the way traditionally oriented Native people and technically oriented modern society think and talk about how they relate to and interact with the natural environment. After listening patiently to an eloquent, if rambling, discourse by Born With A Tooth on the importance of riparian cottonwoods to the spiritual life of the Peigan people, Ross, with apologies for 'jargon that is oriented to the way we think,' characterized Born With A Tooth's offering as a description of 'the use of the resources in the river valley of the Oldman River on your reserve.'[7] The simple emotion and sense of intimacy conveyed by Born With A Tooth's words were entirely lost in Ross' translation. It is not simply that our jargon limits our expression; the way we think, as revealed by the jargon, is severely limited by our technocratic-instrumentalist outlook.

Exaggerating only slightly, what the panel, government bureaucrats, politicians, consultants, the media, and the general public appeared to expect was an estimate of the cubic metres of cottonwoods used for a particular ceremony, the number of Peigans who participated in that ceremony, and the frequency with which they did so, from which could be derived the Peigan's long-term demand for cottonwoods in cubic metres per capita. What Born With A Tooth was saying was that no such data are available, and if they were, they would not serve to define what he was talking about – that cottonwoods are an essential element of Peigan spiritual/cultural existence, and if they cease to exist, Peigan culture and religion will cease to exist. Develon Small Legs was telling the panel the same thing when he said, 'They are telling us, well, identify a spot where you sit and have your quest. We are saying the whole area is a vision quest area,' within which there are innumerable sites, some used, some yet to be discovered, each of which has 'volumes of information for an individual Indian person,' who may 'for one whole lifetime continue to revisit that site.'[8]

A similar difference exists in the way Indians and technocrats, in this case archaeologists, think of artifacts of Indian origin. The Peigan think of them as sacred objects, a tangible tie with their past and vital to their continued existence. The majority of archaeologists look on them as collections of scientific curiosities to be 'salvaged' so that they can be warehoused and studied. In the words of a former head of the Archaeological Survey of Alberta, 'The materials that make up the archaeological record, the stones and bones, really are just things until they are invested with meaning. Archaeological methods and theories are applied to study these materials and the relationships between them, and it is only then that they help us to learn about the human condition in the past.'[9] Similar rationale was offered by those who ravaged the tombs of the pharaohs for the glory of Europe's museums.

The federal government revealed that it shared the technocratic obsession for specific sites when it offered its 'understanding' that neither the Peigan nor the province of Alberta had been able to identify any such sites as part of its rationale for approving the dam prior to the Peigan and Alberta agreeing on compensation for cultural and spiritual losses.[10]

It can be argued that it is not reasonable to expect that evidence of the dam's impact on the Peigan's spiritual beliefs and practices could be gathered, analyzed, documented, and evaluated in the same way as could the impact on, for example, fish habitat or riparian ecosystems. In fact, such arguments were made, and not ineffectively, during the course of informal submissions to the panel by both Milton Born With A Tooth and Develon Small Legs. Speaking of the impact of the dam on the Peigan's spiritual beliefs and practices, Born With A Tooth told the panel that 'there is no written form or no expert analysis from a spiritual or native perspective,' and that even if there had been, 'the EARP process does not have a foundation on how to measure' things like the impact of the loss of riparian cottonwoods on Peigan spiritual life.[11] In his remarks to the panel, Chief Bastien said, 'Our position is not one that can be calculated by outside consultants using exotic economic analysis, cost/benefit ratios or net economic benefits. Our people and our culture have been tied to the land and the rivers and the mountains from time immemorial. We live and have lived in harmony with the land. To the Peigan, land and water do not generate diversification or multiplier effects. Rather it is the foundation of a culture that has existed in this area in harmony with nature for thousands of years.'[12]

And yet, despite these fairly convincing arguments, the official Peigan position persisted with the fiction that the band could and would document the cultural and spiritual impacts of the dam. Between 1986 and 1991, the Peigan undertook two different studies to examine the question of the impact of a dam on the Oldman River on their spiritual and cultural beliefs and practices, neither of which produced any information for the public record.

The Peigan presented some information of a very general nature, for example the use of cottonwoods and willows in certain ceremonies, but there were no studies or documentation presented to the public or to the panel to support the often-repeated claim that the dam 'violated' Peigan spiritual and religious beliefs. Nor, perhaps, could there have been. Small Legs and Born With A Tooth's arguments suggest that there could not have been. Bastien's remarks imply that an understanding of Peigan religion – pantheistic and intimately associated with the immediate environment – and the history of the Peigan's occupation of the Oldman basin, where they practised their religion for 1,000 years or more, should have made the impacts of the dam apparent. But the Peigan religion was either not understood or not accepted by most people. Perhaps in a culture where Hinduism or some other Eastern religion rather than those of the Judeo-Christian community was predominate, people might have more easily understood and related to Native Indian religion. And in a culture where Native Indian religion had not so recently been dismissed as pagan animism, it might have found broader acceptance.

In a technologically oriented society, where people prefer the practical and concrete to the general and abstract, the Peigan's reluctance to speak openly about some aspects of their religion and their vagueness about the location of such things as sacred sites was exasperating to many. There are reasons, again perhaps neither understood nor accepted by most people, that account for these aspects of Peigan behaviour. One very practical reason for vagueness about the location of sacred sites is that the Peigan religion has only recently entered a period of reestablishment and, while the existence of sacred sites has been passed down in oral histories, few Peigan may have actually seen or visited them. As Reeves frequently points out, there was a long period – from the 1880s to the 1950s – when Indians were not allowed to leave the reserve without a pass and they required a good reason to obtain one. A desire to visit a sacred site was not likely to be considered a good reason in the eyes of the Indian agents, whose job was to hasten the assimilation of Indians into Western society. During this period the Peigan lost contact with their sacred sites and have only recently begun to rediscover them.

A second, equally sound, reason is that because the sites are sacred, Indian people are reluctant, even frightened, to reveal them. Reeves and others who have, over the years, gained the confidence of elders and spiritual leaders, often mention privileged information that they have obtained but are not free to pass on. It was, presumably, the absence of objective data and information about the impact of a dam on Peigan spiritual beliefs that dissuaded the Peigan's lawyers from attempting to convince a court that the Oldman River is fundamental to the Peigan religion and that construction of the dam would make it impossible for the Peigan to continue to practise their religion. Nevertheless, it is possible to accept, as did the federal panel, that there are close ties between the Peigan religion and the Oldman River and that the construction of the dam resulted in spiritual losses to the Peigan. The difficulty comes in understanding the magnitude of the loss, both in absolute terms and relative to other gains and losses.

Federal panel Chairman Ross told Milton Born With A Tooth that he did not expect the Peigan's information on cultural/spiritual impacts 'to come to us in the same way [quantitative] that we've received information today.' And the panel accepted the information offered by Small Legs, Born With A Tooth, various elders, and spiritual adherents as a substitute for whatever data the Peigan had collected with panel funding but refused to disclose. As was apparent from its recommendations, the panel took the fact of cultural and spiritual losses on faith and, despite the absence of hard data, put a value on those losses relative to political and economic considerations.

In a submission to the AWRC in 1984, a Peigan spokesperson asked, rhetorically, 'What price can be set on our spiritual and cultural values?'[13] More recently, the Peigan have said that the potential impact of the dam on their cultural and spiritual heritage is 'immeasurable.' The federal panel disagreed. It found the dam 'not acceptable,' but it did not recommend that it be dismantled because it felt that 'would be an inappropriate use of government funds,' nor did the panel seriously recommend that the dam be decommissioned because that '[might] pose insurmountable inter-jurisdictional difficulties.' Thus, in formulating its recommendations, the panel made the implicit judgment that the spiritual losses that would be suffered by the Peigan would be of less consequence than the inappropriate use of government funds or inter-jurisdictional difficulties. It concluded that it was possible to put a price on the Peigan's spiritual losses, and in recommending that federal approval of the dam be contingent on an agreement on compensation to be negotiated between the Peigan and Alberta, it implied that the price was not so great as to upset the economic viability of the project.

From the beginning, the Peigan's willingness to negotiate, which even took them so far as to propose a dam on the reserve, left the impression that they could accept the impacts of the dam if it would provide sufficient benefit to the band. To the cynical, this implied that there was indeed a price on the Peigan's spiritual and cultural values. To the more thoughtful, it simply suggested that the Peigan's experience with governments told them that a dam on the Oldman was inevitable and that, like all cultural or spiritual communities, they understood that economic security is a precondition for cultural and religious independence. In 1988, Bastien said, 'Common sense says they are going to go ahead with the dam, therefore we would like to be given some type of compensation, perhaps a sanctuary in which to practice our spiritual and religious beliefs.'[14] And in 1991, he told the panel, 'we will consider mitigation measures that will compensate the Peigan for the damages caused by the dam.'[15]

Despite the panel's recommendations that the Peigan be compensated for their cultural and spiritual losses, neither Alberta nor Canada have ever acknowledged that the Oldman River Dam will have any impact on the spiritual life of the Peigan. While the irrigation community reaps the economic benefits of the completed dam, the Peigan have yet to receive even an offer of compensation.

24
The Federal Watchdog: I

A good law, however, is not itself enough. It must be enforced –
ruthlessly if need be.

> – The Honourable Tom McMillan, minister of environment[1]

If there be anyone who ought scrupulously to conform to the
official duties that the law casts upon him or her in the role of a
high state official, it is a Minister of the Crown.

> – Mr. Justice Muldoon, Federal Court of Canada[2]

In Canada, minority groups who believe that their interests are neglected
or ignored by provincial governments commonly look to the national
government to intervene on their behalf. Such was the case with the Oldman River Dam. Both the environmentalists and the Peigan appealed to
Ottawa, asking it to take action to reduce the impacts of the project on
areas of federal jurisdiction.

Throughout the controversy, the federal government's actions on Oldman River Dam issues were tempered by its concern about other issues,
the most compelling of which were the increasingly disputatious constitutional debate with the western provinces about jurisdiction over natural
resources and the environment and the never-ending wrangling with Quebec over its place in confederation. The general effect of these larger issues
on the federal government's handling of Oldman Dam issues stemmed
from its determination to avoid, wherever possible, any action that would
annoy provincial governments. Federal agencies were unenthusiastic and
ineffectual in exercising whatever responsibilities for the well-being of
Indian people and the environment that fell within their mandates. Most
of their actions seemed to be directed at abetting Alberta's construction
and operation of the dam.

There are a number of federal laws and policies of greater or lesser import
upon which construction of the Oldman River Dam infringed. Section 5 of
the Navigable Waters Protection Act requires that no work be built or
placed in, on, over, under, through, or across any navigable water unless
approved by the minister of transport. Section 35 of the Fisheries Act
requires that no works that result in the harmful alteration, disruption, or
destruction of fish habitat be placed in a river without the authorization of
the minister of fisheries. Section 91(24) of the Constitution Act, 1867,

assigns to the Parliament of Canada responsibility for 'Indians and Lands reserved for the Indians.' The federal Environmental Assessment and Review Process Guidelines Order (EARPGO)[3] established conditions under which federal departments were required to undertake a public review of projects that might have an impact in areas of federal jurisdiction. Confusion about whether the EARPGO was an order that federal departments were obliged to apply or simply a guideline, which they could apply or not at their discretion, was clarified when the Federal and Supreme Courts ruled that the EARPGO had the force of law. The Department of Fisheries and Oceans' (DF&O's) Policy for the Management of Fish Habitat[4] has as its guiding principle 'no net loss of the productive capacity of habitats' and the 1987 Federal Water Policy[5] commits the federal government to 'review and clarify with native people their water-related issues and interests with respect to their treaty areas.'[6]

The run on Ottawa began in March 1986, when Alberta applied for approval under the Navigable Waters Protection Act to build the Oldman River Dam. In September 1987, with no investigation of the environmental impacts of the dam, Transport Canada issued that approval. The conditions attached to the approval pertained only to safeguards for navigation.

There were at least three instances when DF&O might have been expected to advise Alberta that it required authorization under the Fisheries Act to build the dam. The first was when DF&O first learned of Alberta's intentions, which, at the latest, was in August 1980, when Alberta Ministers Cookson and Schmidt released their joint Ministerial Statement, committing the province to the construction of a dam on the Oldman. The second was in 1987, when at the request of Indian Affairs, DF&O reviewed information on the project provided by Alberta to assess 'potential major impacts' on the fisheries resource and 'the effects on fisheries of the Peigan Indian Reserve.'[7] Since Alberta had provided 'no information on the proposed operating regime for the project,' DF&O was unable to assess the impacts of changes in the flow regime on fish habitat downstream from the dam, where the Peigan Reserve is located. They were, however, able to determine that the dam would 'act as a barrier to fish movements, affecting fish species whose life cycles include habitats above and below the dam.'[8] DF&O passed this information to Indian Affairs but took no action to prevent violation of s. 35 of the Fisheries Act. The third was in September 1988, when FOR filed a complaint with the regional office of DF&O, charging that Alberta had violated s. 35 of the Fisheries Act. Given the shameful performance of the federal government in dealing with Alcan's Kemano Completion Project in British Columbia in 1987, DF&O's inaction on the Oldman was not out of character.[9]

Like Alberta, the minister of fisheries and oceans claimed that responsibility for administration of the Fisheries Act in Alberta had been delegated to the province. This was a weak excuse at best, since even those responsibilities that are exercised by Alberta, such as the formulation of fishing regulations, have the force of law only after they have been proclaimed by the federal government.

In 1987, Environment Canada prepared an evaluation of the environmental impacts of the dam for Indian Affairs.[10] Though it observed that trout and mountain whitefish migrations would be 'completely blocked' by the dam, the evaluation concluded that most of the impacts on the Peigan Reserve would be positive, including increased trout and mountain whitefish populations and opportunities for irrigation expansion on reserve lands. One Environment Canada official, noting an estimate that 21,000 hectares of reserve land could be irrigated, naively concluded that 'this indicates a strong positive benefit of the Dam to the Peigan Reserve.'[11] Indian Affairs referred the Oldman Project to Environment Canada's Regional Screening and Coordinating Committee (RSCC) in 1987. Relying on Environment Canada's evaluation, the RSCC concluded that the project's effects on the Peigan would be either 'favourable or mitigable.'[12]

The federal Department of Justice contributed to the frustration experienced by FOR in trying to prosecute the charges laid against Alberta in 1988 for offences under the Fisheries Act. The department was instrumental in dragging out the RCMP investigation of Kostuch's charges for two years, until July 1990, when the federal attorney general decided that prosecution of Alberta wouldn't 'serve the proper administration of justice.' The 1990 decision notwithstanding, Justice reentered the fray in the summer of 1992 to reconsider the evidence and circumstances of the charges, effectively delaying the process for several months.

The RCMP's part in quelling the Lonefighters' 1990 insurrection, however justified, was played out in such a way as to raise questions about the RCMP's methods and judgment. Its actions appeared to have had more to do with exercising authority and dominance than with *maintiens le droit*.[13] Had the force's esteemed ancestors, the North-West Mounted Police, taken the same approach in dealing with the Blackfoot Nation in the late 1800s, Canada might have a history of Indian wars like that of our neighbour to the south.

A major area of federal constitutional responsibility encroached upon by the Oldman River Dam is Indians and Indian lands. These responsibilities go beyond the specific requirements of the treaties, the constitution, and the Indian Act, placing the federal government in a special position of trust with Canadian Indians – in legal terms, a fiduciary relationship.[14] In exercising this fiduciary duty, the federal government 'is obliged to seek the best possible deal for the Indians.'[15] The conflict between Alberta and the Peigan over the Oldman River Dam placed the federal government in the awkward position of having to take the side of the Indians, which presented a threat to the maintenance of the harmonious federal-provincial relations so essential to the resolution of Canada's ongoing constitutional disputes. The law requires that fiduciaries avoid conflicts of interest. Since the federal Crown faced the possibility of having to defend itself in a water rights claim filed by the Peigan against the minister of Indian affairs, it was of the view that to side with the Peigan in its water rights claim against Alberta would be a conflict of interest.[16] These factors influenced the vigour with which the federal government exercised its fiduciary responsibility to the Peigan.

The agency charged with the execution of the federal government's responsibilities for and fiduciary obligations to Indians is the Department of Indian Affairs (IA), which journalist and author Boyce Richardson has described as 'the nation's most obscurantist and anachronistic government department.'[17] In 1987, IA initiated discussions with Alberta on 'the possible adverse impacts the project could have on the river as it crosses the Peigan Reserve.' The proposed discussions were intended to facilitate exercise of the federal fiduciary duty to the Peigan. The deputy minister advised Alberta Environment, 'My Minister must ensure on behalf of the Federal Crown the protection of federal lands reserved for Indian people.'[18] Alberta refused to discuss matters of substance with IA because it feared that the agency might pass information to the Peigan, who could use it as evidence in their water rights suit against Alberta.[19] Obviously impatient with Alberta's intransigence, the deputy minister of Indian affairs wrote to Alberta Environment in October 1988, noting that since 'Canada has not yet decided on its position with respect to litigation [by the Peigan against Alberta,] a full discussion of these concerns [dam impacts on the Peigan] may be worthwhile.'[20] This veiled threat had the desired effect of getting Alberta back to the table, but it did nothing to soften Alberta's attitude towards discussing impacts on the Peigan.[21]

As events transpired, the province had little to fear from the federal watchdog. Alberta found comfort in a report provided by IA indicating that the 'concerns' it wished to discuss were apparently of no consequence. The report, prepared by federal officials, described 'the specific environmental changes which federal officials consider most relevant to the Peigan Band.'[22] It itemized twelve issues, only one of which, mercury methylation, identified as the key issue, was reported to have a potentially deleterious impact on the Peigan. The report even played down this impact, noting that 'reserve residents are unlikely to be affected to a major extent.'[23] No impacts were identified for the eleven 'residual issues,' with the exception of 'modified flow regime,' for which the 'net impact [is] believed to be 'positive.'[24] In April 1989, a senior IA official expressed the understanding that the inter-departmental review committee, 'accepts the provincial view that the dam will improve management of water and there will not be any affect to [sic] Indian lands.'[25]

Throughout, IA seems to have been preoccupied with maintaining its standing with Alberta officials. The department's attitude is captured in a senior official's conclusion that 'We cannot initiate action that is contrary to reasonable development by the Province of Alberta.'[26] A letter to Alberta Environment from IA's deputy minister expressed 'appreciat[ion]' of Alberta's 'willingness to ensure that the project will not *unnecessarily* adversely impact the reserve [emphasis added].'[27] The obvious inference to be drawn was that developments considered reasonable for Alberta that necessarily had an adverse impact on the reserve were acceptable to IA, Peigan views to the contrary notwithstanding. As the pre-EARPGO phase drew to a close, a working level official in IA noted that he was 'not comfortable that the department has met its obligations to the Band and/or the reserve lands on this issue.'[28]

The federal government largely stayed clear of the Lonefighter affair. The minister of Indian affairs avoided the province whenever possible, and there was no attempt by federal politicians or officials to intervene as an intermediary, nor did the federal government ever object to Alberta's unnecessary, untimely, and provocative raids onto the Peigan Reserve.

Despite its proclaimed intention to cooperate in the application of the EARPGO to the Oldman River Dam, IA did its utmost to avoid any direct involvement in the panel review process. Only at the insistence of the panel did IA agree to appear at the public hearings and then only at the Edmonton sitting. The department refused a 'strong request' by the panel to attend the hearings at Brocket. It was only with great reluctance that the department provided a partial record of documentation pertaining to the department's dealings with the Peigan and with Alberta on matters pertaining to the Oldman Project. However unpleasant or bureaucratically inconvenient it might have been for the department, there can surely be no clearer evidence of dereliction of duty or support for Develon Small Legs' assessment that 'Indian Affairs has more or less thrown the Peigan Nation to the wind.'[29] In its final report, the panel indicated its displeasure with all federal departments involved in the environmental review but 'singled out' IA for its particular 'lack of commitment to the process.'[30]

Lest anyone get the idea that its performance on the Oldman was an isolated event, IA went to even greater lengths to dissociate itself from Peigan opposition to Alberta's Pine Coulee Project. In a letter to the joint review panel chairperson, IA advised that it had not been a partner in initiating the federal EARPGO on the project and that its participation in the review would be neither appropriate nor of assistance to the panel.[31] Amongst the department's reasons for its inability to be of assistance was that it 'neither possesses information nor does it have the specialist expertise to address the topics of ... ethnography and socioeconomics.' While the admission that it understands neither Indians, economics, nor Native social issues might seem strange coming from the department charged with responsibility for the affairs of the nation's Indians, it surprised no one familiar with the department's performance over the years. Perhaps the assessment of IA attributed to the late prime minister Louis St. Laurent is closest to the mark. St. Laurent is reported to have referred to the management of the department as 'an almost continuous state of absence of mind.'[32] There has been no noticeable change in that state since St. Laurent's day. Little wonder that the Honourable A.C. Hamilton, fact finder for the minister of Indian affairs, reports, 'Aboriginal peoples still view the Government and the Department of Indian Affairs and Northern Development as adversaries, who look after the needs and demands of others.'[33]

The 1987 Federal Water policy specified a number of initiatives that the federal government intended to take on Native water rights. Amongst those most relevant to Peigan concerns about the Oldman River Dam were commitments to 'clarify with people their water related issues and interests with respect to their treaty areas ... determine how they [Native people] will participate in resource management programs affecting water resources of interest to them ... [and] encourage greater native participation in water allocation and management decisions involving instream and traditional uses.'[34] At the time the controversy over the dam reached its peak, in the early 1990s, neither Environment Canada nor IA had done anything to implement these policies with the Peigan. As of 1999, the policy has yet to be discussed with the Peigan. There are likely few people in Ottawa who are aware of its existence.

In June 1984, the federal cabinet approved the EARPGO and in 1992, the Supreme Court ruled that the minister of transport was required to apply the EARPGO before issuing an approval for the dam under the Navigable Waters Protection Act.[35] Except that DF&O had never taken the trouble to ask cabinet to make a regulation requiring anyone constructing a work to provide information that would enable it to determine whether the work would disrupt fish habitat, it is likely that the minister of fisheries and oceans would also have been on the hook to apply the EARPGO.

The more fundamental question of whether the ministers had a moral or ethical obligation to require an assessment of the environmental impacts of the dam had earlier been placed before at least three federal ministers. The first appeal was in August 1987, when SAEG wrote to the minister of fisheries and oceans, pointing out that the Oldman Dam would have an impact on fisheries, a federal responsibility, and asking if the minister would call for an evaluation of the environmental impacts of the dam.[36] The minister replied, 'In view of the long-standing administrative arrangements that are in place for the management of fisheries in Alberta and the fact that the potential problems associated with the dam are being addressed, I do not propose to intervene in the matter.'[37]

The 'long-standing administrative arrangements' were exactly that – administrative. They did not absolve the federal government of its constitutional responsibilities for fish, nor did they relieve the minister of his responsibility for the protection of fish habitat as detailed in the Fisheries Act. As for Alberta addressing potential problems, reports from the minister's own department made it clear that Alberta had yet to identify many of the potential problems, and that whatever Alberta was contemplating in the way of mitigation did not address the problem of the obstacle to migration posed by the dam, and was not consistent with the 'no net loss of habitat' policy that the federal department encouraged provincial agencies to implement.[38] In its 1991 submission to the federal panel, DF&O admitted that, despite having made arrangements with Alberta 'for the day to day management of the inland fisheries,' the federal minister remains 'responsible to Parliament for the conservation and protection of fish habitat,' and that the operation of the Oldman River Dam would 'directly affect fish habitat.'[39]

In December 1987, FOR wrote to Environment Canada Minister Tom McMillan, 'pleading for the initiation of a Federal Environmental Assessment Review of this project.'[40] The minister's assistant replied that 'the Oldman River Dam Project falls primarily within provincial jurisdiction ... The federal government is not directly involved with the proposal, and, therefore, it would be inappropriate for Environment Canada or Fisheries and Oceans Canada to intervene directly ... [and that] in view of the longstanding administrative arrangements that are in place for the management of the environmental impact assessment proposals and the fisheries in Alberta, and because the potential problems with the dam are being addressed, it is not appropriate for Environment Canada to intervene.'[41] By this time, the federal government, despite having managed to avoid its responsibilities for fish and Indians, *was* directly involved with the proposal. The previous September, Transport Canada had issued its approval for the dam under the Navigable Waters Protection Act – an event which may not have come to the attention of Environment Canada. The 'longstanding administrative arrangements' argument offered by Siddon to excuse his inaction on fish habitat destruction was endorsed by Environment Canada and extended to include 'the management of environmental impact assessment proposals.' No environmental assessments had ever been carried out under the only existing arrangement with Alberta in the environmental area. In fact, the Canada – Alberta Accord for the Protection and Enhancement of Environmental Quality required only 'adequate discussions on possible environmental effects of proposed major developments.'

Indian Affairs consistently refused to act on or to support the Peigan's requests for a federal assessment of the dam under the EARPGO. The Peigan made the first of several requests to the minister of Indian affairs in 1988.[42] The response, from the environment minister's office, claimed that the federal government had no grounds for invoking the EARPGO on a provincial project.[43] In July 1989, Indian Affairs Minister Cadieux claimed that he could not comment on the request because 'this matter is currently before the courts.'[44]

As FOR's quest for an order requiring the federal government to apply the EARPGO wound its way from the federal courts to the Supreme Court, federal lawyers offered spirited opposition at every stage. While defending the constitutionality, the mandatory nature, and the scope of the EARPGO in general, they put the narrowest possible interpretation on the EARPGO, the Navigable Waters Protection Act, and the Fisheries Act, as they applied to the Oldman Dam. One argument, which was to become a familiar refrain in other appeals to the courts by federal lawyers, was that just because a project might have an environmental impact in an area of federal jurisdiction was not sufficient reason to invoke the EARPGO. Another was that the Fisheries Act is concerned with fish habitat, not the environment, which indicates how far federal lawyers were prepared to go in testing the intelligence of the court. They claimed that Alberta's studies, and its public review, had adequately identified and assessed the impacts of the dam on areas of federal jurisdiction and that further review would be a wasteful duplication. The shallowness of these claims was revealed in evidence placed before the federal review panel by public interest groups, the panel's technical experts, and agencies of the very ministers on whose behalf the claims were made.

There was little more that the federal government could have done to buy time for Alberta to finish building its dam.

25
The Federal Watchdog: II

> Environmental assessment has become a cynical, irrational and
> highly discretionary federal policy in Canada.
>
> – Andrew Nikiforuk, 'The Nasty Game': The Failure of
> Environmental Assessment in Canada [1]

An incident early in the life of the ORDEAP could later be seen as an indication of the panel's concern for maintaining the 'credibility' of the federal
environmental assessment review process.[2] The members of the Environmental Assessment Review Panel accepted their appointment with the
knowledge that construction of the dam would proceed during the review.
As they became familiar with the project, they discovered that outlet
valves would be installed in both diversion tunnels before the 1991 spring
run-off. This would limit the flow that could be passed downstream, and
the reservoir would begin to fill. If the run-off was above normal, the reservoir could fill completely, with the result that 'certain recommendations'
that the panel might otherwise wish to make 'would be precluded.' Anxious to ensure that neither the minister nor the public were harbouring
'impossible expectations of the Panel,' Chairman Ross wrote to the minister on 7 January 1991 to advise him 'and the public of [the] consequences
of the construction schedule.'[3] Ross was clear that, while the panel was
'not in a position to recommend that th[e] second diversion tunnel be left
open,' it would 'be desirable to delay [its] closing.' This somewhat open-
ended advice left many opponents of the dam wondering about the panel's
determination.

Ross says that, given the conditions of their appointment, it 'would
have been wrong' of the panel to ask the minister to stop construction.
Conscious of the circus-like atmosphere surrounding the federal review of
the Rafferty-Alameda Project in Saskatchewan, the panel wished to avoid
the minister being 'embarrassed by having to reiterate ... that construction
would be proceeding while the review was underway.'[4] Minister de
Cotret's response – or his 'nonresponse' as one observer characterized it –
side-stepped the issue entirely, which was potentially less embarrassing
and, perhaps, less damaging to the credibility of the process than a rebuff
by Alberta, the likely consequence of a suggestion that construction be
delayed.[5]

The panel was not required to complete its review by any specific time; its directions were to submit its findings and recommendations 'as expeditiously as possible.'[6] The federal cabinet was in no hurry to receive any recommendations from the panel that might lead to a confrontation with Alberta before the dam was completed. The panel, on the other hand, hoped to minimize the time between the completion of the project and the completion of the review, in the interest of maintaining the credibility of the process. The panel's original schedule, drafted before any public consultation, called for public hearings in June 1991 and the submission of recommendations by September. The early public consultations revealed the inadequacy of much of the information pertaining to project impacts that had been made public by Alberta.[7] To allow time to obtain this information, the panel was forced to push its public hearings back to November 1991. This still left only six months for the panel to obtain and consider the additional information before the hearings, and most of this new information was not available to the public until a month or less before the public hearings were to begin in November. Although the panel was aware of this, it did not consider rescheduling the hearings so that intervenors could consider the additional information in the preparation of their submissions. In instances where submissions for or against the project were based on ideological or political grounds, the availability or otherwise of additional information was of little consequence. As became apparent, however, submissions that dealt in an analytical way with environmental, social, or economic impacts might have benefited from the additional information.

The panel's public hearings were conducted fairly and efficiently and were generally well received by the participating public. Even the environmentalists seemed satisfied to have had their views heard and considered. The Peigan reminded the panel of 'the importance of communications in a cross-cultural context' and urged it to 'present the information it receive[d] in a [sic] 'Indian way.'[8] If the panel failed to achieve this it was not from want of effort. The panel held a day of hearings at Brocket on the Peigan Reserve, during which it suspended its rules of procedure in the interest of giving any Indian person who wished to speak the chance to do so. On other occasions the chairperson was liberal in allowing unscheduled presentations by Peigan people and the panel was courteous and attentive in hearing what the speakers had to say.

The panel tried to give equal weight and attention to scientific, social-cultural, and purely political submissions. According to Ross, this reflected 'a very important principle' to which all panel members subscribed: 'that the expression of the consequences on local people of these projects that come from the local people are at least as valuable as *some* of the scientific and technical stuff.'[9] In Ross' mind, 'that's what this whole process is in large part about; if you want scientific and technical analysis, you don't have to hold public hearings, you can sit in closed rooms and do that. What you get is the public understanding ... a different picture ... different ways of expressing what the impacts are. It is not clear to me that those impacts are less important because people express them in different ways.'[10] Throughout the hearings, Ross tried to convey the message that 'cultural and religious things are just as important [as scientific things].'

The panel felt its 'ability to assess fully the consequences of the dam for the Peigan was somewhat diminished' by the Peigan's refusal to release certain information pertaining to cultural and spiritual impacts.[11] In particular, the Peigan refused to release to the panel information collected through a survey funded by FEARO. The Peigan explained that they withheld the information – which they claimed the right to do because their contract with FEARO gave them 'an editorial right' – because of 'the delicate nature of our court case [against Alberta].'[12] The best indications of the impact of the project on the cultural and spiritual values and practices of the Peigan were provided to the panel in the submissions of Dr. Brian Reeves and individual Peigans.[13] In its final report, the panel noted that 'the Peigan declined to participate fully in the ... assessment undertaken by the Panel.'[14]

Though it did not understand the 'detail' of the impacts on the Peigan's 'cultural and religious association with the [Oldman] river,' the panel 'understood the importance of the issue' and concluded that it was 'one of, if not the single most important issue that was not acceptably dealt with [by the proponent].'[15] That view is reflected in the panel's recommendations.

The panel was unanimous in agreeing that the project, as presented, was unacceptable. What it could not agree on was the remedy. Five of the six panel members agreed that the dam should be decommissioned; the sixth member – Tracy Anderson, the only member with close ties to the agricultural community and a resident of the irrigation community – disagreed. There is little reason to doubt that the majority of the panel's members were sincere in their support of this recommendation. It was acknowledged that decommissioning would mean that 'most benefits of the project would be sacrificed,' and 'that individuals [who] have made investments in anticipation of project operation ... may also suffer losses.' However, the panel concluded that 'on balance ... the social, economic and environmental costs of the project outweigh the social, economic and environmental benefits, *even with the construction costs as sunk costs* [emphasis added].' In the end, the panel recommended that the dam be decommissioned, but, 'recogniz[ing] that [decommissioning might] pose insurmountable interjurisdictional difficulties,' it also recommended a 'secondary set of recommendations' that imposed conditions on the operation of the project 'such that the adverse environmental and socio-economic impacts ... would be acceptably mitigated.'[16]

The panel members believed that, to maintain the 'credibility' of the environmental assessment process, their recommendations must be 'principled and pragmatic' but not constrained by their potential political consequences.[17] Paradoxically, the panel seems to have defined its pragmatism in terms of political consequences. The panel's 'preferred' recommendation, though arguably principled, at least to the environmentalists and the Peigan, was obviously not very pragmatic – it 'posed insurmountable inter-jurisdictional difficulties.' If the federal government endorsed the recommendation, Alberta could be expected to refuse to decommission the dam, leaving the federal government in the uncomfortable position of having either to back down or to somehow enforce its edict. Hence, the secondary recommendations, though these appeared to present inter-jurisdictional obstacles every bit as insurmountable as the preferred recommendation.

The secondary recommendations are those in Recommendations 2 to 5. Recommendation 2 is that federal approvals for the project should be conditional on the proponent incorporating measures to protect against or mitigate environmental impacts and reaching agreement with the Peigan on the operation of the dam. The environmental impacts to be protected against included those on fish habitat and riparian ecosystems downstream from the dam.[18] In Ross' words,

> Recommendation 2 was the pragmatic response (though it was also principled), in the sense that a federal government, faced to choose between telling Alberta to decommission the dam or telling Alberta there were conditions that would have to be met in order to operate it, would choose the latter. The necessary conditions were also pragmatic ... for two reasons: first, because they are tough conditions – the project is not very environmentally acceptable and so tough conditions have to be imposed upon it to make it that way. Secondly, because ... in the process of negotiating the tough conditions some things may get lost and if some things get lost it may not be quite as environmentally acceptable as the Panel would like, but if there are some real benefits achieved, then something will have been achieved by this review, and that is what we were shooting for.[19]

Then why make Recommendation 1? Ross says, 'Because five out of six panel members thought it was better yet ... although there was no hope' that it would be accepted.

Ross agrees that the avoidance of inter-jurisdictional difficulties was not the panel's mandate, but the bottom line was that the recommendations had to be 'pragmatic' in order to preserve the credibility of the process. In Ross' mind, the credibility of the process depends on independent panels making recommendations based on their review of information received. But 'if politicians get embarrassed by having a fair and principled recommendation made that they have to turn down, then the politicians get turned off on the process. The process is damaged because the federal politicians are embarrassed by having to do something distasteful, which they might have avoided had the review not taken place.'[20] Which doesn't say much for the principles of politicians or the utility of the process.

Recommendation 3 was designed to involve all 'stakeholders' in the future operation of the project and in the mitigation of its impacts. It called for the formation of an Environmental Management Committee (EMC) 'with full authority to mitigate and continue mitigating the major environmental impacts.'[21] The EMC's operations were to be funded by the proponent, 'within a reasonable fiscal framework for financial account-ability.'[22] Ross says the panel felt the EMC should have 'a fair bit of author-ity' because 'we didn't want the committee to be in a position where it recommended to the proponent and the proponent said "no we can't afford it" ... at the same time we felt it would be irresponsible to suggest it have the authority to manage, so we included some qualifications about financial responsibility.'[23] Since this [stakeholder management committee] approach 'is widely used with considerable success, and because it's the sort of thing that many proponents and government agencies encourage and are willing to participate in,' Ross felt this recommendation was 'in many ways one of the least controversial.'[24]

The panel recommended that the federal government and the Peigan be included on the committee to protect their interests. The members believed that the 'obvious' choice to look out for environmental interests was FOR but recognized there was 'almost no way' that would be accept-able to Alberta. Instead, they recommended that the Alberta Environmen-tal Network nominate members to represent the environmental interests. What the panel wanted was to 'make sure it wasn't the provincial govern-ment that got to name the delegate from the environmental group, because that would be wrong.'[25]

The panel found the 'project has important adverse consequences for the social and cultural economy [sic] of the Peigan,' and that 'the Peigan were not treated fairly in the decision-making, planning or implementa-tion phases of th[e] project.'[26] It concluded that 'the failure of the propo-nent and the Peigans to come to terms over this project is one of the most significant and unacceptable features of the project.'[27] To compensate for these shortcomings, Recommendation 4 called on the federal government to 'establish a negotiating process by which the proponent and the Peigan can reach an agreement on mitigation and compensation for environmen-tal, social and cultural impacts of the project on the Peigan and Peigan Reserve.'[28] The recommendation 'assumes that the parties will reach an agreement to agree and will be able to negotiate, *in good faith,* a reasonable and equitable settlement [emphasis added].'[29]

Recommendation 5 provided a fallback should Alberta refuse to play ball: 'If the proponent fails to comply with Recommendations 2, 3 and 4 then decommission the dam in accordance with Recommendation 1.' The panel added that the conditions under which the panel 'recommend[ed] that the dam continue to operate ... must be fulfilled within a reasonable time.'[30]

The panel was reasonably satisfied with the contributions of individual Fisheries and Oceans and Transport Canada officials at the public hearings. However, it noted that these departments, as well as Environment and Indian Affairs, 'did not provide departmental positions on the issues to the extent that is normal and desirable in panel reviews.'[31] Environment Canada's limited contribution was excused because of 'poor relations' between that department and Alberta Environment.[32] The panel saved its harshest criticism for the performance of Indian Affairs, which Ross characterized as 'simply embarrassing.'[33] The agency was 'unwilling to participate' and told the panel it had 'no responsibility' to contribute to the review.

The panel concluded that 'the federal government has the authority to impose either decommissioning of the Dam or all the recommended conditions.'[34] What the federal government – both the Conservative and Liberal varieties – lacked was the will to do either.

The federal government's first response to the recommendations rejected the option of decommissioning the dam.[35] The following day, Transport Minister Corbeil assured the House of Commons that, although the government had rejected the panel's first recommendation, 'all other recommendations were retained and we will ensure that they are implemented.'[36] For over a year, Ottawa said nothing further about the Oldman. Finally, in September 1993, prodded by the Federal Court to 'move the matter forward,' the minister released the federal government's formal response to the panel's recommendations.[37] It was a masterpiece in public deception. What the government's news release called 'a reasonable and appropriate answer' to the panel's recommendations offered little or, in the case of the more critical recommendations, nothing in the way of protection for the environment or the interests of the Peigan. The government's initial response had rejected the panel's 'preferred recommendation'; without saying so, its considered Response rejected the panel's 'secondary recommendations.'

The key secondary recommendation, what panel chairman Ross called the 'pragmatic response,' was Recommendation 2. It required that federal approvals for the project be conditional on the dam being operated to 'acceptably mitigate' the adverse environmental and socioeconomic impacts of the dam and on agreement between Alberta and the Peigan on the 'mode of operation of the dam.' The federal response was that approval of the project under the Fisheries Act didn't require an environmental assessment under the EARPGO – implying that when this approval was issued it would not include the conditions recommended by the panel, and that, since negotiations between Alberta and the Peigan 'could take some time,' Transport *might* issue the Navigable Waters Protection Act Approval before those negotiations were completed. Sure enough, the news release that announced the federal Response included the news that 'the approval of the dam under the Navigable Waters Protection Act was also issued today.' The conditions of the Approval made no mention of operation to mitigate environmental or socioeconomic impacts.[38] Negotiations between Alberta and the Peigan, far from being completed, had yet to begin.

In expanding on Recommendation 3, which called for the creation of an Environmental Management Committee (EMC), the panel had stressed that it was important the EMC be independent 'to allay fears that the proponent is itself defining the mitigation measures and determining the success of the programs.'[39] The federal Response endorsed the Environmental Advisory Committee (EAC) announced by Alberta Environment in July 1993. The 'purpose and mandate' of the Alberta committee was to *'advise the Department* [emphasis added]' on matters pertaining to dam operations and mitigation programs; it had *no* authority and its members were appointed exclusively by the Alberta minister for terms 'at the Minister's pleasure.'[40]

The federal Response did support Recommendation 4, the establishment of a process by which the Peigan and Alberta could negotiate an agreement on mitigation of the project's impacts. As the federal government has demonstrated convincingly over the years, when dealing with Native communities, talk comes cheap.

The trump card dealt to the federal government was Recommendation 5. It stated, quite simply, that should Alberta 'fail to comply with' Recommendations 2 through 4, 'then decommission the dam.' The federal Response was that 'decommissioning of the dam would be considered only under subsection 6(1) of the *Navigable Waters Protection Act.*'[41] What this meant was that if Alberta balked at compliance, the federal government would *consider* decommissioning the dam, but only if it was 'not maintained in accordance with' plans approved by the minister. This provision might be stretched to mean if not operated in accordance with the conditions attached to the federal approval but, as has been noted, those conditions required nothing of Alberta with respect to environmental impact or agreement with the Peigan. In rejecting Recommendation 5, the federal government discarded its trump card and denied the Peigan whatever leverage it might have provided them in their negotiations with Alberta.

It was earlier suggested that the panel's secondary recommendations package posed as many 'insurmountable inter-jurisdictional difficulties' as did its preferred recommendation. The federal Response surmounted any such inter-jurisdictional difficulties by the simple expedient of interpreting them in ways that were favourable to Alberta – a degree of pragmatism far in excess of what the panel had in mind. The federal government's acquiescence was subsequently compounded by the issuance of the Navigable Waters Protection Act Approval, with its limited and vague conditions pertaining to the environment; the endorsement of Alberta Environment's June 1994 Operating Strategy for the dam, including the fish rule curve, which, as was earlier observed, has more to do with politics than biology, as the determinant of flow requirements for fish; and the issuance of the Fisheries Act Authorization, which requires that, in operating the Oldman Dam, Alberta need only 'take into account the protection of fish habitat.'

Those, such as FOR, who had hoped for a better federal performance on matters related to the Oldman Dam after the Liberal Party took office in Ottawa were disappointed. The Liberals have supported the federal Response authored under the previous government in its entirety, and, despite the assurances given to FOR while still in opposition, the Liberals in government made no move to influence the operating regime for the dam. Both the endorsement of Alberta's June 1994 Operating Strategy and issuance of the Fisheries Act Authorization occurred under the Liberal government. There has been no meaningful progress towards negotiating an agreement between Alberta and the Peigan.

26
Iniquity and Betrayal

The Panel recommends a partnership be established between a sensitive Alberta government and the Peigan peoples.

– The Environment Council of Alberta, 1979[1]

The Peigan were not treated fairly in the decision making, planning or implementation phases of this project.

– Oldman River Dam Environmental Assessment Panel, 1992[2]

The panel did not say exactly who was responsible for the unfair treatment of the Peigan, nor was there any need to do so. The Government of Alberta was the main decision maker, and its departments of Environment and Public Works were responsible for the planning and implementation of the project. The Government of Canada, by its acquiescence, and its agencies, particularly Indian Affairs, but also Environment, Transport, and Fisheries and Oceans, by dereliction of their duties, aided and abetted Alberta's unfair treatment of the Peigan. Given the history of Indian-government relations in Canada, it was simply business as usual.

Despite this legacy of unfair treatment, the panel believed that the Peigan could yet 'reduce the negative impacts and derive some positive benefits if they were to reach an agreement with the proponent.'[3] Though left unsaid, the clear implication was that the governments that had treated the Peigan so unfairly in the past would have to treat them fairly in the future. Fairness doesn't seem too much to expect of our governments – it's what we expect of our children; its what we all learn in kindergarten.[4] It didn't happen after 1978, of course, nor has it happened since 1992. Anyone who wants to take the time to ponder this might want to consider the explanation offered by one Brian McInnis, who, in 1994, earned brief fame, or notoriety, for blowing the whistle on the Canadian Security Intelligence Service. McInnis said, 'It is easier to do the right thing than the wrong thing. It just rarely occurs to people in government to do the right thing.'[5]

One reason communication and accommodation between the Peigan and the governments is so elusive is because Canada's Indians, in their newly awakened state, think of themselves as nations and would prefer that others do likewise. Governments, on the other hand, though in the interests of political correctness they may refer to Indian bands as Nations, still regard them as troublesome dependants, in the federal case, or, in the Alberta case, as just another interest group. Indian bands, generally, are of the opinion that Canada did not live up to the terms of the treaties, and in the Peigan's case, this view extends to other agreements entered into with the federal government and with Alberta. For example, the Peigan are convinced that the federal government acted outside the law when it authorized the transfer of reserve land for the original LNID weir and that Alberta has reneged on the April 1981 agreement granting it access to the weir. American author Jerry Mander attributes the liberal violation of Indian treaties in the United States to a sense amongst politicians and bureaucrats that 'Indians are somehow not people in the same category as the English [for example], and so deals can be made with them in a less earnest fashion.'[6] The same explanation may hold in Canada. Sociologist Joan Ryan suggests that Canada's Indians are regularly subjected to 'institutionalized racism,' which she defines as a condition where 'an institution such as the courts or the government is not concerned about the rights of the people whom they administer.'[7]

From the Peigan perspective, Alberta's unfairness might, charitably, be characterized as a failure to act in 'good faith.' Alberta's acts of bad faith sometimes marginalized the Peigan by simply ignoring their presence or discounting entirely their interests in the Oldman and in their own heritage. In some instances, however, they involved imposing Alberta's will on the Peigan by using the province's superior position to dictate the terms and conditions for interaction with the Peigan or for entering into negotiations. And at other times, they took the form of overt acts to subjugate the Peigan, as in the two Alberta Environment raids onto the Peigan Reserve in 1990, or to preempt the exercise of some future initiative by the Peigan, as in the allocation of the Oldman River water reserved by the 1991 regulation.

Alberta's exercise of bad faith began in the Lougheed era with the government's dismissal of the Peigan's joint-venture proposal without any attempt to negotiate an arrangement more favourable to the province and with its failure to live up to many of its non-cash covenants under the 1981 LNID weir agreement. Indian Affairs reported in 1991 that 'the Peigans have recently identified a number of areas where the province has not honoured its obligations under this agreement in the areas of Peigan rights, the provision of technical assistance for the development of an irrigation system on the reserve, and the provision of adequate safety precautions.'[8] In the early years of the Getty era, Alberta threw money at the Peigan to buy time to get dam construction under way and avoid negotiation of a settlement. The Peigan countered by launching its court action against the province and the dam in 1986. As it had done in the wake of the Peigan's blockade of the LNID weir, Alberta dug in its heals and refused to negotiate anything as long as the Peigan continued with the threat of a law suit.

Alberta used obstructionist tactics to frustrate the Peigan's attempt to obtain an early decision from the courts on whether the band has reserved water rights. The objective of the Peigan's court action was to obtain a declaration relating to its water rights and to have the court determine the amount of water the band is entitled to. Faced with a long and potentially expensive time before the courts, the Peigan moved to have the case tried in two stages: a first stage to settle the question of whether the Peigan has reserved water rights, and, if the courts ruled in the band's favour, a 'more lengthy and expensive' second stage to determine how much water the band was entitled to. The Peigan entertained the hope that, if the courts ruled in the band's favour at the first stage, it might be possible to negotiate its water entitlement with the province, and thus avoid a costly second round of litigation.[9] The province refused to cooperate and successfully opposed the Peigan's application to have the Court sever the trial. Appealing to the minister of Indian affairs for financial support, Chief Bastien said, 'It is truly open to question whether, without funding, the band will be able to assert its claim to water rights.'[10] Bastien could see 'no apparent reason' for Alberta's actions 'except to obstruct the process of the law suit.' He captured the iniquity of the situation in his observation that 'the Attorney General of Alberta has sought at every stage to make the litigation more expensive, more difficult for the band. This is something the Attorney General of Alberta can do because of course the province has deep pockets. The band is not in the same position.'[11] As was soon to become apparent, Alberta's reason for obstructing the process of the Peigan's law suit had everything to do with the success of its irrigation expansion strategy.

Alberta Environment's mitigation planning program for the project paid no more heed to the interests of the Peigan than had the original decision to build the dam. Given the Peigan's long period of occupation of the Oldman basin and the acknowledged importance of the river, the river valley, and their resources to the history of the Peigan, their traditional way of life, and their religious beliefs and practices, it might be supposed that Alberta would have considered the impact of the dam on these to be major components of its mitigation plan. Such was not the case. There was no Peigan involvement in the design or implementation of the prehistoric (archaeological) portion of Alberta's Historical Resource Impact Assessment. This omission reflected both the philosophy inherent in Alberta's Historical Resources Act and the attitude of the Archaeological Survey of Alberta (ASA). The act claims all archaeological 'resources' for the Crown, and neither the act nor the practices of the ASA make any allowance for the interests of Indian people, who consider those same archaeological resources to be a living record of their culture and history. In contrast, the study of historic, or what Reeves refers to as non-Native or 'white,' resources included the 'involvement of many people throughout the area,' and an extensive program of interviews with community members to 'satisfy the interests and needs of local groups interested in preserving the area's history.'[12]

The Peigan were invited to nominate a representative to sit on the Historical and Archaeological Resources Sub-committee of the Local Advisory Committee, an organization of local people who, among other things, reviewed the mitigation plan. The Peigan, who regarded the invitation to sit as a representative of a local interest group as one more attempt by Alberta to marginalize their interests, reluctantly complied. It was a no-win proposition for the Peigan. Acceptance of a place on the LAC allowed Alberta to offer it as evidence of Peigan acceptance of the project and the mitigation concept; had the Peigan declined representation, they would have stood accused of turning their backs on an opportunity to protect their interests.

The Lonefighters' uprising in 1990 provided Alberta with a number of opportunities to turn the tables on the Peigan. With the unwitting assistance of the federal government, FOR, the local media, and the Peigan themselves, Alberta exploited the situation to its maximum advantage. The right-wing press characterized the Lonefighter leaders as persons of dubious virtue. The diversion attempt did not have the blessing of the Peigan Chief and Council, nor could the Lonefighters claim the support of a majority of reserve residents. The timing was bad. The uprising took place at the same time as the more dramatic events at Oka, which entirely absorbed the attention of the federal government and the national media. The act of diverting the river, had it been successful, would have been a breach of provincial law. The local media, encouraged by Lonefighter rhetoric, focused on the 'circus' aspects of the affair and exaggerated the potential threat posed by the diversion attempt, which by Alberta Environment's own admission was virtually nonexistent.

All of these factors worked in Alberta's favour. The province was able to attack Peigan opposition to the dam, as symbolized by the Lonefighters, without attacking the Peigan Band, its leaders, or reserve residents – something that they had previously been unable to do. Government spokespersons, following the lead of the local media, and spared interference by the federal government or attention from the national media, were able to focus attention on the Lonefighters' potentially illegal act – unauthorized river diversion, so managing to avoid debate about what had motivated the Lonefighters' action – Alberta's unwillingness to negotiate a settlement with the Peigan. The fact that what the Lonefighters were attempting was illegal and posed a threat to third parties – irrigation farmers and communities dependent on the water supply – allowed the government to occupy the high ground, gave it another excuse for refusing to negotiate with the Peigan, and seemed to justify it taking a confrontational rather than a conciliatory approach to resolving the impasse. The Lonefighters' inflated estimates of the progress of the diversion attempt and of its imminent success, dutifully reported by the media, provided public justification for the 7 September Alberta Environment-RCMP raid onto the reserve.

The unnecessary and indefensible nature of this foray onto Peigan land was eclipsed by the mindless and futile action of the Lonefighters' leader, who, in a moment of panic or exuberance, discharged his rifle to the heavens. This inexplicable and pointless act of defiance, which led to what the media characterized as an 'armed stand-off,' was of inestimable good fortune for the government forces. It appeared to justify, however weakly, the government's armed invasion, and allowed the government to portray what was an act of provocation in response to an act of civil disobedience as a show of tolerance and measured restraint in response to reckless and dangerous behaviour. It also provided the government with a long sought-after 'villain,' someone whom they could, and did, prosecute mercilessly as an example to others who might contemplate overt action to stop the dam. Alberta's victory over the Lonefighters was a loss for the Peigan Band and a major setback in its struggle to negotiate some benefit from the dam.

A final example of Alberta's unfairness towards the Peigan during the Getty era went virtually unnoticed, because only those who were reasonably well informed about the practice of water management in Alberta connected it with the dam and the Peigan's water rights suit against the province. The penultimate step in the process that the government had set in motion to expand irrigation in southern Alberta was to ensure that the irrigation community had first call on the water stored by the Oldman River Dam. This was achieved by passing the Order in Council that reserved the water for specified irrigation developments and then licensing the water for exclusive use by those developments. In putting this arrangement into effect, Alberta Environment discriminated against the Peigan by not consulting with them, as it had with the irrigation districts, in establishing the number of hectares to be designated for development and for which water would be reserved. Consequently, though the Peigan had determined that there were 21,000 hectares on the reserve that could be irrigated, Alberta Environment arbitrarily designated only 6,070 hectares of reserve land as eligible for a water allocation. At the same time, 37,000 hectares were designated for irrigation expansion in irrigation districts in the Oldman Basin and the districts were subsequently awarded additional allocations of 370,000 cubic decametres of water to supply the expansion acreage.

This action was taken in full knowledge that the Peigan were in the process of asking the Court of Queen's Bench to award it a water allocation sufficient to irrigate about 21,000 hectares of land. The amount of water that Alberta had reserved for the Peigan – about 55,000 cubic decametres – was substantially less than what Alberta Environment knew the Peigan would be asking the Court to award – something in the neighbourhood of 185,000 cubic decametres. The preemptive allocation to the irrigation districts will make it more difficult for a court to make the award requested by the Peigan. It will be argued that the water could be made available to the Peigan only by taking it away from others to whom it has already been allocated – farmers who, by then, will have invested in the equipment required to irrigate with the water and the success of whose farming operations will have come to depend on that irrigation. Considered in this light, Alberta's determination to delay the settlement of the Peigan's water rights suit was much more than simple bloody-mindedness.

Alberta's unfair treatment of the Peigan continues under the Klein government. In May 1997, Alberta advised Indian Affairs that it was finally ready to open the negotiations with the Peigan recommended by the ORDEAP in 1992. Since the federal government has already issued its approvals for the dam, the Peigan will have little leverage if negotiations ever do get under way.

Testimony at a 1994 federal-provincial hearing on Alberta's Pine Coulee water development project revealed that the province's practice of dealing unfairly with the Peigan on water management issues has become something of a tradition. The project is located within the Peigan's traditional territory and it will deplete the flow of the Oldman River, both of which would suggest that the project has implications for the Peigan.

Despite a claim by Public Works that Pine Coulee would not be a controversial project like the Oldman River Dam, there was little about the way it was handled that wasn't deja vu to the Peigan. Alberta did not formally advise the band of the proposal until the environmental impact assessment, which did not consider any potential impacts on the Peigan, had been completed; the Peigan were not consulted on their historical use of the area, any connections it might have with Peigan cultural or religious practices, the interpretation of the 'archaeological resources' found in the area – some of which are considered sacred by the Peigan – or on the mitigation of impacts on those resources. The additional water that will be allocated to irrigators served by the project will further preempt the Peigan's water rights claim. It was, the Peigan's lawyer said, 'as if the Peigans were invisible.' Lawyers acting for Alberta Environment and Public Works vigorously opposed the Peigan's status as an intervenor and their eligibility for public funding to present their case at the public hearings, claiming that the Peigan would not be affected by the project. During the course of the public hearing – a formally conducted, quasi-judicial process that lent itself more to legal theatrics than to informed communication – Alberta's lawyers expended more effort in attempting to discredit the

Peigan than in defending the shortcomings of the province's studies and procedures. The bullying tactics employed by Alberta's lawyers, which one editorial writer called 'Pine Coulee hardball,' were clearly intended to intimidate the Peigan spokespersons.[13]

Alberta's attitude towards the interests of the Peigan and the public interest in general was effectively summed up in the closing statement of the government lawyer acting for Public Works. He maintained that the department had operated in accordance with 'existing laws,' and that, since those laws claimed ownership of all of the water and all of the archaeological 'resources' affected by the project, the department could 'call the shots' as to how those resources were used.

If Alberta Environment or Alberta Public Works had learned anything from their experience on the Oldman, it was not evident at the Pine Coulee hearings. A Public Works spokesperson was quoted as asking, 'Who in their right mind in government would be proposing a project of this kind if it has major problems?'[14] Who, indeed?

The NRCB/EARP Panel's refusal to comment on the Peigan's claims or to consider them in framing its recommendations on Pine Coulee was an indication of the treatment that the Peigan can expect when Alberta and the federal government implement their plans to 'harmonize' their environmental impact assessment processes.

In November 1997, a joint federal-provincial hearing was held on another Alberta water project (Little Bow Project/Highwood Diversion Plan) that has similar implications for the Peigan. The process leading up to the hearings and the hearings themselves were in most ways a repetition of the Pine Coulee experience. The NRCB/CEAA Little Bow/Highwood Panel reported in May 1998. It dismissed the Peigan's water concerns, having been persuaded by WMS that 'should the outcome of the long-standing litigation favour the Peigan and they receive more water allocation [sic] and a prior right to that water than [sic] almost all present rights holders, sufficient water or an appropriate water management plan can be found or already exists [sic] to accomodate [sic] that eventuality.'[15]

In May 1992, the federal review panel recommended that federal approvals for the Oldman Dam should be withheld until Alberta and the Peigan had agreed on compensation for Peigan 'cultural and spiritual losses in the reservoir area' and on water allocation to the Peigan. As an interim measure until the Peigan's water allocation had been agreed upon, the panel recommended that the ministers 'ensure that the maximum amount of water that might be allocated to the Peigan be reserved and not allocated to others.'[16] In September 1993, though no agreement between Alberta and the Peigan was in sight, Transport Canada issued federal approval for the dam under the Navigable Waters Protection Act. This blatant contradiction of the panel's recommendations, which the federal government rationalized on weak legal grounds, was pointed out in an open letter from Peigan Chief Bastien to the minister of Indian affairs.[17] There was no public response. In August of 1994, with still no agreement between Alberta and the Peigan on water allocation or compensation for cultural and spiritual losses, or even a start to negotiation of these matters, Fisheries and Oceans issued the other federal approval that the panel had recommended be withheld, its authorization to operate the dam under the Fisheries Act. There was no indication that the federal government had made the least attempt to get Alberta to hold in reserve 'the maximum amount of water that might be allocated to the Peigan.' While such an attempt would no doubt have been fruitless, it would, at least, have indicated that the federal government was trying to get 'the best possible deal for the Indians.' To the contrary, its observation that Alberta had 'designated' water for 6,070 hectares of irrigation on the Peigan Reserve signalled that, in the federal view, the Peigan had no entitlement to water beyond that which Alberta might confer upon them, a position consistent with their earlier and ongoing refusal to support the Peigan in their water rights suit against Alberta.[18]

The issuance of these federal approvals before any agreement between the Peigan and Alberta further undercut the Peigan's already weak bargaining position and threw federal support squarely behind Alberta. It also revealed that the federal government discounted the Peigan's cultural and spiritual losses even more than did the panel. To anyone familiar with the federal bureaucracy's unrivalled capacity for avoiding action, the limp excuse that 'the applicable federal legislation does not confer authority to withhold approvals until such agreement is reached' is laughable.[19]

The governments of Canada and Alberta argue that they acted entirely within the law in their dealings with the Peigan on the Oldman issue. Laws, however, generally offer some considerable latitude for their interpretation and most allow for substantial ministerial discretion in their application. Hardly any prohibit governments from doing the right or decent thing. Over the past century, our various federal governments have steadfastly avoided doing the decent thing when it came to dealing with Canada's indigenous peoples on issues ranging from land claims to allowances for war veterans. This regrettable behavioural trait has been adopted and liberally exercised by our provincial governments, nowhere more so than in Alberta. Canadians observing such behaviour in other nations are quick to label it as discrimination and abuse of human rights. Unfortunately, when we see it in our own backyard, we seem willing to accept it as the way things are.

27
The Peigan, Politics, and the Courts

Native peoples' ability to twinge the consciences of Canadians is nearing its limit.

– Richard Gwynn, *Nationalism without Walls*[1]

The Peigan explained to the federal panel in 1991 that they had adopted a two-pronged strategy in working towards the resolution of their concerns with the Oldman Project: political action and legal action. The political action was directed at getting Alberta to negotiate a settlement of the Peigan's compensation claims and their water rights claims. The legal action was directed at getting the courts to declare that the Peigan had treaty rights to the Oldman River and its water and to award the Peigan a specific allocation of water for their exclusive use. Neither proved effective. On the political side, the Peigan lacked the political skills, the federal support, and the bargaining chips required to get Alberta to the table to begin negotiations. It was their perception of these weaknesses and the futility of the Peigan's attempted negotiations that convinced the Lonefighters of the need to adopt more desperate measures. But the Lonefighters' inability to obtain the approval and support of Chief and Council and a clear majority of reserve residents prevented them from presenting the appearance of a united front as the Mohawk Warriors had done so successfully at Oka. Alberta took advantage of the Chief and Council's indecision to force the issue with the Lonefighters and gain the upper hand.

Throughout the Oldman controversy, the federal government consistently refused to exercise its fiduciary duty to support the Peigan or to intervene with Alberta on the Peigan's behalf to 'seek the best possible deal for the Indians.' By disregarding or ignoring the recommendations of the panel and issuing federal approvals for the dam before Alberta and the Peigan reached agreement on compensation, the federal government systematically weakened both its own and the Peigan's bargaining positions.

The Peigans introduced two concepts into the Oldman controversy that are basic to the ongoing misunderstandings between Natives and non-natives in Canada: Aboriginal rights and treaty rights. Though these concepts come up in any discussion of Native rights, they figure most prominently in arguments over Native land claims. In the case of the Oldman

River Dam, the Peigan used these concepts to support their claim to ownership and use of the waters of the Oldman River.

In 1973, the Supreme Court of Canada recognized the legality of Aboriginal rights deriving from the historic occupation and possession of their tribal lands.[2] In its suit against Alberta, the Peigan described the 'tract of land over which the Peigan Nation [historically] owned and exercised jurisdiction' as encompassing the area from the Red Deer River south to the Yellowstone River in the United States, and from the Rocky Mountains east to the Cypress Hills.[3] This is the same territory that most historical accounts refer to as the territorial range of the entire Blackfoot Confederacy, the Canadian portion of which is approximately that ceded by the representatives of the various tribes that signed Treaty 7. Historically, governments have countered with the claim that Aboriginal rights were extinguished when European nations 'discovered' and occupied the lands.[4] A 1985 ruling in Ontario, upheld by the Supreme Court of Canada, established that 'aboriginal rights exist at the pleasure of the Crown and can be extinguished by treaty, legislation or administrative acts.'[5] Native people conceive Aboriginal rights to include, among other things, rights to ownership of land and resources, cultural and spiritual rights, legal recognition of traditional law, and the inherent right of self-government. Frequently, what Native people identify as a right, non-Natives consider a claim. The most familiar example is what are commonly referred to, from the non-Native perspective, as land claims.

Although the Canadian Constitution Act, 1982, recognized the existence of Aboriginal rights and a subsequent amendment to the act set out a process for their definition and identification, there has yet to emerge any general agreement as to what those rights are or what they include. In 1979, the Federal Court set out the conditions that would have to be established for it to recognize the validity of an Aboriginal land title claim. The conditions are that it must be established that the Natives making the claim, and their ancestors, lived within and were members of an organized society; that the society occupied the specific territory over which title was claimed; and that they had exclusive occupation of the territory at the time that the British claimed sovereignty over it.[6]

Over the years, other court decisions have dealt with a variety of questions relating to the rights of Native people, and while there has been some progress in clarifying Aboriginal rights as they pertain to 'traditional practices,' such as hunting and fishing, there have been no startling breakthroughs on ownership of land and resources or the question of Aboriginal rights in general. In 1996, the Supreme Court 'rejected the notion that claims to aboriginal rights could be determined on a general basis'; it ruled that they must be established on 'a case by case basis.'[7] The court said that 'in order to be considered an aboriginal right, an activity must be an

element of a practice, custom or tradition integral to the distinctive culture of the aboriginal group claiming the right ... [and] which has continuity with traditions, customs and practices that existed prior to contact
[with European society].'

One of the most publicized Aboriginal rights cases involves a claim by
the Gitksan and Wet'suwet'en Bands to a large area in British Columbia. In
1991, the BC Supreme Court ruled that the bands' Aboriginal rights had
been 'extinguished' by the European 'discovery' and occupation of lands
in British Columbia before confederation.[8] The BC Court of Appeal partially overturned the judgment in 1993, ruling that British Columbia did
not have the constitutional capacity to extinguish Aboriginal rights but,
since the bands had not proved their ownership of and jurisdiction over
the land, that they were entitled only to use and occupy parts of the territory that they claimed, but had no right to exclude others from the land
and resources, nor to govern, manage, conserve, or transfer them.[9] The
Supreme Court of Canada agreed to hear an appeal of the BC Court of
Appeal's ruling, filed by the Gitskan and Wet'suwet'en, but in June 1994,
the bands and the BC Crown agreed to suspend the hearing while they
attempted to negotiate a settlement to the dispute. After eighteen months
of what it called 'futile' negotiations, British Columbia withdrew from the
talks and the bands reactivated the appeal to the Supreme Court. The
Court heard the appeal and released its ruling on 11 December 1997.[10] It
upheld the BC Appeal Court's ruling that the band's Aboriginal rights had
not been extinguished, and it confirmed the conditions for establishing
Aboriginal title set out by the Federal Court in 1979, but it concluded that
a new trial was required because the trial judge had not taken into account
the oral histories presented by the bands to establish their occupation and
use of the land in question. The Court encouraged the bands to seek a
negotiated settlement of their claims with the federal and provincial governments rather than returning to litigation. Both governments indicated
they would prefer to negotiate settlement of the claim, which is where
things stood in June 1994.

Alberta's official position on Aboriginal water rights is that they were
'extinguished' by the legislation and actions of the Canadian government.[11] This notion that all Aboriginal rights were somehow extinguished
by the actions and legislation of successive rulers of what is now Canada is
adhered to by the federal and most provincial governments in Canada.[12]

Treaty rights are those rights granted to Indian people in treaties entered
into with the Crown – in the Peigan case, Treaty 7. 'Existing' treaty rights,
like Aboriginal rights, are 'recognized and affirmed' in s. 35 of the Constitution Act, 1982. There are large areas of disagreement between Native
people and the federal and provincial governments as to the interpretation of the treaties. In the case of the Peigan and the Oldman River Dam,

there is a major disagreement between the Peigan and the Province of Alberta over the right to the water of the Oldman River.

Indian Reserve No. 147 and the Peigan's occupance thereof, is a consequence of Treaty 7. This particular treaty was negotiated and signed by a group of treaty commissioners, acting on behalf of Queen Victoria, and the chiefs of the five Indian bands that occupied what is now southern Alberta, in 1877.[13] The basics of the treaty are that the Indians agreed to 'cede, release, surrender and [lest there be any doubt] yield up ... forever ... all their rights, titles and privileges whatsoever ... to the lands' within the area encompassed by the treaty or anywhere else.[14] In exchange, the Indians received from 'Her Majesty's bounty and benevolence' the right to hunt, subject to government regulation, on Crown land in the treaty area not taken up for other purposes; reserves 'of sufficient area to allow one square mile for each family of five persons'; and a variety of tools, seed, and livestock 'for the encouragement of the practice of agriculture among the Indians.'[15] The Peigan's reserve was to be 'on the Old Man's River, near the foot of the Porcupine Hills, at a place called 'Crow's Creek.' On 15 May 1889, the federal government passed an Order in Council creating Indian Reserve No. 147, an area of 470 square kilometres in this general location.

By 1882, Crowfoot, the Blackfoot chief who was the nominal head of the Blackfoot Confederacy and whose name heads the list of chiefs who signed the treaty, was accusing the government of breaking the treaty promises. There can be little doubt that the Indian leaders who signed the treaties, though they were aware that they were giving something to the white men, did not have a clear understanding of what was in the treaty.[16] Not only did they neither read nor speak the English language, many of the concepts that are fundamental to the treaties, for example, the exclusive ownership of land, were alien to their culture. Dickason says that the Indians believed that in signing the treaties, 'they were not alienating their lands, but sharing them.'[17]

Authors like Leroy Little Bear argue that the traditional Indian way of thinking about the relationship between human beings and the land did not include the concept of ownership. Rather, they considered land and resources as a gift of the Creator to be shared by all human beings, and other beings as well. Because they did not think of themselves as owners, they could not conceive of giving up something they didn't have, thus alienating themselves from the land and resources. According to Little Bear, the 'norm of the aboriginal peoples' law is that land is not transferable and therefor is inalienable ... the subject of the treaty, from the Indians' viewpoint, was not the alienation of the land but the sharing of the land.'[18]

Much of the debate today revolves around interpretation of the treaty – what it says as opposed to what the Indian leaders who signed it may have believed it to say, and what, though unsaid, is implied by the treaty. The notion that Indian people did not understand what they had agreed to is not of recent origin. Within two years of the treaty having been signed, a Jesuit who was present at the negotiations said, 'unhesitatingly,' that the Indians did not understand the treaty but had signed it because they 'did not wish to offend' the authorities by whom they had been 'kindly dealt with,' and because they hoped that the treaty meant a continuation of that treatment.[19] Historian Hugh Dempsey says 'the speeches of the [Indian] leaders imply that they were signing treaty because of their faith in Colonel Macleod, rather than any comprehension of the terms.'[20] One cannot help but wonder what Colonel Macleod would think of the outcome.

Contemporary Indians, be they elders or younger leaders, claim that many of the things that the signatory chiefs thought that they had agreed to were either not understood in the same way by the commissioners or were simply not recorded in the treaty. For example, Peigan elders claim that the location for a Peigan Reserve stipulated in Treaty 7 was actually Chief Sitting Behind Eagle Tailfeathers' response to an order 'to select a place where he would call home,' and that the area he had in mind was much larger than the 470 square kilometres set aside for the Peigan in Reserve No. 147. In fact, some elders claim that what he really meant was all of the land from Waterton Park to the Porcupine Hills and from the Rocky Mountains to Fort Macleod.[21] In its submission to the NRCB/EARP Panel hearing arguments for and against Alberta's proposed Pine Coulee Project in 1994, the Peigan describe the area selected by the chief as the area in which the Peigan 'would live' and which he understood would be 'reserved for their exclusive benefit' as 'defined by the following natural boundaries: (a) the Oldman River (from the headwaters, including lands and resources encompassed by the Oldman River's tributaries), (b) the Porcupine Hill, and (c) the Crow Lodge River (now called Waterton River).'[22]

Modern-day Peigans also claim that, since Treaty 7 is clear in its intent that the Indians should give up their life as nomadic hunters to practise agriculture on their reserve lands, it can be inferred that the government, having reserved land for the Peigan for that purpose, intended also to reserve sufficient water from the Oldman River for the Peigan to irrigate that land so that they might farm with the same success as their white neighbours.[23] This interpretation was encouraged by the Indian Association of Alberta's 1970 Red Paper, presented to the federal government in response to its 1969 White Paper on the future of the Department of Indian Affairs.[24] The Red Paper petitioned the government to accept that 'the intent and spirit of the treaties must be our guide, not the precise letter of a foreign language' on the grounds that 'treaties that run forever must have room for changes in the conditions of life.' From that perspective, the Red Paper claimed that 'machinery and livestock symbolized economic development.' The Supreme Court of Canada appeared to add its weight to this view when, in a 1990 judgment, it said that the existing Aboriginal rights recognized and affirmed in s. 35(1) of the Constitution Act, 1982, 'must be interpreted flexibly so as to permit their evolution over time.'[25]

Although he thinks it unlikely that the chiefs who signed the treaty comprehended its meaning, Dempsey is of the view that some of the problems of treaty interpretation are the result of 'modern Indians applying their own late twentieth century concepts to nineteenth century situations, crediting to the treaty chiefs an innate knowledge of mineral rights, land leases and property values.'[26] A proposal submitted to the federal government in 1991 offers an example of a twentieth-century Peigan interpretation of Treaty 7: 'Part of the bargain struck between Canada and the Peigan was that, in exchange for a much larger territory possessed by the Peigan and other members of the Blackfoot nation, the smaller territory reserved by [sic] the Band required the use of all its resources (land and water) to develop an economy to sustain a permanent homeland.'[27] This may be implicit in the treaty, and consistent with the Supreme Court's direction that treaties should be 'liberally construed' in the Indian's favour but the words and syntax are clearly late twentieth century.[28]

These interpretations create an embarrassing dilemma for non-Natives and their governments. To deny the inference that Treaty 7 reserved some water for the Peigan is to admit that our ancestors swindled the Indians; to accept the inference is to admit that subsequent generations, including the present one, swindled the Indians by allocating all of the water to non-Natives. Since neither the Indians nor the commissioners had any experience with the practice of agriculture in the Treaty 7 area, it is unlikely that either gave any thought to the need for irrigation, but this may be an instance of what the Supreme Court justices were thinking when they spoke of rights evolving over time.

The particular types of Aboriginal or treaty rights that came to be at issue in the Oldman River Dam controversy were the rights claimed by the Peigan to the use of the water of the Oldman River and to ownership of the river bed on the Peigan Reserve.

In 1988, Richard Bartlett, at the time a law professor at the University of Saskatchewan, published a book on Aboriginal water rights in Canada.[29] Bartlett argued that Indians in Canada have both Aboriginal and treaty rights to water. He concluded that Aboriginal water rights are probably limited in kind and amount by traditional and historic uses, but if a major water resource project was ever challenged in court on the basis of infringement of Aboriginal water rights, those rights would likely prove sufficient to 'restrain' the development of the project. As for treaty rights, Bartlett noted that on numerous occasions the Supreme Court of Canada has stated that the treaties should be interpreted liberally in favour of what the

Indians may have understood at the time of their signing. And since this 'principle of interpretation' is the same as that applied by US courts, it 'suggests the significant precedential value of Indian water law of the United States.' Noting, in particular, the 'Winters doctrine,'[30] Bartlett concluded that 'Canadian law recognizes a treaty right to water for traditional and *contemporary* uses by the Indians [emphasis added].'[31] As persuasive as Bartlett's arguments may seem, the fact is that no water claims similar to those of the Peigan on the Oldman have been adjudicated by the courts in Canada.

As with other kinds of rights, the Indian interpretation of the treaties and Indian oral histories reflect an understanding that is frequently at odds with what modern-day governments and resource managers accept as the case. A survey conducted for the Indian Association of Alberta in the 1970s revealed that most Native people interviewed believed that water had not been given up in the treaties.[32] As time goes on, the claims of Indian people and their leaders more and more reflect the 'sophistication' of their non-Native counterparts. In a 1992 newspaper advertisement objecting to the terms of the Charlottetown Accord, the Treaty 7 First Nations offered an interpretation of the treaty that 'means sharing in the billions of dollars that flow to federal and provincial coffers from industrial and resource development on Crown lands and First Nations' territories.'[33] In October 1994, a report on the federal government's public accounts indicated that Canadian taxpayers might be facing payments of $8 billion in unsettled Native land claims that were then before the courts or in negotiation.[34] There is little wonder that politicians are reluctant to open this can of worms.

Disputes over Aboriginal and treaty rights have taken up substantial amounts of time in the courts in recent years and are likely to take up even more in future. Georges Erasmus, former head of the Assembly of First Nations says, 'There are government lawyers who have made a life's work of finding ways to diminish the rights of aboriginal people.'[35] Others would argue that there are government-funded lawyers working for Indian bands who have made a life's work of embellishing the rights claimed by Aboriginals. One of these might be Mel Smith, who devotes a chapter in his recent book to describing attempts to 'top up' the treaties with 'outlandish specific claims.'[36]

Although the Peigan had asserted their claim to ownership of the Oldman River as early as 1976, it was not until they filed suits against Alberta and Canada in 1986 that Indian water rights emerged as the focal point of the Peigan opposition to the Oldman Dam. By 1991, the question of their 'legal rights, interest and title in the Oldman River' had become the 'key issue for the Peigan Nation.'[37] As noted earlier, 1986 marked a turning point in the Peigan's position on the project. Since 1976, they had cooperated with Alberta in the hope that a dam on the Oldman might bring some economic prosperity to the reserve. Alberta's rejection of the Peigan's Brocket site proposal and refusal to enter into what the Peigan considered meaningful negotiations on mitigation and compensation was compounded by the federal government's reluctance to put pressure on Alberta to deal fairly with the Peigan. Frustrated by the apparent indifference of the two senior governments to their plight, the Peigan decided to exercise what they saw as their only remaining option to get the attention of politicians in Ottawa and Edmonton – the threat of legal action.

The suits against the two governments, although they differ somewhat in form, each asked the Court to declare that the Peigan own the bed and banks of the Oldman River through the Peigan Reserve, that Alberta can not interfere with or impede the flow of the river through the reserve, that the Peigan have rights to the use of the water in the Oldman River flowing through the reserve, and that the Oldman River Dam interferes with or impedes flow through the reserve, causing irreparable damage to the reserve.[38]

In a 1988 letter to federal Justice Minister Hnatyshyn, Thomas Berger, in his capacity as senior counsel for the Peigan, advised that the Peigan's claim of reserved water rights was 'in accordance with the Winters doctrine.' Berger described the Winters doctrine as follows: 'The *Winters* doctrine, established by the Supreme Court of the United States in *Winters* v. *United States* 207 U.S. 564 (1908), is based on the idea that the setting aside of a reserve for an Indian band implies setting aside of waters appurtenant to the reserve to enable the purposes for which the reserve was set aside (agriculture, ranching, etc.) to be fulfilled. In a case where a reserve is set aside for agriculture and ranching purposes, the volume of water which the band may appropriate is whatever volume is needed to irrigate all 'practically [sic] irrigable acreage.'[39] He referred the minister to Bartlett's work for 'a full discussion of the issues raised in this lawsuit.' In a 1990 letter to Indian Affairs Minister Tom Siddon, Chief Bastien wrote that 'the Band's object is to obtain a declaration relating to its water rights and to have the court determine the amount of water the band is entitled to.'[40]

In both suits, the Peigan's original statement of claim declared that they 'traditionally owned and exercised jurisdiction over' a territory of land (referred to as 'Peigan territory') that included the Oldman River Basin and that 'prior to the arrival of non-Indian settlers into the territory the Peigan Nation was organized as a distinct society, exercising exclusive jurisdiction over the Peigan territory and using the resources therein and thereon for their survival.'[41] These are the conditions that an earlier Federal Court ruling established must be met in order for it to find an Aboriginal title to be valid.[42] Both suits maintained that 'the Oldman River sustains the spiritual practices of the Peigan Nation.'

In the first amendment to its statement of claim against Alberta, the Peigan deleted the declaration of traditional ownership and jurisdiction over 'Peigan territory' and altered the declaration of its status before the arrival of non-Indian settlers from that of a distinct society exercising jurisdiction over the Peigan territory to that of having 'an economy based on hunting, trapping, fishing and food gathering.' In so doing, the Peigan have dropped any claim to Aboriginal rights to Oldman water and they appear to have ruled out any claims that agriculture and irrigation were traditional practices of the Peigan. In the light of the Supreme Court's 1996 ruling in *R.* v. *Van der Peet,* this would suggest that the Peigan have no claim to an Aboriginal right to water for irrigation.

In the second amendment to its claim, filed in January 1989, the Peigan also deleted the declaration that the Oldman 'sustains the spiritual practices of the Peigan.' The explanation for this deletion is probably found in a memo written by one of the Peigan's lawyers, offering the opinion that in order for their case to succeed on religious grounds, 'we would have to convince the court that not only is the Oldman River basin absolutely fundamental to the religion of the Peigan, but that there is no possible way for the religious practice to continue should the dam be built ... I am pessimistic that we could support an injunction on the basis of right to freedom [of religion] alone.'[43] Thomas Berger advised the Peigan not to press their application for an injunction on religious grounds, having concluded that it 'will fail' and that the 'balance of convenience' argument favoured the government.[44] He predicted that the Court was likely to say that inconvenience and losses associated with stopping construction would outweigh those associated with the flooding of habitat and sacred sites.

In September 1988, Berger advised the federal justice minister that, although the Peigan claim against Alberta still included 'injunctive relief,' the Peigan were no longer seeking an injunction against the Oldman River Dam.[45] Although the claim for an injunction against dam construction was not deleted from the Peigan's statement of claim until December 1992, and the Peigan continued to tie the water rights issue to the Oldman River Dam (e.g., in their 1991 submission to the Environmental Assessment Review Panel), Berger's advice was consistent with Develon Small Legs' advice to the federal panel that the Peigan's continuing opposition to the dam was symbolic of their concern about the larger question of water rights.

In 1994, the Peigan and Indian Affairs signed a memorandum of understanding pertaining to arrangements for negotiations with Alberta on matters related to the impacts of the Oldman River Dam. One item proposed for negotiation was the 'water rights of the Peigan Nation.'[46] By the summer of 1996, the Peigan's suit against Alberta was still at the 'discovery stage,' and, in the estimation of the Crown's lawyer, still at least a year from trial. Possibly because of the *Bear Island* decisions and the Gitskan's postponement of their appeal of *Delgamuukw* v. *British Columbia,* the Peigan gave the appearance that they would prefer to negotiate their water rights claim with Alberta rather than leave it to the courts.

The most recent clarification of Aboriginal use rights offered by the Supreme Court in its December 1997 ruling in *Delgamuukw* v. *British Columbia* may have given the Peigan new heart. Speculating on the possible impacts of this case on Native rights issues in Alberta, Irene Kwasniak, Staff Counsel for the Alberta Environmental Law Centre, wrote: 'The case might be favourable to potential outstanding Aboriginal title or use claims. For example, the numbered Treaties covering Alberta do not specifically mention water rights or ownership of beds of rivers or other water bodies within reserves. Aboriginal groups subject to numbered Treaties [the Peigan among them] have claimed that they never gave up aboriginal water use rights or aboriginal title to water bodies within reserves ... the *Delgamuukw* case, together with other SCC decisions, could strengthen claims of surviving aboriginal water use and title rights.'[47]

The Peigan's political position has been steadily eroded by the passage of time and the continuing betrayals of the federal government, and Alberta has used the threatened legal action as an excuse for its unwillingness to communicate openly with the Peigan or with Indian Affairs. On a number of occasions, Alberta Environment either refused to meet with Indian Affairs or did so only with tight constraints on the agenda.[48] Alberta was concerned that it might reveal information that could be used by the Peigan in its suit against the province and feared that Indian Affairs' fiduciary responsibility and role as 'alter ego to' the Peigan Band could 'create a situation whereby DIAND could favour the Band's interests.' In November 1991, Chief Bastien told the federal panel that, 'because these [water rights] issues are in litigation, the province has refused to discuss the issues with the Peigan Nation in any meaningful way and has defended as a necessary precondition for administrative and substantive talks the withdrawal of our legal action.'[49]

Talks between Alberta and the Peigan meant to lead into negotiations on the recommendations of the ORDEAP began in 1998, but nothing productive has come of these. Whether Alberta is prepared to negotiate Peigan water rights remains to be seen. Since Alberta has obtained all the federal approvals required for the dam, the Peigan's negotiating position is much weaker than it was in 1992. Meanwhile, the Peigan's water rights suit against Alberta, most recently scheduled to come to trial on 5 October 1998, has again been postponed. This latest postponement is a product of further delaying actions by Alberta. In August 1998, the Court granted an application by the province to have the federal government brought into the action as a co-respondent, which upset the 5 October trial date. The parties recently agreed to a new trial date in January 2000.

There has been no progress in the Federal Court action against Canada. The Peigan appear to have left it on hold, pending the outcome of their Court of Queen's Bench action against Alberta, whether determined by trial or by a negotiated out-of-court settlement.

28
The Environment, Politics, and the Courts

Why should ordinary citizens find it necessary to go to court to force their own government to respect the law?

– *Lethbridge Herald*[1]

Law which can be set aside whenever the government sees fit is no law at all.

– Eugene Forsey

Lobbying of provincial government politicians in Alberta by environmentalists has had a long history of ineffectiveness. In fact, it was that reality as much as anything that propelled FOR into the courts so soon after its formation. FOR did not fare any better with politicians on the government side at the federal level – most were unsympathetic towards environmental issues, and the phalanx of Progressive Conservative MPs representing the irrigation belt had easier access to the cabinet than did FOR.

FOR's greatest hopes lay with the federal Liberal Party, which was the official opposition throughout the years that the Oldman was near the top of the heap of environmental issues. During the run-up to the 1993 federal election, FOR received two letters from the Liberals that were the basis for its belief that the best hope for getting rid of the Oldman Dam lay in a Liberal defeat of Mulroney's Tories. The first of these was written in May by Liberal environment critic Paul Martin, whose post-election emergence as minister of finance confirmed FOR's belief that he would have an influential post in a Liberal government. Martin's letter was written in response to a request for clarification of the Liberal's position on the federal panel's recommendations. The letter was carefully crafted to allow a range of interpretations. Whatever commitments it contained were included in the following:

In approaching this issue, we seek to maintain all options open while conditions are established for federal approvals. We, therefore, accept the Environmental Assessment Panel's recommendation that the federal government should determine the interim operating regime of the dam, while agreement for these conditions are being developed, and that this regime should enable a full range of management and mitigation options ... The

Liberal party is committed to implementing recommendations 2 through 22 of the Panel's report ... The government must reserve the option of acting on the Panel's recommendation to decommission the Oldman River Dam should the proponent fail to cooperate or comply with the implementation. Reserving this option is the best incentive to ensure reaching federal-provincial agreement on the many issues which must be settled.[2]

Confirmation of the apparent Liberal commitment was provided in a letter to Kostuch from Liberal Leader Jean Chrétien, signed on 2 September 1993 – by coincidence the very day that the Tory government released its long-awaited response to the panel's recommendations. Chrétien advised that the Liberal Party's position had been 'effectively summed up' by Martin in his 21 May letter to Kostuch.[3] Kostuch read Martin's letter to say that 'they [a Liberal government] will not licence the dam until the panel's recommendations are implemented, and if they're not implemented in a reasonable time, they will decommission the dam.'[4] Wallis called it a commitment 'to decommission the dam while environmental studies are done.'[5]

As political parties are inclined to do, the Liberals in government failed to act as the party had claimed it would while still in opposition.

With the Supreme Court's decision to not hear Kostuch's Charter appeal, the environmental movement's honeymoon with the courts came to a quiet end, at least as far as the Oldman River Dam was concerned. This brief love affair reached its peak in January 1992, when the Supreme Court rejected Alberta's bid to prevent the application of the EARPGO to the Oldman River Dam, and had been in steady, if unspectacular, decline ever since. There are still those who believe, in the face of overwhelming evidence to the contrary – losses in the PEI Fixed Link action and FOR's attempted Fisheries Act prosecution – that the victories of the late 1980s and early 1990s will continue to happen.[6] This unwarranted optimism is symptomatic of the self-delusion to which many in the environmental movement are prone.

The courts are limited to interpreting the laws passed by governments. If a law works against a government, the government is at liberty to change that law. Canada's national government, determined to do nothing that might offend its provincial counterparts, is quick to enter into accommodations that allow both levels of government to maintain the facade that they are working together to protect the environment when, in fact, they are moving to adopt the 'lowest common law.' Hence the National Accord on Environmental Harmonization and the federal proposal to devolve responsibility for fish habitat to the provinces. The Oldman River Dam experience indicates the type of habitat protection that can be expected of provincial governments. The NRCB/EARP Pine Coulee hearings and the

NRCB/CEAA Little Bow/Highwood hearings, which resulted from the 1993 Canada-Alberta agreement on joint environmental assessments, suggest what can be expected from harmonized environmental assessments.[7] Like the Indian people, some environmentalists are beginning to suspect that they can no longer rely on political systems and political institutions to protect their interests.

Professor Chris Levy, of the Faculty of Law at the University of Calgary, suggests, 'It may be a question of whether the traditional theories of democracy and control are really working. We've got the old patterns, the old forms, the old structures, and it's a serious question whether the control mechanisms that were built into them are still viable. I'm not sure that they are, because, essentially, it seems to me that every four years or so we elect a dictatorship, which I realize is a contradiction of terms.'[8] That, says Levy, 'is one reason why people are turning more and more to the courts, in the hope that the courts will provide a measure of control over government activity that no longer seems to be subject to other traditional forms of scrutiny and control.'[9]

The erosion of traditional controls and the elected dictatorships that concern Levy sounds much like de Tocqueville's 'soft despotism' – not tyranny and oppression, but, rather, government that is 'mild and paternalistic ... may even keep democratic forms, with periodic elections, but ... everything is run by an "immense tutelary power" over which people will have little control.'[10] This, together with a growing sense of powerlessness felt by individuals – the 'fragmentation' of society, which Charles Taylor defines as 'people increasingly less capable of forming a common purpose and carrying it out' – leads to special interest politics and greater reliance on the courts to resolve issues that no longer seem capable of solution through debate and equitable compromise.[11] But there are reasons to question whether our justice systems are any more effective than our political systems when it comes to protecting the environment. There are several reasons why the courts are unable, or unwilling, to prevent the continuance of environmental indiscretions perpetrated by governments. Most megatype projects are sponsored by federal or provincial governments and, so long as they jump through all of the procedural hoops, the courts are not in a position to override the decisions or thwart the will of duly elected governments, nor, in a world where politicians could be trusted, should they be. But politicians and the institutions established to do their will are no longer held in the same high repute that they once were.

As former Peigan Chief Leonard Bastien says, governments have deep pockets. This gives them considerably more staying power than individual citizens or interest groups, which enables them to tie matters up in the courts for years. Mark Freiman, lawyer for Friends of the Island, a public interest group opposed to construction of the bridge to link Prince Edward

Island to the mainland, says, '[Legal] costs are fundamental to the administration of justice in this country. Costs determine for whom the courts are open and for whom the courts are closed.'[12] Frequently, though not for Friends of the Island, courts award costs to interest groups that they believe to have a legitimate case, even if these groups do not succeed in persuading the court that they are in the right. FOR was particularly fortunate in being awarded costs for all of their legal battles over the application of the EARPGO to the Oldman Project. In most instances, FOR was able to find lawyers who provided their services free or at cost, but lawyers' fees are not the full cost of taking a case to court. The cost of providing the documentation required to support the arguments offered can be formidable.

The staying power that governments derive from their relative unconcern with costs gives them a substantial advantage. As Cliff Wallis says, 'Governments control the agenda, we've seen that in the courts time and time again. They have an incredible amount of power to slow things down.'[13] The more government can drag out court proceedings, the more costly they become for interest groups, the less newsworthy they become for the media, and the more time the government buys to implement whatever program or project is at issue. Frequently, and surely in the case of the Oldman River Dam, governments are relieved to have an issue before the courts. Not only can a government then drag out proceedings and wear down its opponents, it can also use the fact that the issue is before the court as an excuse for refusing to debate the issue in public.

The unfettered power of attorneys general, which the courts are not prepared to challenge and which Parliament is not prepared to diminish, allows governments to sidestep their own laws. In explaining the reluctance of the courts to interfere with the prosecutorial discretion of the attorney general, the Alberta Court of Appeal, in its judgment on Martha Kostuch's Charter appeal, made reference to comments by Supreme Court Justice L'Heureux-Dubé in *R. v. Power*.[14] Those comments focus to a great extent on the separation of powers between the judiciary and the executive. The case at issue involved the discretionary actions of the Ontario attorney general with respect to charges brought against a private citizen. The arguments of some of the authorities quoted by Justice L'Heureux-Dubé in defence of noninterference by the courts lend themselves to a much different interpretation in an instance where charges have been brought against the government. For example, L'Heureux-Dubé quotes J.A. Ramsay as follows: 'It is fundamental to our system of justice that criminal proceedings be conducted in public before an independent and impartial tribunal.'[15] In the instance of *Kostuch v. Kowalski*, the executive, in the person of the attorney general of Alberta, faced with an obvious conflict of interest, nevertheless acted on three occasions to prevent the prosecution from proceeding in public before an independent and impartial tribunal.

Madam Justice L'Heureux-Dubé also quotes extensively from an article by Donna Morgan, offering the following comments on the performance expected of attorneys general: 'Along with the exalted status of his office come high expectations as to the Attorney General's performance of his functions ... he bears a heavy responsibility to conduct himself with dignity and fairness. When exercising his "grave" discretion in prosecutorial matters he must take into account ... what the public interest demands. In doing so he must stand alone, acting independently of political or other external influences. He is to be neither instructed or restrained, save by his final accountability to Parliament.'[16] It is unrealistic to expect that any professional politician, which is what most attorneys general are today, will not be influenced by political considerations or that he or she will see any clear distinction between the public interest and the government's interest. The latter is particularly the case where the government in power claims a hefty majority of the seats in the legislature. Nor is it realistic to believe that in the tightly controlled caucuses of modern-day governments he or she will not be amenable to instruction from cabinet and caucus colleagues. It seems especially unlikely that the attorney general will not be influenced or restrained in instances where the government itself is in the dock.

Madam Justice L'Heureux-Dubé expressed her agreement with the view that 'aggressive news coverage or oversight by ... special interest groups affects the exercise of discretion. *Hence, public opinion assumes an increasingly important position in the prosecutor's decisional matrix* [emphasis added by L'Heureux-Dubé].'[17] The change in prosecutorial policies in the United States when it became unpopular to convict Vietnam War protesters and draft evaders is held out as an example of the influence of public opinion. In the less dramatic case of the stays on Kostuch's prosecution attempts entered by the Alberta attorney general, there was no aggressive news coverage – in no small part because of Alberta's success in dragging the proceedings on for so long that the media lost interest, and the only public interest group that spoke out was FOR, which, as a party to the action, could hardly be considered an overseer. Hence, public opinion concerning the attorney general's actions was nonexistent.

Chris Levy suggests that 'the traditional patterns of control on the attorney general,' such as those that influenced the Alberta Court of Appeal, 'either no longer exist, or are dramatically weakened.'[18] Specifically, 'We no longer have the real vision of the attorney general being independent of politics ... the idea of parliamentary control over the attorney general in the context of Alberta is complete nonsense, the idea of press control is not borne out by the realities of press behaviour, and the idea of interest group control, or focusing attention – yes, there is an element of that, but how do you focus attention? You have to do it, in large measure, through parliamentary opposition, which may not be interested, or through the media, which may not be interested.'[19]

The received wisdom common to all courts is that judicial interference is acceptable, even called for, in instances where the attorney general's actions qualify as 'flagrant impropriety.' To a layperson, an attorney general whose actions are not seen to be independent of political influences is at least open to suspicion of flagrant impropriety. The courts, however, take a more charitable view. In Chris Levy's experience, '[If] some senior government politician or civil servant is involved as an accused, [it] certainly raises questions when a stay is entered but it is not, in and of itself, regarded as evidence of the sort of flagrant impropriety that [a court] is looking for.'[20]

The Alberta Court of Appeal observed that the attorney general 'is answerable to the Legislature and finally to the electorate for decisions made.'[21] The message was clear: If the province's electors believe that the attorney general had abused his or her power, they should not look to the courts to rectify matters, but rather, they should vote the attorney general out of office. The short attention span of voters and the low priority of the environment relative to other issues come election time aside, it is difficult for anyone who believes in the democratic principle that those who are elected by the people should not be dictated to by those whom they appoint to high office to quarrel with that observation. The exception, of course, is where the elected official exercises his power improperly, which might reasonably be assumed to include an obvious conflict of interest.

The Alberta situation concerning attorney-general intervention in environmental prosecutions initiated by private citizens is not unique. British Columbia also has a policy whereby the provincial attorney general intervenes in all privately initiated prosecutions. In recent years, the Sierra Legal Defence Fund's (SLDF's) attempts to prosecute both the forest industry giant Fletcher Challenge and the Greater Vancouver Regional District for violations under the Fisheries Act have been sidetracked by intervention and eventual staying of proceedings by the BC attorney general.[22] The SLDF says this 'consistent misuse of Crown power to control what is supposed to be an independent justice system' shows the Crown's 'utter contempt for the public's right to enforce the law when government is implicated in the offence.'[23] The SLDF might as easily have been commenting on the behaviour of the Alberta attorney general in staying the charges brought against the province by Martha Kostuch. Professor Levy says, 'In the case of politically sensitive private prosecutions, it has become increasingly common practice across Canada for Crown prosecutors to step in and, on direction from the centre, to actually terminate those charges. While this practice is clearly legal, and clearly conforms to the historical theory, it is relatively modern.'[24]

The reluctance of almost every judge who was forced to rule on the Alberta attorney general's obvious conflict of interest in this case and the refusal of the Supreme Court to become involved is the final confirmation of the absolute futility of looking to the courts to defend the environment from governments that wish to exploit its economic potential. Martha Kostuch was surprised that the Supreme Court refused to hear her appeal, as were other environmental groups that considered it one of the most important cases of the decade. Chris Levy understands the disappointment of the environmentalists but was not surprised at the Supreme Court's decision. As he says, 'If one is deeply involved in an issue, one tends to assume that it has that sort of transcendent public importance that will automatically justify the Supreme Court hearing it. The Supreme Court may take a somewhat different view of the global significance of the matter.'[25]

The current federal government is clearly not prepared to make any exceptions to the powers of attorneys general to prevent them from shielding the government's ministers, its agencies, and its friends from prosecution for environmental offences. In June 1995, the House of Commons Standing Committee on Environment and Sustainable Development published the results of its review of the Canadian Environmental Protection Act (CEPA). In its report, the committee recalled that the Liberal Party's preelection bible, the infamous Red Book, committed a Liberal government to 'use the forthcoming review of the Canadian Environmental Protection Act to examine giving members of the public access to the courts as a last recourse if the federal government persistently fails to enforce an environmental law.'[26] The committee also observed that citizens who initiate a private prosecution, 'may not be able to see the prosecution through, because of the intervention of the Attorney General for Canada, either by taking over the prosecution or by ordering that it be stayed.'[27] This was FOR's experience when it attempted to prosecute Alberta for its violation of the Fisheries Act. To correct this, the committee recommended that the CEPA be amended to entitle a private citizen, in instances where the attorney general assumes control of a prosecution initiated by the citizen, to 'remain a party to the proceedings.'[28] Although the proposal applied only to the CEPA, and its broader implications were unclear, the Liberal government was having none of it. The official government response to the recommendation was that such an entitlement was 'not appropriate,' since it 'would fetter the discretion of the Attorney General.'[29] That was precisely its intent.

Cliff Wallis says, 'Going to court is a crapshoot. In some cases, the province has been able to snow the courts, pull the wool over their eyes.'[30] Success depends on the judges' knowledge and understanding of matters beyond the law, and on the skills of the opposing lawyers in persuading the judges to accept what may or may not be fact. Environmentalists, like everyone else, have no say in the appointments to the bench and no control over which judge or judges will be assigned to preside over a particular case. Consequently, as was seen time and again in FOR's legal actions, contradictory judgments, whether in the same or different courts, are not uncommon. These invariably lead to appeals on the part of one party or the other, which gets back to the question of which side has the most time and the most money at its disposal.

Martha Kostuch believes that courts are not competent to pass judgment on scientific matters. She is probably right; but that does not dissuade judges from buying into the notion that a pile of 'scientific' reports means a job has been done well. In fact, this goes beyond the hard sciences to the social sciences and human behaviour, individual or collective. Judges can be persuaded by lawyers that things have transpired in a particular way when they did not. Not only do erroneous understandings influence the courts' judgments, they are reported by the courts as facts, go into the record, and are passed on to posterity as such. For example, in Kostuch's Charter appeal, the Alberta Court of Appeal reported that 'the appellant does not suggest that the authorization and approval by Alberta Fish and Wildlife officials was granted other than in good faith. The appellant merely suggests that the delegation of authority to the province was unconstitutional,' and that 'the Federal Minister of Fisheries and Oceans and the Minister of Environment were consistent in the position that jurisdiction for enforcement of the *Fisheries Act* had been transferred to the province.'[31] Whether intended or simply the result of sloppy reporting, these statements, in context, clearly suggest that Alberta Fish and Wildlife, exercising authority delegated to the province by the federal government, had authorized construction of the dam under s. 35(2) of the Fisheries Act. Such was not the case. Authorization for the construction of the Oldman River Dam and the consequent destruction of fish habitat in the Oldman River under the terms of s. 35(2) of the Fisheries Act has never been issued by anyone. The facts are that Alberta applied, retroactively, to the minister of fisheries and oceans for authorization to *construct* the dam and was refused, and that on 2 September 1993, Fisheries and Oceans issued Alberta its authorization to *operate* the illegally constructed dam.

Nor is this the only or the most obvious example of erroneous information that was reported as fact by the Appeal Court and which presumably influenced its decision. (If not, why report it?) The Court reported that Alberta had 'projects planned upstream of the dam to enhance fish population [sic] with objectives of ensuring that there would be no net loss of fish.'[32] In fact, the objective of the Fisheries Component of Alberta's Oldman River Dam Mitigation Plan was to 'achieve no net loss of recreational fishing opportunities,' which is an entirely different kettle of fish – pun intended.[33] The Appeal Court reported that Mr. Justice Power of the Court of Queen's Bench had found that 'the Provincial officials had carried out a complete investigation of the effect of the dam on fish habitat, and they were satisfied that adequate plans had been put in place to protect fish. Therefore no net loss of fish would result from the project.'[34] If Power made such a finding, he did not report it, and if he had, he would have been dead wrong.[35] No such investigation had been undertaken at the time that the river was diverted, nor could there have been in the absence of an operational plan for the dam, which did not materialize until January 1989. As noted above, the Fisheries component of the mitigation plan was not intended to protect fish but to enhance the recreational fishery upstream from the dam.

Since all judges in an earlier incarnation were lawyers, and lawyers, demonstrably and understandably, do not exhibit the depth of understanding of some of the things beyond the law itself that are taken to the courts, why should we expect their understanding to improve simply because they have been appointed to the bench? Yet Canadians invariably defer to the wisdom that flows from the bench. As Richard Gwynn says, 'Deference to judges has become the last manifestation of Canadians' famed deference to authority.'[36]

The weakness in FOR's legal strategy, in the long term, as the Oldman experience demonstrated, is that governments can and do amend their laws to suit their purposes. In the short term, FOR's court actions drew public attention to environmental issues that might otherwise have gone unheeded, and they cast some doubt on the legality and morality of government action. The successful court actions – on application of the EARPGO – may, at best, result in some environmentally beneficial modifications to the operation of the project. The unsuccessful actions – the aborted Fisheries Act prosecution – prompted no changes and drew little public attention, but added substantially to the final bill for the project, borne by the taxpayers.

Martha Kostuch still believes the courts are a vital tool in her crusade to force governments to protect the environment. Without them, governments would be even more likely to disregard the law whenever it suited their purpose to do so. As noted in Chapter 14, as recently as July 1998, Friends of the West Country, another environmental interest group led by Kostuch, convinced the Federal Court to quash approvals issued by DF&O for bridges on a logging road in Alberta. The Federal Court of Appeal upheld the ruling. But, since DF&O can still appeal to the Supreme Court, this may yet prove to be another temporary victory. FOR is planning to mount a campaign to lobby for changes in the Criminal Code that would limit the power of attorneys general to prevent private prosecutions in environmental cases.

29
Information and Disinformation

The Public Affairs Bureau supports the government in its ongoing dialogue with Albertans by providing quality communications services and consulting.

– Mission and Mandate of Alberta's Public Affairs Bureau[1]

Media coverage is spasmodic and seldom establishes a context. A government elected to represent the public interest can get away with shoddy, hypocritical or dishonest behaviour without most of us having any idea what is happening.

– Boyce Richardson[2]

This account would not be complete without a brief look at how each side in the controversy used and misused information to bolster its position and attract supporters to its cause, and at the role played by the media in disseminating that information to a wider audience. The masses of information offered up by governments, interest groups, and the media did little to clarify the issues for the public. Much of that information was contradictory, much was misinformation, and much was propaganda, plain and simple.

By far the most prolific purveyor of information was the Government of Alberta. Bankrolled by the taxpayers, government agencies were most favourably positioned to create and distribute information. As the proponent, Alberta had the advantage of being the initial provider of information about the project, to which others – opponents, neutral parties, and the general public – were obliged to respond. The government created and disseminated this information in a variety of ways.

The earliest information came in the form of studies prepared by government agencies or their consultants. These were offered as the basis for the decision to build the dam and to implement mitigation programs to compensate for its environmental impacts. These studies lent an aura of scientific respectability to what was essentially a political decision. In 1988, Alberta Environment produced a list of over fifty studies related to the dam. Add to this the reports on studies done after 1988, and the total comes closer to 100. These reports were available to anyone who cared to read them, though relatively few people ever did so. The practice of releasing reams of technical information is increasingly common amongst

government agencies. Overwhelming the public with technical information that most people have neither the time nor the background to consider critically is little different from providing no information at all, but
it creates the illusion of an open process. And it benefits the government
by helping to intimidate those inclined to question its actions and
impressing those who are more concerned with quantity than quality.

Alberta regularly submitted batches of study reports to the courts as evidence of the diligence with which its agencies had exercised their responsibilities. The judges, pressured by overcrowded schedules, could not possibly
have taken the time to read and understand them, much less put them
into context. Nonetheless, apparently impressed by the sheer volume of
reports, the courts frequently commented favourably upon them.[3] Because
they were not subjected to strenuous review outside the walls of the agencies that funded them, the limitations and oversights of the studies were
not revealed until very late in the process, if at all.[4]

The government also relied on news releases, official statements,
newsletters, and other literature – including a book – produced by government communication agencies to get its message out to the public. In the
information age, the communications branch is an integral part of most
government departments. Staffed by people trained and experienced in
advertising, public relations, or the media, the task of these agencies is to
cast the decisions and actions of governments in the most favourable
possible light.[5] They accomplish this by the long-established practices of
controlling the flow of information to the public and ensuring that it is
presented with a spin, or interpretation, advantageous to the government.
Alberta's communications gurus tried their best to limit bad news about
the Oldman River Dam. As PWSS Communications Director Jan Berkowski
confessed to Rod Chapman, 'After [1989], we tried to keep the issue local,
and out of the media. That was the only way to reduce the negative coverage. We tried to reduce the visibility of the project, and to hit on the positive aspects.'[6]

The news release is an effective instrument for controlling the flow of
information and ensuring it is delivered with the preferred spin. Joyce
Nelson says the news release is used to 'establish lines of control regarding
information. It initiates the news-making process, and sets ideal boundaries around what is to be known by emphasizing some information and
leaving out other information.'[7] All Alberta Environment and Alberta Public Works news releases concerning the Oldman River Dam followed this
simple formula. They consistently emphasized the benefits, while leaving
out information about adverse social or environmental impacts. News
releases in the early 1980s stressed economic benefits: increased acres of
irrigation, regional economic development, jobs created, or water supply
for small communities. In later years, the litany was extended to include

the environmental benefits of the mitigation program. News releases were most effective in propagating the government's line through smaller media outlets that, strapped for resources, were most likely to print news releases exactly as received and without attributing them to the government.

Ever sensitive to criticism, the government's communication arm frequently wrote to newspapers and periodicals offering hair-splitting arguments in response to information or comments critical of the project levelled in articles, editorials, or even letters to the editor.[8] It also authored articles favourable to the dam, which it offered for publication to the rural weeklies.[9] These were often published without attribution, leaving readers unaware that they were being fed the government line.[10] In 1989, PWSS sent an 'information package' to schools in southern Alberta that included a letter and government-produced videos explaining why the Oldman Dam was needed, extolling the benefits it would provide, and arguing that its environmental impacts would be minimal. Some teachers and FOR voiced their concern that the department was attempting to use the schools to indoctrinate students and, through them, their parents. PWSS's communications manager, Jan Berkowski, was surprised by all the fuss, claiming the department was just trying to give out as much information as possible.[11]

Alberta also used its position to withhold information critical to assessing the impacts of the project. By denying the panel access to Alberta Environment staff and consultants familiar with the computer simulations that were the basis for determination of the impacts of operating the dam, it denied both the panel and the public information vital to the review. And by refusing to participate in the federal review, Alberta avoided having to respond to questions from the public and the interest groups opposed to the dam. Instead, Public Works mounted a dog and pony show that followed the panel into each community where a public hearing was scheduled, wherever possible setting up in the same venue as the panel. Brochures putting the government's spin on various aspects of the project were handed out, and communications staff ensured that project staff were available to the media for interviews.

Most organizations, public or private, large enough to afford a public relations staff to promote the organization's viewpoint, publish a newsletter. Alberta government departments are no exception, and in June 1986, Alberta Environment launched its Oldman River Dam newsletter, *Update*. Over the next five years, twelve issues of *Update* were published. It was a classic of the genre. Although condemned by Andy Russell as 'a rank and misleading piece of propaganda,' *Update*, printed on glossy paper, with well-written articles and lots of pictures – Ken Kowalski and other politicians were common fare – was a well-received and frequently quoted source of information about the Oldman River Dam.[12]

Like the government's news releases, *Update* focused on good news – construction progress, job creation, local economic spin-offs, and the work of the local public advisory committee. Demonstrations in opposition to the dam, court actions, unless they resulted in victory for the government, and the information deficiencies uncovered by the federal review went unreported. The Peigan, the Lonefighters, and the Friends of the Oldman River might not have existed. When bad news could not be avoided, it was presented as good news. In the summer of 1986, the cost of the dam was revised upward. *Update* reported the greater cost together with the results of a new economic study concluding that 'for every dollar spent, the return to the province will be $2.17.'[13] The salvage operation mounted to preserve some examples of the archaeological, palaeontological, and historical artifacts that would be inundated in the reservoir area was 'our past coming to life' and 'a unique opportunity for amateur archaeologists.'[14] Monitoring the results of an experiment to provide upland habitat for wildlife driven from the valley bottom was 'keeping track of success.'[15]

Alberta Environment continues the publication of a dam newsletter in the post-construction era. The *Oldman River Dam EAC Bulletin* is a periodical devoted to 'keep[ing] everyone with a stake in the project's success accurately and factually informed.'[16] Like its predecessor, this newsletter is devoted to spreading good news. Although the initial issue said more about disagreements with the Peigan and environmental interests than any previous government publication, it characterized them as 'cloud[s]' over the project, which disappeared when the dam was 'declared officially finished.'

The most ambitious and shameless of Alberta's information projects was the publication, in 1992, of *The Oldman River Dam: Building a Future for Southern Alberta*, a blatant attempt by the government to imprint its version of the history of the Oldman River Dam Project on the public mind. The book presents an anthropocentric view of 'resource enhancement.' The theme is the triumph of man – the doer, the builder, the regulator – over nature, in the form of an 'erratic' and 'undependable' river. The heroes of the tale are provincial politicians and civil servants, irrigation farmers, and assorted local luminaries (bold, industrious, and visionary all), persevering against and ultimately prevailing over the forces of darkness, represented by environmentalists (selfish and uninformed outsiders), dissident Indians (lawless malcontents), and the big-city media (negative, unbalanced, and unfair). It laments that what was a straightforward, local issue was blown out of proportion and transported onto the national stage by a 'relatively' small number of people – predominantly outsiders – who could not seem to understand why it was necessary to dam the Oldman River. The account focuses on the increases in local employment and economic activity experienced during the construction period and rhapsodizes about a rosy economic future for southern Alberta, brought about by the sound water management made possible by the Oldman Dam. Any irksome social or environmental complications will be transformed into 'enhancements' by the mother of all mitigation programs.

This Alberta-government-authorized version of the events that unfolded during the course of the affair is based on the selected recollections and second thoughts of the politicians and civil servants responsible for the project. The most outstanding example of historical revisionism is the claim that the dam was built for reasons other than to supply water for irrigation expansion; that its primary purpose was to sustain life – both the human and the wild varieties. This convenient afterthought contradicts the rationalization for the dam maintained from 1976 until it was revised in the aftermath of the 1986 court decision quashing the first licence issued for its construction. The project is plainly and simply the manifestation of the government's 1975 Water Management for Irrigation Use policy, which called for a dam on the Oldman to support irrigation. That policy, unlike the government's book, was silent on cottonwood forests, rainbow trout, and world-class canoe runs.

The second-ranking distortion is the claim that Alberta did an environmental impact assessment of a dam at the Three Rivers site before its construction, and that the federal review duplicated the Alberta assessment. Again, as we have seen, the truth is much simpler. The federal review was the only formal public review of the Three Rivers site, and, as the litany of information deficiencies identified at the outset of the federal review made clear, there was little in the way of useful, available information to duplicate.

The book perpetuates the myth that the Oldman Dam makes it easier for Alberta to meet its apportionment flow commitments to Saskatchewan. The best way for Alberta to meet its commitments to Saskatchewan is to divert and store less water, not more. If the irrigation and industrial growth trumpeted as benefits of building the dam are realized, the consumption of water from the Oldman River will increase substantially, making it more difficult for Alberta to meet its flow commitments to Saskatchewan. What *is* a possibility is that meeting this commitment in the post-Oldman Dam era may constrain water-related growth in the Bow and Red Deer basins.

The many lesser fabrications in the book are contradicted by conditions and events either ignored or understated. The claim that legal questions were satisfactorily answered suggests that Alberta successfully repelled all legal challenges. FOR's court setbacks are recounted in detail, but that Alberta fought in vain to prevent a federal review of the dam is glossed over. The three interventions by Alberta's attorney general that prevented FOR from prosecuting Alberta for destroying fish habitat in the Oldman River are not mentioned at all. The claim that the Oldman River Dam was

'widely judged' to be socially acceptable ignores the very strong conclusions to the contrary reached by the federal review panel.

Those who read the book will learn that landowners at the Three Rivers
site and the Peigan were 'satisfied' with their dealings with the government. The federal review panel reported that the Peigan 'were not treated
fairly,' and that 'some displaced landowners believe that they were mis-
treated' by the Alberta government. A claim by Minister Kowalski that the
government ensured that the dam would not have an impact on Peigan
'spiritual grounds' misrepresents the reality and reveals the great gulf in
understanding between the government and the Peigan. In fact, a vast
expanse of the Oldman River valley – a Peigan vision-quest area – has been
inundated. Much of the Peigan cultural legacy within the reservoir area was
'salvaged' (excavated, packed in boxes, and warehoused in Edmonton), an
act the book identifies as one of the benefits of the Oldman Project. The
federal review panel concluded that inundation of the reservoir area
resulted in 'cultural and spiritual losses' to the Peigan.

The most useful information the book might have imparted is the total
cost of the project. Though it was published in 1992, the only cost figure
mentioned is a 1986 estimate. Subsequent legal, mitigation, and other costs
are not even estimated. Disclosure of the intelligence that led to cancellation of the dam opening ceremonies and the evidence linking alleged
threats to the United Church of Canada would have been revealing. The
details of Milton Born With A Tooth's Fort Macleod trial would have proved
instructive to future students of cross-cultural relations in southern Alberta.

In addition to exalting the Oldman Dam, the book pays tribute to Ken
Kowalski (his picture appears six times and his name is mentioned on
twenty-eight occasions – supplemented by a generous sprinkling of personal pronouns in quotes attributed to him, and innumerable references to
'the minister'), who tells readers that he wants to be remembered as the
builder of the dam. Publication of *The Oldman River Dam* probably ensured
that his wish will come true. Former premier Peter Lougheed, whose 1984
cabinet made the decision to build the dam at Three Rivers, is not likely to
complain if posterity associates the furor that followed with Ken Kowalski.[17]

The federal government, whenever possible, avoided public exposure of
its role in the Oldman controversy. It had sound reasons for doing so. Cast
in what was, for the most part, a reactive role, in which it was noticeably
uncomfortable, the federal government took no initiatives and made no
decisions that did anything to enhance its image. On the few occasions
when it was obliged to issue a public statement – such as when the justice
minister decided not to prosecute the charges brought by FOR against
Alberta under the Fisheries Act – it did so with as little fanfare and as much
obfuscation as possible.

The environmental interest groups, the irrigation lobby, and the Peigan used the same means as the Alberta government to get their message to the public. Of these, FOR was by far the most active. With the limited funding available to it, FOR engaged consultants to prepare a number of reports to counter studies done by Alberta. Based for the most part on inadequate or incomplete information, the propaganda value of the studies outweighed their scientific contribution.

Like FOR, the irrigation lobby, represented by the SAWMC and the LNID, hired consultants to make their case before the panel. And like the studies submitted by FOR, they contributed more heat than light to the debate. The greatest number of them were done by the consulting firm then under contract to Alberta to manage construction of the dam. Any doubt that the firm's close association with the project might have cast on the scientific veracity of its reports was reinforced by the comment in a letter from the firm to the SAWMC that one of its reports 'echo[es] the positive outlook that is the trademark of the committee.'[18]

The Peigan were second only to Alberta Environment in the number of dam-related studies undertaken and the quantity of reports produced. These studies were apparently reviewed by the government agencies that funded them – Alberta Environment and Indian Affairs – but those reviews were not made public.[19] Some of the studies were never revealed to the public. In particular, those that stood to offer the most support for the Peigan and to most enlighten the public – studies of the impact of the dam on Peigan cultural and spiritual beliefs and practices – were withheld on the advice of the Peigan's lawyers.

Beginning in 1986, FOR issued a steady stream of news releases to ensure that the Oldman River Dam and FOR's struggles to oppose it remained in the public eye. FOR's news releases, generally prepared by Kostuch, adhered to the formula that emphasized information favourable to FOR's position and ignored or put a negative spin on information that favoured the dam or the Alberta government. In particular, FOR used news releases to keep the media up-to-date on the progress of its various legal actions, something Alberta and Canada, FOR's usual courtroom opponents, did not bother to do. Neither government was anxious to publicize either the issues at stake or its defeats, and when they did emerge from court victorious, it was usually a case of having managed to evade a responsibility or, in the case of Alberta, of having used its power to frustrate FOR's legal initiatives. In these David and Goliath-like encounters, a win for the government was rarely cheered by anyone other than another government.

The Peigan were adept at conveying their message verbally but made little use of written communications to sell their position to the general public. Lonefighter leader Milton Born With A Tooth issued a few news releases, but these long, rambling epistles, if not incomprehensible, lacked the succinctness that appeals to the news media.

Opponents of the dam, most of them either members or friends of FOR, made extensive use of magazines, journals, and newspapers to get their message to the public. Articles or columns arguing against the dam appeared in popular magazines such as *Harrowsmith,* periodicals such as *Borealis, Trout Canada, Environment Network News,* and *World Rivers Review,* in newsletters published by the Alberta Wilderness Association and the Canadian Parks and Wilderness Society, and in daily and weekly newspapers.

The pro-dam literature produced by the government and the irrigation lobby was generally technical in nature, emphasizing the economic benefits that the dam would bring to southern Alberta. It was crafted to appeal to the reader's reason. Those writing on the other side of the issue were more likely to appeal to their readers' emotions by describing the responses of families displaced by the dam and its assault on Native culture and the natural order of things.[20] One of the Lonefighters' earliest news releases, believed to have been penned by Milton Born With A Tooth, included the following: 'For the misty fume clouds the environment which shows my true identity. My Blackfoot mind is my sword, the History is my Shield. The animals, the earth, the air and the universe are my supporters, who justify my reason for battle. For the systematical dragon seeks only to conqueror and to destroy. It does not wish to live in peace with Creation. Therefore, it is inevitable that the dragon will be slain by what it fears most, 'One who is One with the Earth and its Environment.'[21] This passage may have been what inspired the Anglican Church's Reverend Peter Hamel to say, 'Milton speaks in parables.'[22]

In 1987, naturalist and author Andy Russell, a founding member of FOR, released a new book – a mixture of natural history, Indian folklore, anecdote, and personal reminiscence – that presented a decidedly different view of the Oldman River.[23] Russell's Oldman was home to Indians of the noble savage variety, polo-playing ranchers, and eccentric anglers, who lived in harmony with the river's erratic nature; a place where irrigation farmers and government bureaucrats compelled to regulate its flow are johnnies-come-lately. If the government's book overstates the dam as the saviour of southern Alberta and the heroism of the politicians and bureaucrats who made it possible, Russell's book stretches things in the opposite direction. He portrays the dam as a desecration that spells the death of the river, and its patrons as villains. Nor is Russell's book any less given to exaggeration and imagination, though presented with more humour than the government's tome. His anecdotes about thirsty deputy ministers falling from the sky and secret plans in plain, brown envelopes sliding through his mail slot make entertaining reading, but, despite his publisher's claim that the book 'could change history and save half a billion dollars in the process,' it added nothing of substance to the debate. One reviewer, perhaps with tongue in cheek, declared *The Life of a River* to be 'of epic proportions.'[24]

With few exceptions, the media provided shallow coverage of the Oldman struggle. Controversial events, such as the earlier court cases, the Lonefighter' diversion attempt, and the Environmental Assessment Panel's hearings were given fairly extensive coverage by the southern Alberta media. However, reporting and comment focused mainly on the confrontational aspects of these events; they provided little in the way of clarification of the broader water management, environmental, or Native issues. Follow-up on the continued development and operation of the project or on the resolution of issues since the review panel reported in May 1992 has been spasmodic and then only when prompted by dam opponents.[25]

That the urban media were more interested in fuelling controversy than in objective reporting was most apparent in their coverage of the Lonefighters' attempt to divert the river. As was clear from the assessments of government officials, the reliability of which could easily have been confirmed by independent sources, there was little or no possibility that the Lonefighters' attempt to divert the river would be successful. Yet the media, in its collective frenzy for a story that imitated, if it failed to rival, the events at Oka, persisted in reporting that the diversion was imminent. In the process, they created the illusion that the government used to justify its 7 September raid onto the Peigan Reserve. Ironically, in his testimony at Milton Born With A Tooth's second trial, RCMP Sergeant Mills, who witnessed most events during the Lonefighter escapade, called the media's reporting 'irresponsible.'

The *Lethbridge Herald,* located in the heart of the irrigation community, provided more extensive reporting of the controversy and more in-depth discussion of the issues surrounding it than did Alberta's other daily newspapers. Editorially, the *Lethbridge Herald* took a very hard line in questioning the basis for the government's decision to build a dam at the Three Rivers site. When it did not receive what it considered satisfactory answers, the *Herald* persisted in asking the questions and became progressively more critical of the Alberta government's lack of openness, the timing and inadequacy of its environmental impact studies, its unwillingness to address the issues raised by environmental interests and the Peigan, and the performance of the various cabinet ministers responsible for the project. While critical of the Lonefighters' methods and timing, the *Herald* blamed the government for creating the circumstances that led to their protest.

The *Herald*'s lead editorial writer, Joanne Helmer, regularly authored a column in which she was even more critical of the government and more probing in her questioning than were the paper's editorials. From 1984 onwards, Helmer, more than any media person, was a constant thorn in the government's side. Helmer also used her column to set out and explain the issues behind the Lonefighters' uprising; the only attempt by any element of the media to do more than report the confrontational aspects of the affair. Helmer was one of the few media people to openly express sympathy for the Lonefighters. She explained her motivation as follows: 'I'm not ever sympathetic towards violence, but they weren't a violent group of people. My sympathy for the Lonefighters came from the frustration I saw among the people there [on 7 September] who were trying to do something, believing that they had a very legitimate cause, and not getting anybody to understand what they were doing.'[26]

Helmer attributed her persistence to the stonewalling she experienced in response to her early inquiries about matters pertaining to the dam. Generally, only senior government officials were authorized to speak on the record to the media, and as the controversy became more heated, officials became more selective in their choice of reporters to whom they were willing to grant interviews. As the controversy over the dam intensified, Helmer, who had been identified by the Iron Triangle as a threat to the dam, found it increasingly difficult to arrange interviews with senior government officials or to keep herself informed of upcoming events, such as meetings of the SAWMC, where her attendance was not welcome.

The Alberta Irrigation Projects Association (AIPA) and the SAWMC were highly critical of coverage by all the urban media but took particular exception to Helmer's editorials and columns in the *Lethbridge Herald*. At one point, they were so incensed by what they called the *Herald*'s 'anti-dam' attitude that they sent a delegation to complain to the publisher and to convince him to bring the *Herald* 'on-side' on dam issues.[27] Although the *Herald* published a somewhat conciliatory editorial in the wake of this meeting, there was no discernible softening or reduction in its persistent questioning of the government's performance with respect to the project.

WMS head Peter Melnychuk refused interviews with Helmer, whom he characterized as 'dishonest' and described as having a 'personal bias against the project.'[28] On the other hand, Melnychuk judged *Herald* agriculture editor Ric Swihart's reporting to have been 'fair.' Swihart promoted the dam at every opportunity, complemented the government on its environmental impact studies and its mitigation program, and cheered its decision to continue construction without federal approval. He raged against outsiders and the 'yapping' Friends of the Oldman River, who wouldn't accept that the dam meant 'life in southern Alberta.'

The Calgary and Edmonton dailies, further removed from the action and less informed on local issues and events, covered them in less detail than did the *Lethbridge Herald*. They were, however, equally as critical of the government's handling of the affair, and, in particular, of Minister Kowalski. Rural weeklies in the region generally reflected the support for the project and for the government that prevailed over most of rural southern Alberta.

Alberta Report, an Edmonton-based far-right weekly magazine with wide circulation in Alberta, lent its unqualified support to the government and to the Oldman River Dam Project. Its anti-eastern establishment mindset resulted in predictable knee-jerk opposition to any decision made in Ottawa, whether by the federal government or the Supreme Court. Its reports on the dam controversy derided the actions of environmentalists and the Peigan, and its editorial comment on these camps bordered on the hysterical.

Windspeaker, a Native weekly little read outside the Native community, represented the extreme viewpoint on Peigan issues and was very support-ive of the Lonefighters. Milton Born With A Tooth, the Lonefighter leader, was martyred in reports, columns, and editorials appearing in *Windspeaker.* Born With A Tooth's Fort Macleod trial and the subsequent tribulations of Mr. Justice MacLean were given more extensive coverage and comment by *Windspeaker* than by other news media.

Media coverage of Oldman issues and events was sporadic in other parts of Canada. Milestone events like the legal debate on the application of the EARPGO, which made it all the way to the Supreme Court and had reper-cussions for resource management throughout the country, were widely reported. Others, like Martha Kostuch's attempts to bring Alberta to trial for violation of the Fisheries Act, equally as important, if not more impor-tant in the long term, and the armed raids onto the Peigan Reserve by Alberta Environment and the RCMP, received little coverage. The Lone-fighters' uprising, which at any other time would probably have received exhaustive coverage, coincided with events at Oka and couldn't compete for attention with the Mohawk Warriors. Had the Supreme Court agreed to hear Toronto lawyer Clayton Ruby argue against the Alberta Court of Appeal's 1995 ruling against Martha Kostuch in her battle with Alberta's attorney general, that issue, which the Canadian Environmental Defence Fund called 'the environmental case of the decade,' would undoubtedly have received extensive media coverage.[29] The Supreme Court's refusal to hear the appeal, if reported at all, was relegated to the back pages.

The media is notably deficient in reporting and commenting on how environmental issues are dealt with by the justice system. Once an envi-ronmental issue gets on a court docket, it is to a very great extent out of the public eye until a judgment is handed down. Parties to a dispute, in particular government politicians and bureaucrats, acting on the advice of their lawyers, refuse public discussion of embarrassing questions, and arguments and evidence presented in the courts, if reported at all, gener-ally escape criticism by the media. There are many reasons for this. With the exception of cases concerning violent crime, the process within the walls of a courtroom can be mind-numbingly boring and slow to unfold. This is normally the case with environmental issues, which often get bogged down in technical details. Drawn out court proceedings are expen-sive for the media to cover – a full day in court might not produce a single item of interest to most people. Often by the time a court hearing takes place, the event that precipitated the legal action has faded from public memory and is no longer news. The entire process – from the initial filing of charges to the final appeal – can drag out over a period of years, which often means different reporters covering the case and therefore a lack of continuity in reporting. These practical reasons aside, some critics argue that the media 'rarely challenge the dominant institutions in society,' which include the courts amongst their number.[30]

Chief Justice Lamer of the Supreme Court of Canada blames the failure of the media to adequately report court proceedings, in part, on a 'clash of cultures' between the news media, in a hurry and looking for a story, and the judiciary, with its 'reasoned elaboration.'[31] He has expressed concern that the work behind the decisions of the Court is not being communicated adequately to the public. Lamer says that, 'too often still there is a failure to get the basic facts straight. There is the ongoing problem that the process itself is not treated with sufficient understanding or respect.'[32] The Chief Justice's observations could as well apply to courts other than the Supreme Court.

Highlights or summaries of the decisions or outcomes of significant cases are usually reported in the media, but little information on the issue in question or on the arguments of the opposing sides is offered. Often reporters lack the background knowledge required to fully understand the issues and arguments, or to comment critically on outcomes. This is less because they are incapable of obtaining the background and acquiring the knowledge than because the measured pace and formality of the process (Chief Justice Lamer's 'reasoned elaboration') and the moderate level of public interest in anything other than the final decision, do not justify the effort. The complete texts of most significant court decisions are published in a variety of law reports. These, however, are not available until some months after the decisions are rendered. Some reports include useful background, but none offer critical comment on decisions. Critical comment occasionally appears in scholarly law journals, but these usually appear well after the fact and, like the law reports, are not readily accessible to the general public. The result is that, even in cases where the outcome has substantial implications, the protagonists are spared the embarrassment they might experience if the issue were in the public spotlight rather than confined to the relative obscurity of the courts.

More critical reporting by the media might discourage governments from offering narrowly legalistic explanations in defence of actions that defy common sense. A case in point is the questionable arguments frequently put forward by lawyers acting for the Crown in defence of a government stretching the truth to fit its purposes or unwilling to exercise its responsibilities. As Boyce Richardson observed of a case involving the federal

Crown, 'the arguments that the government brought to court would be a source of deep shame to Canadians, if only more of us knew about them.'[33] Examples abounded in the Oldman Dam cases.

Another case in point is Martha Kostuch's attempts to prosecute Alberta for its violations of the Fisheries Act. Although not reported as such by the media, the major issues in this series of actions became the right of a private citizen to prosecute the government, the determination of the provincial attorney general to use his power to prevent that prosecution, and the reluctance of the courts to exercise their power to overrule the attorney general. By not pointing out what is really going on in these instances, the media inadvertently support the manipulations of morally bankrupt politicians and bureaucrats, the clever footwork of their ethically challenged legal representatives, and the timidity of the bench.

30
Does It Matter?

> This dispute is not about facts. It is not even about water, which
> can be provided in many ways. It is about the privileges that flow
> from political power. It's an exchange of public money for
> political support. Politicians are always hungry for votes and
> southern Alberta is always hungry for more water.
>
> – Joanne Helmer, *Lethbridge Herald*[1]

The Oldman River Dam stands. In the end the Alberta government won;
the people of Three Rivers, the environment, the Peigan, and, in a larger
sense, the people of Canada lost. Does it really matter? Alberta's Oldman
River Dam Project pales in comparison with China's Three Gorges Project,
which will create a 660-kilometre-long reservoir submerging 450 towns
and villages and displacing 1.2 million people, or India's Narmada River
Project, which will flood 4,000 square kilometres of land and displace 1.5
million people. The twenty-one families whose lives were disrupted to
make way for the Oldman Dam have been resettled; if life is not as pleasant for them in their new locations as it was at Three Rivers, at least they
have homes and they are no worse off economically. Anglers still cast their
lines in the Oldman, Castle, and Crowsnest Rivers; if the fish are not as
abundant or the scenery as grand as in former times, they are still able to
land their quota, and the valleys away from the reservoir are as beautiful
as they ever were. The Peigan still live on their reserve below the dam; they
have reaped no benefits from the project and they have lost a part of their
spiritual geography; otherwise, they are no worse off than before the dam
was built. The Lonefighters have faded into obscurity and Milton Born
With A Tooth is all but forgotten. The riparian ecosystems downstream
from Three Rivers remain intact; only time will tell if the operation of the
dam will destroy the cottonwood forests and upset the biological diversity
of the Oldman River valley. The environmentalists have moved on to fight
other battles: Special Places, Cheviot, Kananaskis, and the West Country.
Meanwhile, the amount of irrigated land in the Oldman basin has increased substantially, the livestock industry is thriving, and agriculture is
again on a sound footing in southern Alberta. But despite all of this, there
are things about the Oldman Project that really do matter.

It matters that Canadians continue to two-bit the environment into submission. If Planet Earth is taken to be Hardin's commons, the Oldman Project is an element, albeit a small one, in an unfolding tragedy.[2] Politicians

mouth all the correct words about environmental protection, sustainable development, and human rights, while cynically manipulating the framework of laws established to provide these things in order to encourage and facilitate the systematic exploitation of publicly owned resources, frequently for the benefit of a limited few at the expense of the common good.

Ken Kowalski said he could 'think of no more important environmental improvement or enhancement project that has been undertaken in a great length of time in North America than that of the Oldman River Dam.'[3] Martha Kostuch called it 'an unmitigated disaster.' Which of them is right? To irrigation farmers and engineers in the water management business, any project in the water-deficient southern Prairies that makes more water available to grow crops enhances what they see as a harsh and barren environment. For business interests, any project that injects provincial money into the local economy is good, and for politicians, if it buys votes in a concentrated area it is even better. At the other end of the spectrum, the environmentalists believe that any project that dramatically alters the existing environmental balance is a desecration, especially if it is for the benefit of a privileged minority.

Whatever their perspective, no one denied that construction of a dam on the Oldman River at a point where the water in its reservoir would inundate parts of three river valleys, and operation of the dam to regulate the flow of the river downstream would alter the environment. What was at issue was the extent and significance of the consequences of those alterations. To the proponents, the impacts were minor, entirely mitigable with measures devised and implemented by WMS, and strictly of local concern. To those opposed to the project, the impacts were severe, they were not amenable to mitigation, and at least of national concern. Beyond that, they saw the project as a violation of the concept of sustainable development.

The ORDEAP did not address, directly, the issue of sustainable development. It did, however, conclude that the 'known losses of river valley ecosystem' resulting from the project were 'significant,' and that the potential losses of 'riparian forest and native prairie' were 'of even greater significance.'[4] It acknowledged that there would be benefits from irrigation – the sole reason for building the dam – but said that in the prevailing climate of economic diversification in Alberta, there was 'little need to promote new irrigation agriculture to support economic growth.'[5] In sum, the panel found that 'the social, economic and environmental costs of the project outweigh the social, economic and environmental benefits.'[6] In other words, the Oldman River Dam Project is not sustainable from any perspective.

It matters that our governments lie, break the law, abuse their powers, and manage information to serve their political ends. I said at the outset that this book is not for or against the Oldman River Dam, it is about how the protagonists conducted themselves. The evidence suggests that while none of them conducted themselves entirely with honour, the two governments behaved most shamefully. Alberta was bold and aggressive. It manoeuvred around its own laws and policies, it violated federal laws, it used its power to avoid being prosecuted for a crime it had clearly committed, it lied to the Peigan, and it withheld information from the federal government, from the courts, and from the public inquiry. The federal government was meek and submissive. For several years it pretended that whatever was going on in the Oldman was none of its business, it acted to enforce its laws only when ordered to do so by the courts, it failed to exercise its fiduciary duty to the Peigan, and it disregarded the recommendations of its environmental assessment panel. Both governments blatantly raided the public purse to defend themselves against attempts by citizens to make them obey the law and follow the dictates of the courts. And in the aftermath they colluded, in the name of harmony, to preclude independent federal intervention in environmental assessments of projects proposed by the province so that in future they could stand together in the face of opposition rather than apart, as had been the case in the Oldman. As demonstrated by the joint Pine Coulee review, harmony was achieved by subordinating the federal process to that of the province and by erecting barriers to participation in those processes by Native people and broadly based public interest groups. The steps taken to ensure harmony between governments will result in disharmony between the people of Canada and the environment in which they live.

It matters that governments have been able to render ineffective the efforts of interest groups that challenge their management of our environment. The coalition of environmental interest groups active in the Oldman controversy accomplished three things: it brought the project and the shameful performances of the federal and provincial governments to public attention; it forced the federal government to apply its EARPGO to the project; and, though that was not its intent, it exposed the ineffectiveness of the environmental impact assessment process. It was unable to prevent the construction of the Oldman Dam or the environmental destruction that will ensue from the project. Some will argue, and they may well be right, that the intervention of FOR prompted the Alberta government to do more to mitigate the environmental impacts of the dam than it might otherwise have done. Whether Alberta will persist in the implementation of mitigative measures and how effective they will be remains to be seen.

Because governments have virtually unlimited access to the public purse, they are able to outlast public interest groups in the conduct of legal actions and the management of information. Only the unselfish dedication and public-spirited, hard work of individual FOR members, the willingness of some of their legal advisors and counsel to work at reduced fees, and the support of other environmental organizations allowed FOR to fight the two governments in court for so long.

FOR's one successful legal action, that over the application of the EARPGO, initially held out some promise for stopping construction of the dam, but in the long run it accomplished nothing. Once a dispute over a development project becomes the subject of legal action, governments commonly excuse themselves from commenting publicly on the issue on the grounds that their lawyers have advised them to do so. The absence of public debate on the issue limits its news value, sparing the governments and the project much of the bad publicity they might otherwise have received. Once the issue is before the courts, governments can, and frequently do, delay the culmination of the action until the media and the public have lost interest or until the project is built and the 'balance of convenience' has shifted to the project. Such was the case in the Oldman Project. The Supreme Court's final ruling on application of the EARPGO was delayed until February 1992, by which time the dam was virtually completed. Alberta had managed to buy the time it needed before the weight of the law, the environmental review, and public pressure forced it or the federal government to bring the project to a halt.

It is futile to look to the courts to protect the environment over the long term. The courts can be very inconsistent, as the various judgments on the Oldman demonstrated. At best they may force governments to abide by their own laws. They can't create law, and they can't prevent governments from changing laws (nor should they be able to do so); and they are clearly not prepared to limit interventions by attorneys general to prevent the criminal prosecution of their governments (as in Oldman) and others (as in British Columbia) for breaking laws (as in the federal Fisheries Act) intended to protect the environment.

It matters that the process of environmental impact assessment, which was introduced as a means of protecting the environment, has become simply another bureaucratic obstacle to be overcome in the continuing quest by the greedy to get more than their share of the nation's natural endowment while bearing a diminishing share of the cost. Ironically, the most important and lasting legacy of the Oldman controversy, and probably the most threatening to the environment, is the 'harmonization' of provincial and federal laws, policies, and arrangements for environmental protection. The federal government's willingness to 'harmonize' its environmental assessment process with those of the provinces and the drive by the Department of Fisheries and Oceans to delegate responsibility for s. 35 of the Fisheries Act to the 'inland provinces' indicate that there are strong forces within the federal bureaucracy and at the cabinet table who would be content to see the federal role in environmental assessment revert to what it was assumed to be in the days before Rafferty-Alameda and the Oldman. They regard environmental assessment as an obstacle to politically motivated economic development and a source of conflict with the provinces that they could do without.

The 1993 Canada-Alberta Agreement for Environmental Assessment Co-operation, in practice, effectively subordinates the federal process for assessing the impact of projects on areas of federal jurisdiction in Alberta to that of the province. This was demonstrated convincingly by the joint NRCB/EARP review of the Alberta government's Pine Coulee Project. The joint review panel, comprised of one federal and two provincial appointees, and chaired by one of the provincial appointees, operated in accordance with a process and rules of procedure developed by the province. Though the federal government contributed to the terms of reference for the review, areas of federal responsibility were given little or no attention.

The contrast between the performance of the joint Pine Coulee panel and the federal Oldman panel with regard to the Peigan was particularly striking. While the Oldman panel went out of its way to accommodate participation by the Peigan, the joint Pine Coulee panel placed the Peigan in the all too familiar role of cultural outsider. Where the Oldman panel did its best to understand the impact of the Oldman Dam on the Peigan, the Pine Coulee panel refused to accede to a Peigan request that Alberta present the results of an analysis that would have indicated the relationship between the Pine Coulee Project and the Peigan's water rights claims.[7] And where the Oldman panel reflected its understanding of issues raised by the Peigan in its report and recommendations, the Pine Coulee panel pointedly refused to comment on two of the main Peigan concerns: Alberta's failure to communicate with the Peigan about the project and the impact of the project on Peigan water rights.[8] The panel's failure to explain why it refused to comment on these concerns added insult to injury. Alberta excused its failure to consult with the Peigan on the archaeological resources in the Pine Coulee area with the explanation that while 'it may be that there is an evolution in thinking and that there should be consultation with aboriginals at early stages of the review process ... this is not the present law in Alberta.' How any panel, much less one with federal representation, could avoid comment on that claim is beyond comprehension. Though it was somewhat more attentive to Native concerns about archaeological resources, the 1998 NRCB/CEAA review of Alberta's Little Bow Project/Highwood Diversion Plan was largely a repeat performance.

The environmental assessment industry (consisting of government agencies, consultants, academics, quasi-judicial panels and their burgeoning support staffs, lawyers, and public interest groups) was spawned by good intentions, but as it becomes increasingly adversarial in its conduct, reductionist in its outlook, and complex in its processes, it has become a large part of the problem. This is most apparent in the harmonized reviews that are now the norm in Alberta.

It matters that the protagonists in disputes over the management of publicly owned resources regard information management as a legitimate tool for achieving their objectives. In so doing they deny the rest of us access to information that would help us to draw our own conclusions about whether a proposal is in the public good or otherwise. In the Oldman, the Alberta government, as the proponent of the project and the regulator of the resource, had a monopoly on information pertinent to the dam project and its potential impact. It used its monopoly position to withhold and control access to that information, and it spent liberally of public funds to disseminate information casting the project in a favourable light. Environmental interest groups and Indian bands, while equally willing to use information management as a tool, do not have comparable resources at their disposal.

It matters that our governments continue to treat Canada's Indian people unfairly. Their persistent refusal to do the decent thing and to be honest and open in dealings with Indians does nothing to pave the way to a just and peaceful settlement of the issues that come between Indian people and other Canadians. Politicians say all the right things about Native peoples and their aspirations, while failing to defend their rights and extending the practices of paternalism begun in the last century. In the Oldman, decisions were made and the dam was constructed without any meaningful consultation between Alberta and the Peigan. Meanwhile, federal bureaucrats and politicians strained their necks looking the other way, doing their utmost to pretend that the project would have no impact on the Peigan. In so doing, they failed abysmally to exercise their fiduciary duty to the Peigan to ensure that the project was in their interest.

What was learned from this controversy? On the positive side, precious little. On the negative side, a lot – perhaps *confirmed* is a better word than *learned*, since most of it we knew already.

We learned that greed and avarice are nothing to be ashamed of and that, as always, the squeaky wheels, if they are sufficiently concentrated to represent a significant voting bloc, will get the grease. We learned that politicians and bureaucrats, federal and provincial, can break the rules, misuse the system, and manage information to their advantage without the risk of serious repercussions. We learned that lawyers need not be deterred by their ignorance of matters beyond the law from attempting to sway the views of their betters on the bench. We learned that the means the public has at its disposal to protect the environment – laws, environmental impact assessments, access to the courts, public opinion – are not effective in preventing governments from having their way. We learned that, despite the recommendations of government enquiries, the rulings of the courts and the urging of fair-minded citizens and institutions, those who govern Canada continue to bully and lie to our Indian population as they have done for the past 500 years. If anyone doubts this, let them examine the behaviour of the Alberta and federal governments in the conduct of the Pine Coulee Project.

The people of Alberta and Canada, whether supporters of the governments in power or otherwise, learned that what those governments say about the importance of protecting the environment and ensuring that Indian people are treated fairly and with respect is not borne out by their actions. They might also have learned that if they wish to conserve the natural environment, they cannot leave the job to special interest groups, which can easily be isolated and marginalized and ultimately overwhelmed by governments. In the words of Canadian philosopher Charles Taylor, 'The mills of democratic politics ineluctably grind such small islands of resistance into powder.'[9]

As citizens in a democratic society, we must hope and trust that those whom we elect to represent our interests will see to it that our publicly owned resources are protected and conserved. But Canada's present governments, federal and provincial, not only lack the will to enforce the measures they have enacted to protect the environment, but they also seem to believe that the people of Canada do not really expect them to do so. According to the polls, and politicians are devout students of the polls, our governments may be right. Although Canadians continue to identify environmental protection as a concern, we assign it a much lower priority than other issues. Polls conducted in late 1997 indicated that less than 2 percent of Canadians rated the environment as a top priority concern, which is about where it stood in 1986, in the trough between waves of environmental concern, when construction of the Oldman Dam began.[10]

The last word goes to Charles Taylor, who warns that 'the battle of isolated communities or groups against ecological desolation [is] bound to be a losing one until such time as some common understanding and a common sense of purpose forms in society as a whole about the preservation of the environment.'[11]

Notes

Introduction

1 Canada, Oldman River Dam Environmental Assessment Panel, *Compendium of Submissions* (Vancouver: Federal Environmental Assessment Review Office, 22 October 1991), 489.

Chapter 1: The Oldman River Basin

1 Kevin Van Tighem, 'Who Speaks for Running Waters,' *Coming West: A Natural History of Home* (Canmore, AB: Altitude Publishing, 1997), 192.

2 This is about 36 percent of the mean annual flow of the South Saskatchewan River. The Bow contributes 44 percent; the Red Deer the remaining 20 percent.

3 *Master Agreement on Apportionment* (Regina: Prairie Provinces Water Board, 30 October 1969).

4 Ibid., Schedule A, s. 2(c). The confluence of the Red Deer and South Saskatchewan Rivers is in Saskatchewan, a few miles downstream from the Alberta/Saskatchewan boundary.

5 Alberta, Alberta Environment, *Water Resource Management Principles for Alberta* (Edmonton, n.d. [1980?]), 10.

6 Liz Bryan, *The Buffalo People: Prehistoric Archaeology on the Canadian Plains* (Edmonton: University of Alberta Press, 1991), 5 ff.

7 Hugh A. Dempsey, *Indian Tribes of Alberta* (Calgary: Glenbow Museum, 1979), 8.

8 Ibid., 9.

9 Ibid., 11.

10 This was reduced in 1909, when a portion of the reserve was ceded to the federal government and 4,654 hectares were sold to local ranchers. The Peigan later claimed that this transaction was not legal because proper procedures were not followed, and in 1987, the federal government paid the Peigan $6 million in compensation.

11 Dempsey, *Indian Tribes of Alberta*, 33.

12 The CPR had earlier been opposed to any 'talk' of irrigation in the west, on the grounds that it 'would do a lot of damage to land sales.' (Letter, Burgess/Pearce, 12 February 1891, *William Pearce Papers*, File 13 A. 1, Rare Book Room, University of Alberta).

13 North-west Irrigation Act, 57-58 Vict., c. 30.

14 Prairie Farm Rehabilitation Act, 25-26 George V, c. 23, s. 4.

15 R.S.C. 1952, c. 214, s. 4.

16 The federal works included the St. Mary and Waterton Dams; the Belly River Diversion and the St. Mary Main Canal in the Oldman basin; and the WID (Western Irrigation District) and Carseland headworks, including McGregor and Travers Reservoirs, in the Bow Basin.

17 Alberta, Alberta Environment and Alberta Agriculture, *Water Management for Irrigation Use*, Alberta Sessional Paper 502/75, 20 May 1975.

18 Canada, Department of the Interior, *Report on Irrigation Surveys and Inspection, 1915-1916* (Ottawa, 1916).

19 Canada, Department of the Interior, *Report on Irrigation Surveys and Inspections, 1916-1917* (Ottawa, 1917).

Chapter 2: In the Beginning

1 Alberta, Alberta Environment and Alberta Agriculture, *Water Management for Irrigation Use*, Alberta Sessional Paper 502/75, 20 May 1975.
2 See various statements by Alberta Environment Minister Bill Yurko in Alberta Department of Environment and the Canadian Council of Resource and Environment Ministers, *Proceedings of the Alberta Prairie Water Seminar-Third Tier*, Banff, AB, 1-3 December 1971.
3 Alberta, Alberta Environment and Alberta Agriculture, *Water Management for Irrigation Use*, Alberta Sessional Paper 502/75, 20 May 1975.
4 Alberta, Alberta Environment, *Oldman River Flow Regulation Preliminary Planning Studies*, vol. 1 (Edmonton, June 1976), letter of transmittal.
5 Ibid., 79.
6 Ibid., 161.
7 Ibid., 53.
8 Alberta Environment, *Red Deer River Flow Regulation Planning Studies* (Edmonton, June 1975).
9 'LNID canals may close to let reservoir fill,' *Lethbridge Herald*, 14 July 1976.
10 'Cost questioned on Oldman water storage plans,' *Lethbridge Herald*, 21 July 1976.
11 Editorial, 'Build the dam,' *Lethbridge Herald*, 15 July 1976.
12 'Conflicting statistics traded at dam meeting,' *Lethbridge Herald*, 2 December 1976.
13 'Reserve dam site not counted out,' *Lethbridge Herald*, 24 November 1976.
14 Alberta, Oldman River Study Management Committee, *Oldman River Basin: Phase II Studies: Report and Recommendations* (Lethbridge, 1978), 1.
15 Ibid., Appendix 1, 70. The civil servants on the committee were Peter Melnychuk and Henry Theissen of Environment and Cy McAndrews of Agriculture, all ADMs, and Dick Bennett of Environment, who was also an irrigation farmer. The private citizens were Jack Brewin, an irrigation farmer and chairman of the board of directors of the SMRID and of the AIPA; John Zoeteman, an irrigation farmer in the LNID; Jim Almond, a Lethbridge businessman; Lawrence Barany, a dryland farmer from Taber; Ron Buchanan, a rancher in the Three Rivers area and a member of the Committee for the Preservation of Three Rivers; and Hilton Pharis, a rancher from the Cowley area. Buchanan subsequently resigned from the committee.
16 'Between the Guidelines,' *Environment Views* 3, 2: 8-9.
17 Alberta, Oldman River Study Management Committee, *Oldman River Basin: Phase II Studies*, 60 ff.
18 'Debris removal allows LNID water,' *Lethbridge Herald*, 3 June 1978.
19 Alberta, Oldman River Study Management Committee, *Oldman River Basin: Phase II Studies*, 62.

Chapter 3: The ECA Review

1 Alberta O.C. 803/78, 17 July 1978.
2 Environment Conservation Authority, *First Annual Report* (Edmonton, November 1971), 10.
3 Environment Conservation Authority, *Flood Control and Water Management in the Paddle River Basin: Report and Recommendations* (Edmonton, March 1975).
4 'Notley raps ECA demise,' *Calgary Herald*, 10 August 1977.
5 Ibid.
6 'Oldman hearing panel nomination deadline set,' *Lethbridge Herald*, 21 April 1978.
7 Alberta, Environment Council of Alberta, *Management of Water Resources within the Oldman River Basin: Report and Recommendations* (Edmonton, 1979).
8 Ibid., 196.
9 Ibid., 150.
10 *Onstream storage* involves the construction of a dam across a river valley to capture some portion of the river's flow, which is stored in the reservoir that forms in the valley behind the dam. Water stored in an onstream reservoir can be released into the river downstream from the dam or conveyed by a canal or other means to some other destination. *Offstream storage* normally involves the construction of a weir in a river to divert some portion of

the river's flow into a canal or pipeline for conveyance to a reservoir (usually an existing lake, depression, or coulee that has been diked to enhance its storage capability) some distance from the river. Because river flows in southern Alberta are high for such a short period, where river valley conditions are favourable to the formation of a large reservoir, more water can be captured and stored onstream than can be diverted for storage off-stream. The creation of either onstream or offstream storage has environmental implications. Both obstruct streamflow, an onstream dam more so than a diversion weir. Water stored onstream can be released into the river to maintain streamflow at times when natural flow would be low (a capability often offered in support of onstream storage); whether this actually happens is of course an operating decision. Water diverted to off-stream storage is not available to maintain streamflow in the donor river, since works are not normally built to convey water from offstream storage back to the river. Water stored in a reservoir, whether onstream or offstream, inundates the land within the reservoir area. However, river valley land is usually of greater value for wildlife habitat or recreational use than is the land in areas converted to offstream storage.

11 Alberta, Environment Council of Alberta, *Management of Water Resources within the Oldman River Basin: Report and Recommendations* (Edmonton, 1979), 196, 197. The only instance in which the panel could see a need for a dam on the Oldman was if the government and the Peigan were unable to agree on access to the LNID weir, in which case it saw a dam at Fort Macleod as the only alternative to abandoning the LNID (ibid., 150.)
12 Ibid., 28.
13 Ibid., 182.
14 Ibid., 145.
15 Ibid., 146, 148.
16 Ibid., 146.
17 Supplementary Brief No. 218, submitted by John W. Smith, in Environment Council of Alberta, *Supplementary Briefs to Public Hearings on Management of Water Resources within the Oldman River Basin* (Edmonton, n.d.), 54. This document was published in 1978.
18 Alberta, Environment Council of Alberta, *Management of Water Resources within the Oldman River Basin: Report and Recommendations* (Edmonton, 1979), 171, 198.
19 'Environmental chief still eyes a dam,' *Lethbridge Herald*, 27 August 1979, and Editorial, 'The crucial problem,' *Lethbridge Herald*, 29 August 1979.
20 *Alberta Hansard*, 19th Legislature, 2nd Session (20 March 1980): 4.
21 'Water use plan to be proposed,' *Calgary Herald*, 11 April 1980.
22 *Alberta Hansard*, 19th Legislature, 2nd Session (28 April 1980): 607.
23 'Plans for dam far from certain,' *Calgary Herald*, 9 June 1980.
24 'Oldman dam still undecided, says Cookson,' *Calgary Herald*, 12 August 1980.

Chapter 4: A Dam on the Oldman
1 Richard C. Bocking, *Canada's Water: For Sale?* (Toronto: James Lewis and Samuel, 1972), 126.
2 'Water Resources and Irrigation Development in Southern Alberta,' *Ministerial Statement*, by J.W. (Jack) Cookson, minister of environment, and Dallas Schmidt, minister of agriculture, 29 August 1980.
3 In 1980, the irrigation districts that obtained their water supply from the Oldman River were committed to supply water to 229,000 hectares of land (Alberta Agriculture, Irrigation Branch, *Alberta Irrigation Districts Acreages, Water Rates and Crop Summaries, 1994*, Lethbridge, May 1995).
4 'The river's closed says rancher,' *Lethbridge Herald*, 29 August 1980, 1.
5 Ibid.
6 Ibid.
7 'Dam decision will not deter recommendations,' *Lethbridge Herald*, 4 September 1980.
8 Letter from Hon. John W. (Jack) Cookson, minister of environment, to Dr. D. Thompson, 16 September 1980.
9 'Build the dam,' *Lethbridge Herald*, 15 July 1976.
10 'Dam decision,' *Lethbridge Herald*, 2 September 1980.

11 'Turning irrigation tap,' *Calgary Herald,* 6 September 1980.
12 'Peigans willing to discuss dam on reserve,' *Lethbridge Herald,* 30 August 1980.
13 Ibid.
14 This account draws on information in a report prepared by Alberta's native affairs secretariat, *Peigan Indian Band/Government of Alberta Resolution of the Oldman River Irrigation System Dispute: A Case Study,* rev. ed. (Edmonton, 1984); and the sworn testimony of Henry Theissen at Milton Born With A Tooth's trial in Alberta Court of Queen's Bench, Calgary, 22 February to 11 March 1994.
15 Woods Gordon Management Consultants, *Summary Consolidation of Consultant's Reports on the Impacts of the Proposed Brocket Reservoir, Oldman River* (Edmonton, 1983).
16 Letter from Peigan Band Administration to the minister of environment and Members of the Alberta Legislative Assembly, 10 November 1983 (Exhibit CC to Lorand K. Szojka's Affidavit to Federal Court of Canada, Trial Division, T-865-89, 15 June 1989).
17 'Prayers ask for rain,' *Lethbridge Herald,* 16 July 1984.
18 'Lougheed's gesture will be remembered,' *Lethbridge Herald,* 11 August 1984.
19 Peter Melnychuk, personal interview, 14 June 1994.
20 Bradley's letter advised that cabinet had 'examined the Weasel Valley study summary report and the Band conditions for reservoir development at Brocket, as identified in your letter of 10 November, 1983, and concluded that the interests of Albertans would best be served by a dam constructed at the Three Rivers site' (Alberta Sessional Paper No. 555/84, 2 Session, 20 Legislature).
21 'Peigans plan to build dam on reserve,' *Lethbridge Herald,* 11 August 1984.
22 'Dam plan angers fish, game group,' *Calgary Herald,* 14 August 1984.
23 'Dam on the way' and 'Lougheed promises more water security,' *Lethbridge Herald,* 11 August 1984.
24 'Oldman Dam Announcement,' Alberta Environment *News Release* (9 August 1984).
25 Editorial, 'Dam's enormous benefits don't answer all questions,' *Lethbridge Herald,* 10 August 1984.
26 Ibid., and Editorial, 'Other costs possible at Three Rivers site,' *Lethbridge Herald,* 10 August 1984.

Chapter 5: Interlude
1 *Edmonton Journal,* quoted in *AWA Wise Use Newsletter* 1 (Spring 1991).
2 Alberta, Alberta Environment, *South Saskatchewan River Basin Planning Program: Summary Report* (Edmonton, 1984).
3 Included amongst the senior bureaucrats on the commission were Peter Melnychuk, head of Environment's Water Management Service, and Doug Radke, head of Agriculture's Planning and Development Sector, the agencies responsible for implementing the government's 1975 *Water Management for Irrigation Use* policy.
4 Henry Kroeger served as minister of transport from 1979 to 1982. He died in November 1987.
5 When interviewed for this book in October 1993, Jensen was president of Unifarm, the major lobby group for agricultural commodity producers in Alberta.
6 Alberta Water Resources Commission, *Re: South Saskatchewan River Basin Planning Program, Public Hearings,* Lethbridge, AB, 13 November 1994, Vol. I (Edmonton: November-December, 1984), 137-40.
7 'That dam issue,' originally published as an editorial in the *Tabor Times,* reprinted in the *Pincher Creek Echo,* 15 September 1982.
8 Alberta Water Resources Commission, *Re: South Saskatchewan River Basin Planning Program, Public Hearings,* Lethbridge, AB, 13 November 1994, Vol. I (Edmonton: November-December, 1984), 183.
9 Alberta, Alberta Water Resources Commission, *Water Management in the South Saskatchewan River Basin: Report and Recommendations* (Edmonton, n.d.), 76. This report was released in October 1986.
10 Alberta Environment, *Update* (June 1986): 3.
11 'Peigan people battling for survival,' *Lethbridge Herald,* 3 January 1986.

12 *Proclamation, Peigan Indian Nation, Respecting Title to Water and Water Rights in the Oldman River,* January 1986.
13 Peter Lougheed resigned as head of Alberta's Progressive Conservatives in the fall of 1985, and the party selected Don Getty to take his place.
14 The cabinet approved the proposal on 20 May 1986.
15 *Chief Peter Yellowhorn of the Peigan Indian Band on behalf of himself and all other members of the Peigan Indian Band* v. *Her Majesty the Queen in the Right of the Province of Alberta,* Statement of Claim filed in the Alberta Court of Queen's Bench, Calgary, on 11 April 1986 (8601-06578).
16 *Chief Peter Yellowhorn of the Peigan Indian Band on behalf of himself and all other members of the Peigan Indian Band* v. *Her Majesty the Queen in the Right of Canada and the Honourable David Crombie, Minister of Indian Affairs and Northern Development,* Statement of Claim filed in the Federal Court of Canada, Trial Division, Montreal, on 19 June 1986 (T-1486-86).
17 Alberta Environment, 'Main engineering report complete,' *Update* (November 1986).
18 Committee for the Preservation of Three Rivers, 'Submission to the Hon. Dave Russell, minister of environment, Regarding Oldman River Flow Regulation Planning Studies' (12 November 1976) and Committee for the Preservation of Three Rivers, 'Presentation to the Provincial Cabinet' (Lethbridge, AB: 20 September 1977).
19 There are two songs on the 45 RPM recording, produced by A. Westrop and recorded at Southern Sound Studios in Lethbridge, AB, in 1978: *Three Rivers,* written by Dan Reeder, and *Misty Dreams,* written by Dan Reeder and D. Bly. The songs are sung by Dan Reeder, a local country and western singer, who performed free of charge.
20 Marie Louise Million, '"It Was Home": A Phenomenology of Place and Involuntary Displacement as Illustrated by the Forced Dislocation of Five Southern Alberta Families in the Oldman River Dam Flood Area,' (PhD dissertation, Saybrook Institute Graduate School and Research Centre, San Francisco [1991]), 284.
21 The figure of sixteen families (a total of sixty-one people) is taken from Audrey Westrop's submission to the panel (Canada, Oldman River Dam Environmental Assessment Panel, *Addendum to Compendium of Submissions Dated October 22, 1991,* vol. 2 [Vancouver: Federal Environmental Assessment Review Office, 31 December 1991], 1158). Westrop says fifteen farmsteads were taken in total; the government puts the figure at eighteen farmsteads (Alberta, Alberta Public Works, Supply and Services, *The Oldman River Dam: Building a Future for Southern Alberta* [Edmonton, 1992], 44).
22 Peter Melnychuk, personal interview, 15 June 1994.
23 Louise Million recorded one landowner's description of attending information meetings with government bureaucrats during the course of the land acquisition process. He describes a scene where the bureaucrats sat at the front of the room facing the landowners and conducted *their* meeting according to *their* agenda (Million, 'It Was Home,' 409). Another recorded his disillusionment on finding that while the government was paying the lawyers it had contracted $200 per hour for negotiating with the landowners, including their time spent 'sitting on a plane,' the landowners got 'zip' for their time (ibid., 298).
24 Alberta, Public Works Supply and Services, Oldman River Dam Environmental Advisory Committee, *Oldman River Dam Social and Landuse Impact Study* by Linda D. Cerney (September 1994).
25 Million, 'It Was Home,' Appendix.
26 Memo from Dr. George Kupfer to Patricia Woodward, Federal Environmental Assessment Review Office, 5 November 1991, included as an Addendum to Section 10.0 of Canada, Oldman River Dam Environmental Assessment Panel, *Response to the Panel's Additional Information Requirements Document* (Vancouver: Federal Environmental Assessment Review Office, 1991).

Chapter 6: The Battle Joined
1 Luna B. Leopold, 'Ethos, Equity, and the Water Resource,' *Environment* 32 (March 1990): 37.
2 Interim Licence pursuant to the Water Resources Act No. 14628, issued 18 August 1987. The Water Resources Act (R.S.A. 1980, c. W-5, s. 16) directs the minister to require an

applicant to give public notice of an application filed under the act, and, for thirty days thereafter, the minister is obliged to receive objections from anyone opposed to the application. The minister may, however, waive the requirement to give notice, 'if he considers it expedient and fit and proper to do so' (ibid., s. 19).

3 FOR *News Release* (September 1987).
4 Editorial, 'Why do we need dam on Oldman,' *Lethbridge Herald*, 10 September 1987.
5 'Friends of Oldman River called "social anarchists,"' *Lethbridge Herald*, 12 September 1987.
6 Ibid.; 'The dam dispute won't die,' *Alberta Report* (26 October 1987); and *Trout Canada* (Spring 1988): 3.
7 The CEDF says its 'purpose is to provide funding, fund-raising assistance, legal, scientific, planning and engineering referrals and organizational support to grass-roots groups pursuing nationally significant environmental law cases.'
8 'Scientists fear loss of historic artifacts,' *Calgary Herald*, 18 October 1987.
9 'Health, safety officials shut down dam tunnel,' *Lethbridge Herald*, 23 October 1987.
10 B.O.K. Reeves, *Oldman River Dam Phase II Archaeological and Historical Resources Inventory and Assessment of Pre-historic Sites: Recommendations* (Calgary: Lifeways Canada Ltd., February 1987), 1.
11 'Oldman River Dam Project Historical Resources Impact Assessment,' Alberta Environment *News Release* (18 November 1987): 1.
12 Ibid., 2.
13 'Archaeological Survey of Alberta approves continued construction of Oldman River Dam,' *Lethbridge Herald*, 21 November 1987.
14 'Oldman River Dam Project Historical Resources Impact Assessment,' Alberta Environment *News Release* (18 November 1987): 1.
15 The 'no net loss' concept was borrowed from Canada, Department of Fisheries and Oceans, *Policy for the Management of Fish Habitat* (Ottawa, 7 October 1986). DF&O, however, used the term to describe its policy of no net loss of the productive capacity of habitats.
16 'Scientists fear loss of historic artifacts,' *Calgary Herald*, 18 October 1987.
17 'FOR wants energy board to decide dam issue,' *Lethbridge Herald*, 21 December 1987.
18 'Decline of downstream poplars a concern,' *Lethbridge Herald*, 22 December 1987, and Stewart Rood, Letters, 'Biologist explains facts of poplar stands,' *Lethbridge Herald*, 8 December 1987.
19 Cheryl Bradley's research in the Milk River valley had produced similar results. See C. Bradley and D. Smith, 'Plains Cottonwood Recruitment and Survival on a Prairie Meandering River Floodplain, Milk River, Alberta and Northern Montana,' *Canadian Journal of Botany* 64 (1985): 1433-42.
20 'Oldman dam site flooded with counterclaims,' *Calgary Herald*, 18 October 1987; 'Irrigation controversies worry EID manager,' *Brooks Bulletin*, 4 November 1987.
21 'AIPA fails to offset concentrated barrage of distorted news,' *Brooks Bulletin*, 18 November 1987.
22 'Irrigation controversies worry EID manager,' *Brooks Bulletin*, 4 November 1987.
23 *Friends of the Oldman River Society* v. *Alberta (Minister of Environment)* (1987), 56 Alta. L.R. (2d) 368 (Q.B.).
24 'Oldman permits not valid,' *Edmonton Journal*, 10 December 1987, and *Alberta Hansard* 21st Legislature, 2nd Session, Vol. III (9 December 1987): 2285, 2290.
25 Editorial, 'Bumbling for all to see,' *Calgary Herald*, 10 December 1987.
26 'Group backs Alberta dam project,' *Globe and Mail*, 17 December 1987.
27 *Alberta Hansard*, 21st Legislature, 2nd Session, Vol. III (10 December 1987): 2318-29.
28 'Dam action questioned,' *Calgary Sun*, 16 December 1987.
29 Interim Licence pursuant to the Water Resources Act, No. 15410, issued 5 February 1988.
30 'Kowalski brushes off opposition to project,' *Calgary Herald*, 9 February 1988.
31 *Friends of the Oldman River Society* v. *Alberta (Minister of Environment)* (1988), 89 A.R. 339 (Q.B.).
32 Ibid.

33 'Decision brings disbelief,' *Calgary Herald,* 10 December 1987, and 'Opening cracks in the Oldman,' *Alberta Report* (21 December 1987): 20.

34 'Story of water management relayed to province, public,' *Lethbridge Herald,* 23 December 1987.

35 'FOR just a new face put on for government lobby,' *Lethbridge Herald,* 23 December 1987.

36 Included among those supporters were staff from Alberta Environment's Lethbridge office, whose attendance, at government expense, the *Lethbridge Herald* claimed, had been 'strongly suggested' by departmental officials ('Dart,' *Lethbridge Herald,* 12 March 1988).

37 Fisheries Act, R.S.C. 1985, c. F-14, s. 35.

38 The various 'habitat enhancement structures' are described in Alberta, Public Works, Supply and Services, *A Strategy for Fisheries Mitigation in the Oldman River Basin, Volume I: Upstream Component* (Edmonton, May 1988). The plan included the selective placement of rocks and boulders in the stream to create 'boulder gardens,' 'flow deflectors,' and 'rock weirs.'

39 Editorial, 'Getty clears deadwood,' *Calgary Herald,* 8 September 1988.

40 'Getty to walk tightrope between environment, economy,' *Edmonton Journal,* 8 September 1988.

41 'Environmentalists praise ousting of Kowalski,' *Lethbridge Herald,* 9 September 1988.

42 Bob Kambeitz, 'Fairness and the Water Resources Act,' *Trout Canada* (Summer 1988).

Chapter 7: The EARPGO Challenge

1 Mr. Justice Stone, Federal Court of Appeal, *Friends of the Oldman River Society* v. *Canada (Minister of Transport),* [1990] 2 F.C. 40 (F.C.A.).

2 *Canada Gazette, Part II* (11 July 1984), Environmental Assessment and Review Process Guidelines Order, SOR/84-467.

3 *Canadian Wildlife Federation Inc., et al.* v. *Canada (Minister of the Environment) and Saskatchewan Water Corp.,* Federal Court (T.D.), 28 April 1989, 26 F.T.R. 245.

4 Not all Saskatchewan members of the CWF were pleased with the Court's ruling. As was later to happen in Alberta, when local and provincial members of the AF&GA took opposing stands on the Oldman Dam, CWF members in the project area supported the dam in contradiction of the national and provincial wings of the federation.

5 Navigable Waters Protection Act, R.S.C. 1985, c. N-22.

6 Letter from Mary E. Bailey, president, SAEG, to Hon. Tom Siddon, minister of fisheries and oceans, August 1987, quoted in *Friends of the Oldman River Society* v. *Canada (Minister of Transport),* [1990] 2 F.C. 29.

7 Letter from Hon. Tom Siddon, minister of fisheries and oceans, to Mary Bailey, president, SAEG, 25 August 1987, quoted in *Friends of the Oldman River Society* v. *Canada (Minister of Transport),* [1990] 2 F.C. 29.

8 Letter from Holly Martell, special assistant, Office of the Minister of Environment, to Cliff Wallis, FOR, 15 January 1988, included in Annex C to letter from Garry Wouters, regional director general, INAC, to Dr. W.A. Ross, chairman, ORDEAP, 31 December 1991.

9 Letter from Hon. Pierre Cadieux, minister of Indian affairs, to Chief Peter Yellowhorn, Peigan Nation, 9 March 1989, included in Annex C to letter from Garry Wouters, regional director general, INAC, to Dr. W.A. Ross, chairman, ORDEAP, 31 December 1991.

10 'Federal court protects province's rivers,' *Calgary Herald,* 20 April 1989.

11 'Friends of the Oldman challenge dam licence in new court action,' *Edmonton Journal,* 25 April 1989.

12 'Alberta won't let ruling halt dam,' *Calgary Herald,* 18 May 1989.

13 Ibid.

14 Andrew Nikiforuk and Ed Struzik, 'The Great Forest Sell-off,' *Report on Business Magazine* (November 1989): 57-66.

15 *Canadian Wildlife Federation Inc., et al.* v. *Canada (Minister of the Environment) and Saskatchewan Water Corp.,* (F.C.A.), 22 June 1989, 99 N.R. 73.

16 *Friends of the Oldman River Society* v. *Canada (Minister of Transport),* [1990] 1 F.C. 248 (F.T.D.).

17 Scott was later elected to the Saskatchewan Legislature and was appointed minister of environment in Saskatchewan's NDP government in 1995.
18 *Friends of the Oldman River Society* v. *Canada (Minister of Transport)*, [1990] 2 F.C. 18 (F.C.A.).

Chapter 8: Carry On Regardless
1 *Alberta Hansard*, 22nd Legislature, 2nd Session, Vol. I (13 March 1990): 45.
2 'Bouchard hints at early dam decision,' *Lethbridge Herald*, 14 April 1990.
3 Editorial, 'Stop construction of Oldman Dam,' *Lethbridge Herald*, 15 March 1990, and Editorial, 'Respect the law,' *Lethbridge Herald*, 27 March 1990.
4 Editorial, 'Stop dam work now,' *Calgary Herald*, 14 March 1990.
5 *Alberta Hansard*, 22nd Legislature, 2nd Session, Vol. I (13 March 1990): 45.
6 Ibid., 54.
7 Ibid., 55-65.
8 Ibid., 57.
9 'Horseman says dam crucial for survival,' *Calgary Sun*, 15 March 1990.
10 'Dam not vital to survival,' *Lethbridge Herald*, 16 March 1990.
11 'Supporters oppose threat to halt dam work,' *Lethbridge Herald*, 27 March 1990.
12 Editorial, 'Respect the law,' *Lethbridge Herald*, 27 March 1990.
13 Column, Joanne Helmer, 'The Oldman Dam show,' *Lethbridge Herald*, 29 March 1990.
14 Ibid.
15 'Bouchard hints at early dam decision,' *Lethbridge Herald*, 14 April 1990.
16 'Ottawa won't halt dam,' *Lethbridge Herald*, 25 May 1990.
17 'Rafferty dam deal worries Bouchard,' *Lethbridge Herald*, 1 May 1990.
18 Alberta, Alberta Environment, *Water Management Policy for the South Saskatchewan River Basin*, Alberta Environment fact sheet, attachment to *News Release*, no. 28 (28 May 1990).
19 FOR's appeal of Harvie's decision was denied. *Kostuch* v. *Kowalski*, decided in the Alberta Court of Queen's Bench on 24 July 1990, Mr. Justice Paul Chrumka (unreported) (9001-1156 C1A01).
20 'No action planned on Alberta,' *Globe and Mail*, 11 July 1990.

Chapter 9: The Lonefighters
1 Canada, Oldman River Dam Environmental Assessment Panel, *Addendum to Compendium of Submissions Dated October 22, 1991*, vol. 2 (Vancouver: Federal Environmental Assessment Review Office, 31 December 1991), 801.
2 'Ottawa on the Oldman,' *Alberta Report* (26 March 1990). In January 1989, Leonard Bastien was elected chief of the Peigan Band, replacing Peter Yellowhorn.
3 For example, see 'End of the uprising,' *Alberta Report* (8 April 1991).
4 Vicki English, quoted in 'Personal Life, Public Property,' *Calgary Herald*, 16 January 1994, B3. Also see Rupert Ross, *Dancing with a Ghost* (Markham, ON: Octopus Publishing Group, 1992), 60 ff.
5 Joanne Helmer, 'Lonefighters protecting Peigan interests,' *Lethbridge Herald*, 13 August 1990.
6 Some Peigans who claimed to be legitimate members of the Lonefighters Society said that since not all of Born With A Tooth's followers were Lonefighters Society members, it was incorrect for the group to call itself the Lonefighters Society.
7 'Debris removal allows LNID water,' *Lethbridge Herald*, 3 June 1978.
8 This commitment was confirmed in an RCMP news release issued on 6 August 1990.
9 Annex A to Briefing for Harry Swain, deputy minister, INAC, 21 August 1990, included in Annex C to letter from Garry Wouters, regional director general, INAC, to Dr. W.A. Ross, chairman, ORDEAP, 30 December 1991.
10 Peter Melnychuk, testimony at Milton Born With A Tooth's trial in Calgary, 23 February 1994.
11 Joanne Helmer, personal interview, 5 April 1994.
12 Ibid.

13 Briefing for Harry Swain, 21 August 1990, 5.
14 'Klein charged with genocidal act,' *Kainai News*, 16 August 1990.
15 Ibid.
16 'LNID ready to sue if water diverted,' *Fort Macleod Gazette*, 15 August 1990. When interviewed in the fall of 1993, both Jensen and Don Lebaron remained convinced that FOR had masterminded the Lonefighters' diversion attempt.
17 'LNID ready to sue if water diverted,' *Fort Macleod Gazette*, 15 August 1990.
18 'RCMP have no proof yet of any native illegalities,' *Lethbridge Herald*, 17 August 1990.
19 'River diversion "going nowhere," says Rostad,' *Lethbridge Herald*, 21 August 1990.
20 'Province won't tolerate bid to divert river,' *Lethbridge Herald*, 14 August 1990.
21 'Peigans dig in to finish channel,' *Calgary Herald*, 26 August 1990.
22 Letter from James D. Horseman, deputy premier, to Chief Leonard Bastien, Peigan Nation, 21 August 1990, included in Annex C to letter from Garry Wouters, regional director general, INAC, to Dr. W.A. Ross, chairman, ORDEAP, 30 December 1991.
23 Letter from Chief Leonard Bastien, Peigan Nation, to Hon. James Horseman, deputy premier, 22 August 1990, included in Annex C to letter from Garry Wouters, regional director general, INAC, to Dr. W.A. Ross, chairman, ORDEAP, 30 December 1991.
24 Doug Clark, testimony at Milton Born With A Tooth's trial in Calgary, 23 February 1994.
25 'Militant Peigans say they'll die for cause,' *Calgary Herald*, 30 August 1990; 'Injunction halts bid to divert river,' *Globe and Mail*, 31 August 1990. It turned out that this estimate had been provided by the Lonefighters.
26 Doug Clark, testimony at Milton Born With A Tooth's trial in Calgary, 22 February 1994.
27 Ibid.
28 An injunction is issued ex parte in an instance where the party to whom the injunction applies, in this case the Lonefighters, is not present at the hearing. 'Generally, such an application [for an ex parte injunction] is only made in cases of emergency, where it is not possible to give the adverse party notice of the proceeding.' John A. Yogis, QC, *Canadian Law Dictionary* (Toronto: Barron's Educational Series, 1983), 81.
29 'Minister postpones meeting with natives,' *Lethbridge Herald*, 6 September 1990.

Chapter 10: 7 September 1990
1 Column, Joanne Helmer, 'Can Alberta recognize its real enemy?' *Lethbridge Herald*, 11 September 1990.
2 This declaration was probably borrowed from Crazy Horse, chief of the Oglala Sioux, who is said to have so described the 25 June 1876, the day on which the Sioux routed Custer at the Battle of the Little Big Horn. Like Crazy Horse, Born With A Tooth meant it was a good day for him to die; his opponents and the media chose to interpret him to mean it was a good day for his enemies to die.
3 Much of the following account is based on the testimony of witnesses at Milton Born With A Tooth's retrial, *R. v. Born With A Tooth*, before Mr. Justice Willis O'Leary in Alberta Court of Queen's Bench, Calgary, 22 February 1994 to 11 March 1994.
4 The media reported the size of the RCMP contingent commanded by Maguire as numbering from 70 to 200 officers. RCMP evidence given in court the following February established that 88 officers had participated in the operation.
5 *Lethbridge Herald* columnist Joanne Helmer later tried to find out from the RCMP who was in charge at the weir that morning but was unable to get a straight answer. (Joanne Helmer, personal interview, 5 April 1994.)
6 The Alberta Court of Appeal was later to observe that '*as a matter of law* ... no notice need have been given by Alberta to the accused [Born With A Tooth] about its proposed exercise of its right of entry' [emphasis added] (131 A.R. 198). The Court was not asked to venture an opinion as to whether, under the circumstances, Alberta might, *as a matter of common sense*, have been expected to give such notice.
7 The Crown prosecutor at Born With A Tooth's Calgary trial claimed the women and children were moved to high ground to act as a shield – an idea attributed by *Alberta Report* ('The Lonefighters' folly,' 10 September 1990) to a Lonefighter leader. Born With A Tooth

claimed they were moved to where they would be seen and not accidentally shot by the invading forces.
8 Joanne Helmer, personal interview, 5 April 1994.
9 'Police leave diversion site,' *Lethbridge Herald,* 10 September 1990.
10 Column, Joanne Helmer, 'Can Alberta recognize its real enemy?' *Lethbridge Herald,* 11 September 1990.

Chapter 11: In the Aftermath
1 *Windspeaker,* 7 June 1991, 1.
2 'Peigan Band backs Lonefighters,' *Lethbridge Herald,* 11 September 1990.
3 Briefing for Hon. Tom Siddon, minister of Indian affairs, 30 April 1991, included in Annex C to letter from Garry Wouters, regional director general, INAC, to Dr. W.A. Ross, chairman, ORDEAP, 30 December 1991.
4 Letter from Don Getty, premier, to Chief Leonard Bastien, Peigan Nation, 2 November 1990, included in Annex C to letter from Garry Wouters, regional director general, INAC, to Dr. W.A. Ross, chairman, ORDEAP, 30 December 1991.
5 Letter from Hon. Tom Siddon, minister of Indian affairs, to Hon. Ken Rostad, undated (received by Rostad on 9 November 1990, see reference in Letter, Rostad to Siddon, dated 28 November 1990), both included in Annex C to letter from Garry Wouters, regional director general, INAC, to Dr. W.A. Ross, chairman, ORDEAP, 30 December 1991.
6 Letter from James D. Horseman, deputy premier, to Chief Leonard Bastien, Peigan Nation, 21 August 1990, included in Annex C to letter from Garry Wouters, regional director general, INAC, to Dr. W.A. Ross, chairman, ORDEAP, 30 December 1991.
7 'Lonefighters spurned by province,' *Lethbridge Herald,* 15 November 1990.
8 Letter from Ken Rostad, Alberta attorney general and minister responsible for Native affairs, to Hon. Tom Siddon, minister of Indian affairs and northern development, dated 28 November 1990, included in Annex C to letter from Garry Wouters, regional director general, INAC, to Dr. W.A. Ross, chairman, ORDEAP, 30 December 1991.
9 'What they are saying,' *Calgary Herald,* 1 December 1990.
10 'Lonefighter granted release,' *Lethbridge Herald,* 20 December 1990.
11 'Lonefighter to be tried in Fort Macleod,' *Lethbridge Herald,* 16 February 1991.
12 'Lonefighter lawyer spars with judge,' *Lethbridge Herald,* 4 March 1991.
13 Notice of Appeal of the 25 March 1991, Court of Queen's Bench conviction of Milton Born With A Tooth, filed in the Alberta Court of Appeal, Calgary, 28 March 1991.
14 'Lonefighter supporters to file complaint,' *Lethbridge Herald,* 9 April 1991.
15 'Judicial bias investigation on hold until fall,' *Calgary Herald,* 27 May 1991.
16 'Oldman Dam foe vows to fight arms conviction,' *United Church Observer,* May 1991, 13.
17 'The "other" justice system,' *Catalyst,* May 1991.
18 Linden Willms, *Report to the Mennonite Central Committee,* April 1990. Unpublished.
19 'Peigan symbolizes year,' *Calgary Herald,* 30 December 1990; 'Peigan a powerful symbol,' *Windspeaker,* 18 January 1991.
20 Letter from Elizabeth May, executive director, Cultural Survival (Canada), to Hon. Tom Siddon, minister of Indian affairs, 27 February 1991, included in Annex C to letter from Garry Wouters, regional director general, INAC, to Dr. W.A. Ross, chairman, ORDEAP, 30 December 1991.
21 'Lonefighter leader warns of loss of life,' *Lethbridge Herald,* 22 May 1991.
22 'Peigan ceremony held at dam,' *Lethbridge Herald,* 27 May 1991.
23 Reverend Peter Hamel, personal interview, 4 August 1993.
24 'Natives lash out at "police harassment,"' *Calgary Herald,* 30 May 1991. The *Herald* said the RCMP also questioned Fulton.
25 *R. v. Born With A Tooth* (1992), 131 A.R. 193 (C.A.).
26 Ibid., 198.
27 Letter from Jeannie Thomas, executive director, Canadian Judicial Council, to members of the CASNP, Lethbridge, 6 April 1993.
28 Ibid.
29 Ibid.

Chapter 12: The Federal Review

1 Dr. W.A. Ross, panel chairman, quoted in *Release* (Ottawa: Minister of Environment, Canada, 16 November 1990).

2 'Dam review awaits ruling from court,' *Lethbridge Herald,* 16 July 1990.

3 'Province's court action delaying dam review,' *Lethbridge Herald,* 24 October 1990.

4 The panel's complete terms of reference are in Appendix A to Canada, Oldman River Dam Environmental Assessment Panel, *Report of the Environmental Assessment Panel* (Hull: Federal Environmental Assessment Review Office, 1992).

5 'Judge orders Oldman dam review continue,' *Lethbridge Herald,* 21 December 1990.

6 Canada, Oldman River Dam Environmental Assessment Panel, *Compendium of Submissions* (Vancouver: Federal Environmental Assessment Review Office, 11 February 1990).

7 Ibid., 5.

8 Ibid., 329.

9 Ibid., 118.

10 Ibid., 107.

11 Ibid., 176. Table 2 in this report indicates that the available information was deficient in all but 2 of 120 categories of biological/ecological data examined by Horesji.

12 Ibid., 393-409.

13 Ibid., 396.

14 Ibid., 390. The operating plan provided to the panel was Alberta, Alberta Environment, *Oldman River Reservoir Operational Plan: Water Supply, Flow Regulation and Interprovincial Apportionment* (Edmonton, January 1989).

15 Canada, Oldman River Dam Environmental Assessment Panel, *Additional Information Requirements* (Vancouver: Federal Environmental Assessment Review Office, 1991).

16 Ibid., 7.

17 Ibid., 18 and 19.

18 Ibid., 20.

19 Ibid., 21.

20 Ibid., 1.

21 Canada, Oldman River Dam Environmental Assessment Panel, *Newsletter,* no. 1 (March 1991): 2.

22 'Federal dam case hailed by Kostuch,' *Calgary Herald,* 30 January 1991.

23 The Native groups were the Assembly of First Nations, the National Indian Brotherhood, the Dene Nation, the Metis Association of the Northwest Territories, and the Native Council of Canada (Alberta). The environmental interest groups included the Sierra Legal Defence Fund, the Canadian Environmental Law Association, Friends of the Earth, the Sierra Club of Western Canada, and Cultural Survival Canada.

24 The federal panel's hearings were held in six centres in southern Alberta and in Edmonton during the period from 5 November to 20 November. Alberta Environment's workshops were held in seventeen centres across the province during the period from 30 October to 11 December.

25 Canada, Oldman River Dam Environmental Assessment Panel, *Response to the Panel's Additional Information Requirements Document* (Vancouver: Federal Environmental Assessment Review Office, 1991). This document was supplemented by: Canada, Oldman River Dam Environmental Assessment Panel, *Addendum and Erratum Material for the Response to the Panel's Additional Information Requirements Document, September 1991* (Vancouver: Federal Environmental Assessment Review Office, 1991).

26 Canada, Oldman River Dam Environmental Assessment Panel, *Response to the Panel's Additional Information Requirements Document,* 4.

27 Ibid., 4 and 2.3-2.

28 FEARO promised to place transcripts of the hearings in the Calgary, Edmonton, Lethbridge, and Pincher Creek public libraries (Canada, Oldman River Dam Environmental Assessment Panel, *Newsletter,* no. 4 [December 1991]: 2). None of these libraries ever received copies of the transcripts; they are available only in the CEAA Reference Library in Edmonton. Interestingly, none of the public libraries could recall anyone but me ever having inquired about the transcripts.

29 Canada, Oldman River Dam Environmental Assessment Panel, *Compendium of Submissions,* and Canada, Oldman River Dam Environmental Assessment Panel, *Addendum to Compendium of Submissions Dated October 22, 1991,* 2 vols. (Vancouver: Federal Environmental Assessment Review Office, 31 December 1991). Annexes A, B, and C to Indian Affairs 30 December 1991 submission to the panel (INAC 5-NC-31/12/91) were not published by FEARO. These annexes and the three volumes of documents attached to Annex C are held in the CEAA Reference Library in Edmonton.

30 One of the SAWMC's submissions included copies of over fifty letters to the committee from IDs, towns, MDs, agricultural producer groups, chambers of commerce, and Alberta cabinet ministers, all indicating support for the project.

31 Including four submissions by consultants under contract to Alberta Public Works, Supply and Services.

32 'Decision leaves dam vulnerable,' *Globe and Mail,* 24 January 1993.

Chapter 13: The Panel Reports

1 Canada, Oldman River Dam Environmental Assessment Panel, *Report of the Environmental Assessment Panel* (Hull: Federal Environmental Assessment Review Office, 1992), 32.
2 Ibid., 23.
3 Ibid., 22.
4 Ibid., 23.
5 Ibid., 5.
6 Ibid.
7 Ibid., 25.
8 Ibid., 6.
9 Ibid.
10 Ibid.
11 Ibid., 6-8.
12 Ibid., 12.
13 Ibid.
14 Government of Canada, *News Release,* no. 79/92 (21 May 1992).
15 Interview on CBC Radio, 22 May 1992; 'Battle rages on at feds inaction,' *Calgary Herald,* 22 May 1992.
16 *Alberta Hansard,* 22nd Legislature, 4th Session, Vol. II (22 May 1992): 1057.
17 Ibid.
18 'Alberta sniffs at need for approvals,' *Calgary Herald,* 12 June 1992.
19 Ibid.
20 'Ottawa, Alberta reject opening dam flood gates,' *Globe and Mail,* 22 May 1992.
21 Editorial, 'Closing the Oldman,' *Calgary Herald,* 22 May 1992.
22 Ibid.
23 'Oldman Dam tests Alberta's mettle,' *Calgary Herald,* 22 May 1992.
24 Alberta Environment, *Update* (August 1991): 3.
25 'Oldman Dam festival "trouble."' *Calgary Herald,* 20 May 1992.
26 Martha Kostuch, personal interview, 6 June 1993.
27 'Oysters clam up over dam,' *Calgary Herald,* 30 June 1992.
28 'Threat cancels dam's party,' *Calgary Herald,* 5 July 1992.
29 Roy Jensen, personal interview, 20 October 1993.
30 'Kowalski defends claims,' *Calgary Herald,* 9 July 1992.
31 Editorial, 'Where's proof, Ken?' *Calgary Herald,* 10 July 1992.
32 'An Oldman celebration after all,' *Alberta Report* (27 July 1992): 12. The MLA in attendance was Tom Musgrove, PC, Little Bow.

Chapter 14: And Thereafter

1 Kevin Van Tighem, *Coming West: A Natural History of Home* (Canmore, AB: Altitude Publishing, 1997), 194.
2 The ill-starred Charlottetown Accord.
3 The Licence to Divert and Use Water Pursuant to The Water Resources Act, No. 15410, 18

August 1992, included the condition that 'within one year after full supply level of the works is reached (Elevation 1118.6 m), the licensee shall provide the Controller with an updated operational strategy in a form acceptable to the Controller.'

4   *Friends of the Oldman River Society* v. *Canada (Minister of Environment)* (1993), 105 D.L.R. (4th) 444 (F.T.D.).

5   Canada, Transport Canada, *Federal Government Response to the Oldman River Dam Project Environmental Review Panel Report* (Ottawa, 30 August 1993).

6   Government of Canada, *News Release*, no. 190/93 (2 September 1993): 1.

7   Navigable Waters Protection Act Approval, Oldman River Dam, 8200-86-370 (AMAP), 1 September 1993. The Fisheries Act Authorization for Works or Undertakings Affecting Fish Habitat, Oldman River Dam (operation and maintenance) was issued on 16 August 1994, with still no indications of progress in negotiations between Alberta and the Peigan.

8   Alberta Environmental Protection, *News Release*, no. 93-065 (29 July 1993).

9   Ibid.

10   Familiar faces on the EAC included Hilton Pharis, Dr. Stewart Rood, Don Lebaron, Roy Jensen, and Jake Theissen. In 1997, the Peigan appointed a member to the committee.

11   Letter from Hilton Pharis, chairman, EAC, to Hon. Brian Evans, minister of environmental protection, 2 June 1994.

12   This would comply with Recommendation 7 of the ORDEAP.

13   Letter from Chief Leonard Bastien, Peigan Nation, to Hon. Pauline A. Browes, minister of Indian affairs, *Globe and Mail*, 13 October 1993.

14   Memorandum of understanding between Her Majesty the Queen in Right of Canada (minister of Indian affairs and northern development) and the Peigan Band, 8 February 1994.

15   Following the 1997 provincial election, Kowalski started a comeback when his peers elected him Speaker of the Legislature.

16   Memorandum on the Decision of Hon. Justice V.W.M. Smith, Court of Queen's Bench of Alberta, Judicial District of Edmonton, in the case of *Friends of the Oldman River* v. *Minister of Alberta Environmental Protection and Controller of Water Resources*, December 1993 (unreported). In FOR papers held by Dr. Martha Kostuch, Rocky Mountain House, AB.

17   *Friends of the Oldman River Society* v. *Alberta (Minister of Environmental Protection)* (1996), 181 A.R. 306 (C.A.).

18   Canada, Statutes 40-41 Elizabeth II, c. 37.

19   'All resolute on the western front,' *Alberta Report* (11 March 1991): 16.

20   Peter Melnychuk, personal interview, 14 June 1994.

21   Bora Laskin, *Resources for Tomorrow*, Conference Background Papers, vol. 1 (Ottawa: Queen's Printer, 1961), 219.

22   Sierra Legal Defence Fund, 'Feds Caught Flaunting Fisheries Law,' *Newsletter*, no. 17 (July 1997): 7.

23   *Friends of the West Country Association* v. *Minister of Fisheries and Oceans* decided in the Federal Court of Canada, Trial Division, on 7 July 1998, Mr. Justice Frederick Gibson (unreported) (T-1893-96).

24   'Alberta activists jubilant over court ruling on environment,' *Globe and Mail*, 11 July 1998; 'Court ruling against logging firm's bridges delights environmentalists,' *Vancouver Sun*, 11 July 1998.

25   *Friends of the West Country* v. *Minister of Fisheries and Oceans*, decided in the Federal Court of Appeal on 23 November 1998, Chief Justice Julius A. McIsaac (unreported) (T-1893-96).

26   Environmental Protection and Enhancement Act, S.A. 1992, c. E-13.3.

27   National Resources Conservation Board Act, S.A. 1990, c. N-5.5.

28   As of October 1998, Environment Department officials had no clear indication of when the new act would be promulgated.

29   Natural Resources Conservation Board Act, S.A. 1990, c. N-5.5, s. 8(2) and s. 10(1).

30   The lack of participation by high profile, provincially or nationally based environmental interest groups at the Pine Coulee and Little Bow/Highwood public hearings suggests that the 'directly affected' requirement is working as the province intended.

31 A subsidiary agreement entered into at the same time, designated either the NRCB or the ERCB to enter into agreements with Canada to conduct joint assessments.

32 The provincial members of the panel were Ken Smith, chairman of the NRCB, and Charles Weir, the permanent member of the NRCB. The federal member was Dr. George Kupfer, a consultant in private practice.

33 Subsequently the Peigan and the Pine Coulee Coalition received funding under the Federal Participant Funding Program that brought their funding up to 50 percent and 80 percent, respectively, of what they had requested of the board.

34 Alberta, Natural Resources Conservation Board/Environmental Assessment Review Process Joint Review Panel, *Report of the NRCB/EARP Joint Review Panel: Pine Coulee Water Management Project* (Edmonton, 1995).

35 The NRCB may refuse approval for a project but may issue an approval for a project only with the prior authorization of the cabinet (NRCB Act, s. 9[1]).

36 Alberta, Natural Resources Conservation Board/Canadian Environmental Assessment Act Joint Review Panel, *Report of the NRCB/CEAA Joint Review Panel: Little Bow Project/Highwood Diversion Plan* (Edmonton, 1998).

37 Canada, Alberta *News Release*, No. 98-089 (December 1998).

38 Canada, Department of Fisheries and Oceans, *Authorization for Works or Undertakings Affecting Fish Habitat*, issued to Alberta Environmental Protection for the operation and maintenance of the Oldman River Dam, 16 August 1994.

39 A 1992 manuscript, produced by the Fish and Wildlife Division, concerning fish rule curves developed for use in the Highwood River (Alberta, Alberta Forestry, Lands and Wildlife, Fish and Wildlife Division, *The Highwood River: Instream Flow Needs for Fish and Flow Scenario Evaluations,* by Allan G.R. Locke, draft no. 16-09-92 [Edmonton, 1992]) includes the following comments: 'The philosophy employed in the development of these instream flow requirements for the protection of the fisheries resource is one of making the *best use* of water in the basin. When water is abundant, optimal conditions are requested for the fishery resource, while during average water years, average habitat conditions are specified. During drought years, only the amount of habitat required to keep the fish alive is requested [p. 87]. These curves represented ... the *initial negotiating position* of the Fish and Wildlife Division [p. 64]. If these demands could not be met *in view of the demands of other water users*, then the AFWD was willing to evaluate alternative water management scenarios [p. 80]' [emphasis added].

40 The total assessed acreage in those districts (LNID, SMRID, TID, MID, RID) in 1997 was 654,400 acres (264,800 hectares) (Alberta Agriculture, Food and Rural Development, Irrigation Branch, *Alberta Irrigation Information: 1997* [Lethbridge, n.d.]).

41 The total acreage specified for those districts (LNID, SMRID, TID, MID, RID) by Alberta Regulation 307/91 is 686,000 acres (277,600 hectares).

42 Kyle McNeilly, 'The Nosedive of the Bull Trout,' *Environment Views* 17 (Fall 1994): 10.

Chapter 15: The Iron Triangle and the Oldman River Dam

1 Owen G. Holmes, 'Courage Mr. Minister: stay dam work,' Personal Opinion, *Lethbridge Herald,* 16 April 1986.

2 On the Bow River system, development for hydroelectric generation was an early competitor with development for irrigation. The last hydro dam was built on the Bow (at Bearspaw immediately upstream from Calgary) in the 1950s, primarily to regulate flow through the city of Calgary to reduce winter flooding.

3 Robert Gottlieb, *A Life of Its Own: The Politics and Power of Water* (New York: Harcourt Brace Jovanovich Publishers, 1988), 47.

4 Alberta, Alberta Environment, *Environmental Impact Assessment Guidelines* (Edmonton, February 1977).

5 Alberta Environment, *Environmental Impact Assessment,* Water Management in Alberta Background Paper, vol. 9 (August 1991), 3. In 1978, *Requirements for the Identification, Analysis and Evaluation of Community Impacts* was adopted as a modification to the February 1977 *Guidelines.*

6 Alberta, Alberta Environment, *Environmental Impact Assessment Guidelines,* 1.

7 Ibid.
8 Ibid.
9 Ibid., Executive Summary.
10 Land Surface Conservation and Reclamation Act, R.S.A. 1980, c. L-3, s. 8(1).
11 Alberta, Alberta Environment, *Water Resource Management Principles for Alberta* (Edmonton, n.d.), Principle 14, p. 13. This document was published in 1980.
12 Peter Melnychuk, personal interview, 14 June 1994.
13 Water Resources Act, R.S.A. 1980, c. W-5, s. 11.
14 Water Resources Act, s. 83.
15 Ibid., s. 16(1) and (2). Ministerial Order 8/82 delegated the minister's authority under the act to the controller.
16 Ibid., s. 16(4) and s. 18(1). The minister is not, however, obliged to acknowledge their receipt, much less offer any explanation of why the objections might have been accepted or rejected.
17 Ibid., s. 19.
18 Interim Licence Pursuant to The Water Resources Act, No. 14628, 18 August 1987.
19 Interim Licence Pursuant to The Water Resources Act, No. 15410, 5 February 1988.
20 In fact, a list of studies released by PWSS four years later, in February 1990, still included none that addressed the potential impact of dam operations on environmental concerns downstream.
21 *Friends of the Oldman River Society* v. *Alberta (Minister of the Environment)* (1987), 56 Alta. L.R. (2d) 375 (Q.B.).
22 Ibid.
23 In the process of certiorari (essentially a judicial review), the court is not at liberty to change a purely discretionary decision that does not exceed the authority of the decision maker.
24 The reasons were failure to refer the application to ERCB as required by s. 17 and failure to seek the written permission of the MD of Pincher Creek, which had jurisdiction over road allowances that would be affected by the project, as required by s. 15(8)(b).
25 Jonathon Scarth, 'The Oldman Dam Decisions,' *Resources: The Newsletter of the Canadian Institute of Resources Law* 22 (Spring 1988); Bob Kambeitz, 'The Three Rivers Dam: *Friends of the Oldman River Society vs. The Minister of the Environment, et al.*, Part II,' *Trout Canada* (Spring 1988): 21.
26 Scarth, 'The Oldman Dam Decisions,' 5.
27 *Friends of the Oldman River Society* v. *Alberta (Minister of Environment)* (1988), 89 A.R. 339 (Q.B.).
28 Ibid., 343.
29 In his 16 September 1980 letter to Dixon Thompson, Environment Minister Cookson said any reasons for building the dam other than irrigation were 'peripheral.' Also see Government of Alberta, 'Oldman Dam Announcement,' *News Release* (9 August 1984): 2.
30 The information required to accompany an application to divert water is specified in the Water Resources Regulations, Alta. Reg. 91/58.
31 Alberta, Alberta Environment, *Water Management Policy for the South Saskatchewan River Basin*, 28 May 1990. The policy was released with Alberta Environment, 'Water Management Policy Announced for South Saskatchewan River Basin,' *News Release*, no. 28 (28 May 1990).
32 Ibid., 2. When read in its entirety, the somewhat disjointed flow of this policy statement suggests a compromise between conflicting interests on the drafting committee or around the cabinet table.
33 Ibid.
34 Alberta Environment/AWRC, *Planning and Management Strategy for Establishing Instream Flow Needs for Alberta Streams*, November 1988. The Water Management Service presented this policy document to Highwood River Basin and Little Bow River Basin 'stakeholders' at a public meeting in High River, on 1 May 1989.
35 Water Resources Act, R.S.A. 1980, c. W-5, s. 12(1).
36 South Saskatchewan Basin Water Allocation Regulation, Alta. Reg. 307/91, s. 4.

37 Section 11 of the Water Resources Act listed the purposes for which a water right can be obtained. The only purpose on the list which was *not* included in s. 6 of the regulation as a purpose for which the reserved water could be allocated was use of water 'in its natural state [i.e., instream flow] for the purpose of conservation, recreation or the propagation of fish and wildlife, or for any like purpose.'

38 South Saskatchewan Basin Water Allocation Regulation, s. 7(2) and Canada, Oldman River Study Management Committee, *Oldman River Basin-Phase II Studies: Report and Recommendations* (Lethbridge: 1978), 14.

39 Alberta, Alberta Environment, *Water Management Policy for the South Saskatchewan River Basin*, 3.

40 Don Pike, general manager of Trout Unlimited, quoted in 'River standards set before consultation,' *Calgary Herald*, 18 January 1992.

41 Taber Irrigation District, *Annual Report* (Taber, AB: 1990), 7.

42 Alberta Environment, *Water Management in Alberta: Challenges for the Future* (Edmonton, n.d.), 6. This document was released with Alberta Environment *News Release*, no. 71 (4 July 1991).

43 Letter from Lew Fahner, controller of Water Resources, to Dr. Martha Kostuch, 17 February 1993, in FOR papers held by Dr. Martha Kostuch, Rocky Mountain House, AB.

44 Letter from H. Johnson, provincial ombudsman, to Dr. Martha Kostuch, 21 December 1992, in FOR papers, held by Dr. Martha Kostuch, Rocky Mountain House, AB.

45 Notices of the district's applications were published in the *Lethbridge Herald* as follows:

District	Allocation applied for	Dates of publication	
SMRID	222,000 acre-feet	29 Aug. and 5 Sept. 1991	[273,800 cubic decameters]
MID	4,000 acre-feet	29 Aug. and 5 Sept. 1991	[4,900 cubic decametres]
TID	8,000 acre-feet	29 Aug. and 5 Sept. 1991	[9,900 cubic decametres]
LNID	50,000 acre-feet	30 Aug. and 6 Sept. 1991	[61,700 cubic decametres]
RID	26,000 acre-feet	23 and 30 Sept. 1991	[32,800 cubic decametres]

46 The licences were issued to the IDs for the amounts applied for as indicated in note 45 above.

47 *Friends of the Oldman River Society* v. *Alberta (Minister of Environment)* (1988), 89 A.R. 341.

Chapter 16: The Environment and Its Friends

1 Charles Taylor, *The Malaise of Modernity* (Concord, ON: House of Anansi Press, 1994), 9.

2 Ibid., 95.

3 Results of an Angus Reid poll, reported in the *Calgary Herald*, 14 March 1995.

4 *Maclean's* 108, 52 (26 December 1995): 22; *Maclean's* 109, 53 (30 December 1996/6 January 1997): 46.

5 For example, see Robert Paehlke, 'Eco-History: Two Waves in the Evolution of Environmentalism,' *Alternatives* 19 (1992) and Lynton K. Caldwell, '20 Years with NEPA Indicates the Need,' *Environment* 31 (1989): 10.

6 Robert Paehlke, 'Eco-History,' 18.

7 Alberta, Alberta Environment, *Environmental Impact Assessment Guidelines* (Edmonton: 1977).

8 *Canada Gazette, Part II*, vol. 118, no. 14 (11 July 1984), Environmental Assessment and Review Process Guidelines Order, SOR 84/467, at 2794.

9 World Commission on Environment and Development, *Our Common Future* (New York: Oxford University Press, 1987).

10 Planning was under way for the UN's 1992 Earth Summit in Rio de Janeiro, the centrepiece of which was to be the *Convention on Biological Diversity*, which Canada signed and ratified in 1992.

11 Edward O. Wilson, *The Diversity of Life* (Cambridge: Belknap Press of Harvard University Press, 1992), 15 and 283.

12 Cliff Wallis, personal interview, 2 October 1995.

13 Dr. Martha Kostuch, personal interview, 6 July 1993.

14 The entertainers performed free of charge as a favour to Tyson, a wilderness buff and FOR supporter. David Suzuki and the other speakers also appeared at their own expense.

15 Alberta Wilderness Association, Wise Use Newsletter, *Action Alert* 2 (Spring 1991), 1.
16 The Sierra Club Legal Defence Fund, a US organization, and the Sierra Legal Defence Fund in Canada are not affiliated.
17 Dr. Martha Kostuch, personal interview, 6 July 1993.

Chapter 17: Archaeology

1 *Alberta Hansard,* 22nd Legislature, 4th Session, Vol. II (21 May 1992): 1023.
2 Alberta Wilderness Association, Wise Use Newsletter, *Action Alert* 2 (Spring 1991), 1.
3 It was not until he was doing research at the Oldman River Dam site in 1985 that Reeves learned from Peigan elders that the correct name for the UNESCO site is The Buffalo Jump. There is a buffalo jump that the Indians called Head-Smashed-In, but it is some distance west of the UNESCO site.
4 Alberta Environment defined prehistoric resources as those 'containing evidence of human activity in the period before the arrival of Europeans,' and historical resources as 'artifacts or structures representing the period since the arrival of the Europeans' *(Oldman River Dam Historical Resources,* n.d. This is one of a series of information brochures prepared and distributed by Alberta Environment's Oldman River Dam Project Office during the period that the dam was under construction).
5 Dr. Brian Reeves, personal interview, 19 January 1995. In their student days, in the early 1960s, Reeves and Bill Byrne, who later became deputy minister of Alberta culture, participated in a 'cursory' archaeological survey of the Three Rivers and Gap sites, funded by a National Museum of Canada grant to Dr. Richard Forbis, then head of the archaeology department at the University of Alberta at Calgary. In the late 1970s, working for LGL Ltd., Reeves conducted limited archaeological surveys of the various Oldman River Dam sites for the Oldman River Study Management Committee.
6 Brian Reeves, 'The Oldman River Dam and Alberta's Heritage: Conservation or Desecration?' in *Economic, Environmental and Social Aspects of the Oldman River Dam Project,* edited by Stewart B. Rood and Frank J. Jankunis (Lethbridge: University of Lethbridge, 1988), 83. The second was at the confluence of the Bow and Highwood Rivers.
7 B.O.K. Reeves, *Oldman River Dam Phase II Archaeological and Historic Resources Inventory and Assessment, Volume II, Prehistoric Sites Part I* (Calgary: Lifeways Canada Ltd., February 1987), 1.
8 Ibid.
9 Historical Resources Act, R.S.A. 1980, s. 33(2)(c); Jack Ives, 'Evaluation and Mitigation of Historical Resources Affected by the Oldman River Dam Project,' in *Economic, Environmental and Social Aspects of the Oldman River Dam Project,* edited by Stewart B. Rood and Frank J. Jankunis (Lethbridge: University of Lethbridge, 1988), 105.
10 'Gov't to study Oldman dam site historic resources,' *Lethbridge Herald,* 19 November 1987.
11 Ives, 'Evaluation and Mitigation,' 100.
12 Ibid., 102.
13 Ibid.
14 Reeves, personal interview, 19 January 1995.
15 Ives, 'Evaluation and Mitigation,' 101.
16 Reeves, personal interview, 19 January 1995.
17 Ibid.
18 Peigan Nation, Band Council Resolution, No. 2017/88-89, 24 February 1989 in Annex C to letter from Garry Wouters, regional director general, INAC, to Dr. W.A. Ross, chairman, ORDEAP, 30 December 1991. Band council resolutions (BCRs) have no force in law. In some instances the federal government converts them into regulations under the Indian Act. Since that was not the case with this BCR, the government agencies and their contractors were not acting illegally.
19 Historical Resources Act, R.S.A. 1980, s. 28(1).
20 Which prompted the Peigan's lawyer to observe that 'one way to find out if you have an integrated site is to ask someone who might know.'
21 Letter from W.J. Byrne, deputy minister, Alberta Community Development, to D. Bader, assistant deputy minister, Alberta PWSS, 5 January 1994 (Exhibit #24, NRCB/EARP Public

Hearings, Pine Coulee Project).
22 Heritage Conservation Act, R.S.B.C. 1979, c. 165, s. 7(5) and s. 5(5).
23 Ibid., s. 3.1(1) and (4).
24 Reeves, personal interview, 19 January 1995.
25 Alberta Environment, *Oldman River Dam Historical Resources.*
26 Oldman River Dam Local Advisory Committee, *Final Report and Recommendations to the Ministers of Alberta Public Works, Supply and Services and Alberta Environmental Protection,* January 1993, 19-22.
27 Hilton Pharis, personal interview, 19 October 1993.
28 Letter from Bill Yeo, Parks Canada, to David Donald, Inland Waters and Lands, Environment Canada, 29 February 1988 (included in Annex C to letter from Garry Wouters, regional director general, INAC, to Dr. W.A. Ross, chairman, ORDEAP, 30 December 1991).
29 Canada, Oldman River Dam Environmental Assessment Panel, *Compendium of Submissions* (Vancouver: Federal Environmental Assessment Review Office, 11 February 1990), 98.
30 Canada, Oldman River Dam Environmental Assessment Panel, *Public Hearings Proceedings, November 5-20, 1991,* vol. 5 (Vancouver: Federal Environmental Assessment Review Office, 7 November 1991), 1069.
31 David Meyer, 'Archaeological and Historical Resources,' in Canada, Oldman River Dam Environmental Assessment Panel, *Addendum and Erratum Material for the Response to the Panel's Additional Information Requirements Document, September 1991,* Addendum 3 (Vancouver: Federal Environmental Assessment Review Office, 1991), 9.
32 Ibid., 1.
33 Canada, Oldman River Dam Environmental Assessment Panel, *Report of the Environmental Assessment Panel* (Hull: Federal Environmental Assessment Review Office, 1992), 23.
34 Ibid.
35 Reeves, personal interview, 19 January 1995.

Chapter 18: Biological Diversity
1 Paul R. Ehrlich, *The Machinery of Nature* (New York: Simon and Schuster, Touchstone Books, 1986), 239.
2 Aldo Leopold, *A Sand County Almanac* (New York: Oxford University Press, 1968), 224.
3 Alberta, World Wildlife Fund Canada and Alberta Energy/Alberta Forestry, Lands and Wildlife, *Conservation and Management Strategy For Riparian Forests in Southern Alberta* (Edmonton, 1992), 4.
4 World Wildlife Fund Canada, *Prairie Conservation Action Plan, 1989-1994* (Toronto: World Wildlife Fund Canada, n.d.), 18. The term 'threatened' is used in its generic sense in this publication – neither the cottonwood ecosystem nor any of the species associated with it were listed in the Canadian Species at Risk, produced by the Committee on the Status of Endangered Wildlife in Canada (COSEWIC).
5 Alberta Environment, *Oldman River Dam Vegetation,* n.d. This is one of a series of information brochures prepared and distributed by Alberta Environment's Oldman River Dam Project Office during the period that the dam was under construction.
6 Cheryl Bradley, Frances Reintjes, and John Mahoney, *The Biology and Status of Riparian Poplars in Southern Alberta* (Edmonton: World Wildlife Fund Canada and Alberta Forestry, Lands and Wildlife, 1991), 64.
7 Alberta, World Wildlife Fund Canada and Alberta Energy/Alberta Forestry, Lands and Wildlife, *Conservation and Management Strategy,* 16.
8 For information on the various species of plant and animal life associated with the riparian cottonwood forest ecosystems see Bradley et al., *The Biology and Status of Riparian Poplars;* Environmental Management Associates, 'A Review of Potential Impacts on the Riparian Downstream of the Oldman Dam (Addendum Report),' in *Addendum and Erratum Material for the Response to the Panel's Additional Information Requirements Document, September 1991,* by Oldman River Dam Environmental Assessment Panel (Vancouver: Federal Environmental Assessment Review Office, 1991); Alberta, Alberta Environment, *Vegetation Inventory: Oldman River Dam,* by Hardy Associates (Edmonton, 1986); Trevor

Rhodes, 'The Importance of Cottonwoods to Wildlife,' and Keith Shaw, 'Ecology of the River Bottom Forest on the St. Mary River, Lee Creek and Belly River in southern Alberta,' in *The Biology and Management of Southern Alberta's Cottonwoods*, edited by Stewart B. Rood and John M. Mahoney (Lethbridge: University of Lethbridge, 1991).

9 Bradley et al., *The Biology and Status of Riparian Poplars*, 5.
10 Alberta, Alberta Environment, 1986 study *Vegetation Inventory: Oldman River Dam*, by Hardy Associates, noted the potential impact of the dam on downstream riparian forests but this work was not widely distributed.
11 Stewart B. Rood and Sig Heinz-Milne, 'Abrupt Downstream Forest Decline Following River Damming in Southern Alberta,' *Canadian Journal of Botany* 67 (1989): 1744-9.
12 See Rood and Mahoney, eds., *The Biology and Management of Southern Alberta's Cottonwoods*.
13 Stewart B. Rood and John M. Mahoney, 'The Importance and Extent of Cottonwood Forest Decline Downstream from Dams,' in *The Biology and Management of Southern Alberta's Cottonwoods*, edited by Rood and Mahoney, 6.
14 Alberta Environment, 'Protection and Preservation part of the plan,' *Update* (June 1986): 4; Alberta, Alberta Environment, Water Management Services, *Oldman River Reservoir Operational Plan: Water Supply, Flow Regulation and Interprovincial Apportionment* (Edmonton, 1989).
15 Dr. Stewart Rood, personal interview, 21 October 1993.
16 S. Rood, Letters, *Lethbridge Herald*, 8 December 1987, A7.
17 Stewart B. Rood and John M. Mahoney, 'Impacts of the Oldman River Dam on Riparian Cottonwood Forests Downstream,' in *Addendum to Compendium of Submissions Dated October 22, 1991*, vol. 2, by Canada, Oldman River Dam Environmental Assessment Panel (Vancouver: Federal Environmental Assessment Review Office, 31 December 1991), 1080-1114.
18 Ibid., 1089.
19 Canada, Oldman River Dam Environmental Assessment Panel, *Response to the Panel's Additional Information Requirements Document* (Vancouver: Federal Environmental Assessment Review Office, 1991), 2.3-1-2.3-2. The computer model used to develop the plan is the Water Resources Management Model, developed by the WMS's Planning Division for its South Saskatchewan River Basin Planning Program, 1981-4. WMS's January 1989 operational plan for the dam was based on simulation ODO4. Another simulation, ODO5, was completed prior to the federal panel's review, some output from which was made available to Rood and to the panel's technical experts. Rood's analysis of the operational plan for the dam was based on the ODO5 simulation. The panel was given to understand that 'the outputs from the ODO4 and ODO5 simulations are very similar, and that the written description in the 1989 plan is still representative.'
20 Rood and Mahoney, 'Impacts of the Oldman River Dam on Riparian Cottonwood Forests Downstream,' 1103. The pages of the Rood and Mahoney paper in ORDEAP, *Submissions Addendum*, vol. 2, December 1991, are out of sequence; p. 1103 is the twenty-third page of the Rood and Mahoney paper.
21 Ibid., 1105.
22 Ibid., 1109.
23 'Oldman River Dam Project: The Cottonwood Story,' PWSS *FACT SHEET*, 30 October 1991.
24 See figures for Fort Macleod Reach in Alberta, Alberta Environment, *Oldman River Reservoir Operational Plan* (Edmonton, January 1989), 23, Table 5, and Alberta, Alberta Environment, *Oldman River Dam Operational Strategy* (Edmonton, March 1991), 20. These minimum flows were further reduced by the fish rule curve adopted in June 1994: Alberta, Alberta Environmental Protection, *Oldman River Dam and Reservoir Operational Strategy (June 1994)* (Edmonton, June 1994), Appendix 1, segment 4.
25 Canada, Oldman River Dam Environmental Assessment Panel, *Addendum and Erratum Material for the Response to the Panel's Additional Information Requirements Document, September 1991* (Vancouver: Federal Environmental Assessment Review Office, 1991), 49.
26 Canada, Committee on the Status of Endangered Wildlife in Canada, *Canadian Species at Risk* (Ottawa: April 1994).

27 David W. Mayhood, 'Fishes Threatened, Vulnerable or of Special Concern in Relation to the Oldman River Dam,' in *Addendum to Compendium of Submissions Dated October 22, 1991*, vol. 1, by Canada, Oldman River Dam Environmental Assessment Panel (Vancouver: Federal Environmental Assessment Review Office, 31 December 1991), 309.
28 Alberta Energy and Natural Resources, *Status of the Fish and Wildlife Resource in Alberta* (Edmonton, 1984), 35.
29 Canada, Oldman River Dam Environmental Assessment Panel, *Public Hearings Proceedings, November 5-20, 1991*, vol. 6 (Vancouver: Federal Environmental Assessment Review Office), 1193.
30 Mayhood, 'Fishes Threatened, Vulnerable or of Special Concern in Relation to the Oldman River Dam,' 31.
31 Ibid., 35.
32 Alberta, Alberta Environment, *Oldman River Dam and Reservoir Operational Plan*, 24.
33 Cliff Wallis, personal interview, 2 October 1995.

Chapter 19: EARPGO and the Courts

1 *Friends of the Oldman River Society* v. *Canada (Minister of Transport)*, [1992] 1 S.C.R. 16.
2 *Canada Gazette, Part II*, v. 118, n. 14 (11 July 1984), Environmental Assessment and Review Process Guidelines Order, SOR/84-467.
3 Ibid., ss. 2, 3, 4, and 6.
4 *Canadian Wildlife Federation Inc.* v. *Canada (Minister of the Environment) and Saskatchewan Water Corp.* (1989), 26 F.T.R. 245 (F.T.D.).
5 Ibid.
6 Fisheries Act, s. 35.
7 *Friends of the Oldman River Society* v. *Canada (Minister of Transport)*, [1990] 1 F.C. 261 (F.T.D.).
8 *Friends of the Oldman River Society* v. *Alberta (Minister of Environment)* (1987), 56 Alta. L.R. (2d) 368 (Q.B.) and *Friends of the Oldman River Society* v. *Alberta (Minister of Environment)* (1988), 89 A.R. 339 (Q.B.).
9 *Friends of the Oldman River Society* v. *Canada (Minister of Transport)*, [1990] 1 F.C. 264.
10 Ibid., 267.
11 Ibid., 273.
12 Ibid.
13 *Friends of the Oldman River Society* v. *Canada (Minister of Transport)*, [1990] 2 F.C. 18 (F.C.A.).
14 Ibid., 51, note 16.
15 Ibid., 50.
16 The intervening provinces and territories were Newfoundland and Labrador, New Brunswick, Quebec, Manitoba, Saskatchewan, British Columbia, and the Northwest Territories. There were persistent rumours that Ontario would also intervene but, in the end, Ontario chose to observe from the sidelines. Ontario's reluctance was in part because it was not averse to the notion of federal intervention in cases where another province might do something inimical to Ontario's interests, for example Quebec's Great Whale Project.
17 Intervenors on FOR's side included the Alberta Wilderness Association, the Friends of the Earth, Cultural Survival (Canada), the Sierra Club of Western Canada, the Canadian Environmental Law Association, the Sierra Legal Defence Fund, the Native Council of Canada (Alberta), the Dene Nation and the Metis Association of the Northwest Territories, and the National Indian Brotherhood/Assembly of First Nations.
18 *Friends of the Oldman River Society* v. *Canada (Minister of Transport)*, [1992] 1 S.C.R. 3. The information presented here is drawn from the reasons for the judgment in this case written by Mr. Justice La Forest.
19 Ibid., Notice of Application, Affidavit of Vance MacNichol, sworn 18 April 1990 (to which are attached letters from the deputy environment ministers of BC, Manitoba, Quebec, and Newfoundland), 1.
20 *Friends of the Oldman River Society* v. *Canada (Minister of Transport)*, [1992] 1 S.C.R. 71.

21 Section 92 of the Constitution Act, 1867, sets out areas in which the provinces have exclusive powers of legislation. Section 91 of the act denotes areas in which the federal government has the exclusive right to legislate and gives the federal government the power to 'make laws for the peace, order and good government of Canada' in all matters not assigned exclusively to the provinces (commonly referred to as the 'residual power'). The environment is not listed in either section 91 or 92. As noted by Mr. Justice La Forest, the environment, in its generic sense, touches on powers assigned to both levels of government. [1992] 1 S.C.R. 63.
22 Constitution Act, 1867, s. 92(16). Alberta's argument was at least consistent with its position in the earlier cases before the Alberta Court of Queen's Bench that the dam was really of no concern to anyone beyond the narrow confines of southern Alberta.
23 *Friends of the Oldman River Society* v. *Canada (Minister of Transport)*, [1992] 1 S.C.R. 70.
24 Ibid., 75.
25 Ibid., 80.
26 *Friends of the Oldman River Society* v. *Canada (Minister of Environment)* (1993), 105 D.L.R. (4th) 454 (F.T.D.).

Chapter 20: FOR and the Attorney General
1 *Kostuch* v. *Kowalski* (1991), 78 Alta. L.R. (2d) 146.
2 Dr. Martha Kostuch, personal interview, 6 July 1993.
3 Constitution Act, 1867, s. 91(12) and the Fisheries Act, R.S.C. 1985, c. F-14.
4 Canada/Alberta Fisheries Agreement, 9 January 1987.
5 Letter from Hon. Romeo Leblanc, minister of fisheries and environment, to Hon. D.J. Russell, minister of environment, Alberta, 3 August 1978, quoted in *Kostuch* v. *Alberta (Attorney General)* (1993), 143 A.R. 168 (Q.B.).
6 Canada, Oldman River Dam Environmental Assessment Panel, *Compendium of Submissions* (Vancouver: Federal Environmental Assessment Review Office, 11 February 1990), 396; Canada, Oldman River Dam Environmental Assessment Panel, *Compendium of Submissions* (Vancouver: Federal Environmental Assessment Review Office, 22 October 1991), 144.
7 Letter from Hon. John Crosbie, minister of fisheries and oceans, to Mr. James Fulton, MP, 30 December 1992, in FOR papers, held by Dr. Martha Kostuch, Rocky Mountain House, AB; letter from David J. Robinson, chief, Western Operations and Chemical Hazards, DF&O, to the author, 6 December 1994.
8 Department of Fisheries and Oceans, *Authorization for Works or Undertakings Affecting Fish Habitat* issued to Alberta Environmental Protection for operation and maintenance of the Oldman River Dam, 16 August 1994.
9 Criminal Code, R.S.C. 1985, c. C-46, s. 504.
10 Lord Wilberforce in *Gouriet* v. *Union of Post Office Workers*, [1978] A.C. 477.
11 For information on private prosecutions in general, and, in particular, on the powers of attorneys general to intervene, with specific references to Alberta, see Linda F. Duncan, *Enforcing Environmental Law: A Guide to Private Prosecution* (Edmonton: Environmental Law Centre [Alberta] Society, 1990), upon which most of this discussion is based.
12 A stay of proceedings may be temporary; however, if the proceedings are not reactivated within a period of time specified by the Criminal Code, the charges against the accused lapse and the opportunity to prosecute on that particular information is lost.
13 Provincial Court Judge John Harvie in *Kostuch* v. *Kowalski* (1990), 75 Alta. L.R. (2d) 119 Prov.
14 Supreme Court Chief Justice Dickson in *R* v. *Jewitt*, quoted in *Kostuch* v. *Kowalski* (1991), 81 Alta. L.R. (2d) 219 (Q.B.).
15 *Kostuch* v. *Kowalski* (1990), 75 Alta. L.R. (2d) 115 and 118. Also see Duncan, *Enforcing Environmental Law*, 37.
16 John Swaigen, former general counsel for the Canadian Environmental Law Association, in Duncan, *Enforcing Environmental Law*, x.
17 Duncan, *Enforcing Environmental Law*, 36.
18 *Kostuch* v. *Kowalski* (1991), 81 Alta. L.R. (2d) 219.
19 Under ss. 35 and 40 of the Fisheries Act, it is an 'offence' for any person 'to carry on any

work or undertaking that results in the harmful alteration, disruption or destruction of fish habitat,' except 'under conditions authorized by the Minister [of Fisheries and Oceans].'

20 Fisheries Act, R.S.C. 1985, c. F-14, s. 3(2).
21 *Kostuch* v. *Kowalski* (1991), 78 Alta. L.R. (2d) 135.
22 *Kostuch* v. *Kowalski* (1990), 75 Alta. L.R. (2d) 116.
23 Provincial Court Judge Fradsham later observed of this move that 'the Attorney General was of the view that he did not have enough information to commence his own prosecution but he wanted to control somebody else's' (78 Alta. L.R. [2d] 137).
24 *Kostuch* v. *Kowalski* (1990), 75 Alta. L.R. (2d) 121.
25 Ibid., 119.
26 Ibid., 125.
27 The characterization of these events as coincidental is borrowed from Judge Fradsham (78 Alta. L.R. [2d] 137).
28 The 10 July 1990 statement is reproduced in its entirety in 78 Alta. L.R. (2d) 137, and was reported in 'No action planned on Alberta,' *Globe and Mail,* 11 July 1990.
29 *Kostuch* v. *Kowalski* decided in the Alberta Court of Queen's Bench on 19 October 1990, Mr. Justice Sulatycky (unreported) (9001-14507).
30 *Kostuch* v. *Kowalski* (1991), 81 Alta. L.R. (2d) 221.
31 *Kostuch* v. *Kowalski* (1991), 78 Alta. L.R. (2d) 131.
32 Ibid., 152.
33 *Kostuch* v. *Kowalski* (1991), 81 Alta. L.R. (2d) 214.
34 *Kostuch* v. *Alberta* (1992), 125 A.R. 214 (C.A.).
35 Ibid., 218.
36 *Kostuch* v. *Alberta (Attorney General)* (1992), 125 A.R. 214.
37 Ibid., 167.
38 Ibid., 170.
39 Ibid., 173.
40 Ibid.
41 Martha Kostuch's Factum in *Kostuch* v. *Alberta (Attorney General),* [1996] 1 W.W.R. 292 (Alta. C.A.).
42 *Kostuch* v. *Alberta (Attorney General),* [1996] 1 W.W.R. 301 (Alta. C.A.).
43 Ibid., 300.
44 'Top lawyer takes on Oldman dam,' *Calgary Herald,* 28 November 1995.

Chapter 21: The Peigan Indians

1 Public Works and Government Services Canada, *Canada and Aboriginal Peoples: A New Partnership,* Report of Hon. A.C. Hamilton (Ottawa: Indian Affairs and Northern Development, 1995), 12.
2 Royal Commission on the South Saskatchewan River Project, *Report of the Royal Commission on the South Saskatchewan River Project* (Ottawa: Queen's Printer and Controller of Stationery, 1952) and Zenon Pohorecky, 'The Great Cree Stone,' *Canadian Geographical Journal* 73 (1966): 88-91. Other dams built downstream from the Gardner Dam in subsequent years added to the impact on the Cumberland House Band.
3 Larry Krotz, 'Dammed and Diverted,' *Canadian Geographic* 111 (February/March 1991): 36-44.
4 Canada, Alberta, Saskatchewan Peace Athabasca Delta Project Study Group, *The Peace Athabasca Delta: A Canadian Resource* (Ottawa, 1972).
5 'Watery Grave Finally Consecrated,' *Alberta Native News,* August 1993; 'Kemano: SLDF Investigates the Legal Options,' *SLDF Newsletter,* no. 7 (June 1994); Bev Christiansen, *Too Good To Be True: Alcan's Kemano Completion Project* (Vancouver: Talonbooks, 1995).
6 Chief John Snow, *These Mountains are our Sacred Places* (Toronto: Samuel-Stevens, Publishers, 1977), 128-31.
7 Olive Patricia Dickason, *Canada's First Nations: A History of Founding People from Earliest Times* (Toronto: McClelland and Stewart, 1992), 402.
8 Alberta Environment Conservation Authority, *Flow Regulation of the Red Deer River: Report and Recommendations* (Edmonton, June 1977), 7.

9 Stephen Leacock, *Canada: The Foundations of Its Future* (Montreal: House of Seagram, 1941), 19. This book was reprinted and distributed free of charge, as a centennial year promotion by Seagrams Distillers, in 1967.
10 'Peigan hurt by lack of housing,' *Lethbridge Herald,* 2 June 1992.
11 Canada, Oldman River Dam Environmental Assessment Panel, *Addendum to Compendium of Submissions Dated October 22, 1991,* vol. 2 (Vancouver: Federal Environmental Assessment Review Office, 31 December 1991), 800.
12 For example, Dickason, *Canada's First Nations;* Grand Council of Treaty 8 Nations Environment Committee, *Grand Council of Treaty 8 First Nations Great Bear Environmental Health Study* (Edmonton, May 1993); Jerry Mander, *In the Absence of the Sacred* (San Francisco: Sierra Club Books, 1992); Rupert Ross, *Dancing with a Ghost: Exploring Indian Reality* (Markham: Octopus Publishing Group, 1992); and Duncan M. Taylor, 'Disagreeing on the Basics,' *Alternatives* 18 (1991): 3.
13 Adapted from Grand Council of Treaty 8 Nations Environment Committee, *Grand Council of Treaty 8 First Nations Great Bear Environmental Health Study* (Edmonton, May 1993).
14 Mander, *In the Absence of the Sacred,* 260.
15 Snow, *These Mountains Are Our Sacred Places,* 4.
16 Ross, *Dancing with a Ghost,* 91.
17 During the period from 1982 to 1991, the Peigan undertook three studies to document the impact of the Oldman River Dam on their cultural and spiritual beliefs and values – in the Weasel Valley study, the Peigan RDI studies, and a survey funded by the ORDEAP. They have been unwilling to make the results of those studies public.
18 The discussion that follows draws on the following sources: Betty Bastien, 'Native Spiritual Links to Rivers,' in *Flowing to the Future,* edited by Cheryl Bradley et al. (Edmonton: University of Alberta, Faculty of Extension, 1989); Dickason, *Canada's First Nations;* Brian Reeves, 'The Oldman Dam and Traditional Piikani Religious Values,' in Canada, Oldman River Dam Environmental Assessment Panel, *Addendum to Compendium of Submissions Dated October 22, 1991,* vol. 2, 829-38; Reeves' verbal submission to the federal panel in Canada, Oldman River Dam Environmental Assessment Panel, *Public Hearings Proceedings, November 5-20, 1991,* vol. 5 (Vancouver: Federal Environmental Assessment Review Office, November 1991), 1077 ff.; Ross, *Dancing with a Ghost;* Snow, *These Mountains Are Our Sacred Places;* and *The Sacred Tree,* 2nd ed. (Lethbridge: Four Winds Development Press, University of Lethbridge, 1985).
19 Snow, *These Mountains Are Our Sacred Places,* 146.
20 'The Politics of Water,' on *Ideas,* CBC Radio, 8 March 1993.
21 Four Worlds Development Project, *The Sacred Tree* (Lethbridge, AB: Four Worlds Development Press, University of Lethbridge, 1984), 76.
22 Reeves, 'The Oldman Dam and Traditional Piikani Religious Values,' in Canada, Oldman River Dam Environmental Assessment Panel, *Addendum to Compendium of Submissions Dated October 22, 1991,* vol. 2, 3.

Chapter 22: The Peigan and the Oldman River Dam: I
1 Joan Ryan, *Wall of Words: The Betrayal of the Urban Indian* (Toronto: PMA Books, 1978), xvii.
2 The Peigan's 1986 water rights suit against Alberta included a request for an injunction to halt construction, which was withdrawn while the dam was still under construction.
3 For an account of the events that led to Nelson Small Legs, Jr.'s suicide see Ryan, *Wall of Words.*
4 George Kupfer, personal interview, 18 June 1994.
5 Environment Council of Alberta, *Proceedings of Public Hearings on the Management of Water within the Oldman River Basin,* Brief No. 91, presented by Albert Yellowhorn Sr. and Percy Smith at Pincher Creek, AB, 20 November 1978.
6 Ibid., Supplementary Brief, No. 218, submitted by John W. Smith.
7 Peter Boothroyd and Co-West Associates (George Kupfer, Robert Langin), *Oldman River Basin Study: Phase II – Social Impact Assessment* (Lethbridge: Oldman River Study Management Committee, 1978), 95 and 96.

8 Peigan Band Administration, 'Proposed Statement of Position,' January 1981.
9 Ibid., 4-5.
10 Barry Barton, 'Water Resources and Native People' (paper presented to a conference called Canadian Waters: The State of the Resource, sponsored by the Rawson Academy of Aquatic Science, Toronto, 26-9 May 1985).
11 Letter from Peigan Chief Peter Yellowhorn to Hon. Fred Bradley, Alberta minister of environment, dated 10 November 1983 (attached as Exhibit CC to Lorand Szojka's 15 January 1989 Affidavit to the Federal Court, T-865-89). Although Chief Yellowhorn was adamant that the 'summary' of the Weasel Valley study attached to his letter that detailed what the Peigan might expect in compensation for a dam on the reserve should not be considered a proposal, it was considered as such by the government and was the source of the Peigan compensation demands evaluated by government analysts.
12 Ibid.
13 Alberta Water Resources Commission, *Re: South Saskatchewan River Basin Planning Program Public Hearings*, Red Deer, AB, 12 December 1994, Vol. III (Edmonton: November-December 1984), 436, 438.
14 *Chief Peter Yellowhorn v. The Queen (in Right of Alberta)*, Statement of Claim filed in the Alberta Court of Queen's Bench, Calgary, on 11 April 1986 (8601-06578).
15 *Chief Peter Yellowhorn v. The Queen (in Right of Canada) and Hon. David Crombie*, Statement of Claim filed in the Federal Court of Canada, Trial Division, Montreal, on 19 June 1986 (T-1486-86).
16 Peigan Nation, *Oldman River Investigations: Community Impact Management and Development Programme*, 13 vols. (Brocket, AB, May 1987). (Also referred to as Resource Development Impact [RDI] Studies.)
17 Peigan Nation, *A Proposal for Resolution of the Major Issues Relating to the Oldman River Dam* (Brocket, AB, April 1987).
18 Ibid., 15. The 'major issues' are identified at three different places in the proposal. The list on p. 15 is the most comprehensive.
19 Ibid., 5, Table 2. The Peigan estimated the total cost of construction for the 2,670-hectare irrigation project at $13.6 million; the $5 million requested in the proposal was for 'initial funding' of this construction. (Ibid., 6.)
20 Peigan Nation, *Oldman River Investigations: Community Impact Management and Development Programme: Final Report*, vol. 13c (Brocket, AB, May 1987), 19-28, included in Annex C to letter from Garry Wouters, regional director general, INAC, to Dr. W.A. Ross, chairman, ORDEAP, 30 December 1991. The estimated construction costs for the development of 17,800 hectares of this land was $94.4 million.
21 Alberta Environment, *Update* (November 1986): 7.
22 'Peigans awaiting ruling on Oldman dam petition,' *Lethbridge Herald*, 17 April 1989, A3.
23 'Lonefighters oppose Chief's dam position,' *Lethbridge Herald*, 24 May 1991.
24 Letter from Chief Leonard Bastien, Peigan Nation, to Hon. Tom Siddon, minister of Indian affairs, 22 August 1991.
25 Canada, Oldman River Environmental Assessment Panel, *Public Hearings Proceedings, November 16, 1991*, vol. 10 (Vancouver: Federal Environmental Assessment Review Office, n.d.), 2215-8.
26 Rick J. Ponting, ed., *Arduous Journey: Canadian Indians and Decolonization* (Toronto: McClelland and Stewart, 1986), 238.
27 Letter from Chief Leonard Bastien, Peigan Nation, to Hon. Pauline A. Browse, minister of Indian affairs, *Globe and Mail*, 13 October 1993.

Chapter 23: The Peigan and the Oldman River Dam: II

1 *Windspeaker*, 7 June 1991, 1.
2 Brian Reeves, 'The Oldman River Dam and Alberta's Heritage: Conservation or Desecration?' in *Economic, Environmental and Social Aspects of the Oldman River Dam Project*, edited by Stewart B. Rood and Frank J. Jankunis (Lethbridge: University of Lethbridge, 1988), 99.
3 For example, see Gordon Merrick, 'Organization direction to be decided Thursday,' *Lethbridge Herald*, 17 February 1988; John-Scott Black, 'The Old Man's Blessing,' *Borealis*

(Spring 1991): 18-9; *Flowing to the Future,* ed. Bradley et al. (Edmonton: University of Alberta, Faculty of Extension, 1990).

4 'Peigans' future lies ahead of new chief,' *Lethbridge Herald,* 6 January 1989.

5 *Chief Peter Yellowhorn* v. *The Queen (in Right of Alberta),* Statement of Claim filed in the Alberta Court of Queen's Bench, Calgary, on 11 April 1986 (8601-06578). Reply to Demand for Particulars, 13 June 1986, 3.

6 Canada, Oldman River Dam Environmental Assessment Panel, *Public Hearings Proceedings, November 5-20, 1991,* vol. 5 (Vancouver: Federal Environmental Assessment Review Office, n.d.), 1088-9.

7 Ibid., vol. 6, 1364 ff.

8 Ibid., vol. 5, 1109-10.

9 Jack Ives, 'Evaluation and Mitigation of Historical Resources Affected by the Oldman River Dam Project,' in *Economic, Environmental and Social Aspects of the Oldman River Dam Project,* edited by Stewart B. Rood and Frank J. Jankunis (Lethbridge: University of Lethbridge), 109.

10 Canada, Transport Canada, *Federal Government Response to the Oldman River Dam Project Environmental Review Panel Report* (Ottawa, 30 August 1993), 18.

11 Canada, Oldman River Dam Environmental Assessment Panel, *Public Hearings Proceedings, November 5-20, 1991,* vol. 6, 1364-5.

12 Ibid., vol. 10, 2142.

13 Environment Council of Alberta, *Transcripts of Public Hearings on Management of Water Resources within the Oldman River Basin* (Edmonton, 1979), Supplementary Brief No. 218, 54.

14 'Peigans plan court fight,' *Lethbridge Herald,* 17 May 1989.

15 Canada, Oldman River Dam Environmental Assessment Panel, *Public Hearings Proceedings, November 5-20, 1991,* vol. 10, 2142.

Chapter 24: The Federal Watchdog: I

1 Government of Canada *News Release* announcing the proposed federal Environmental Protection Act (December 1986).

2 *Canadian Wildlife Federation Inc., et al., v. Canada (Minister of the Environment) and Saskatchewan Water Corp.,* Federal Court (T.D.), 28 December 1989, 31 F.T.R. 15.

3 *Canada Gazette, Part II,* v. 118, n. 14 (11 July 1984), Environmental Assessment and Review Process Guidelines Order, SOR/84-467.

4 Canada, Department of Fisheries and Oceans, *Policy for the Management of Fish Habitat* (Ottawa, 1986).

5 Canada, Environment Canada, *Federal Water Policy* (Ottawa, 1987).

6 Ibid., 31.

7 Canada, Department of Fisheries and Oceans, Central and Arctic Region, *Comments on the Oldman River Dam Proposal* (Ottawa, 24 February 1987), included in Annex C to letter from Garry Wouters, regional director general, INAC, to Dr. W.A. Ross, chairman, ORDEAP, 30 December 1991.

8 Ibid., 2.

9 For a discussion of DF&O's dealings with Alcan see Bev Christiansen, *Too Good To Be True: Alcan's Kemano Completion Project* (Vancouver: Talonbooks, 1995).

10 Canada, Environment Canada, *Environmental Impact Evaluation: The Three Rivers Dam Project,* rev. ed. (Ottawa, 9 July 1987), included in Annex C to letter from Garry Wouters, regional director general, INAC, to Dr. W.A. Ross, chairman, ORDEAP, 30 December 1991.

11 R.A. Halliday, Conservation and Protection, Western and Northern Region, *Three Rivers Dam Issue,* 5 May 1987, included in Annex C to letter from Garry Wouters, regional director general, INAC, to Dr. W.A. Ross, chairman, ORDEAP, 30 December 1991.

12 *Friends of the Oldman River Society* v. *Canada (Minister of Transport),* [1992] 1 S.C.R. 22.

13 The RCMP's motto, which translated into English is 'Uphold the Right.'

14 The Supreme Court in *Guerin* v. *The Queen* declared that the Crown's fiduciary duty to Indians with respect to Indian land arises from s. 18(1) of the Indian Act, which confirms 'the historic responsibility which the Crown has undertaken to act on behalf of the

Indians so as to protect their interests in transactions with third parties' (13 D.L.R. [4th] 340). For a discussion of the Crown's fiduciary duty to Indians see Public Works and Government Services Canada, *Canada and Aboriginal Peoples: A New Partnership*, Report of Hon. A.C. Hamilton (Ottawa: Indian Affairs and Northern Development, 1995).

15 Rick J. Ponting, ed., *Arduous Journey: Canadian Indians and Decolonization* (Toronto: McClelland and Stewart, 1986), 239.

16 A briefing note prepared by federal bureaucrats for Minister Landry in May 1991 includes the following: 'The [Peigan] band may wish to pursue the federal crown in respect of the permits issued for the irrigation system which is the subject of the band's action against the province. Given this possibility and the band's now dormant action against the federal crown, *direct involvement in negotiations toward settlement of the band's action against the province would surely result in conflict of interest.*' In Annex C to letter from Garry Wouters, regional director general, INAC, to Dr. W.A. Ross, chairman, ORDEAP, 30 December 1991. The italicized portion of the above quotation is blacked out in the copy of the briefing note held by FEARO, but if the page is held in front of a light, the wording is easily discernible.

17 Boyce Richardson, 'Concealed Contempt,' *Canadian Forum* (December 1989): 18.

18 Letter from Fred Drummie, associate deputy minister, Indian Affairs, to Vance MacNichol, deputy minister, Alberta Environment, 9 June 1987, in Annex C to letter from Garry Wouters, regional director general, INAC, to Dr. W.A. Ross, chairman, ORDEAP, 30 December 1991.

19 Letter from Vance MacNichol, Alberta Environment, to Fred Drummie, Indian Affairs, 3 July 1987; letter from Peter Melnychuk, Alberta Environment, to Elizabeth Turbayne, Indian Affairs, 22 August 1988; memorandum Keith MacDonald, Indian Affairs, to Gerry Throndson, Indian Affairs, 13 February 1989; all in Annex C to letter from Garry Wouters, regional director general, INAC, to Dr. W.A. Ross, chairman, ORDEAP, 30 December 1991.

20 Letter from Fred Drummie, Indian Affairs, to Vance MacNichol, Alberta Environment, 24 October 1988, in Annex C to letter from Garry Wouters, regional director general, INAC, to Dr. W.A. Ross, chairman, ORDEAP, 30 December 1991.

21 By this time, Alberta had decreed that its lawyers must be in attendance at any meetings with Indian Affairs concerning the Peigan and the Oldman River Dam.

22 'Environmental Assessment Considerations Respecting The Three Rivers Dam Project Alberta,' September 1988, attached to letter from Fred Drummie, Indian Affairs, to Vance MacNichol, Alberta Environment, 24 October 1988, in Annex C to letter from Garry Wouters, regional director general, INAC, to Dr. W.A. Ross, chairman, ORDEAP, 30 December 1991.

23 Ibid., 1.

24 Ibid., 4.

25 Letter from Doug Kane, A/Director, Environment Directorate, Lands Revenues and Trusts, Indian Affairs, to Gerry Thorndson, director, Alberta Region Lands, Revenues and Trusts, Indian Affairs, 7 April 1989, in Annex C to letter from Garry Wouters, regional director general, INAC, to Dr. W.A. Ross, chairman, ORDEAP, 30 December 1991.

26 Memorandum from D. Wallace, regional director general, Indian Affairs, to Gerry Thorndson, Indian Affairs, 16 February 1988, in Annex C to letter from Garry Wouters, regional director general, INAC, to Dr. W.A. Ross, chairman, ORDEAP, 30 December 1991.

27 Letter from Fred Drummie, Indian Affairs, to Vance MacNichol, Alberta Environment, 9 June 1987, in Annex C to letter from Garry Wouters, regional director general, INAC, to Dr. W.A. Ross, chairman, ORDEAP, 30 December 1991.

28 Memorandum from K. Grady, Indian Affairs, to Keith MacDonald, Indian Affairs, 14 October 1989, in Annex C to letter from Garry Wouters, regional director general, INAC, to Dr. W.A. Ross, chairman, ORDEAP, 30 December 1991.

29 Canada, Oldman River Dam Environmental Assessment Panel, *Public Hearings Proceedings, November 16, 1991*, vol. 10 (Vancouver: Federal Environmental Assessment Review Office, n.d.), 2218.

30 Canada, Oldman River Dam Environmental Assessment Panel, *Report of the Environmental Assessment Panel* (Hull: Federal Environmental Assessment Review Office, 1992), 33.

31 Letter from K.C. Kirby, Indian Affairs, to K. Smith, Pine Coulee NRCB/EARP Joint Review Panel chairman, dated 7 September 1994. (Pine Coulee NRCB/EARP Hearing Exhibit No. 50).
32 'Story of the originals,' a review of Canada's First Nations by Leslie Hall in the *Globe and Mail,* 29 August 1992.
33 Public Works and Government Services Canada, *Canada and Aboriginal Peoples: A New Partnership* (Ottawa: 1995), 11.
34 Canada, Environment Canada, *Federal Water Policy,* 31.
35 *Friends of the Oldman River Society* v. *Canada (Minister of Transport),* [1992] 1 S.C.R. 3.
36 Letter from Mary Bailey, Southern Alberta Environmental Group, to Hon. Tom Siddon, minister of fisheries and oceans, August 1987, in Annex C to letter from Garry Wouters, regional director general, INAC, to Dr. W.A. Ross, chairman, ORDEAP, 30 December 1991.
37 Letter from Hon. Tom Siddon to Mary Bailey, Southern Alberta Environmental Group, 25 August 1987, in Annex C to letter from Garry Wouters, regional director general, INAC, to Dr. W.A. Ross, chairman, ORDEAP, 30 December 1991.
38 Canada, Department of Fisheries and Oceans, Central and Arctic Region, *Comments on the Oldman River Dam Proposal* (Ottawa, 24 February 1987), in Annex C to letter from Garry Wouters, regional director general, INAC, to Dr. W.A. Ross, chairman, ORDEAP, 30 December 1991. The department's 'No net loss of the productive capacity of habitats' policy, and its expectations for provincial agencies in this respect are set out in the Policy for the Management of Fish Habitat that Minister Siddon himself had presented to Parliament in October 1986.
39 'DF&O Submission to the ORDEAP Panel,' 23 October 1991, in Canada, Oldman River Dam Environmental Assessment Panel, *Compendium of Submissions* (Vancouver: Federal Environmental Assessment Review Office, 22 October 1991, 144.
40 Letter from Cliff Wallis, FOR, to Hon. Tom McMillan, minister of environment Canada, 3 December 1987, in Annex C to letter from Garry Wouters, regional director general, INAC, to Dr. W.A. Ross, chairman, ORDEAP, 30 December 1991.
41 Letter from Holly Martell, special assistant, Office of the Minister of Environment, to Cliff Wallis, FOR, 15 January 1988, in Annex C to letter from Garry Wouters, regional director general, INAC, to Dr. W.A. Ross, chairman, ORDEAP, 30 December 1991.
42 Letters from the Peigan Nation to the minister of Indian affairs, 9 November 1988, 29 March 1989, and 3 April 1989, and Peigan BCRs 1896/88-89, 1999/88-89 and 2015/88-89, in Annex C to letter from Garry Wouters, regional director general, INAC, to Dr. W.A. Ross, chairman, ORDEAP, 30 December 1991.
43 Letter from Anne Marie Jean, special assistant, Office of the Minister of the Environment, to Nelbert Little Moustache, Peigan Band Council, 27 February 1989, in Annex C to letter from Garry Wouters, regional director general, INAC, to Dr. W.A. Ross, chairman, ORDEAP, 30 December 1991.
44 Letter from Hon. Pierre Cadieux, minister of Indian affairs, to Nelbert Little Moustache, Peigan Band councillor, 26 July 1989, in Annex C to letter from Garry Wouters, regional director general, INAC, to Dr. W.A. Ross, chairman, ORDEAP, 30 December 1991.

Chapter 25: The Federal Watchdog: II
1 Andrew Nikiforuk, *'The Nasty Game': The Failure of Environmental Assessment in Canada* (Toronto: Walter and Duncan Gordon Foundation, 1997), i.
2 Concern for maintaining the credibility of the process was a dominant theme expressed by Dr. W.A. Ross during the course of my interviews with him.
3 Letter from Dr. W.A. Ross, chairman, ORDEAP, to Hon. Robert de Cotret, minister of the environment, 7 January 1991. This letter was placed on the panel's public file and reported in Oldman River Dam Environmental Assessment Panel *Newsletter,* no. 1 (March 1991).
4 Dr. W.A. Ross, personal interview, 22 July 1993. For one account of the circumstances surrounding the Rafferty-Alameda review, see George N. Hood, *Against the Flow: Rafferty-Alameda and the Politics of the Environment* (Saskatoon: Fifth House Publishers, 1994).
5 Canada, Oldman River Dam Environmental Assessment Panel, *Newsletter,* no. 1: 3.

6 Federal Environmental Assessment Review Office, *Terms of Reference for the Oldman River Dam Environmental Assessment Panel,* Vancouver, n.d. (attached to minister of environment *Release: Minister Names Panel to Review the Oldman River Dam Project,* 16 November 1990).

7 Canada, Oldman River Dam Environmental Assessment Panel, *Additional Information Requirements* (Vancouver: Federal Environmental Assessment Review Office, 1991).

8 Canada, Oldman River Dam Environmental Assessment Panel, *Compendium of Submissions* (Vancouver: Federal Environmental Assessment Review Office, 11 February 1990), 312.

9 Dr. W.A. Ross, personal interview, 20 July 1993.

10 Ibid.

11 Canada, Oldman River Dam Environmental Assessment Panel, *Public Hearings Proceedings, November 5-20, 1991* (Vancouver: Federal Environmental Assessment Review Office, n.d.), 26, and Dr. W.A. Ross, personal interview, 20 July 1993.

12 Canada, Oldman River Dam Environmental Assessment Panel, *Public Hearings Proceedings, November 5-20, 1991,* vol. 10, 2212.

13 Brian Reeves, 'The Oldman Dam and Traditional Piikani Religious Values,' in Canada, Oldman River Dam Environmental Assessment Panel, *Addendum to Compendium of Submissions Dated October 22, 1991,* vol. 2 (Vancouver: Federal Environmental Assessment Review Office, 31 December 1991), 829-38, and Reeves' verbal submission to the panel at the hearings in Calgary on 7 November 1991, in Canada, Oldman River Dam Environmental Assessment Panel, *Public Hearings Proceedings, November 5-20, 1991,* vol. 5, 1077-1104; Develon Small Legs' verbal submission to the panel in Calgary on 7 November 1991, in ibid., vol. 5, 1108-10; Milton Born With A Tooth's verbal submission to the panel in Calgary on 8 November 1991, in ibid., vol. 6, 1363-72; and the verbal submissions of several Peigan at Brocket, AB, on 16 November 1991, in ibid., vol. 10.

14 Canada, Oldman River Dam Environmental Assessment Panel, *Report of the Environmental Assessment Panel* (Hull: Federal Environmental Assessment Review Office, 1992), 26.

15 Dr. W.A. Ross, personal interview, 20 July 1993.

16 Oldman River Dam Environmental Assessment Panel, *Report of the Environmental Assessment Panel,* 6.

17 Dr. W.A. Ross, personal interview, 20 July 1993.

18 Canada, Oldman River Dam Environmental Assessment Panel, *Report of the Environmental Assessment Panel,* Recommendations 7, 10, 11, 13, and 17.

19 Dr. W.A. Ross, personal interview, 20 July 1993.

20 Ibid.

21 Canada, Oldman River Dam Environmental Assessment Panel, *Report of the Environmental Assessment Panel,* 7.

22 Ibid., 8.

23 Dr. W.A. Ross, personal interview, 20 July 1993.

24 Ibid.

25 Ibid.

26 Canada, Oldman River Dam Environmental Assessment Panel, *Report of the Environmental Assessment Panel,* 26.

27 Ibid., 5.

28 Ibid., 8.

29 Ibid.

30 Ibid., i.

31 Ibid., 33.

32 Ibid.

33 Dr. W.A. Ross, personal interview, 22 July 1993.

34 Canada, Oldman River Dam Environmental Assessment Panel, *Report of the Environmental Assessment Panel,* i.

35 Government of Canada, *News Release,* no. 79/92 (21 May 1992): 1.

36 Canada, Parliament, House of Commons, *Commons Debates,* 34th Parliament, 3rd Session, vol. ix (22 May 1992) (Ottawa: 1992), 11080. A similar response appears on p. 11073.

37 Canada, Transport Canada, *Federal Government Response to the Oldman River Dam Project*

. *Environmental Review Panel Report* (Ottawa, 30 August 1993). Released by Transport Minister Corbeil, with Government of Canada, *News Release,* no. 190/93 (2 September 1993).

38 Letter from R. Kingston, director general, Marine Navigation Services Directorate, Transport Canada, to J.W. Theissen, assistant deputy minister, Water Resources Services, Alberta Environmental Protection, 2 September 1993, File 8200-86-370 (AMAP).

39 Canada, Oldman River Dam Environmental Assessment Panel, *Report of the Environmental Assessment Panel,* 8.

40 Alberta Environment, Ministerial Order 55/93.

41 Canada, Transport Canada, *Federal Government Response,* 4.

Chapter 26: Iniquity and Betrayal

1 Alberta, Environment Council of Alberta, *Management of Water Resources within the Oldman River Basin: Report and Recommendations* (Edmonton, 1979), 198.

2 Canada, Oldman River Dam Environmental Assessment Panel, *Report of the Environmental Assessment Panel* (Hull: Federal Environmental Assessment Review Office, 1992), 26.

3 Ibid., 5.

4 Anyone familiar with the recent fate of Alberta's kindergartens will understand that the concepts taught there are not necessarily deemed of importance to Alberta's government.

5 'Whistle blower,' *Globe and Mail,* 1 October 1994, D1.

6 Jerry Mander, *In the Absence of the Sacred* (San Francisco: Sierra Club Books, 1992), 199.

7 'Face to Face,' *Lethbridge Herald,* 12 December 1987. In recent years, the courts have shown greater sensitivity to Indian problems; governments have shown even less.

8 'Status Briefing' for ADM Goodleaf, Indian Affairs, 11 December 1991, p. 3, in Annex C to letter from Garry Wouters, regional director general, INAC, to Dr. W.A. Ross, chairman, ORDEAP, 30 December 1991.

9 The cost of expert testimony in similar cases in the United States has ranged from $250,000 to $1 million.

10 Letter from Chief Leonard Bastien, Peigan Nation, to Hon. Thomas Siddon, minister of Indian affairs, 27 September 1990, in Annex C to letter from Garry Wouters, regional director general, INAC, to Dr. W.A. Ross, chairman, ORDEAP, 30 December 1991.

11 Ibid.

12 Alberta Environment, *Oldman River Dam Historical Resources* (Edmonton, n.d.). This is one of a series of information brochures prepared and distributed by Alberta Environment's Oldman River Dam Project Office during the period that the dam was under construction.

13 Editorial, 'Pine Coulee Hardball,' *Claresholm Local Press,* 5 October 1994, 2.

14 'Province defends proposed dam project,' *Lethbridge Herald,* 28 September 1994.

15 Alberta, Natural Resources Conservation Board/Canadian Environmental Assessment Act Joint Review Panel, *Report of the NRCB/CEAA Joint Review Panel: Little Bow Project/Highwood Diversion Plan* (Edmonton, 1998), 6-71.

16 Canada, Oldman River Dam Environmental Assessment Panel, *Report of the Environmental Assessment Panel,* Recommendations 9 and 18.

17 Letter from Chief Leonard Bastien, Peigan Nation, to Hon. Pauline Browes, minister of Indian affairs, *Globe and Mail,* 13 October 1993.

18 Canada, Transport Canada, *Federal Government Response to the Oldman River Dam Project Environmental Review Panel Report* (Ottawa: 30 August 1993), 5.

19 Ibid.

Chapter 27: The Peigan, Politics, and the Courts

1 Richard Gwynn, *Nationalism Without Walls: The Unbearable Lightness of Being Canadian* (Toronto: McClelland and Stewart, 1995), 239.

2 *Calder* v. *Attorney General of B.C.,* [1973] S.C.R. 313.

3 *Chief Peter Yellowhorn* v. *Alberta,* Statement of Claim filed in the Alberta Court of Queen's Bench, Calgary, on 11 April 1986 (8601-06578), and Reply to Demand for Particulars, 13 June 1986.

4 Originally established by the Privy Council in 1888 *(St. Catharine's Milling and Lumber Co.* v. *The Queen* (1888), 14 A.C. 46 [P.C.]).

5 *Attorney General for Ontario* v. *Bear Island Foundation,* [1985] 1 C.N.L.R. 1 (Ont. S.C.). This judgment was upheld by the Ontario Court of Appeal and, in 1991, by the Supreme Court of Canada.

6 *Hamlet of Baker Lake* v. *Minister of Indian Affairs and Northern Development,* [1979] 3 C.N.L.R. 17 (F.T.D.).

7 *R.* v. *Van der Peet,* [1996] 2 S.C.R. 507.

8 *Delgamuukw* v. *British Columbia,* [1991] 3 W.W.R. 97 (B.C.S.C.).

9 *Delgamuukw* v. *British Columbia,* [1993] 5 W.W.R. 97 (B.C.C.A.).

10 *Delgamuukw* v. *British Columbia,* [1997] 3 S.C.R. 1010.

11 Alberta Environmental Protection, 'Aboriginal Water Issues' in *Water Management in Alberta,* Background Paper, vol. 3 (Edmonton, August 1991).

12 Public Works and Government Services Canada, *Canada and Aboriginal Peoples: A New Partnership* (Ottawa: 1995), 71.

13 The Stoney, Sarcee, Blackfoot, Blood, and Peigan.

14 Approximately everything between the International Boundary, the Cypress Hills, the Rocky Mountains, and the North Saskatchewan River Basin.

15 In addition, the treaty promised that the Crown would pay the salaries of teachers to educate the children and provide money for the purchase of ammunition, as well as a collection of baubles for the chiefs who signed the treaty.

16 The courts have taken this view in some cases. For example, in 1973, the Supreme Court of the NWT. ruled in a case concerning the Dene that the leaders who signed the treaties didn't understand what was in the official English version of the treaties, and that no one had bothered to tell them. See *Re Paulette,* [1973] 6 W.W.R. 97 (N.W.T.S.C.).

17 Olive Patricia Dickason, *Canada's First Nations: A History of Founding People from Earliest Times* (Toronto: McClelland and Stewart, 1992), 353.

18 Leroy Little Bear, 'Aboriginal Rights and the Canadian Grundnorm,' in *Arduous Journey: Canadian Indians and Decolonization,* edited by J. Rick Ponting (Toronto: McClelland and Stewart, 1986), 244 ff. Little Bear puts a distinctly Aboriginal spin on the idea of sharing what the Creator 'gave to all living creatures' when he says that 'sharing here cannot be interpreted as meaning that Europeans got the same rights as any other native person' (ibid., 246).

19 Father John Scollen, quoted by Donald B. Smith, 'The Original Peoples of Alberta,' in *Peoples of Alberta: Portraits of Cultural Diversity,* edited by Howard and Tamara Palmer (Saskatoon: Western Producer Books, 1985), 63.

20 Hugh A. Dempsey, 'Treaty Research Report: Treaty 7,' (Ottawa: Treaties and Historical Research Centre, Comprehensive Claims Branch, Self-Government, 1987), 44.

21 See the statements of various Peigan elders in Canada, Oldman River Dam Environmental Assessment Panel, *Public Hearings Proceedings,* vol. 10 (Vancouver: Federal Environmental Assessment Review Office, n.d.), 2146-95. The elders' accounts are generally based on oral histories passed on to them by their parents or a previous generation of elders. However, in one of the accounts referred to above, the elder attributes his information to 'what I heard from this historian on TV' (ibid., 2149).

22 'Submissions of the Peigan Nation' to the Pine Coulee NRCB/EARP Joint Review Panel, 12 September 1994 (Hearing Exhibit No. 39). The submission does not offer an explanation of when or by whom the Waterton River was known as the Crow Lodge River.

23 For an example of this claim, see 'Scope of Work: Peigan Rights to the Use of Water of the Oldman River as Confirmed by Treaty 7,' in Canada, Oldman River Dam Environmental Assessment Panel, *Addendum to Compendium of Submissions Dated October 22, 1991,* vol. 2 (Vancouver: Federal Environmental Assessment Review Office, 31 December 1991), 796. This interpretation owes much to the Winters doctrine, a US Supreme Court ruling, which is discussed later in this chapter.

24 Department of Indian Affairs and Northern Development, *White Policy Paper on Indian Affairs* (Ottawa: Queen's Printer, 1969).

25 *R.* v. *Sparrow,* [1990] 3 C.N.L.R. 171 (S.C.C.).

26 Dempsey, 'Treaty Research Report: Treaty 7,' 52.

27 'Scope of Work - Peigan Rights to Use the Water of the Oldman River As Confirmed by

Treaty 7,' in Canada, Oldman River Dam Environmental Assessment Panel, *Addendum to Compendium of Submissions Dated October 22, 1991*, vol. 2 (Vancouver: Federal Environmental Assessment Review Office, 31 December 1991), 796.

28 *Nowegijick v. The Queen*, [1983] 2 C.N.L.R. 1994 (S.C.C.).

29 Richard H. Bartlett, *Aboriginal Water Rights in Canada: A Study of Aboriginal Title to Water and Indian Water Rights* (Calgary: The Canadian Institute of Resources Law, University of Calgary, 1988).

30 The so-called Winters doctrine, based on a 1908 ruling by the US Supreme Court in *Winters v. United States* (207 U.S. 564 [1908]), says that when the US government set aside land for Indian reservations, it also reserved sufficient water for the use of the inhabitants of the reservation 'to enable the purpose for which the land was set aside,' i.e., the practice of agriculture, so they might become a 'pastoral and civilized people.' In 1963, the US Supreme Court extended the Winters doctrine by ruling that sufficient water had been reserved 'to satisfy the future as well as the present needs,' which, in the case in question, included water to irrigate 'all the practicably irrigable acreage on the reservations.' (*Arizona v. California*, 373 U.S. 546 [1963]).

31 Bartlett, *Aboriginal Water Rights in Canada*, 52

32 John L. Taylor, *Understanding the Treaties* (Edmonton: Indian Association of Alberta, 1975). (See Bartlett, *Aboriginal Water Rights in Canada*, 28, fn 26.)

33 *Globe and Mail*, advertisement, 24 September 1992, A5.

34 'Unsettled land claims hit $8 billion,' *Calgary Herald*, 21 October 1994. Melvin Smith suggests that the total could reach $15 billion in British Columbia alone. (Melvin H. Smith, *Our Home or Native Land?: What Government Aboriginal Policy is Doing to Canada*. [Victoria: Crown·Western, 1995], 98.)

35 Boyce Richardson, 'Government Greenwash,' *Canadian Forum* (November 1993): 13.

36 Melvin H. Smith, *Our Home or Native Land?*, 109.

37 Canada, Oldman River Dam Environmental Assessment Panel, *Addendum to Compendium of Submissions Dated October 22, 1991*, vol. 2, 804.

38 *Chief Peter Yellowhorn v. The Queen (in Right of Alberta)*, Statement of Claim filed in the Alberta Court of Queen's Bench, Calgary, on 11 April 1986 (8601-06578); *Chief Peter Yellowhorn v. The Queen (in Right of Canada) and the Hon. David Crombie*, Statement of Claim filed in the Federal Court of Canada, Trial Division, Montreal, on 19 June 1986 (T-1486-86).

39 Letter from Thomas Berger to Hon. Ray Hnatyshyn, minister of justice, 22 September 1988, in Annex C to letter from Garry Wouters, regional director general, INAC, to Dr. W.A. Ross, chairman, ORDEAP, 30 December 1991. Berger's explanation of how much water a band might be entitled to is drawn from another US Supreme Court ruling, *Arizona v. California*, 373 U.S. 546 (1963), where the reference is to 'practicably irrigable acreage.'

40 Letter from Chief Leonard Bastien, Peigan Nation, to Hon. Tom Siddon, minister of Indian affairs, 27 September 1990, in Annex C to letter from Garry Wouters, regional director general, INAC, to Dr. W.A. Ross, chairman, ORDEAP, 30 December 1991.

41 The suit against Alberta omits the adjective 'exclusive,' perhaps because jurisdiction was shared with the Peigan Band now resident in the United States.

42 *Hamlet of Baker Lake v. Minister of Indian Affairs and Northern Development*, [1979] 3 C.N.L.R. 17.

43 Memorandum from Louise Mandell to Thomas Berger, re: Native Religious Freedoms and Charter, 9 August 1988. This view was supported by the law firm Code, Hunter in a 5 January 1989 letter to FOR. Both in FOR papers held by Dr. Martha Kostuch, Rocky Mountain House, AB.

44 Letter from Thomas Berger to Chief Peter Yellowhorn, 5 August 1988, in Annex C to letter from Garry Wouters, regional director general, INAC, to Dr. W.A. Ross, chairman, ORDEAP, 30 December 1991. A US Supreme Court decision reinforced Berger's opinion that an application based on religious grounds would fail. In a 1988 decision (G-O Road) overturning a lower court ruling that would have prevented the US Forest Service from constructing a road through a National Forest in California on the grounds that the road

would run through a sacred place used for vision quests, the Court said that only actions that directly and intentionally disrupt religious practices are prohibited. This ruling put the Indian bands in the position of having to prove that the US Forest Service wished to build the road for the express purpose of disrupting their religious practices. (*Lyng* v. *Northwest Indian Cemetery Protective Association,* 485 U.S. 439, 19 April 1988 [G-0 Road]).

45   Letter from Thomas Berger to Hon. R. Hnatyshyn, 22 September 1988.
46   Memorandum of Understanding between Her Majesty the Queen in Right of Canada and The Peigan Band, 6 February 1994.
47   'Supreme court Clarifies Aboriginal Title and Use Rights,' *Environmental Law Centre News Briefs* 13, 2: 7.
48   For example, see letters from Peter Melnychuk, Alberta Environment, to E. Tremayne, Indian Affairs, 22 August 1988 and 14 April 1989, and a memorandum from Keith Mac-Donald, Indian Affairs, to Gerry Throndson, Indian Affairs, 13 February 1989, both in Annex C to letter from Garry Wouters, regional director general, INAC, to Dr. W.A. Ross, chairman, ORDEAP, 30 December 1991.
49   Canada, Oldman River Dam Environmental Assessment Panel, *Public Hearings Proceedings, November 5-20, 1991,* vol. 10 (Vancouver: Federal Environmental Assessment Review Office, n.d.), 2141.

Chapter 28: The Environment, Politics, and the Courts

1   From an editorial in the *Lethbridge Herald,* January 1993.
2   Letter from Paul Martin, Liberal Opposition Environment Critic, to Martha Kostuch, 21 May 1993, in FOR papers held by Dr. Martha Kostuch, Rocky Mountain House, AB.
3   Letter from Jean Chrétien, Liberal Party Leader, to Dr. Martha Kostuch, 2 September 1993, in FOR papers held by Dr. Martha Kostuch, Rocky Mountain House, AB.
4   Dr. Martha Kostuch, personal interview, 6 July 1993.
5   Cliff Wallis, 'Keeping the Oldman River Rolling Along: The Courts as a Tool for Riparian Habitat Protection,' *Environment Network News* (May/June 1993): 21.
6   For example, see 'Editor's Notebook,' *Environmental Views* (Spring 1996): 3.
7   Canada-Alberta *Agreement for Environmental Assessment Co-operation,* 6 August 1993. The Pine Coulee hearings are discussed in Chapters 30 and 33.
8   Professor J.C. Levy, personal interview, 10 July 1996.
9   Ibid.
10   Charles Taylor, *The Malaise of Modernity* (Concord, ON: House of Anansi Press, 1994), 9.
11   Ibid., 113.
12   'PEI group loses right to court costs,' *Globe and Mail,* 14 December 1995.
13   Cliff Wallis, personal interview, 2 October 1995.
14   *Kostuch* v. *Alberta (Attorney General),* [1996] 1 W.W.R. 301 (Alta. C.A.).
15   *R.* v. *Power,* [1994] 1 S.C.R. 623.
16   Ibid., 622. The quotation is attributed to Donna C. Morgan, 'Controlling Prosecutorial Powers - Judicial Review, Abuse of Process and Section 7 of The Charter,' *Criminal Law Quarterly* 29 (1986-7): 18-9.
17   Ibid., 628-9.
18   Professor J.C. Levy, personal interview, 10 July 1996.
19   Ibid.
20   Ibid.
21   *Kostuch* v. *Alberta (Attorney General),* [1996] 1 W.W.R. 301.
22   John Werring, Sierra Legal Defence Fund, telephone interview, 9 June 1995.
23   Sierra Legal Defence Fund, *Newsletter,* no. 10 (July 1995): 2.
24   Professor J.C. Levy, personal interview, 10 July 1996.
25   Ibid.
26   Canada, House of Commons Standing Committee on Environment and Sustainable Development, *It's About Our Health! Towards Pollution Prevention; CEPA Revisited* (Ottawa: Public Works and Government Services, June 1995), 225; Liberal Party of Canada, *Creating Opportunity, The Liberal Plan for Canada* (Ottawa, 1993), 69.

27 Ibid., 231.
28 Ibid., 232.
29 Canada, Environment Canada, *CEPA Review: The Government Response,* Response to the Recommendations of the House of Commons Standing Committee on Environment and Sustainable Development outlined in its Fifth Report (Ottawa: Supply and Services Canada, 15 December 1995), 28.
30 Cliff Wallis, personal interview, 2 October 1995.
31 *Kostuch v. Alberta (Attorney General),* [1996] 1 W.W.R. 304.
32 Ibid., 297.
33 Alberta Environment, *Update* (November 1986): 5; Alberta Environment, *Oldman River Dam Fisheries* (Edmonton, n.d. [1988?]), 1; statement attributed to Alberta Fish and Wildlife officials, *Kostuch v. Alberta (Attorney General)* (1993), 143 A.R. 166 (Q.B.).
34 *Kostuch v. Alberta (Attorney General),* [1996] 1 W.W.R. 298.
35 Power's judgment is reported in 143 A.R. 161.
36 Richard Gwynn, *Nationalism Without Walls: The Unbearable Lightness of Being Canadian* (Toronto: McClelland and Stewart, 1995), 168.

Chapter 29: Information and Disinformation
1 Government of Alberta, Executive Council, *A Better Way: A Plan for Securing Alberta's Future* (Edmonton: 24 February 1994), 12.
2 Boyce Richardson, 'Government Greenwash,' *The Canadian Forum* (November 1993): 12.
3 For example, see *Friends of the Oldman River Society v. Canada (Minister of Transport),* [1990] 1 F.C. 273 (F.T.D.); and *Friends of the Oldman River Society v. Canada (Minister of Transport),* [1990] 2 F.C. 50 (F.C.A.).
4 See the comments of the panel's technical specialists and federal agencies in Canada, Oldman River Dam Environmental Assessment Panel, *Compendium of Submissions* (Vancouver: Federal Environmental Assessment Review Office, 11 February 1990); *Response to the Panel's Additional Information Requirements Document* (Vancouver: Federal Environmental Assessment Review Office, 1991) and *Public Hearings Proceedings,* vol. 6 (Vancouver: Federal Environmental Assessment Review Office, n.d.).
5 Kevin Taft, *Shredding the Public Interest* (Edmonton: University of Alberta Press and Parkland Institute, 1997), 73-9, provides an interesting description of the Alberta Public Affairs Bureau's role in massaging information disseminated by Alberta government politicians and agencies.
6 Rod Chapman, 'A Case Study of How Two Newspapers Covered the Oldman Dam Controversy' (COMS Final Project, graduate program in Communication Studies, University of Calgary, 1994), 122.
7 Joyce Nelson, *Sultans of Sleaze: Public Relations and the Media* (Toronto: Between the Lines, 1989), 44.
8 For example, see Letters, 'Oldman River Revisited,' *Western Living* (May 1990): 12; 'Court didn't order halt to work on dam,' *Calgary Herald,* Letters, 11 May 1991; Letters, 'Province not breaking law,' *Calgary Herald,* 1 August 1991; Forum, 'Oldman Dam defended,' *Trout Canada* (winter 1988).
9 Letter from Paula Power, Alberta Public Works, Supply and Services, Communications, attaching an article: 'Oldman River Dam draws visitors from around the world,' sent to a number of rural weeklies in southern Alberta, 9 June 1994, with the request that 'I hope you can publish [this] ... as I think it would be of interest to your readers.'
10 'Dam draws visitors from around the world,' *Regional,* 27 June 1994. The *Regional* is included as a supplement to a number of rural weeklies, including the *High River Times* and the *Nanton News* published in southern Alberta. The article, a faithful reproduction of that offered by Public Works (see note 9), was published without attribution to Public Works.
11 'Dam package "propaganda,"' *Calgary Herald,* 20 April 1989.
12 'If PRIME was a crime, what changes,' *Lethbridge Herald,* 21 October 1987.
13 Alberta Environment, *Update* (November 1986).
14 Ibid., October 1987 and September 1988.

15 Ibid., July 1989.
16 *Oldman River Dam EAC Bulletin* (September 1994): 1.
17 As chairman of the mining company that, in 1997, won approval to develop a strip mine adjacent to Jasper National Park, Lougheed is in the process of creating his own environmental legacy.
18 Letter from K.R. Craig, manager, Lethbridge Operations, UMA Engineering Ltd., to D.M. Lebaron, chairman, Southern Alberta Water Management Committee, 18 October 1991, in Canada, Oldman River Dam Environmental Assessment Panel, *Compendium of Submissions* (Vancouver: Federal Environmental Assessment Review Office, 22 October 1991), 511.
19 A summary of a review of the Peigan's RDI studies by Environment Canada was included in the documents submitted to the panel by Indian Affairs. It is doubtful that more than a few people outside the federal government ever viewed these documents.
20 For example, see Stewart B. Rood and Frank J. Jankunis, eds., *Economic, Environmental and Social Aspects of the Oldman River Dam Project* (Lethbridge: University of Lethbridge, 1988); Cheryl Bradley et al., eds., *Flowing to the Future* (Edmonton: University of Alberta, Faculty of Extension, 1989).
21 Lonefighters' *Press Release/Legal Notice,* May 1990.
22 Reverend Peter Hamel, personal interview, 4 August 1993.
23 Andy Russell, *Life of a River* (Toronto: McClelland and Stewart, 1987).
24 'Russell takes readers for ride on Oldman,' *Lethbridge Herald,* 16 January 1988.
25 For example, see 'Oldman River's health worries environmentalists,' *Calgary Herald,* 21 November 1997.
26 Joanne Helmer, personal interview, 5 April 1994.
27 Ibid. and Don Lebaron, personal interview, 20 October 1993.
28 Peter Melnychuk, personal interview, 14 June 1994.
29 FOR *News Release* (27 October 1993).
30 Rod Chapman, 'A Case Study of How Two Newspapers Covered the Oldman Dam Controversy' (COMS Final Project, graduate program in Communication Studies, University of Calgary, 1994), 88.
31 'Lamer judges critics severely,' *Globe and Mail,* 14 October 1994.
32 Ibid.
33 Boyce Richardson, 'Government Greenwash,' *Canadian Forum* (November 1993): 12.

Chapter 30: Does It Matter?

1 Joanne Helmer, 'Heart of dam dispute more basic than water,' *Lethbridge Herald,* 6 June 1992.
2 Garrett Hardin, 'The Tragedy of the Commons,' *Science* 162 (13 December 1968): 1243-8.
3 *Alberta Hansard,* 22nd Legislature, 2nd Session, Vol. I (14 March 1990): 64.
4 Canada, Oldman River Dam Environmental Assessment Panel, *Report of the Environmental Review Panel* (Hull: Federal Environmental Assessment Review Office, 1992), 30.
5 Ibid., 31.
6 Ibid.
7 The chairperson's explanation of why the panel refused to require Alberta to produce an analysis illustrating the relationship between the project and Peigan water rights claims is recorded in transcripts of the public hearings as follows: 'We believe at this stage that in light of the evidence that's currently before us, that we have sufficient information to give [the matters raised by the Peigan] appropriate regard and to be able to take [them] into consideration in our decision.' Whatever information the panel might have had, or thought it had, pertaining to the question raised by the Peigan was never revealed, nor did the panel report what consideration it gave the matter.
8 Alberta, Natural Resources Conservation Board/Environmental Assessment Review Process Joint Review Panel, *Report of the NRCB/EARP Joint Review Panel: Pine Coulee Water Management Project,* NRCB Application #9401 (Edmonton, 1995), 8-17.
9 Charles Taylor, *The Malaise of Modernity* (Concord, ON: House of Anansi Press, 1991), 100.
10 'Environment slipping as priority,' *Calgary Herald,* 12 December 1997; 'Public willing to act to protect environment,' *Globe and Mail,* 16 December 1997.
11 Taylor, *The Malaise of Modernity,* 111.

A Note on Sources

The primary source for much of the information that is presented in *Once upon an Old-man* was the documentation published or otherwise made available to the public by the Oldman River Dam Environmental Assessment Panel (ORDEAP), which operated under the auspices of the Federal Environmental Assessment Review Office (FEARO) from November 1990 until the summer of 1992. The documentation produced by the ORDEAP is of five types. The first is a newsletter, four issues of which appeared between March and December 1991. The newsletters include information of a general nature about the panel, its members, mandate, procedures, schedule, activities, and documents produced by the panel and available to the public. The second type is written submissions to the panel by individuals, interest groups, government agencies, and the panel's technical specialists. There are two sets of these submissions: the first consists of responses to the panel's invitation to 'identify issues, concerns and gaps in information that the public would like to see the panel address'; the second consists of all written submissions received in response to a solicitation by the panel for 'comment on all issues regarding the Oldman Dam within the panel's mandate.' Some of these submissions were in response to specific requests for information by the panel. The third type of documentation includes a specification by the panel of the additional information it believed it required to conduct its assessment, and a compilation of the additional information that the panel's technical experts were able to obtain. The fourth is the transcribed proceedings of the public hearings held by the panel at seven locations in Alberta from 5 November to 20 November 1991. Though the ORDEAP announced that they would be placed in the Calgary, Edmonton, Lethbridge, and Pincher Creek Public Libraries and the FEARO Library in Vancouver, only the FEARO Library received the twelve volumes of transcripts. Finally, there are the two reports published by the panel outlining its findings and recommendations.

One of the most useful sources of information in the ORDEAP documentation is a three volume attachment to Annex C of a letter from Garry Wouters, regional director general of INAC, to Dr. W.A. Ross, chairman, ORDEAP, dated 30 December 1991. Annex C itself is a chronological list of the documents included in the attachment: correspondence to and from federal and provincial cabinet ministers, the Peigan Chief and Council, interest groups, and individual citizens; intra- and inter-departmental and intergovernmental correspondence between federal and provincial public servants; and briefs and reports prepared by federal government agencies on matters pertaining to the Oldman River Dam. A copy of the 30 December 1991 letter from Wouters to Ross is included in the ORDEAP publication *Addendum to Compendium of Information Dated October 22, 1991*, vol. 1, which received wide distribution; the annexes and the three-volume attachment to Annex C were not included.

Some, though not all, of the ORDEAP documentation is held by the Calgary and Lethbridge Public Libraries. As of 1 January 1999, all of the ORDEAP documentation, including the attachment to Annex C noted above and the twelve volume *Public Hearings Proceedings* will have been transferred from the CEAA (formerly FEARO) Library in Vancouver to the Canadian Environmental Assessment Agency Reference Library, Suite 100, Revillon Building, 10237 - 104 St. NW, Edmonton, AB, T5J 1B1, where it will be available for public perusal.

Another valuable source of information is the papers of the Friends of the Oldman River (FOR), which include correspondence with federal and provincial cabinet ministers and public servants, and copies of documents emanating from or pertaining to the multitude of legal actions and court cases related to the Oldman River Dam, from 1987 to the present day, in which FOR or Dr. Kostuch was or continues to be involved. These papers are in the possession of Dr. Martha Kostuch, PO Box 1288, Rocky Mountain House, AB, T0M 1T0, and are available, on appointment, for public perusal. Some documents from the FOR papers are cited in the present work with the permission of Dr. Kostuch.

Much undocumented information and many interesting interpretations and points of view were obtained through interviews with a number of people who were in some way involved on one side or the other of the Oldman Dam controversy, about twenty of which were recorded. Where information from these interviews is used in the book, the person interviewed is named in the citation. The recordings are in the possession of the author and are available for listening to on request.

The following newspapers and magazines were valuable sources of information and opinion: *Lethbridge Herald, Calgary Herald, Edmonton Journal, Globe and Mail, Vancouver Sun, Windspeaker, Claresholm Local Press, Taber Times, Pincher Creek Echo, Crowsnest Pass Promoter, Brooks Bulletin,* and *Alberta Report.*

Bibliography

Government Documents and Reports

Canada
Berger, Mr. Justice Thomas R. *Northern Frontier, Northern Homeland: The Report of the Mackenzie Valley Pipeline Inquiry.* 2 vols. Ottawa: Supply and Services Canada, 1977.
Canada, Alberta, Saskatchewan Peace Athabasca Delta Project Group. *The Peace Athabasca Delta: A Canadian Resource.* Ottawa, 1972. Summary report of the study group.
Canada, Environment Canada. *CEPA Review: The Government Response.* Ottawa: Supply and Services Canada, 1995.
Committee on the Status of Endangered Wildlife in Canada. *Canadian Species at Risk.* Ottawa, April 1996 (amended 17 September 1996).
Department of Agriculture. Prairie Farm Rehabilitation Administration. *Annual Report on Prairie Farm and Related Rehabilitation Activities: 1958-59.* Regina, 1959.
Department of Fisheries and Oceans. Central and Arctic Region. *Comments on the Oldman River Dam Proposal.* Ottawa, 24 February 1987.
–. *Policy for the Management of Fish Habitat.* Ottawa, 1986.
Department of the Interior. *Report on Irrigation Surveys and Inspections, 1915-1916.* Ottawa, 1916.
–. *Report on Irrigation Surveys and Inspections, 1916-1917.* Ottawa, 1917.
Environment Canada. *Environmental Impact Evaluation: The Three Rivers Dam Project.* Rev. ed. Ottawa, 9 July 1987.
–. Canadian Wildlife Service. *Endangered Species Legislation in Canada: A Discussion Paper.* Ottawa, 17 November 1994.
–. *Federal Water Policy.* Ottawa, 1987.
–. *Peigan Nation Oldman River Investigation: A Review.* Ottawa, 8 May 1987.
–. *A Wildlife Policy for Canada.* Ottawa, 1990. Adopted by the Wildlife Ministers' Council of Canada at its meeting on 26-7 September 1990.
House of Commons. Standing Committee on Environment and Sustainable Development. *It's About Our Health! Towards Pollution Prevention: CEPA Revisited.* Ottawa: Public Works and Government Services Canada, June 1995.
Oldman River Dam Environmental Assessment Panel. *Addendum and Erratum Material for the Response to the Panel's Additional Information Requirements Document, September 1991.* Vancouver: Federal Environmental Assessment Review Office, 1991.
–. *Addendum to Compendium of Submissions Dated October 22, 1991.* 2 vols. Vancouver: Federal Environmental Assessment Review Office, 31 December 1991.
–. *Additional Information Requirements.* Vancouver: Federal Environmental Assessment Review Office, March 1991.
–. *Compendium of Submissions.* Vancouver: Federal Environmental Assessment Review Office, 11 February 1990.

–. *Compendium of Submissions*. Vancouver: Federal Environmental Assessment Review Office, 22 October 1991.

–. *Dam Safety and Design: Interim Report of the Environmental Assessment Panel*. Hull: Federal Environmental Assessment Review Office, June 1991.

–. *Newsletter,* nos. 1-4 (March/April/September/December 1991).

–. *Public Hearings Proceedings, November 5-20, 1991*. 12 vols. Vancouver: Federal Environmental Assessment Review Office (transcribed by Total Reporting Service Ltd., Vancouver), n.d.

–. *Report of the Environmental Assessment Panel*. Hull: Federal Environmental Assessment Review Office, May 1992.

–. *Response to the Panel's Additional Information Requirements Document*. Vancouver: Federal Environmental Assessment Review Office, September 1991.

Prairie Farm Rehabilitation Administration. *History of Irrigation in Western Canada*. Regina, 1982.

Public Works and Government Services Canada. *Canada and Aboriginal Peoples: A New Partnership*. Ottawa, 1995. Report of Honourable A.C. Hamilton, Fact Finder for Minister of Indian Affairs and Northern Development.

Rafferty-Alameda Project Environmental Assessment Panel. *Rafferty-Alameda EIA Summary*. Ottawa: Federal Environmental Assessment Review Office, 1989.

–. *Report of the Environmental Assessment Panel*. Hull: Federal Environmental Assessment Review Office, 1991.

Royal Commission on the South Saskatchewan River Project. *Report of the Royal Commission on the South Saskatchewan River Project*. Ottawa: Queen's Printer and Controller of Stationery, 1952.

St. Mary and Milk Rivers Water Development Committee. *Report on Further Storage and Irrigation Work Required to Utilize Fully Canada's Share of International Streams in Southern Alberta*. Ottawa: King's Printer, 1942.

Saskatchewan-Nelson Basin Board. *Water Supply for the Saskatchewan-Nelson Basin*. Ottawa, 1972. A Canada, Alberta, Saskatchewan, and Manitoba report.

Special Parliamentary Committee on Indian Self-Government. 'Proposals for Indian Self-Government. In *Arduous Journey: Canadian Indians and Decolonization,* edited by J. Rick Ponting. Toronto: McClelland and Stewart, 1986.

Transport Canada. *Federal Government Response to the Oldman River Dam Project Environmental Review Panel Report*. Ottawa, 30 August 1993.

Alberta

Alberta Environment. *Environmental Impact Assessment Guidelines*. Edmonton, 1977.

–. WRMS. *Oldman River Flow Regulation Preliminary Planning Studies*. Edmonton, 1976.

–. *Water Management Policy for the South Saskatchewan River Basin*. Edmonton, 28 May 1990. Distributed with Alberta, *News Release,* no. 28.

–. Community Affairs Branch. *Public Participation in the Oldman River Dam Project,* by Kerry Lowe and Shauna Peets. Edmonton, 1987.

–. WRMS, Planning Division. *Vegetation Inventory - Oldman River Dam,* by Hardy Associates. Edmonton, 1986.

–. WRMS, Planning Division. *Water Resource Management Principles for Alberta*. Edmonton, n.d. [1980?].

–. WRMS, Planning Division. Oldman River Dam Local Advisory Committee. *Report and Recommendations to the Minister of Environment*. Edmonton, 1988.

–. WRMS, Planning Division. *Oldman River Dam Operational Strategy*. Edmonton, 1991.

–. WRMS, Planning Division. *Oldman River Reservoir Operational Plan: Water Supply, Flow Regulation and Interprovincial Apportionment*. Edmonton, 1989.

–. WRMS, Planning Division. *South Saskatchewan River Basin Planning Program: Summary Report*. Edmonton, 1984.

–. WRMS, Planning Division. *Review of Historical Investigations Undertaken by Provincial Agencies on Water Diversions to the Special Areas,* by Lois Collier. Edmonton, 30 May 1988.

Alberta Environment and Alberta Agriculture. *Water Management for Irrigation Use.* Alberta Sessional Paper 502/75. Edmonton, 20 May 1975.

Alberta Environmental Protection. Water Resources Services. *Oldman River Dam and Reservoir Operational Strategy (June 1994).* Edmonton, 1994.

Alberta Forestry, Lands and Wildlife. Fish and Wildlife Division. *The Highwood River. Instream Flow Needs for Fish and Flow Scenario Evaluations,* by Allan G.R. Locke. Draft no. 16-09-92. Edmonton, 1992.

Alberta Native Affairs Secretariat. *Peigan Indian Band/Government of Alberta Resolution of the Oldman River Irrigation System Dispute: A Case Study.* Rev. ed. Edmonton, 1984.

Alberta Public Works, Supply and Services. *The Oldman River Dam: Building A Future for Southern Alberta.* Edmonton, 1992.

–. Oldman River Dam Environmental Advisory Committee. *Oldman River Dam Social and Land-Use Impact Study,* by Linda D. Cerney. Edmonton, 1994.

–. Oldman River Dam Local Advisory Committee. *Final Report and Recommendations to the Ministers of Alberta Public Works, Supply and Services and Alberta Environmental Protection.* Edmonton, 1993.

Alberta Water Resources Commission. *Water Management in the South Saskatchewan River Basin: Report and Recommendations.* Edmonton, n.d. (This report was released in October 1986.)

Boothroyd, Peter, and Co-West Associates (George Kupfer and Robert Langin). *Oldman River Basin Study: Phase II – Social Impact Assessment.* Lethbridge: Oldman River Study Management Committee, 1978.

Cerney, Linda D. *See* Alberta. Alberta Public Works, Supply and Services.

Collier, Lois. *See* Alberta. Alberta Environment. Water Resources Management Services. Planning Division.

Department of Agriculture. *Report of the Irrigation Study Committee on Problems of Irrigation Farming and Administration,* by W.R. Hansen et al. Edmonton, 1958.

–. Water Resources Division. *PRIME: Alberta's Blueprint for Water Development.* Edmonton, 1969. Brochure.

–. *Water Diversion Proposals of North America.* Edmonton, December 1968. Prepared for the Canadian Council of Resource Ministers.

Environment Council of Alberta. *Management of Water Resources within the Oldman River Basin: Report and Recommendations.* Edmonton, 1979.

Government of Alberta. *Report of the Commission Appointed to Report on the Lethbridge Northern and Other Irrigation Districts in Alberta,* by M.L. Wilson, Edmonton, 1930.

Hansen, W.R., et al. *See* Alberta. Department of Agriculture.

Hardy Associates. *See* Alberta. Alberta Environment. WRMS, Planning Division.

Locke, Allan G.R. *See* Alberta. Alberta Forests.

Lowe, Kerry, and Shauna Peets. *See* Alberta. Alberta Environment. Community Affairs Branch.

Marv Anderson and Associates Ltd. *Oldman River Basin Study Phase II: Economic Analysis of Water Supply Alternatives.* Willingdon, AB: Oldman River Study Management Committee, 1978.

Natural Resources Conservation Board/Canadian Environmental Assessment Act Joint Review Panel. *Report of the NRCB/CEAA Joint Review Panel: Little Bow Project/Highwood Diversion Plan.* NRCB Application #9601. Edmonton, 1998.

Natural Resources Conservation Board/Environmental Assessment Review Process Joint Review Panel. *Report of the NRCB/EARP Joint Review Panel: Pine Coulee Water Management Project.* NRCB Application #9401. Edmonton, 1995.

Oldman River Study Management Committee. *Oldman River Basin: Phase II Studies: Report and Recommendations.* Lethbridge, 1978.

Widstoe, John A. *An Examination Into Conditions on the Lethbridge Northern Irrigation District.* Edmonton: King's Printer, 1925.

World Wildlife Fund Canada and Alberta Forestry, Lands and Wildlife, Fish and Wildlife Division. *Conservation and Management Strategy for Riparian Forests in Southern Alberta.* Edmonton: Alberta Energy/Forestry, Lands and Wildlife, 1992.

Books and Articles

Assembly of First Nations. *Backgrounder on the Current Crisis in First Nations: Canada Relations*. Ottawa, 1990.

Bankes, Nigel. 'Water Law Reform in Alberta: Paying Obeisance to the "Lords of Yesterday," or Creating a Water Charter for the Future?' *Resources: The Newsletter of the Canadian Institute of Resources Law* 49 (Winter 1995): 1-8.

Bartlett, Richard H. *Aboriginal Water Rights in Canada: A Study of Aboriginal Title to Water and Aboriginal Water Rights*. Calgary: Canadian Institute of Resources Law, University of Calgary, 1988.

Barton, Barry. 'Water Resources and Native People.' Paper presented at Canadian Waters: The State of the Resource, a conference sponsored by the Rawson Academy of Aquatic Science, Toronto, 26 to 29 May 1985.

Bastien, Betty. 'Native Spiritual Links to Rivers.' In *Flowing to the Future*, edited by Cheryl Bradley et al., 127-30. Edmonton: University of Alberta, Faculty of Extension, 1989.

Bocking, Richard C. *Canada's Water: For Sale?* Toronto: James Lewis and Samuel, 1972.

Born With A Tooth, Milton. 'Messenger for the River.' *Semiotext(e)* 6, (1994): 17.

Born With A Tooth, Milton, and Vicki English. 'Bridges and Barricades: The Crossing Over.' *Border/Lines* (Winter 1991/92): 46-8.

Bourassa, Robert. *James Bay*. Montreal: Harvest House, 1973.

–. *Power for the North*. Scarborough, ON: Prentice-Hall, 1985.

Bradley, Cheryl, Frances Reintjes, and John Mahoney. *The Biology and Status of Riparian Poplars in Southern Alberta*. Edmonton: World Wildlife Fund Canada and Alberta Forestry, Lands and Wildlife, 1991.

Bradley, C., and D. Smith. 'Plains Cottonwood Recruitment and Survival on a Prairie Meandering River, Milk River, Southern Alberta and Northern Montana.' *Canadian Journal of Botany* 64 (1985): 1433-42.

Bradley, Cheryl, Albert Einsiedel, Tim Pyrch, and Kevin Van Tighem, eds. *Flowing to the Future*. Edmonton: University of Alberta, Faculty of Extension, 1990.

Bryan, Liz. *The Buffalo People: Prehistoric Archaeology on the Canadian Plains*. Edmonton: University of Alberta Press, 1991.

Caldwell, Lynton K. '20 Years with NEPA Indicates the Need.' *Environment* 31 (1989): 10.

Canadian Council of Resource and Environment Ministers (CCREM). *Report of the National Task Force on Environment and Economy*. September 1987.

Chapman, Rod. 'A Case Study of How Two Newspapers Covered the Oldman Dam Controversy,' COMS Final Project, graduate program in Communication Studies, University of Calgary, 1994.

Christiansen, Bev. *Too Good to Be True: Alcan's Kemano Completion Project*. Vancouver: Talonbooks, 1995.

Collingwood, Bruce. 'The "Mandatory" Environmental Impact Assessment?' *Environment Network News* 33 (June 1994): 17-8.

Committee for the Preservation of Three Rivers. 'Presentation to the Provincial Cabinet,' Lethbridge, 20 September 1977.

–. 'Submission to the Hon. Dave Russell, Minister of Environment Regarding Oldman River Flow Regulation Planning Studies,' 12 November 1976.

Dempsey, Hugh A. *Indian Tribes of Alberta*. Calgary: Glenbow Museum, 1979.

–. 'Treaty Research Report: Treaty 7.' Ottawa: Treaties and Historical Research Centre, Comprehensive Claims Branch, Self-Government, 1987.

Devine, Grant. 'Political and Historical Perspective of the Rafferty Alameda Dams in Saskatchewan.' Notes for an address by Dr. Grant Devine to Faculty of Management, University of Calgary, 7 and 8 December 1993.

Dickason, Olive Patricia. *Canada's First Nations: A History of Founding Peoples from Earliest Times*. Toronto: McClelland and Stewart, 1992.

Duncan, Linda F. *Enforcing Environmental Law: A Guide to Private Prosecution*. Edmonton: Environmental Law Centre (Alberta) Society, 1990.

Echohawk, John E. 'The Current Status of Tribal Water Rights in the United States.' *Resources: The Newsletter of the Canadian Institute of Resources Law* 18 (Spring 1987).

Ehrlich, Paul R. *The Machinery of Nature*. New York: Simon and Schuster, Touchstone Books, 1986.

Environmental Management Associates. 'A Review of Potential Impacts on the Riparian Downstream of the Oldman Dam (Addendum Report).' In *Addendum and Erratum Material for the Response to the Panel's Additional Information Requirements Document, September 1991*, by Canada, Oldman River Dam Environmental Assessment Panel. Vancouver: Federal Environmental Assessment Review Office, 1991.

Feldman, David Lewis. *Water Resources Management: In Search of an Environmental Ethic*. Baltimore: Johns Hopkins University Press, 1991.

Frideres, James S. *Native Peoples in Canada: Contemporary Conflicts*. 3rd ed. Scarborough, ON: Prentice-Hall Canada, 1988.

Getty, Ian L., and Antoine S. Lussier, eds. *As Long as the Sun Shines and Water Flows: A Reader in Canadian Indian Studies*. Nakota Institute Occasional Paper No. 1. Vancouver: University of British Columbia Press, 1983.

Gittinger, J. Price. *Economic Analysis of Agricultural Projects*. 2nd ed. Economic Development Institute of the World Bank. Baltimore: Johns Hopkins University Press, 1982.

Gottlieb, Robert. *A Life of Its Own: The Politics and Power of Water*. New York: Harcourt Brace Jovanovich, 1988.

Gray, James H. *Men against the Desert*. Saskatoon: Western Producer Prairie Books, 1967.

Gwynn, Richard. *Nationalism without Walls: The Unbearable Lightness of Being Canadian*. Toronto: McClelland and Stewart, 1995.

Hardin, Garrett. 'The Tragedy of the Commons.' *Science* 162 (13 December 1968): 1243-8.

Hood, George N. *Against the Flow: Rafferty-Alameda and the Politics of the Environment*. Saskatoon: Fifth House Publishers, 1994.

Ives, Jack. 'Evaluation and Mitigation of Historical Resources Affected by the Oldman River Dam Project.' In *Economic, Environmental and Social Aspects of the Oldman River Dam Project*, edited by Stewart B. Rood and Frank J. Jankunis, 100-10. Lethbridge: University of Lethbridge, 1988.

Kambeitz, Bob. 'The Three Rivers Dam: *Friends of the Oldman River Society vs. The Minister of Environment, et al.*, Part II.' *Trout Canada* (Spring 1988): 21.

Krotz, Larry. 'Dammed and Diverted.' *Canadian Geographic* 111 (February/March 1991): 36-44.

Leacock, Stephen. *Canada: The Foundations of Its Future*. Montreal: House of Seagram, 1941.

Leopold, Aldo. *A Sand County Almanac*. New York: Oxford University Press, 1968.

Leopold, Luna B. 'Ethos, Equity, and the Water Resource.' *Environment* 32 (March 1990): 16.

Liberal Party of Canada. *Creating Opportunity: The Liberal Plan for Canada* (The Red Book). Ottawa, 1993.

Linnemae, Urva, and Kim E.H. Jones, eds. *Out of the Past: Sites, Digs and Artifacts in the Saskatoon Area*. Saskatoon: Saskatoon Archaeological Society, 1988.

Little Bear, Leroy. 'Aboriginal Rights in the Canadian Grundnorm.' In *Arduous Journey: Canadian Indians and Decolonization*, edited by J. Rick Ponting, 243-59. Toronto: McClelland and Stewart, 1986.

McNeilly, Kyle. 'The Nosedive of the Bull Trout.' *Environment Views* 17 (1994): 8-10.

Mander, Jerry. *In the Absence of the Sacred*. San Francisco: Sierra Club Books, 1992.

Mayhood, David W. 'Fishes Threatened, Vulnerable or of Special Concern in Relation to the Oldman River Dam.' In *Addendum to Compendium of Submissions Dated October 22, 1991*, vol. 1, by Canada, Oldman River Dam Environmental Assessment Panel, 271. Vancouver: Federal Environmental Assessment Review Office, 31 December 1991.

Million, Marie Louise. '"It Was Home": A Phenomenology of Place and Involuntary Displacement as Illustrated by the Forced Dislocation of Five Southern Alberta Families in the Oldman River Dam Area.' PhD dissertation, Saybrook Institute Graduate School and Research Centre, San Francisco, n.d. [1991?].

Mitchener, E. Alyn. *The Development of Western Waters, 1885-1930*. Edmonton: Department of History, University of Alberta, 1973.

Nelson, Joyce. *Sultans of Sleeze: Public Relations and the Media*. Toronto: Between the Lines, 1989.

Nikiforuk, Andrew. *'The Nasty Game': The Failure of Environmental Assessment in Canada*. Toronto: Walter and Duncan Gordon Foundation, 1997.

Nikiforuk, Andrew, and Ed Struzik. 'The Great Forest Sell-Off.' *Report on Business Magazine* (November 1989): 57-66.

Paehlke, Robert. 'Eco-History: Two Waves in the Evolution of Environmentalism.' *Alternatives* 19 (1992): 18-23.

Paul, Bernadette. *The Peigan: A Nation in Transition*. Edmonton: Plains Publishing, 1986.

Pohorecky, Zenon. 'The Great Cree Stone.' *Canadian Geographic Journal* 73 (1966): 88-91.

–. 'Saskatchewan Stonehenge.' *Saskatchewan Archeaology Newsletter* 12 (1965): 5-8.

Ponting, J. Rick. 'Relations Between Bands and DIAND: A Case of Internal Colonialism.' In *Arduous Journey: Canadian Indians and Decolonization*, edited by J. Rick Ponting. Toronto: McClelland and Stewart, 1986.

–, ed. *Arduous Journey: Canadian Indians and Decolonization*. Toronto: McClelland and Stewart, 1986.

Ponting, J. Rick, and Roger Gibbons, eds. *Out of Irrelevance: A Socio-political Introduction to Indian Affairs in Canada*. Toronto: Butterworths, 1980.

Raby, Stewart, 'Alberta and the Prairie Provinces Water Board.' *Canadian Geographer* 7 (1964): 85-91.

Reeves, Brian. 'The Oldman River Dam and Alberta's Heritage: Conservation or Desecration?' In *Economic, Environmental and Social Aspects of the Oldman River Dam Project*, edited by Stewart B. Rood and Frank J. Jankunis, 81-99. Lethbridge: University of Lethbridge, 1988.

Reeves, B.O.K. *Oldman River Dam Phase II Archaeological and Historic Resources Inventory and Assessment, Volume II, Prehistoric Sites Part I*. Calgary: Lifeways Canada Ltd., February 1987.

Rhodes, Trevor, R. 'The Importance of Cottonwoods to Wildlife.' In *The Biology and Management of Southern Alberta's Cottonwoods*, edited by Stewart B. Rood and John M. Mahoney. Lethbridge: University of Lethbridge, 1991.

Richardson, Boyce. 'Concealed Contempt.' *Canadian Forum* (December 1989): 15-20.

–. 'Government Greenwash.' *Canadian Forum* (November 1993): 11-5.

Rood, Stewart B., and Sig Heinz-Milne. 'Abrupt downstream forest decline following river damming in southern Alberta.' *Canadian Journal of Botany* 67 (1989): 1744-9.

Rood, Stewart B., and Frank J. Jankunis, eds. *Economic, Environmental and Social Aspects of the Oldman River Dam Project*. Lethbridge: University of Lethbridge, 1988.

Rood, Stewart B., and John M. Mahoney. 'Impacts of the Oldman River Dam on Riparian Cottonwood Forests Downstream.' In *Addendum to Compendium of Submissions Dated October 22, 1991*, vol. 2, by Canada, Oldman River Dam Environmental Assessment Panel, 1080-114. Vancouver: Federal Environmental Assessment Review Office, 31 December 1991.

–. 'The Importance and Extent of Cottonwood Forest Decline Downstream from Dams.' In *The Biology and Management of Southern Alberta's Cottonwoods*, edited by Stewart B. Rood and John M. Mahoney. Lethbridge: University of Lethbridge, 1991.

–, eds. *The Biology and Management of Southern Alberta's Cottonwoods*. Lethbridge: University of Lethbridge, 1991.

Ross, Rupert. *Dancing with a Ghost: Exploring Indian Reality*. Markham, ON: Octopus Books Publishing Group, 1992.

Russell, Andy. *Life of a River*. Toronto: McClelland and Stewart, 1987.

Ryan, Joan. *Wall of Words: The Betrayal of the Urban Indian*. Toronto: PMA Books, 1978.

Ryder, Grainne, and Margaret Barber, eds. *Damming the Three Gorges; What Dam Builders Don't Want You to Know*. 2nd ed. Toronto: Earthscan Canada, 1993.

Samoil, Howard. 'Harmonization and Environmental Management in Canada.' *Environment Network News* 38 (March/April 1995): 4-5.

Scarth, Jonathon. 'The Oldman Dam Decisions.' *Resources: The Newsletter of the Canadian Institute of Resources Law* 22 (Spring 1988): 4-6.

Shaw, Keith. 'Ecology of the River Bottom Forest on the St. Mary River, Lee Creek and Belly River in southern Alberta.' In *The Biology and Management of Southern Alberta's Cottonwoods*, edited by Stewart B. Rood and John M. Mahoney, 79-84. Lethbridge: University of Lethbridge, 1991.

Sierra Legal Defence Fund. *Newsletter*, nos. 1-16 (Spring 1992-March 1997).

Smith, Donald B. 'The Original Peoples of Alberta.' In *Peoples of Alberta: Portraits of Cultural Diversity*, edited by Howard and Tamara Palmer. Saskatoon: Western Producer Prairie Books, 1985.

Smith, Melvin H., QC. *Our Home or Native Land?: What Government Aboriginal Policy Is Doing to Canada*. Victoria: Crown Western, 1995.

Snow, Chief John. *These Mountains Are Our Sacred Places*. Toronto: Samuel-Stevens, Publishers, 1977.

Taft, Kevin. *Shredding the Public Interest*. Edmonton: University of Alberta Press and Parkland Institute, 1997.

Taylor, Charles. *The Malaise of Modernity*. Concord, ON: House of Anansi Press, 1991.

Taylor, Duncan M. 'Disagreeing on the Basics.' *Alternatives* 18 (1991): 3.

Taylor, John L. *Understanding the Treaties*. Edmonton: Indian Association of Alberta, 1975.

Van Tighem, Kevin. *Coming West: A Natural History of Home*. Canmore, AB: Altitude Publishing, 1997.

–. 'Alberta's Rivers Tomorrow: Plumbing Systems or Ecosystems?' In *Flowing to the Future*, edited by Cheryl Bradley, Albert Einsiedel, Tim Perch, and Kevin Van Tighem, 353-63. Edmonton: University of Alberta, Faculty of Extension, 1990.

Wallis, Cliff. 'Keeping the Oldman River Rolling Along: The Courts as a Tool for Riparian Habitat Protection.' *Environment Network News* (May/June 1993): 18-21.

Warkentin, John. *The Western Interior of Canada*. Toronto: McClelland and Stewart, Carleton Library No. 15, 1964.

White, Lynn, Jr. 'The Historical Roots of Our Ecological Crisis.' *Science* 155 (10 March 1967): 1203-7.

Wilkinson, Charles F. 'Aldo Leopold and Western Water Law.' *Land and Water Law Review* 24 (1989): 1-38.

–. 'Crossing the Next Meridian: Sustaining the Lands, Waters and Human Spirit in the West.' *Environment* 32 (1990): 14.

Wilson, Edward O. *The Diversity of Life*. Cambridge: Belknap Press of Harvard University Press, 1992.

Woods Gordon Management Consultants. *Summary Consolidation of Consultant's Reports on the Impacts of the Proposed Brocket Reservoir, Oldman River*. Edmonton: Woods Gordon Management Consultants, 1983.

World Wildlife Fund Canada. *Prairie Conservation Action Plan*. Toronto: World Wildlife Fund Canada, n.d. [1988].

York, Geoffrey. *The Dispossessed*. Toronto: Lester and Orpen Dennys, 1989.

York, Geoffrey, and Loreen Pindera. *People of the Pines: The Warriors and the Legacy of Oka*. Toronto: Little, Brown and Co. (Canada), 1991.

Court Cases

Arizona v. California, 373 U.S. 546 (1963), 10 L.Ed. 2d 542.

Attorney General for Ontario v. Bear Island Foundation, [1985] 1 C.N.L.R. 1 (Ont. S.C.), 49 O.R. (2d) 353.

Calder v. Attorney General of B.C., [1973] S.C.R. 313, [1973] 4 W.W.R., 34 D.L.R. (3rd) 145.

Canadian Wildlife Federation Inc., et al., v. Canada (Minister of the Environment) and Saskatchewan Water Corp., Federal Court (T.D.), 10 April 1989, 26 F.T.R. 245.

Canadian Wildlife Federation Inc., et al., v. Canada (Minister of the Environment) and Saskatchewan Water Corp. (F.C.A.), 22 June 1989, 99 N.R. 72.

Canadian Wildlife Federation Inc., et al., v. Canada (Minister of the Environment) and Saskatchewan Water Corp., Federal Court (T.D.), 28 December 1989, 31 F.T.R. 1.

Chief Peter Yellowhorn of the Peigan Indian Band on behalf of himself and all other members of the Peigan Indian Band v. Her Majesty the Queen in the Right of the Province of Alberta,

Statement of Claim filed in the Alberta Court of Queen's Bench, Calgary, on 11 April 1986 (8601-06578).

Chief Peter Yellowhorn of the Peigan Indian Band on behalf of himself and all other members of the Peigan Indian Band v. *Her Majesty the Queen in the Right of Canada and the Honourable David Crombie, Minister of Indian Affairs and Northern Development,* Statement of Claim filed in the Federal Court of Canada, Trial Division, Montreal, on 19 June 1986 (T-1486-86).

Delgamuukw v. *British Columbia,* [1991] 3 W.W.R. 97 (B.C.S.C.).

Delgamuukw v. *British Columbia,* [1993] 5 W.W.R. 97 (B.C.C.A.), [1993] 5 C.N.L.R., Special Edition.

Delgamuukw v. *British Columbia,* [1997] 3 S.C.R. 1010.

Dowson v. *The Queen,* [1983] 2 S.C.R. 144.

Friends of the Oldman River Society v. *Alberta (Minister of the Environment)* (1987), 56 Alta. L.R. (2d) 368 (Q.B.), 85 A.R. 321.

Friends of the Oldman River Society v. *Alberta (Minister of the Environment)* (1988), 89 A.R. 339 (Q.B.).

Friends of the Oldman River Society v. *Alberta (Minister of Environmental Protection)* (1996), 181 A.R. 306 (C.A.).

Friends of the Oldman River Society v. *Energy Resources Conservation Board* (1988), 89 A.R. 280 (C.A.), 58 Alta. L.R. (2d) 286.

Friends of the Oldman River Society v. *Canada (Minister of Transport),* [1990] 1 F.C. 248 (F.T.D.), [1990] 2 W.W.R. 150, 30 F.T.R. 108, 70 Alta. L.R. (2d) 289, 4 C.E.L.R. (N.S.) 137.

Friends of the Oldman River Society v. *Canada (Minister of Transport),* [1990] 2 F.C. 18 (F.C.A.), 68 D.L.R. (4th) 375, [1991] 1 W.W.R. 352, 108 N.R. 241, 76 Alta. L.R. (2d) 289, 5 C.E.L.R. (N.S.) 1.

Friends of the Oldman River Society v. *Canada (Minister of Transport)* (1992), 88 D.L.R. (4th) 1, [1992] 1 S.C.R. 3, 7 C.E.L.R. (N.S.) 1, 3 Admin. L.R. (2d) 1, [1992] 2 W.W.R. 193.

Friends of the Oldman River Society v. *Regina, Minister of Environment* (1992), 127 A.R. 400 (S.C.C.).

Friends of the Oldman River Society v. *Canada (Minister of Environment)* (1993), 61 F.T.R. 74 (F.T.D.).

Friends of the Oldman River Society v. *Canada (Minister of Environment)* (1993), 62 F.T.R. 255 (F.C.A.).

Friends of the Oldman River Society v. *Canada (Minister of Environment)* (1993), 105 D.L.R. (4th) 444 (F.T.D.).

Friends of the West Country Association v. *Minister of Fisheries and Oceans* decided in the Federal Court of Canada, Trial Division, on 7 July 1998, Mr. Justice Frederick Gibson (unreported) (T-1893-96).

Friends of the West Country v. *Minister of Fisheries and Oceans,* decided in the Federal Court of Appeal on 23 November 1998, Chief Justice Julius A. McIsaac (unreported) (T-1893-96). FCA Docket A-550-98.

Guerin v. *The Queen* (1984), [1985] 1 C.N.L.R. 120 (S.C.C.), 13 D.L.R. (4th) 321, [1984] 6 W.W.R. 481.

Hamlet of Baker Lake v. *Minister of Indian Affairs and Northern Development* (1979), 107 D.L.R. (3rd) 513 (F.T.D.), [1979] 3 C.N.L.R. 17.

Kostuch v. *Kowalski* (1990), 75 Alta. L.R. (2d) 110 (Prov. Ct.), 107 A.R. 60.

Kostuch v. *Kowalski,* decided in the Alberta Court of Queen's Bench on 24 July 1990, Mr. Justice Chrumka (unreported) (9001-1156 C1A01).

Kostuch v. *Kowalski,* decided in the Alberta Court of Queen's Bench on 19 October 1990, Mr. Justice Sulatycky (unreported) (9001-14507).

Kostuch v. *Kowalski* (1991), 78 Alta. L.R. (2d) 131 (Prov. Ct.), 112 A.R. 283.

Kostuch v. *Kowalski* (1991), 81 Alta. L.R. (2d) 214 (Q.B.), 121 A.R. 219.

Kostuch v. *Alberta* (1992), 125 A.R. 214 (C.A.).

Kostuch v. *Alberta (Attorney General)* (1993), 143 A.R. 161 (Q.B.).

Kostuch v. *Alberta (Attorney General),* [1996] 1 W.W.R. 292 (Alta. C.A.).

Lyng v. *Northwest Indian Cemetery Protective Association,* 485 U.S. 439, 19 April 1988 [G-O Road].

Nowegijick v. *The Queen*, [1983] 2 C.N.L.R. 89 (S.C.C.).

R. v. *Born With A Tooth* (1992), 131 A.R. 193 (C.A.).

R. v. *Born With A Tooth* (1993), 139 A.R. 394 (Q.B.).

R. v. *Horseman*, [1990] 3 C.N.L.R. 95 (S.C.C.).

R. v. *Power*, [1994] 1 S.C.R. 601.

R. v. *Sioui*, [1990] 3 C.N.L.R. 127 (S.C.C.).

R. v. *Sparrow*, [1990] 3 C.N.L.R. 160, [1990] 1 S.C.R. 1075.

R. v. *Van der Peet*, [1996] 2 S.C.R. 507.

Re Paulette, [1973] 6 W.W.R. 97 (N.W.T.S.C.).

St. Catharine's Milling and Lumber Co. v. *The Queen* (1888), 14 A.C. 46 (P.C.).

Sask. Water Corp. v. *Canadian Wildlife Federation* (1989), 99 N.R. 72 (F.C.A.).

Sparrow v. *R.*, [1987] 1 C.N.L.R. 145 (B.C.C.A.).

Winters v. *United States*, 207 U.S. 564 (1908), 52 L.Ed. 340, aff'g 143 F.740 (9th Cir. 1906).

Index

Alberta Report, 116, 266-7
Calgary Herald, 38, 40, 55, 114, 116
Kainai News, 81
Lethbridge Herald, 27, 38, 42, 51, 69, 265-6
Taber Times, 44
Update, 259-60
Windspeaker, 267
Meech Lake Accord, 73, 74
Melnychuk, Peter, 28-9, 120, 266
and Alberta Environment/RCMP operations, 87, 89, 91, 98
and dam, 35-6, 41, 48
and Lonefighters, 79-80
Merrick, Gordon, 44
Meyer, David, 156
Miller, Tevie, 176, 180-1
Mills, Sergeant, 91, 265
Mitigation planning program, 44-5, 52-4, 58-9, 113, 231-2
Mohawk Indians (Quebec), 74, 75, 84, 232
Moore, Kenneth, 54-5, 56, 135
Muldoon, Francis, 213
Mulvain, James, 39

National Accord on Environmental Harmonization, 124, 249-50
National Accord for the Protection and Enhancement of Environmental Quality, 219
Native issues, public support, 196-7, 200
Natural Resources Conservation Board (NRCB), 125, 126, 127
Navigable Waters Protection Act (NWPA), 47, 61-6, 76, 104, 118-9, 165-73, 220, 227
New Democratic Party (NDP), 32, 95
Newspapers. *See* Media
North Peigan, Glen, 77, 103
North-West Irrigation Act, 20, 130
North-West Mounted Police (NWMP), 18, 19
NWPA. *See* Navigable Waters Protection Act

Offstream storage, 33
Oka crisis, 74, 75, 84, 232
Oldman River
diversion projects, 23-4, 176-7
natural water flow, 12-4, 25
significance to Peigans, 4, 107, 193-4
Oldman River Basin, 5, 12-24
riverine forest ecosystem, 12-7, 54, 157-63
wildlife, 15

Oldman River Dam Environmental Advisory Committee (EAC), 119-20
Oldman River Dam Environmental Assessment Panel (ORDEAP), 103-10, 111-4, 117-9, 221-8
Oldman River Dam Project
announcement, 41, 199
construction, 47, 57, 59-60, 64-5, 176, 255
cost, 47
diversion tunnels, 49, 176
land acquisition, 48-9
location, 17, 26-30
official opening, 114-6
ownership, 110
reservoir, 4
Oldman River Study Management Committee (ORSMC), 28-30
ECA review, 31-6
O'Leary, Willis, 123
Onstream storage, 278
Operations Strategy (1994) (Alberta), 128, 228
ORDEAP. *See* Oldman River Dam Environmental Assessment Panel
ORSMC. *See* Oldman River Study Management Committee

Paddle River dam, 31
Paetz, Martin, 54
Peigan Indians, 34-5, 186-212
and Brocket joint dam development, 40-2, 195, 198-9, 230
co-existence with dam, 196
compensation for cultural and spiritual losses, 118, 156, 212, 235-6
compensation in LNID headworks agreement, 39-40
cultural and spiritual beliefs, 150-6, 191-4, 205-12, 223
demonstration (1991), 101-2
and EARPGO, 201, 203, 213-20
and ECA review, 33-4
history, 17-9
ill treatment of by governments, 229-36
and Little Bow Project/Highwood Diversion Plan, 235
and LNID diversion weir, 23, 29-30, 36, 38-40, 103, 198
and Lonefighters' protest, 76-86, 94, 201-2
and mitigation planning program, 231-2
and Oldman River Dam Phase studies, 26-7, 28

Set in Stone by Brenda and Neil West, BN Typographics West

Printed and bound in Canada by Friesens

Copy editor: Judy Phillips

Proofreader: Lynne McNeill

Indexer: Elizabeth Bell

Date Due

JAN 0 6 2000		
JAN 2000		
JAN 3 1 2000		
JAN 1 6 2001		
JUN 1 2 2001		

PRINTED IN U.S.A.   CAT. NO. 24 161   BRO DART